# Outcome Measures and Innovative Approaches in Rehabilitation

# Outcome Measures and Innovative Approaches in Rehabilitation

Editors

**Marco Tramontano**
**Giovanni Galeoto**

MDPI

Basel • Beijing • Wuhan • Barcelona • Belgrade • Novi Sad • Cluj • Manchester

*Editors*

Marco Tramontano
Department of Biomedical
and Neuromotor Sciences
University of Bologna
Bologna
Italy

Giovanni Galeoto
Department of Human
Neurosciences
Sapienza University of Rome
Rome
Italy

*Editorial Office*
MDPI AG
Grosspeteranlage 5
4052 Basel, Switzerland

This is a reprint of articles from the Special Issue published online in the open access journal *Healthcare* (ISSN 2227-9032) (available at: https://www.mdpi.com/journal/healthcare/special_issues/3L2Y82YIM1).

For citation purposes, cite each article independently as indicated on the article page online and as indicated below:

| Lastname, A.A.; Lastname, B.B. Article Title. *Journal Name* **Year**, *Volume Number*, Page Range. |
|---|

**ISBN 978-3-7258-1630-9 (Hbk)**
**ISBN 978-3-7258-1629-3 (PDF)**
**doi.org/10.3390/books978-3-7258-1629-3**

# Contents

**About the Editors** . . . . . . . . . . . . . . . . . . . . . . . . . . . . . . . . . . . . . . . . **vii**

**Preface** . . . . . . . . . . . . . . . . . . . . . . . . . . . . . . . . . . . . . . . . . . . . . **ix**

**Nathaniel Riemann, Jack Coursen, Laura Elena Porras, Bryan Sabogal, Xin-Hua Liang, Christian Guaraca, et al.**
Redesigned Electrodes for Improved Intraoperative Nerve Conduction Studies during the Treatment of Peripheral Nerve Injuries
Reprinted from: *Healthcare* **2024**, *12*, 1269, doi:10.3390/healthcare12131269 . . . . . . . . . . . . . **1**

**Maria Elena Pugliese, Riccardo Battaglia, Maria Ursino, Lucia Francesca Lucca, Maria Quintieri, Martina Vatrano, et al.**
Prevalence and Risk Factors of Deep Venous Thrombosis in Intensive Inpatient Neurorehabilitation Unit
Reprinted from: *Healthcare* **2024**, *12*, 936, doi:10.3390/healthcare12090936 . . . . . . . . . . . . . **15**

**Carla Vanti, Silvano Ferrari, Marco Chiodini, Cesare Olivoni, Arianna Bortolami and Paolo Pillastrini**
Sexual Disability in Low Back Pain: Diagnostic and Therapeutic Framework for Physical Therapists
Reprinted from: *Healthcare* **2024**, *12*, 80, doi:10.3390/healthcare12010080 . . . . . . . . . . . . . . **26**

**Anna Latajka, Małgorzata Stefańska, Marek Woźniewski and Iwona Malicka**
Walking Speed and Risk of Falling Patients Operated for Selected Malignant Tumors
Reprinted from: *Healthcare* **2023**, *11*, 3069, doi:10.3390/healthcare11233069 . . . . . . . . . . . . . **45**

**Hadeel R. Bakhsh, Nouf S. Aldajani, Bodor Bin Sheeha, Monira I. Aldhahi, Atheer A. Alsomali, Ghada K. Alhamrani, et al.**
Arabic Translation and Psychometric Validation of PROMIS General Life Satisfaction Short Form in the General Population
Reprinted from: *Healthcare* **2023**, *11*, 3034, doi:10.3390/healthcare11233034 . . . . . . . . . . . . . **57**

**Ahmad Zaheer Qureshi, Hasan Shacfe, Amara Ilyas, Saeed Bin Ayaz, Khalid Yousef Aljamaan, Imad Saeed Moukais, et al.**
Complications of Intrathecal Baclofen Pump Therapy: An Institutional Experience from Saudi Arabia
Reprinted from: *Healthcare* **2023**, *11*, 2820, doi:10.3390/healthcare11212820 . . . . . . . . . . . . . **69**

**Anna Ortega-Martínez, Rocío Palomo-Carrión, Carlos Varela-Ferro and Maria Caritat Bagur-Calafat**
Feasibility of a Home-Based Mirror Therapy Program in Children with Unilateral Spastic Cerebral Palsy
Reprinted from: *Healthcare* **2023**, *11*, 1797, doi:10.3390/healthcare11121797 . . . . . . . . . . . . . **85**

**Matteo Tamburlani, Rossana Cuscito, Annamaria Servadio and Giovanni Galeoto**
Effectiveness of Respiratory Rehabilitation in COVID-19's Post-Acute Phase: A Systematic Review
Reprinted from: *Healthcare* **2023**, *11*, 1071, doi:10.3390/healthcare11081071 . . . . . . . . . . . . . **99**

**Karolina Szuflak, Roksana Malak, Brittany Fechner, Dorota Sikorska, Włodzimierz Samborski, Ewa Mojs and Karolina Gerreth**
The Masticatory Structure and Function in Children with Cerebral Palsy—A Pilot Study
Reprinted from: *Healthcare* **2023**, *11*, 1029, doi:10.3390/healthcare11071029 . . . . . . . . . . . . . **121**

**Paolo Brasiliano, Martina Alvini, Eugenio Di Stanislao, Giuseppe Vannozzi, Giuseppe Di Rosa and Valentina Camomilla**
Ankle Kinematics Characterization in Children with Idiopathic Toe Walking: Does the Foot Model Change the Clinical Evaluation?
Reprinted from: *Healthcare* **2023**, *11*, 873, doi:10.3390/healthcare11060873 . . . . . . . . . . . . . . **132**

**Erasmo Galeno, Edoardo Pullano, Firas Mourad, Giovanni Galeoto and Francesco Frontani**
Effectiveness of Vestibular Rehabilitation after Concussion: A Systematic Review of Randomised Controlled Trial
Reprinted from: *Healthcare* **2023**, *11*, 90, doi:10.3390/healthcare11010090 . . . . . . . . . . . . . . . **142**

**Mohammad Etoom, Alhadi M. Jahan, Alia Alghwiri, Francesco Lena and Nicola Modugno**
Ataxia Rating Scales: Content Analysis by Linking to the International Classification of Functioning, Disability and Health
Reprinted from: *Healthcare* **2022**, *10*, 2459, doi:10.3390/healthcare10122459 . . . . . . . . . . . . . **158**

**Eduardo Espinosa-Garamendi, Norma Angélica Labra-Ruiz, Lizbeth Naranjo, Claudia Andrea Chávez-Mejía, Erika Valenzuela-Alarcón and Julieta Griselda Mendoza-Torreblanca**
Habilitation of Executive Functions in Pediatric Congenital Heart Disease Patients through LEGO®-Based Therapy: A Quasi-Experimental Study
Reprinted from: *Healthcare* **2022**, *10*, 2348, doi:10.3390/healthcare10122348 . . . . . . . . . . . . . **168**

**Gianluca Giordani, Sara De Angelis, Annunziata Isabella Parisi, Andrea Cosimo D'amico, Moira Di Re, Chiara Liumbruno, et al.**
Manual Physiotherapy Combined with Pelvic Floor Training in Women Suffering from Stress Urinary Incontinence and Chronic Nonspecific Low Back Pain: A Preliminary Study
Reprinted from: *Healthcare* **2022**, *10*, 2031, doi:10.3390/healthcare10102031 . . . . . . . . . . . . . **183**

**Masatoshi Koumo, Akio Goda, Yoshinori Maki, Kouta Yokoyama, Tetsuya Yamamoto, Tsumugi Hosokawa, et al.**
Clinical Items for Geriatric Patients with Post-Stroke at Discharge or Transfer after Rehabilitation Therapy in a Chronic-Phase Hospital: A Retrospective Pilot Study
Reprinted from: *Healthcare* **2022**, *10*, 1577, doi:10.3390/healthcare10081577 . . . . . . . . . . . . . **193**

# About the Editors

**Marco Tramontano**

Marco Tramontano is a distinguished physiotherapist dedicated to both research and clinical practice. After earning his degree in Physiotherapy, he began his career at IRCCS Santa Lucia in Rome, one of Italy's foremost centers for neurological and orthopedic rehabilitation. In this role, Tramontano contributed to the development of innovative rehabilitation programs for patients with various neurological and musculoskeletal conditions. Tramontano has authored over 97 scientific articles published in peer-reviewed international journals, focusing on topics such as neurological rehabilitation, the effectiveness of physical therapies, and new technologies in physiotherapy. His research has significantly advanced clinical practices through rigorous studies and systematic reviews. In 2020, Tramontano took on the role of Researcher in Physiotherapy at the University of Bologna, where he engages in academic research and teaching. In this position, Tramontano explores new advancements in rehabilitation and collaborates with colleagues and students on innovative research projects. His teaching emphasizes the practical application of scientific evidence in clinical settings, preparing future physiotherapists for success. With a strong professional background and a career dedicated to excellence, Marco Tramontano continues to be a key figure in physiotherapy, contributing to both clinical practice and scientific research.

**Giovanni Galeoto**

Dr. Giovanni Galeoto is a physiotherapist with extensive clinical experience and a successful career in research within the field of Orthopedic and Neurological Rehabilitation. After earning his degree in Physiotherapy, Dr. Galeoto began his professional career with a strong focus on multidisciplinary rehabilitation, contributing to numerous studies and publications that have enriched the field of physiotherapy. Since 2014, Dr. Galeoto has been working at Sapienza University of Rome, where he is engaged in both teaching and research. As a professor and researcher, he has led several advanced research projects in Orthopedic and Neurological Rehabilitation, collaborating with national and international universities and research institutions. His work extends across a broad network of collaborations with leading universities and research centers worldwide. In 2021, Dr. Galeoto was appointed as the World Health Organization (WHO) Focal Point for "Rehabilitation 2023", a prestigious role that recognizes his significant contributions to the global field of rehabilitation. In this position, he is involved in promoting international standards and defining best practices to enhance rehabilitation strategies on a global scale. Dr. Galeoto has authored numerous scientific publications in peer-reviewed international journals, addressing multidisciplinary topics in rehabilitation. His research covers the effectiveness of physical therapies and technological innovations, and he has made a significant impact on improving clinical practices and training professionals in the field. With a career marked by a constant pursuit of excellence and international collaboration, Dr. Giovanni Galeoto remains a leading figure in physiotherapy and rehabilitation, contributing to scientific research and clinical practice on a global level.

# Preface

It is with great pleasure that we introduce this volume, "Outcome Measures and Innovative Approaches in Rehabilitation," a collection of 15 articles published as a Special Issue in *Healthcare*.

This volume compiles articles that explore a wide range of crucial topics. These include the analysis of traditional outcome measures, which remain essential for monitoring patient progress, as well as the introduction of new tools and methodologies that offer a more detailed and precise view of rehabilitation outcomes. Among these are advanced assessment technologies, which are transforming the landscape of rehabilitation.

Furthermore, this collection examines innovative approaches aimed at optimizing rehabilitation interventions. The integration of interdisciplinary techniques and the adoption of personalized strategies are concrete examples of how innovation can enhance the effectiveness of rehabilitation. These articles demonstrate how collaboration across disciplines and the customization of treatments can lead to significantly better outcomes for patients.

A particularly noteworthy aspect of this collection is the variety of contexts in which outcome measures and innovations are applied. From hospital settings to long-term care facilities and from private clinics to home rehabilitation programs, each article offers a unique perspective on addressing the specific challenges of each setting. This diversity of experiences and approaches enriches the content of the reprint, providing readers with a deep and multidimensional understanding of modern rehabilitation.

We would like to express our gratitude to the authors who contributed to this Special Issue. Their commitment and dedication to research and innovation have been fundamental to the realization of this volume. Each article represents countless hours of work, including the design and execution of studies, the analysis and interpretation of data, and the careful crafting of manuscripts.

We also extend our thanks to the reviewers and the editorial team of *Healthcare* for their tireless work in ensuring the quality of the published articles. The peer review process is a critical component of scientific publishing, and the reviewers' constructive feedback and rigorous standards have helped to enhance the quality and clarity of the articles in this volume.

In conclusion, we hope that this reprint will serve as a valuable resource for rehabilitation professionals, researchers, and students. The knowledge and experiences shared in these pages are intended to inspire new ideas and promote further advancements in the field. We are confident that "Outcome Measures and Innovative Approaches in Rehabilitation" will help improve clinical practice and, ultimately, enhance the quality of life for patients.

**Marco Tramontano and Giovanni Galeoto**
*Editors*

*healthcare*

MDPI

*Article*

# Redesigned Electrodes for Improved Intraoperative Nerve Conduction Studies during the Treatment of Peripheral Nerve Injuries

**Nathaniel Riemann [1,*], Jack Coursen [1], Laura Elena Porras [1], Bryan Sabogal [1], Xin-Hua Liang [1], Christian Guaraca [1], Allan Belzberg [2], Matthias Ringkamp [2], Gang Wu [2], Lily Zhu [1], Samantha Weed [1] and Constanza Miranda [1]**

1 Department of Biomedical Engineering, Johns Hopkins University, Baltimore, MD 21218, USA; constanzamiranda@jhu.edu (C.M.)
2 Department of Neurosurgery, School of Medicine, Johns Hopkins University, Baltimore, MD 21287, USA
* Correspondence: nrieman1@alumni.jh.edu

**Abstract:** Traumatic peripheral nerve injuries (PNI), present with symptoms ranging from pain to loss of motor and sensory function. Difficulties in intraoperative visual assessment of nerve functional status necessitate intraoperative nerve conduction studies (INCSs) by neurosurgeons and neurologists to determine the presence of functioning axons in the zone of a PNI. This process, also referred to as nerve "inching", uses a set of stimulating and recording electrode hooks to lift the injured nerve from the surrounding surgical field and to determine whether an electrical stimulus can travel through the zone of injury. However, confounding electrical signal artifacts can arise from the current workflow and electrode design, particularly from the mandatory lifting of the nerve, complicating the definitive assessment of nerve function and neurosurgical treatment decision-making. The objective of this study is to describe the design process and verification testing of our group's newly designed stimulating and recording electrodes that do not require the lifting or displacement of the injured nerve during INCSs. Ergonomic in vivo analysis of the device within a porcine model demonstrated successful intraoperative manipulation of the device, while quantitative nerve action potential (NAP) signal analysis with an ex vivo simulated "inching" procedure on healthy non-human primate nerve tissue demonstrated excellent reproducible recorded NAP fidelity and the absence of NAP signal artifacts at all points of recording. Lastly, electrode pullout force testing determined maximum forces of 0.43 N, 1.57 N, and 3.61 N required to remove the device from 2 mm, 5 mm, and 1 cm nerve models, respectively, which are well within established thresholds for nerve safety. These results suggest that these new electrodes can safely and successfully perform accurate PNI assessment without the presence of artifacts, with the potential to improve the INCS standard of care while remaining compatible with currently used neurosurgical technology, infrastructure, and clinical workflows.

**Keywords:** peripheral nerve; nerve conduction study; electrode; intraoperative neuromonitoring; action potential; signal artifact; nerve trauma injury; neurosurgical treatment; design process; clinical need

**Citation:** Riemann, N.; Coursen, J.; Porras, L.E.; Sabogal, B.; Liang, X.-H.; Guaraca, C.; Belzberg, A.; Ringkamp, M.; Wu, G.; Zhu, L.; et al. Redesigned Electrodes for Improved Intraoperative Nerve Conduction Studies during the Treatment of Peripheral Nerve Injuries. *Healthcare* **2024**, *12*, 1269. https://doi.org/10.3390/healthcare12131269

Academic Editors: Marco Tramontano, Giovanni Galeoto and Abdel-Latif Mohamed

Received: 29 February 2024
Revised: 12 April 2024
Accepted: 23 June 2024
Published: 26 June 2024



## 1. Introduction

Peripheral nerve injuries (PNIs) affect 20 million Americans, disproportionately affecting young individuals subject to motor vehicle accidents, falls, and industrial accidents [1,2]. The clinical presentation of PNIs varies from symptoms of mild discomfort to pain and loss of function that limits daily activities [3]. Muscles without nerve reinnervation typically exhibit irreversible deterioration after 12 to 18 months; therefore, PNI treatments are limited by the time necessary to reinnervate the muscle connected to the injured nerve [3]. As axons regenerate at a rate of about one inch per month, an injury further from the site of nerve–muscle innervation will take longer to fully regenerate, thereby shortening treatment time and requiring earlier clinical decision-making and intervention [3].

Once a nerve injury is identified, surgeons wait for a period of 3 to 6 months to provide time for potential axon self-regeneration, after which the nerve is reassessed using intraoperative nerve conduction studies (INCSs) to determine whether the nerve axons are successfully self-regenerating (requiring no further surgical intervention) or whether further surgical intervention is required to reinnervate the muscle with functional nerves [3]. During INCSs, the neurosurgeon first dissects into the surgical field until the injured nerve is identified and isolated. Next, the continuity of nerve action potential (NAP) propagation is assessed along the site of nerve injury using a tripolar stimulating electrode and bipolar recording electrode (Figure 1). During this procedure (also referred to as nerve "inching"), the neurosurgeon places the electrodes on each side of the predicted zone of injury, and an electrical stimulus is sent via the stimulating electrode. If a stimulated NAP successfully propagates through the injured nerve region and is recorded by the bipolar electrode (Figure 1a), successful nerve function is confirmed; conversely, the absence of a recorded signal (Figure 1b) indicates nerve discontinuity (lack of axonal function) through the injury, requiring further surgical treatment (e.g., direct nerve repair and autologous nerve grafting—current gold-standard treatments) [4–8]. Following this single assessment, the nerve inching procedure is continued by incrementally moving the stimulating electrode closer towards the recording electrode and repeating the aforementioned procedure at these subsequent electrode positions to precisely define the zone of injury, guiding the neurosurgeon's clinical decision-making [9].

INCSs are a key and standard electrophysiological technique used to determine internal nerve axonal functionality. Other methods, including advanced functional imaging technologies, do not have the resolution necessary to assess internal axonal structure, and EMG only provides general information regarding nerve function at the late stage when muscle reinnervation is expected to occur [10,11]. Current INCSs are problematic due to electrical artifacts distorting the NAP recording, making definitive nerve assessment difficult [8]. Inching is sensitive to various disruptions:

- Nerve Lifting: Gently lifting the nerve via the electrodes will remove the electric ground from the electrophysiological nerve system, which disrupts the recorded signal by introducing signal artifacts in the NAP recording [12].
- Electrode Spacing: The spacing between the signal artifact and NAP on the recorded signal is proportional to the distance between the recording and stimulating electrodes on the nerve. Distances less than 4 cm between the electrodes can cause the NAP recording to be masked by a signal artifact; distances too long between the electrodes may allow the signal to interact with extrinsic factors [4].
- Isolation of the Electrode-Contact Sites: The currently used electrodes must isolate the nerve through gentle lifting and suspension from the surgical field, distancing the sites of stimulation and recording from surrounding tissues that may produce a misleading NAP signal. This may result from "spread", where the signal propagates through surrounding muscle tissue instead of the nerve [4,11].
- Nerve–Electrode Contact: The prongs of the stimulating and recording electrodes must have proper contact with the nerve for stimulation and NAP recording. This includes minimizing contact with surrounding fluids in the body, as these mediums can disrupt the NAP [4].

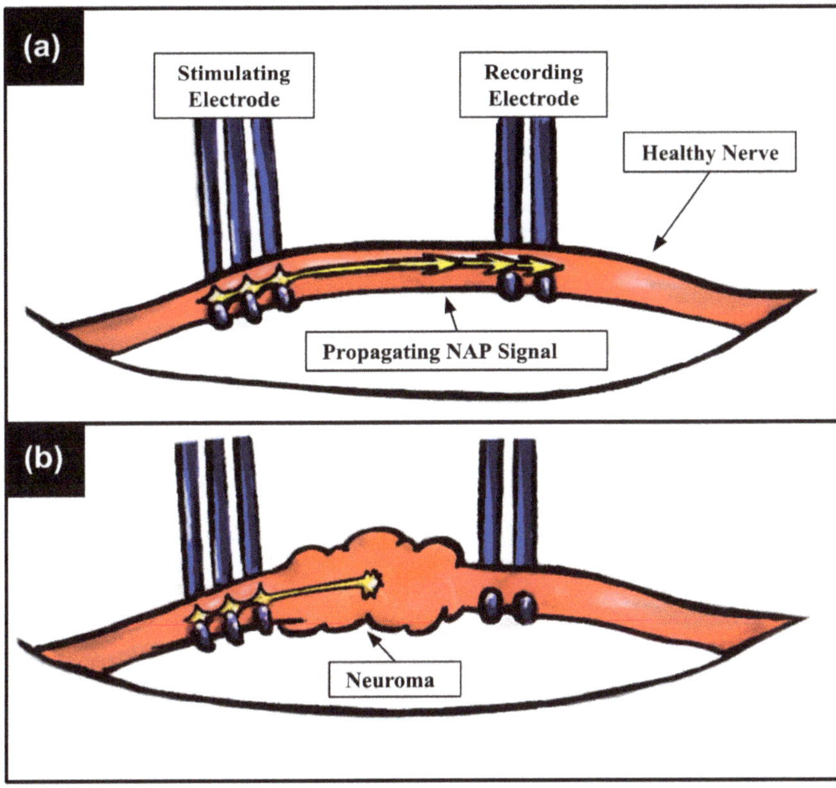


**Figure 1.** Current setup and method of peripheral INCSs. The injured nerve is lifted from the surrounding surgical field using a pair of standard intraoperative neuromonitoring (IONM) electrodes. (**a**) A tripolar stimulating electrode is used to induce nerve action potential (NAP) propagation down the nerve, which is later recorded by the bipolar recording electrode. A healthy nerve exhibits continuity of signal propagation, which is determined by the presence of a recorded NAP. (**b**) In a damaged nerve, the axons within the nerve sheath lose the ability to continuously propagate NAPs to the recording electrode, and for this reason, no signal is recorded. This stimulating and recording procedure is repeated as the stimulating electrode is incrementally moved across the site of nerve injury.

The combination of a limited time frame for successful PNI treatment and nerve assessment inaccuracies can be detrimental to clinical outcomes. False-positive NAPs can result in a lack of surgical intervention in a non-regenerating axon, and false-negative NAPs can result in unnecessary surgery on nerves that would have regenerated on their own; both of these scenarios would restart the treatment process, providing less time for further intervention and full nerve regeneration before the innervated muscle exhibits irreversible atrophy. When patients wait to seek medical attention after injury or when an iatrogenic PNI is sustained through a different operation and the clinician waits to assess the development and extent of the injury, avoiding any further delays to muscle reinnervation may be critical to final functional outcomes [3,10,11].

To perform this nerve "inching" procedure, the current standard of care involves a set of standard IONM hook electrodes. The length of each electrode is electrically insulated, while the hook structure is fully uninsulated; this requires the neurosurgeon to lift the nerve up from the surrounding surgical field to (1) maximize the sufficient quality of electrode contact with the nerve and (2) to ensure that electrical stimulation and recording are limited exclusively to the nerve (as opposed to any surrounding tissue). Unfortunately, this workflow also exposes the nerve to additional strain via nerve lifting.

Through a structured investigation of background research, clinical observation, and a structured design process, our team identified the existence of a clinical need: PNI patients, neurosurgeons, and their operating team require a more accurate and consistent method of determining the presence or absence of functioning axons in a zone of injury to guide further treatment decisions. The objectives of our group were to implement a rigorous design process to create new stimulating and recording IONM electrodes that do not require the displacement/lifting of the nerve. Our group developed, fabricated, and verified our novel electrode design in terms of ergonomics, signal accuracy, and safety of implementation utilizing in vivo, ex vivo, and stimulated nerve experimental setups, respectively.

## 2. Materials and Methods

Section 2 describes the design process that our interdisciplinary team of biomedical engineers and end-users went through to develop our novel IONM electrode design, as proposed by Miranda et al. 2020 to increase the likelihood of final device adoption [13,14].

### 2.1. *Identifying the Clinical Need and Establishing Design Requirements*

We were first approached by scientists and a neurosurgeon from the Neurosurgery Department at a prominent research institution's hospital who needed a better way to assess nerve function in the setting of PNI and to assess the need for surgical intervention. After an extensive literature search across journals of clinical and surgical medicine, biomedical research, and national biostatistics reports regarding the physiopathology of peripheral nerve injuries, we engaged in applied ethnographic methods [13,14], such as participant and non-participant observation in the field [15,16] and open-ended interviews [17,18].

Our sample of participants consisted of 15+ neurosurgeons, neurologists, physician's assistants, electrophysiologists, and additional operating team staff (i.e., circulating nurses, technicians, anesthesiologists, residents, and medical school students) with whom we observed the neurosurgical workflow across a variety of neurosurgical procedures (e.g., nerve tumor removal, nerve decompression surgery, autologous nerve grafting treatment of acute peripheral nerve trauma), including pre-operative clinic visits, patient consent, anesthesia, peripheral nerve assessment, and the ultimate neurosurgical treatment. Our firsthand observations into the technical and ergonomic challenges of peripheral nerve assessment included induced nerve tension from the hook electrodes, ergonomic inefficiency (two surgeons were required to perform the two electrode nerve assessments), and ambiguity of recorded nerve action potential signals due to electrical artifacts that resultantly complicated and delayed surgical treatment decision-making. Further collaboration with electrophysiologists provided insight into the bioelectrical basis of observed clinical pinch-points, how to mitigate emergent signal artifacts, and improved ergonomics within the clinical workflow.

All of this information was collected and interpreted in our Design History File, where our team documented all steps undertaken in the development of our medical device and in synthesizing actionable design requirements (Table 1) for our novel solution via converging ideation by the team [19–22].

**Table 1.** Design criteria and corresponding design affordances regarding electrode ideation and development. The six design requirements (left column) represent a comprehensive set of considerations by our group when ideating a new solution concept. The corresponding design affordances (right column) articulate the means by which each design criterion will be addressed in the ideated solution.

| Design Requirement | Corresponding Design Affordance |
| --- | --- |
| DR01. Minimize invasiveness/disruption to the surgeon's workflow | The principle of the instrument is kept in line with older solutions. The neurosurgeon should be capable of using our new device without substantial new training, thereby streamlining clinical adoptability. |
| DR02. Minimize/eliminate nerve lifting and perturbation to the surgical field | Electrode placement/securement should not require lifting of the nerve and should minimally perturb the surrounding surgical field, both mechanically and electrically. This will both minimize the physical risk to the wounded area and improve recorded signal quality by the surgeon. |
| DR03. Accounting for variable nerve diameters | The differences in physiology between patients and within patients at different points of the body require a device that accounts for the variability in nerve diameters. This design will improve the safety of the device by ensuring that safe compressive forces are exerted on the nerve. This newly designed electrode will also improve upon the adaptability of the device by reducing decision-making in the workflow when choosing which electrode size to use for the nerve at hand. |
| DR04. Ergonomic use of device control using a single hand | To accommodate a set of two electrodes used during peripheral nerve assessment, as well as the added functionality of the new device, each electrode should be ergonomically operable with a single hand. |
| DR05. Sufficient electrical contact between nerve and electrode. | Optimal, reproducible quality of nerve stimulation and NAP recording should be accomplished via secure, consistent physical contact between the electrodes and the assessed nerve; this can be indicated by the metric of constant contact surface impedance of this interface. |
| DR06. Direct control of forces exerted on the nerve via fine motor control. | In the setting of sufficient electrode securement for adequate nerve stimulation and NAP recording, our solution should provide surgeons with extremely fine control of the forces exerted on the nerve by the electrodes, i.e., via fine motor control. |

### 2.2. Prototyping and Fabrication of the Device

Addressing DR02, we ideated and vetted several electrode configurations, settling on a flat "sandwich" or chopstick-style clamp electrode to fasten around the nerve from above to facilitate disengagement in the event of emergency electrode removal. The electrode leads were electrically insulated aside from precise contact areas designated for nerve contact only, thereby isolating NAP stimulation and recording to only the nerve itself. We designed a slider component to be controlled by one's index finger, thereby providing a neurosurgeon with fine motor control over the exerted forces on the nerve by the electrode and the expanding/retracting fastening mechanism of the device (DR04, DR06). The electrode leads and slider mechanism were within an original handle structure designed to support the fastening mechanism. The initial iterative prototyping stage of the design process was facilitated using 3D printing software and printers to quickly produce the electrode slider and housing components.

The overall finalized design (Figure 2) comprised four primary structural components: a "pencil grip"-style handle, an index finger-adjusted linear sliding mechanism to open and close the electrode clamp around the nerve, embedded stainless steel electrode leads for nerve stimulation and recording, and polyolefin electrode insulation around each electrode lead, with cut-outs for necessary sites of stimulation and recording.

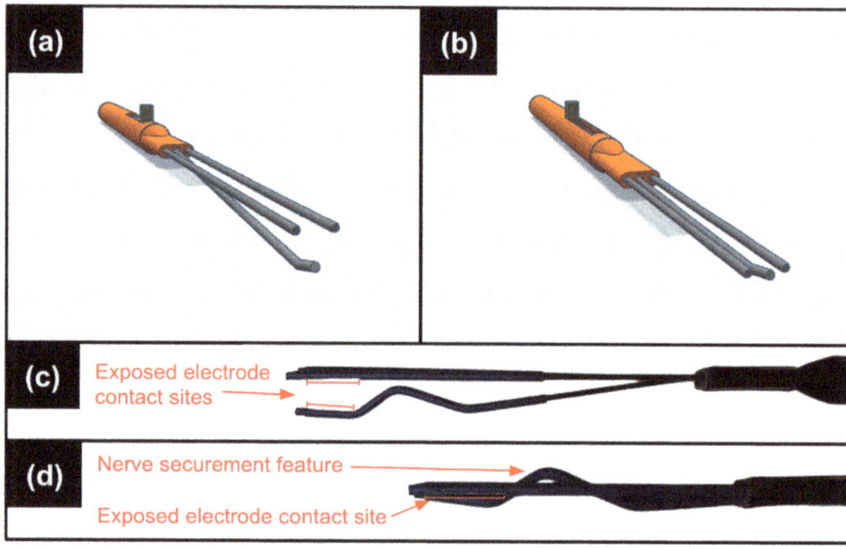


**Figure 2.** Electrode design prototypes. (**a**) Computer-aided design (CAD) render of the electrode prototype used in in vivo preliminary ergonomic analysis (see Figure 3) with uninsulated leads fully extended. Electrode leads extend 9 cm from the handle, with a 1.5 cm spacing between the top two parallel leads and bottom lead. The handle is 15.5 cm in length and 1 cm in diameter. (**b**) CAD render of aforementioned electrode prototype with the slider and leads fully retracted. Electrode leads extend 6 cm outside the handle in this position. (**c**) Side view image: fully extended stimulating electrode leads of the finalized prototype. (Note: the electrode handle, slider components, and lead extension lengths remain unchanged from the previous iteration.) (**d**) Side view image: fully retracted electrode leads of the aforementioned electrode. This iteration contains a nerve securement "hump" feature that prevents the nerve from sliding backwards into the device. Note that the recording electrode is dimensionally identical to the stimulating electrode but uses a fully insulated middle electrode lead for physical support only and has no electrical activity.

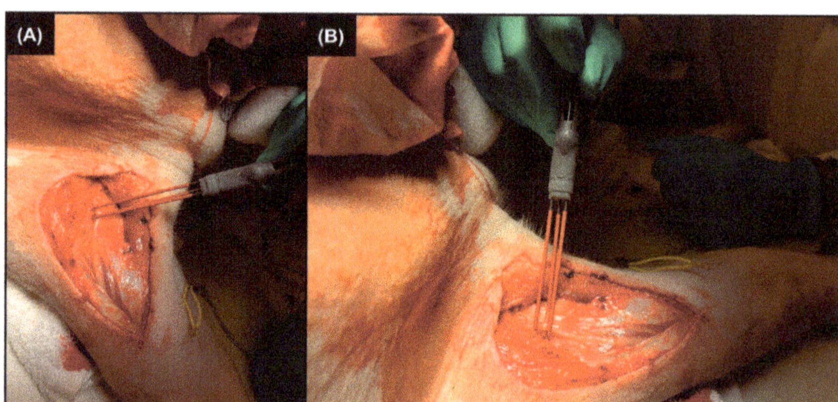


**Figure 3.** Preliminary ergonomic analysis within an animal model. (**A**) Aerial view of the electrode prototype secured on the ulnar nerve of a pig; the surgeon retracted the slider mechanism until the electrode device was safely secured onto the nerve. (**B**) Frontal view of electrode securement on the ulnar nerve.

Many dimensions and materials of the electrode components were chosen to be similar to the currently adopted IONM Cadwell Disposable 180° Degree Double Hook (Cadwell Industries Inc., Kennewick, WA, USA), with 1.5 mm diameter stainless steel electrode leads, a fully extended length of 9 cm outside the handle, and 5 mm spacing between recording electrode leads [12]. The prototype fabrication process was as follows: The electrode handle/housing and slider component were printed using a PLA 3D printer (with later iterations using a resin 3D printer). Next, the stainless steel electrode leads were manually cut to the desired length and shaped with pliers to their desired form (such that the middle electrode lead would expand downwards as the electrode was expanded to a maximum width of 1.5 cm). The electrode leads were glued into the 3D-printed slider component, after which polyolefin insulation was applied to each lead using a heat gun. Flexible 17-gauge tin-plated copper wires were soldered to the back of the electrode leads—on the recording electrode, individual wires were soldered to the right- and left-most leads, while the middle lead was fully insulated; on the recording electrode, the right- and left-most leads were soldered to one wire, while the middle lead was soldered to a separate wire. Electrode-nerve contact areas were manually cut out of the insulation (1 mm by 6 mm) using a hobby knife. Lastly, the electrode lead and slider assembly were sealed within the electrode handle/housing.

Upon completion of an initial functional prototype of the electrode design (represented by Figure 2a,b but with polyolefin lead insulation), our electrophysiologist and neurosurgeon clinical mentors performed a preliminary ergonomic analysis of the device within an in vivo porcine model (Figure 3); the animal had been recently euthanized following the end of a different experimental study. (This animal study protocol PR21M249 was officially approved by the Animal Care and Use Committee of the Johns Hopkins University on 09/14/21.) Using the electrode sliding mechanism, the leads of a single electrode were gently secured by the neurosurgeon onto an exposed, non-injured ulnar nerve; no electrical stimulation or recording was performed, as indicated by the visible yellow disconnected electrode wires. Following this preliminary analysis, a final iteration of electrode design was developed (Figure 2b,c) to further improve the securement of the nerve on the points of the exposed electrode lead contacts.

### 2.3. Ex Vivo Verification Testing

Upon completed design and assembly of the finalized electrode prototype that addressed our aforementioned needs criteria, our team performed ex vivo verification testing on a healthy (i.e., non-injured) monkey tibial nerve to ensure that the devices could successfully stimulate and record NAPs without the presence of signal artifacts. (This animal study protocol SW23M55 was officially approved by the Animal Care and Use Committee of the Johns Hopkins University on 03/17/23.) The tibial nerve was placed on a 10 by 10 cm square of gauze (representing the surrounding surgical tissue within an in vivo surgical field) immersed in a normal saline (synthetic interstitial fluid) solution bath. The experimental setup is shown in Figure 4. A simulated nerve "inching" procedure was performed, using the following procedure: First, the stimulating and recording electrodes were secured onto the nerve and placed 66 mm apart from one another; this was considered the first of six electrode positions of the inching procedure. At each position, a 4 mA, 0.05 ms pulse width constant current stimulus was delivered every 5 s (0.2 Hz) via the stimulating electrode, from which a resulting NAP was recorded via the recording electrode. Following this, the recording electrode remained stationary, while the stimulating electrode was "inched" into the next position, moving 10 mm closer towards the recording electrode. (I.e., the electrodes were 56 mm apart in position two, 46 mm apart in position 3, etc.) Saline solution was periodically applied to the nerve to preserve the physiological properties of the setup. This procedure was repeated through the sixth electrode position, at which the electrodes were placed 16 mm apart. At this final position, the electrical stimulus polarity was reversed to further investigate the presence or absence of signal artifacts.

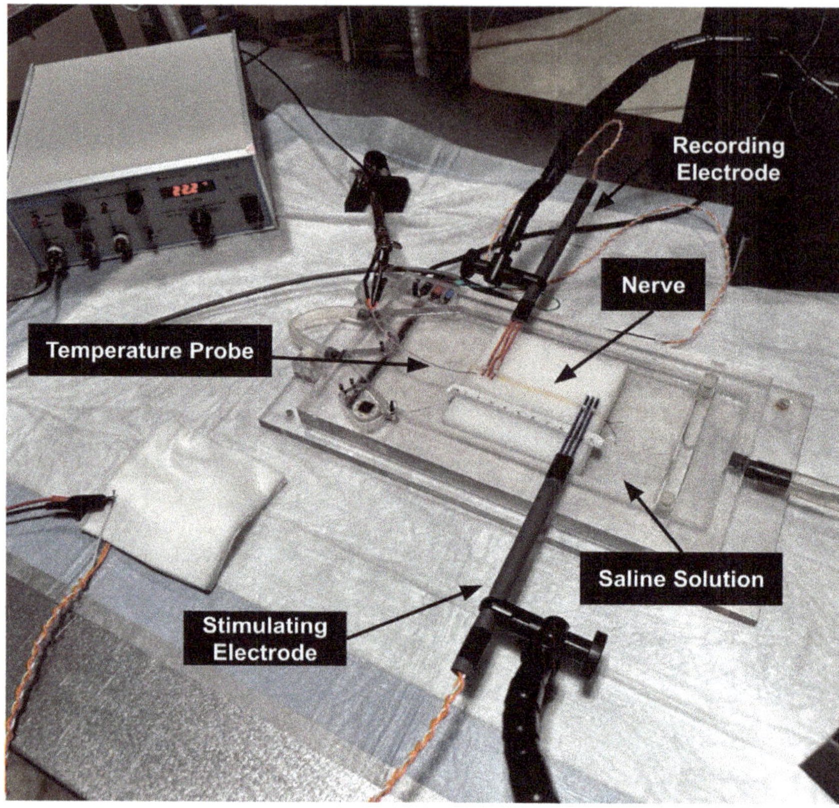


**Figure 4.** Ex vivo experimental setup. Note that the standard "normal" stimulation convention was with the middle electrode lead as negative and the left- and right-most leads as positive; this was then flipped during the reversed stimulation polarity. Both electrodes were secured onto the nerve in such a way that the nerve was not lifted.

### *2.4. Electrode Pullout Force Testing*

Following ex vivo verification testing, the electrodes were tested to determine the force needed for emergency device removal from the nerve by a surgeon. Three-dimensionally -printed molds were used with Smooth-Sil 940 silicone to form three nerve models approximately 7 cm in length and of varying diameters: 2 mm, 5 mm, and 1 cm.

An ESM303 Mark-10 Motorized Test Stand and Model M5-20 Force Gauge (Mark-10 Corporation, Copiague, NY, USA) were used to measure the force required to remove the electrode from the nerve model. First, the nerve model was fixed/clamped to a stage at the base of the Mark-10; next, the electrode was similarly clamped to the movable strain-gauge component of the sensor. Upon securement of the electrode and nerve model, the electrode was fastened and fully retracted onto the nerve model. Under the default settings of the Mark-10, the movable strain gauge component was adjusted to the initial position (Figure 5), and the force gauge was calibrated, from which the electrode was incrementally pulled upwards at a constant rate with linear movement. This was stopped once the electrode detached from the nerve model. The plots and data tables for each run were saved, and this procedure was performed for $n$ = 6, $n$ = 6, and $n$ = 8 trials for the 2 mm, 5 mm, and 1 cm diameter nerve models, respectively.

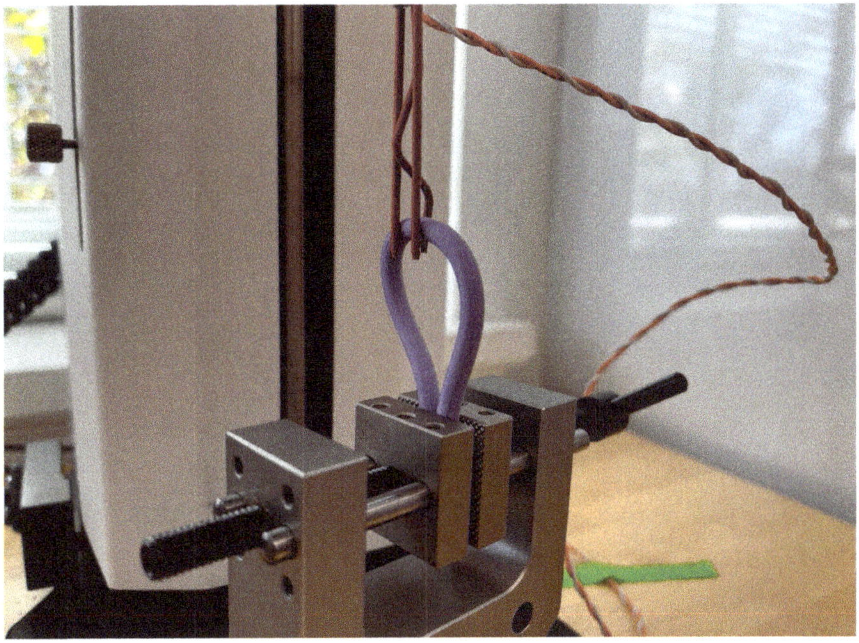

**Figure 5.** Experimental setup for electrode pullout force testing on a 5 mm diameter nerve model. The electrode leads were fully retracted back for a standardized maximum securement on the nerve model for each testing trial; a 5 mm nerve model is shown here; 2 mm and 1 cm nerve models were tested as well.

## 3. Results

Successful completion of our final design yielded a device which directly satisfied all of our articulated design requirements (Table 1). With respect to maximizing the ease of adoptability and minimizing change/disruption to the current surgical workflow (DR01), we designed the device to remain compatible with existing signal reading and stimulation infrastructure while maintaining the critical dimensions and two-electrode setup of the currently used tripolar stimulating and bipolar recording IONM hook electrodes. As a result, the integration of these devices into the current surgical workflow should only require replacing the current IONM electrodes with our new electrode.

Regarding the mitigation of nerve lifting and surgical perturbations (DR02), our electrodes are designed to easily secure around an individual nerve resting within the surgical field rather than requiring lifting force to pull the nerve up and away. This "sandwich" or "chopstick"-like securement onto the nerve allows vertical surgical-accessible, nerve-specific securement while the nerve rests in place, thereby allowing NAP stimulation and recording while minimizing nerve lifting and perturbation within the surgical field (as demonstrated by the preliminary in vivo ergonomic analysis shown in Figure 3). We demonstrated minimal perturbations of the nerve and surgical field as a method of recorded artifact mitigation/prevention, as shown in published academic literature and our collected ex vivo data (Figure 6), as well as a step further towards patient safety, as current methods of peripheral nerve surgery can commonly cause nerve scar tissue formation [11,23].

This newly designed fastening mechanism is precisely engineered to extend and retract along a continuous range of securement sizes (DR03)—from a smaller nerve diameter of 1–3 mm to large (e.g., sciatic) nerve diameters of over 1 cm—allowing the device to accommodate various peripheral nerve diameters in a 'one-size-fits-all' manner (Figure 2) [24]. The extension and retraction of our variable-diameter fastening mechanism is operated by a sliding element integrated into the electrode handle; operation of this mechanism with the lateral side of the surgeon's index finger while the device is held with the thumb, similar to the grip of a pen or pencil, provides fine motor control and thereby precise control of the forces exerted on the nerve by the surgeon/electrode (DR04), as seen in Figure 3 [25]. Furthermore, full use of the device is accomplished using only one hand, thereby allowing simultaneous manipulation of a tripolar stimulating and bipolar recording electrode during the peripheral nerve assessment procedure by a single surgeon, eliminating the need for two operating surgeons for IOMN assessment (DR06).

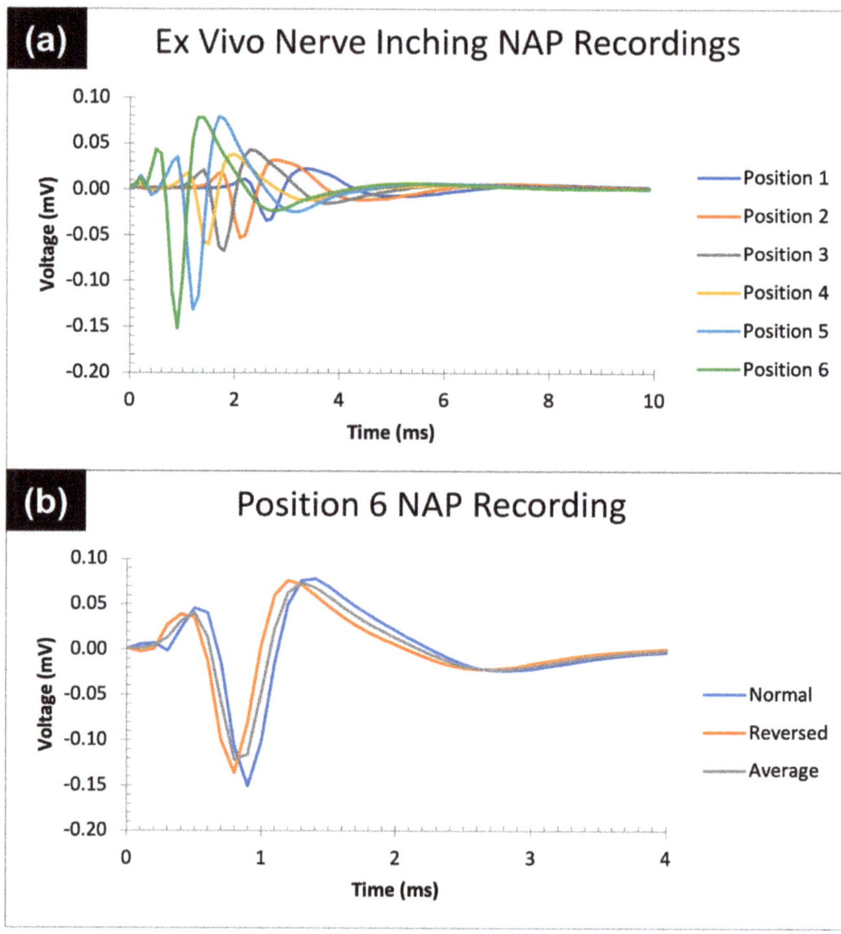


**Figure 6.** Recorded ex vivo NAP signals throughout the nerve inching procedure. (**a**) Recorded NAP signals for each of the six electrode inching positions. (**b**) Recorded NAP at the sixth and final electrode position produced by normal (blue) and reversed polarity (orange) electrical stimulations; an average of the two is shown as well (gray).

Regarding the ex vivo data collection, six NAP signals were recorded from the six total electrode inching positions to verify successful electrode stimulation and recording function, as well as to verify recorded signal quality without artifact presence. Additionally, an extra NAP from a polarity-switched stimulus in the sixth (final) electrode position was recorded with the intention of investigating artifact presence/absence. The recorded waveforms are shown in Figure 6.

As the electrodes were inched closer together, the NAP amplitude increased from a depolarized peak of −0.034 mV in position 1 to a depolarized peak of −0.15 mV in position 6, and the NAP latency shortened from approximately 1.7 ms in position 1 to approximately 0.1 ms in position 6. This is bioelectrically justified, as bringing the point of electrical current stimulation closer to the site of NAP recording should yield a faster presence of NAP signal at the recording electrode, as well as a higher measured potential. Additionally, repositioning of the stimulating electrode throughout the inching procedure did not at all affect or compromise the quality of NAP recordings. Even when the stimulating electrode was brought the closest to the recording electrode, the recorded NAP remained consistent, without any trace of nerve-lifting artifacts or electrical stimulus artifacts (i.e., when the site of stimulation is brought too close), as shown by the consistent NAP signal from normal- and reverse-polarity stimulations in Figure 6b.

With respect to the electrode pullout force testing, the average required forces to remove the electrode from the 2 mm, 5 mm, and 1 cm nerve models were 0.43 N, 1.57 N, and 3.61 N, respectively (Figure 7).

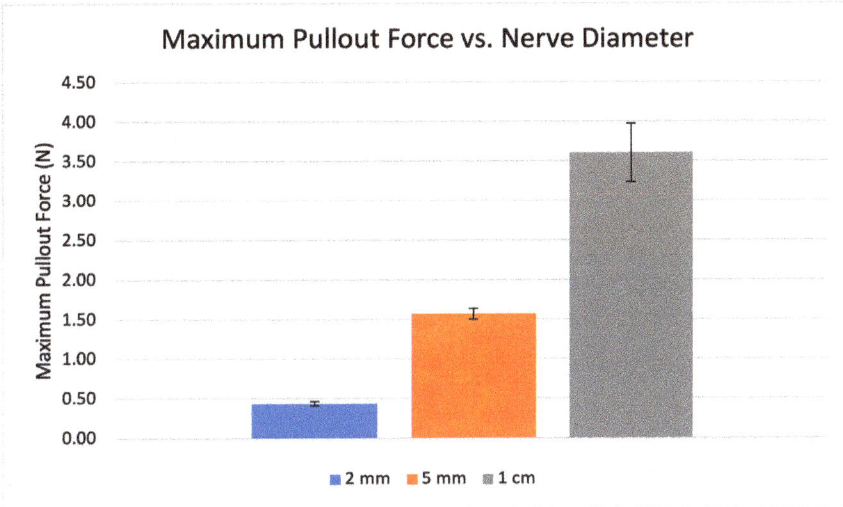


**Figure 7.** Recorded maximum pullout forces required for electrode removal from nerve models of three different diameters. Error bars represent standard error. Statistically significant differences in average pullout forces between the three groups ($p < 0.001$) were calculated using a two-tailed, unpaired *t*-test.

## 4. Discussion

The ex vivo nerve inching procedure verification testing quantitatively verified the stimulation and recording functionalities of our electrodes. As shown in Figure 6a, each of the six NAP recordings throughout the nerve inching procedure yielded clean signals without the presence of artifacts, due to the non-lifting method of electrode engagement with the nerve. The data also demonstrate that the repositioning of the electrodes across different positions during an "inching" procedure does not affect or compromise the recorded signal quality, showing a robustness in accurate signal recording throughout the electrode manipulation within the surgical environment. The absence of the recorded signal artifact is further shown in Figure 6b, showing consistency in the recorded NAP signal from a normal vs. reverse polarity of electrical stimulation, even when the stimulating electrode is brought closest to the recording electrode.

In the case of a clinical emergency in which the electrodes are quickly removed from the nerve—or if the electrodes/wires are pulled by accident—it is important that minimal force be required to disengage our electrodes from the nerve to avoid further nerve injury. Our collected pullout force testing demonstrates that this is the case with the newly designed electrodes via a quantitative maximum pullout force experiment across different nerve diameters, similar to the investigation performed by Lamadé et al. 2011 (which cites a maximum nerve tensile force of 21 $N/mm^2$ of the median nerve) [26]. Our collected results (Figure 7) were then compared to the data published by Rickett et al., in which the NAP amplitude remained statistically unchanged at a 5% strain but diminished at a 10% strain [27]. This suggests that a minimum threshold for stretched nerve damage on NAP amplitude occurs between these two values, which corresponds to calculated stress forces of 1.1 to 2.5 $N/mm^2$, respectively, incorporating the average 1.135 $mm^2$ guinea pig cross-sectional nerve area from the study. The calculated stress forces of our electrode (0.03, 0.02, and 0.01 $N/mm^2$ for the 2 mm, 5 mm, 1 cm diameter nerve models, respectively) lie well within the published safety guinea pig nerve threshold and further suggests that this will remain the case for larger human nerves. It is worth noting that this maximum pullout force was measured with the electrodes exerting their maximum securement at a full lead retraction onto the nerve model; in reality, the nerve can be secured with less than full retraction, thereby requiring even less force for emergency removal.

Alongside these benefits demonstrated by the verification of our design criteria in the final electrode design (Table 1; see Section 3), there still currently remain limitations in our assessment of the device. Namely, functional testing is still required to fully verify ergonomic electrode manipulation during simultaneous successful electrical stimulation and NAP recording within an in vivo surgical field, instead of verifying these design criteria separately (and partially within an ex vivo setup), as shown in this study. Additionally, the reproducibility of simultaneous ergonomic and functional electrode verifications within an in vivo setting should be shown across different anatomical sites of surgery, demonstrating that the electrodes can robustly function across intraoperative settings. Because our electrodes are manipulated via fine motor control, this requires neurosurgeons to actively perform precise surgical technique in order to ensure IONM success and maximize patient safety; this may likely require a degree of training/familiarization with this new instrument.

## 5. Conclusions

This study introduces a novel IONM electrode design to improve intraoperative NAP recording during the treatment of PNIs, in which current electrodes perturb the surgical environment, resulting in signal artifacts and potential iatrogenic nerve damage from surgical lifting. In collaboration with a team of electrophysiologists, neurosurgeons, and neurologists, our team articulated this clinical need and developed a set of design requirements to guide the development of redesigned stimulating and recording electrodes. Our redesign incorporated improved ergonomic design factors to ensure ease of surgical use and successful electrode contact across all diameters of nerves while allowing nerve contact with minimal nerve and surgical field perturbation/displacement; this ultimately addressed every ideated design requirement. Quantitative verification testing demonstrated the proper electrical function and ergonomic device manipulation on nerve tissue and an excellent safety profile with pullout force testing well within established safety limits. Ultimately, this innovation has the potential to improve the standard of care in peripheral nerve assessment, providing neurosurgeons and their operating teams with a valuable tool when making critical surgical decisions.

**Author Contributions:** Conceptualization, N.R., J.C., L.E.P., B.S., X.-H.L., C.G., A.B., M.R., G.W., L.Z., S.W. and C.M.; methodology, N.R., J.C., L.E.P., B.S., X.-H.L., C.G., A.B., M.R., G.W. and C.M.; validation, N.R., J.C., L.E.P., B.S., X.-H.L., C.G., A.B., M.R. and G.W.; formal analysis, N.R. and G.W.; investigation, N.R., J.C., L.E.P., B.S., X.-H.L., C.G., M.R., G.W., L.Z., S.W. and C.M.; resources, A.B., M.R., G.W. and C.M.; data curation, N.R. and G.W.; writing—original draft, N.R., J.C., L.E.P., B.S., X.-H.L., C.G., L.Z., S.W. and C.M.; writing—review and editing, N.R., J.C., L.E.P., B.S., X.-H.L., C.G., M.R., G.W. and C.M.; supervision, N.R., A.B., M.R., G.W. and C.M.; project administration, N.R., A.B.,

M.R., G.W. and C.M.; funding acquisition, N.R. and C.M. All authors have read and agreed to the published version of the manuscript.

**Funding:** This research received internal funding for Biomedical Engineering Design Teams at the Johns Hopkins University. Additional funding was provided by a 2022–2023 VentureWell IDEA International award. APC is funded by Nathaniel Riemann.

**Institutional Review Board Statement:** The animal study protocols were officially approved by the Animal Care and Use Committee of the Johns Hopkins University (protocol SW23M55 was approved on 03/17/23, and PR21M249 was approved on 09/14/21).

**Informed Consent Statement:** Not applicable.

**Data Availability Statement:** Data supporting the results are stored on the personal computers of co-authors Nathaniel Riemann, Matthias Ringkamp, and Gang Wu and are backed up on a personal Google Drive. The data are available upon request.

**Conflicts of Interest:** The authors declare no conflicts of interest.

## References


1. Robinson, L.R. Traumatic injury to peripheral nerves. *Muscle Nerve* **2000**, *23*, 863–873. [CrossRef]
2. Althagafi, A.; Nadi, M. Acute Nerve Injury. In *StatPearls*; StatPearls Publishing: Tampa, FL, USA, 2023.
3. Grinsell, D.; Keating, C.P. Peripheral nerve reconstruction after injury: A review of clinical and experimental therapies. *BioMed Res. Int.* **2014**, *2014*, 698256. [CrossRef]
4. Robert, E.G.; Happel, L.T.; Kline, D.G. Intraoperative nerve action potential recordings: Technical considerations, problems, and pitfalls. *Neurosurgery* **2009**, *65* (Suppl. S4), A97–A104. [CrossRef] [PubMed]
5. Tezcan, A.H. *Peripheral Nerve Injury and Current Treatment Strategies*; InTech: Houston TX, USA, 2017. [CrossRef]
6. Simon, N.G.; Spinner, R.J.; Kline, D.G.; Kliot, M. Advances in the neurological and neurosurgical management of peripheral nerve trauma. *J. Neurol. Neurosurg. Psychiatry* **2016**, *87*, 198–208. [CrossRef] [PubMed]
7. Barnes, S.L.; Miller, T.A.; Simon, N.G. Traumatic peripheral nerve injuries: Diagnosis and management. *Curr. Opin. Neurol.* **2022**, *35*, 718–727. [CrossRef] [PubMed]
8. Mandeville, R.; Sanchez, B.; Johnston, B.; Bazarek, S.; Thum, J.A.; Birmingham, A.; See, R.H.B.; Leochico, C.F.D.; Kumar, V.; Dowlatshahi, A.S.; et al. A scoping review of current and emerging techniques for evaluation of peripheral nerve health, degeneration, and regeneration: Part 1, neurophysiology. *J. Neural Eng.* **2023**, *20*, 041001. [CrossRef] [PubMed]
9. Campbell, W.W.; Sahni, S.K.; Pridgeon, R.M.; Riaz, G.; Leshner, R.T. Intraoperative electroneurography: Management of ulnar neuropathy at the elbow. *Muscle Nerve* **1988**, *11*, 75–81. [CrossRef]
10. Kamble, N.; Shukla, D.; Bhat, D. Peripheral Nerve Injuries: Electrophysiology for the Neurosurgeon. *Neurol. India* **2019**, *67*, 1419–1422. [CrossRef] [PubMed]
11. Strommen, J.A.; Skinner, S.; Crum, B.A. Neurophysiology during peripheral nerve surgery. *Handb. Clin. Neurol.* **2022**, *186*, 295–318. [CrossRef] [PubMed]
12. Wu, G.; Belzberg, A.; Nance, J.; Gutierrez-Hernandez, S.; Ritzl, E.K.; Ringkamp, M. Solutions to the Technical Challenges Embedded in the Current Methods for Intraoperative Peripheral Nerve Action Potential Recordings. *J. Neurosurg.* **2020**, *133*, 884–893. [CrossRef] [PubMed]
13. Miranda, C.; Goñi, J.; Labruto, N. Five Qualitative Research Concepts Grounded in Anthropological Methods for Teaching Design in Healthcare. *Healthcare* **2022**, *10*, 360. [CrossRef] [PubMed]
14. Miranda, C.; Altermatt, F.; Villagran, I.; Goñi, J. Developing an Innovative Medical Training Simulation Device for Peripheral Venous Access: A User-Centered Design Approach. *Healthcare* **2020**, *8*, 420. [CrossRef] [PubMed]
15. Bernard, R.H. *Research Methods in Anthropology: Qualitative and Quantitative Approaches*; AltaMira Press: Lanham, MD, USA, 2006.
16. Wolcott, H.F. *Ethnography: A Way of Seeing*, 2nd ed.; AltaMira Press: Lanham, MD, USA, 2008. Available online: http://www.amazon.com/Ethnography-Seeing-Harry-F-Wolcott/dp/0759111693 (accessed on 11 December 2023).
17. Schensul, S.L.; Schensul, J.J.; LeCompte, M.D. *Essential Ethnographic Methods: Observations, Interviews, and Questionnaires (Vol. 2)*; AltaMira Press: Lanham, MD, USA, 1999.
18. Adler, P.A.; Adler, P. The Promise and Pitfalls of Going Into the Field. *Contexts* **2003**, *2*, 41–47. [CrossRef]
19. Yock, P.; Zenios, S.; Makower, J.; Brinton, T.; Kumar, U.; Watkins, F.; Kurihara, C. *Biodesign: The Process of Innovating Medical Technologies*, 2nd ed.; Cambridge University Press: Cambridge, UK, 2015. [CrossRef]
20. Maiden, N.; Gizikis, A. Where do requirements come from? *IEEE Softw.* **2001**, *18*, 10–12. [CrossRef]
21. van de Poel, I. *Translating Values into Design Requirements BT—Philosophy and Engineering: Reflections on Practice, Principles and Process*; Michelfelder, D.P., McCarthy, N., Goldberg, D.E., Eds.; Springer: Dordrecht, The Netherlands, 2013; pp. 253–266. [CrossRef]
22. Kelley, T.; Littman, J. *The Art of Innovation: Lessons in Creativity from IDEO, America's Leading Design Firm*; Currency/Doubleday: New York, NY, USA, 2001.

23. Aman, M.; Mayrhofer-Schmid, M.; Schwarz, D.; Bendszus, M.; Daeschler, S.C.; Klemm, T.; Kneser, U.; Harhaus, L.; Boecker, A.H. Avoiding scar tissue formation of peripheral nerves with the help of an acellular collagen matrix. *PLoS ONE* **2023**, *18*, e0289677. [CrossRef] [PubMed]
24. Davis, D.; Maini, K.; Vasudevan, A. Sciatica. In *StatPearls*; StatPearls Publishing: Tampa, FL, USA, 2022.
25. McDonnell, M.N.; Ridding, M.C.; Flavel, S.C.; Miles, T.S. Effect of human grip strategy on force control in precision tasks. *Exp. Brain Res.* **2005**, *161*, 368–373. [CrossRef] [PubMed]
26. Lamadé, W.; Ulmer, C.; Rieber, F.; Friedrich, C.; Koch, K.P.; Thon, K.-P. New Backstrap Vagus Electrode for Continuous Intraoperative Neuromonitoring in Thyroid Surgery. *Surg. Innov.* **2011**, *18*, 206–213. [CrossRef] [PubMed]
27. Rickett, T.; Connell, S.; Bastijanic, J.; Hegde, S.; Shi, R. Functional and mechanical evaluation of nerve stretch injury. *J. Med. Syst.* **2011**, *35*, 787–793. [CrossRef] [PubMed]

healthcare

MDPI

*Article*

# Prevalence and Risk Factors of Deep Venous Thrombosis in Intensive Inpatient Neurorehabilitation Unit

**Maria Elena Pugliese [1,*], Riccardo Battaglia [1], Maria Ursino [1], Lucia Francesca Lucca [1], Maria Quintieri [1], Martina Vatrano [1], Paolo Tonin [1] and Antonio Cerasa [1,2,3,*]**

1 Intensive Rehabilitation Unit, S'Anna Institute, 88900 Crotone, Italy; dr.riccardo.battaglia@gmail.com (R.B.); m.ursino@isakr.it (M.U.); l.lucca@istitutosantanna.it (L.F.L.); m.quintieri@isakr.it (M.Q.); m.vatrano@isakr.it (M.V.); patonin18@gmail.com (P.T.)
2 Institute for Biomedical Research and Innovation (IRIB), National Research Council of Italy, 98164 Messina, Italy
3 Pharmacotechnology Documentation and Transfer Unit, Preclinical and Translational Pharmacology, Department of Pharmacy, Health Science and Nutrition, University of Calabria, 87036 Rende, Italy
* Correspondence: me.pugliese@isakr.it (M.E.P.); antonio.cerasa@irib.cnr.it (A.C.)

**Abstract:** Venous thromboembolism (VTE) (deep vein thrombosis and its complication, pulmonary embolism) is a major cause of morbidity and mortality in hospitalized patients and about 7% of these cases are due to immobility secondary to a neurological impairment. Acquired brain injury (ABI) has also been recognized as one of the main risk factors for VTE. Numerous epidemiological studies have been conducted to assess the risk factors for VTE in institutionalized polytrauma patients, although there is a lack of information about neurorehabilitation wards. Since VTE is often undiagnosed, this prospective study aimed to determine the prevalence and clinical characteristics of lower-limb deep venous thrombosis (DVT) in ABI patients at neurorehabilitation admission. Methods: ABI patients were screened for DVT on admission to the intensive rehabilitation unit (IRU) with compression ultrasonography and basal D-dimer assay and were daily clinically monitored until discharge. A total of 127 consecutive ABI patients (mean age: 60.1 ± 17.6 years; 63% male; time from event: 30.9 ± 22.1 days; rehabilitation time in IRU: 84.6 ± 58.4 days) were enrolled. Results: On admission to the IRU, the DVT prevalence was about 8.6%. The mean D-dimer level in patients with DVT was significantly higher than in patients without DVT (6 ± 0.9 vs. 1.97 ± 1.61, $p$-value = 0.0001). ABI patients with DVT did not show any significant clinical characteristics with respect to ABI without DVT, although a prevalence of hemorrhagic strokes and patients originating from the Intensive Care Unit and Neurosurgery ward was revealed. During the rehabilitation period, patients with DVT showed a significant difference in pharmacological DVT prophylaxis (high prevalence of nadroparin with 27.3% vs. 1.7%, $p$-value = 0.04) and a prevalence of transfers in critical awards (36% versus 9.5% of patients without DVT, $p$-value = 0.05). The mortality rate was similar in the two groups. Conclusions: Our research offers a more comprehensive view of the clinical development of DVT patients and confirms the prevalence rate of DVT in ABI patients as determined upon IRU admission. According to our findings, screening these individuals regularly at the time of rehabilitation admission may help identify asymptomatic DVT quickly and initiate the proper treatment to avoid potentially fatal consequences. However, to avoid time-consuming general ultrasonography observation, a more precise selection of patients entering the rehabilitation ward is required.

**Keywords:** deep venous thrombosis; rehabilitation; D-dimer; compressive ultrasonography; severe brain injury; stroke

**Citation:** Pugliese, M.E.; Battaglia, R.; Ursino, M.; Lucca, L.F.; Quintieri, M.; Vatrano, M.; Tonin, P.; Cerasa, A. Prevalence and Risk Factors of Deep Venous Thrombosis in Intensive Inpatient Neurorehabilitation Unit. *Healthcare* **2024**, *12*, 936. https://doi.org/10.3390/healthcare12090936

Academic Editors: Marco Tramontano and Giovanni Galeoto

Received: 21 February 2024
Revised: 30 April 2024
Accepted: 30 April 2024
Published: 1 May 2024



## 1. Introduction

The third most common acute cardiovascular condition worldwide, after myocardial infarction and stroke, is venous thromboembolism (VTE) [1], which can present clinically as deep vein thrombosis (DVT) or pulmonary embolism (PE) [2]. VTE can be fatal for medical inpatients, although there is evidence that pharmacologic VTE prophylaxis can effectively prevent VTE if started 24 to 72 h after admission [3], decreasing symptomatic PE by 58%, fatal PE by 64%, and symptomatic DVT by 53% [4]. However, roughly only 50% of qualified hospitalized patients receive the recommended thromboprophylaxis.

DVT and PE are generally acknowledged as serious side effects in acquired brain injury (ABI) patients. According to earlier research, polytrauma patients may have a lower-extremity DVT incidence of up to 20% [5–7], and DVT is also the leading cause of death for individuals who survive their initial traumatic injuries [7]. One of the main risk factors for VTE is hospitalization. Indeed, Heit and colleagues [8] demonstrated that 48% of the cases of VTE in the community could be attributed to hospitalization for surgery (24%) or for medical illness (22%). In chronic brain injury patients, the incidence of VTE increases [9]. Indeed, because prolonged immobility causes venous stasis and decreased blood flow, it is frequently associated with an increased risk of VTE [8–10]. Pottier and colleagues [11] performed a meta-analytic evaluation of epidemiological studies investigating the incidence of VTE in institutionalized patients, demonstrating that prolonged immobility (>3 days) is associated with a two- to three-fold increase in VTE risk.

DVT is more prevalent in traumatic brain injury patients but it has also been reported in individuals with other neurological conditions like spinal injuries, stroke, and Guillain–Barre syndrome that are characterized by acute paralysis [12–16], whereas it is less common in patients with neurodegenerative diseases [17]. The strict correlation between the time elapsed since the traumatic event and the rate at which immobility begins has been demonstrated to influence the occurrence of DVT in several studies [18,19]. For instance, Engbergs et al. [20] demonstrated that within two weeks of being released from the hospital, there was a fifteen-fold greater risk of thrombosis. Over a period of three months, thrombosis risk was linked to minor leg injuries, plaster casts, surgery fractures, and temporary immobilization at home. For in-hospital immobility, the population-attributable risks were 27%, and for immobility outside of hospitals, they were 15%. Again, Sartori and colleagues [21], evaluating 252 acutely ill medical inpatients, suggested that just 3 days of immobilization should be considered a risk factor for DVT.

Despite many epidemiological investigations evaluating the prevalence and risk factors of DVT in ambulatory or hospitalized cohorts, few prospective studies have been conducted in the post-acute rehabilitation phase. DVT is a significant contributor to morbidity and mortality in individuals who have had significant orthopedic surgery, severe trauma, or an acute stroke [22]. Given the potentially fatal consequences of undetected DVT after failed prophylaxis, some clinicians routinely screen patients with TBI who are asymptomatic by using venous doppler ultrasound (VDU). However, VDU is costly and may have limited sensitivity for asymptomatic DVT. There is no consensus regarding appropriate screening, prophylaxis, or treatment during acute rehabilitation [23,24]. For these reasons, in this study, we aim to evaluate DVT's local prevalence in asymptomatic ABI patients on admission to an intensive rehabilitation unit (IRU) by using a combination of VDU and D-dimer dosing, and to study DVT patient outcomes.

## 2. Methods

### 2.1. Clinical Enrollment

ABI patients were consecutively admitted to the IRU of the Institute S. Anna (Crotone, Italy) between June 2021 and May 2022. We enrolled only those who met the following inclusion criteria: (1) age $\geq$ 18 years; (2) acute brain injury, including trauma, hemorrhagic or ischemic stroke, spinal cord injury, anoxia, polyneuritis, or central nervous system infections; (3) written informed consent. The exclusion criteria were as follows: (1) acute brain injury > 90 days; (2) pre-existing severe disability; (3) diagnosis of DVT in an acute setting before rehabilitation admission; (4) neurodegenerative diseases (i.e., Parkinson's Disease). All patients were transferred directly from the hospital after the medical and neurosurgery complications had been stabilized. The departments transferring patients more frequently were the Intensive Care Unit, Neurosurgery, Neurology, Geriatric, and the Internal Medicine ward. The data from the acute hospital ICU were retrieved from patient files.

The present study was carried out following the rules of the Declaration of Helsinki and was approved by the local ethics committee of "Regione Calabria Comitato Etico Sezione Area Centro", n.320, 21 December 2017. Written informed consent was obtained from the patients' authorized representatives before study enrollment.

### 2.2. Procedure and Clinical Evaluations

This was a monocentric prospective observational study. On admission to the neurorehabilitation unit, all patients underwent a detailed anamnesis and clinical evaluation. Specifically, demographic data (sex, age, and body mass index), comorbidities, risk factors for VTE (i.e., SEPSI or fractures) and DVT-related clinical assessment data were collected.

Diagnosis of DVT was accomplished using an integrated clinical, biochemical, and instrumental evaluation. The DVT screening protocol consisted of the following:

- An evaluation of DVT clinical signs, such as leg asymmetry with unilateral edema, erythema, and pain, and the presence of Buer and Homans signs.
- A single quantitative D-dimer assay performed within 24 h of rehabilitation admission. The LIATEST D-dimer assay, which is an immuno-turbidimetric quantitative assay method based on a latex microparticle agglutination test, was used, with a positive D-dimer test for values > 0.5 g/mL [25,26].
- A compressive leg ultrasound performed on all eligible patients admitted to the rehabilitation unit, irrespective of the D-dimer value (normal value < 0.5 g/mL) [27]. All venous duplex ultrasonography studies were performed by the same radiographer with specific experience and reported by trained radiologists using a Canon Aplio 300 ultrasound machine during the entire study period. A compressive ultrasound was performed on each patient within 72 h of admission. The presence of DVT was determined by a positive venous duplex ultrasonography result [28].

Clinical assessment on admission also included the following:

(A) A motor functional evaluation with the Barthel Index.
(B) A thrombosis/hemorrhagic risk evaluation with PADUA scores including the improve bleeding risk prediction score, improve associative score for VTE, and improve DD scale [29,30].
(C) A laboratory screening protocol on admission included complete blood count, levels of creatinine, azotemia, electrolytes, and reactive C protein (RCP), erythrocyte sedimentation rate (ESR), PT, and aPTT.

Patients who had DVT evidence (DVT+) started anticoagulation therapy, if clinically feasible. In addition, the treatment protocol included highly compressive (23–32 mmHg) monolateral or bilateral socks and early mobilization. Throughout their entire rehabilitation stay, each DVT-negative enrolled patient had a daily clinical evaluation to check the appearance of DVT signs/symptoms (Figure 1). In cases of clinical suspicion, D-dimer testing and compressive leg ultrasound were performed. The diagnosis of PE was made on clinical grounds and investigated accordingly.

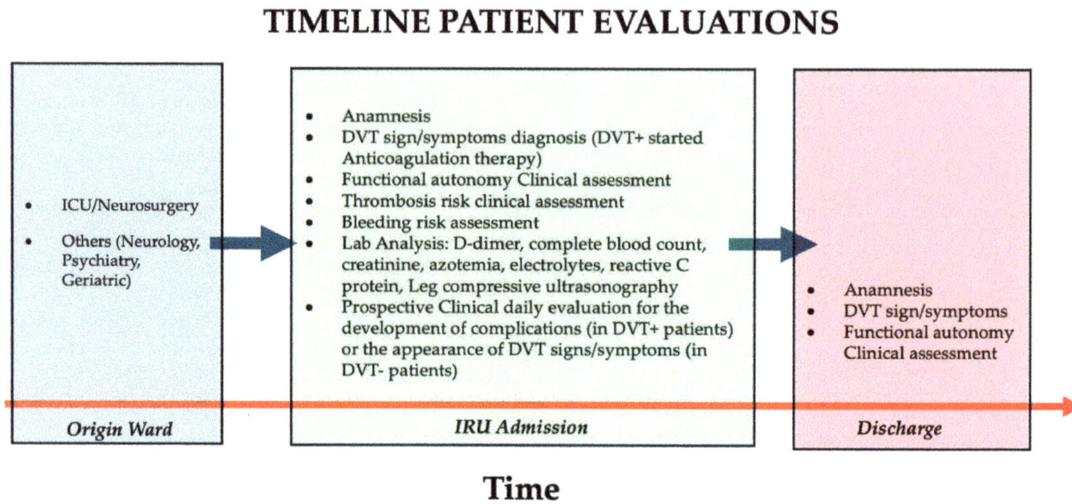


**Figure 1.** Procedural phases of patient evaluations from origin ward (blue box), during the neurorehabilitation stay in the IRU (green box) and at discharge (rose box). Clinical, laboratory, and ultrasonography evaluations were performed on admission to determine the prevalence of ABI patients with (DVT+) or without (DVT−) lower-limb deep venous thrombosis. Before discharge, a daily clinical evaluation was carried out to assess the development of new DVT symptoms in the enrolled ABI population or the occurrence of complications in DVT+ patients.

### 2.3. *Statistical Analysis*

Statistical analysis was performed using SPSS v26 package for Windows (Statistical Package for Social Sciences; www.spss.it (accessed on 1 January 2024); Chicago, IL, USA). Assumptions for normality were tested for all continuous variables. Normality was tested using the Kolmogorov–Smirnov test. Chi2 was used to analyze variations in the distribution of clinical (i.e., risk factors and etiology) and demographic (i.e., gender) characteristics. Both the parametric statistical analysis (unpaired *t*-test) and the non-parametric statistical analysis (Mann–Whitney U-tests and the Wilcoxon signed-rank test) were used for other variables. A $p < 0.05$ cut-off was considered statistically significant for every test.

## 3. Results

Table 1 reported the demographical and clinical information acquired on admission to the IRU. The prevalence of DVT was 8.6%, with only two patients showing clinical signs of DVT (1.45%). ABI patients with DVT tended to be more hemorrhagic and came from the ICU/Neurosurgery ward (Figure 2), although a significant difference with respect to other patients was not revealed (*p*-value = 0.36 and 0.21, respectively, for etiology and origin ward). Similarly, no significant risk factors were detected also considering additional clinical parameters such as thrombophilia, active cancer, estrogen contraceptive therapy, cardiac insufficiency, previous stroke, hypertension, smoking habit, obesity, and pressure wounds.

ABI patients with DVT are characterized by higher values in the D-dimer assay ($6 \pm 0.9$) and PCR test ($5.5 \pm 4.2$) with respect to ABI patients without DVT ($1.97 \pm 1.61$ and $3.31 \pm 3.8$; *p*-values = 0.0001 and = 0.03; respectively, for D-dimer assay and PCR). The totality of patients ($n = 11$) diagnosed with DVT by means of color doppler ultrasonography had positive D-dimer tests on admission (sensibility: 100%). No false negative D-dimer result was reported (negative predictive value (NPV): 100%). A total number of 105 patients with a positive D-dimer value were negative upon ultrasound examination (sensibility: 10.25%), with only 12 patients with a negative D-dimer value and negative ultrasound (positive predictive value (PPV): 9.48%).

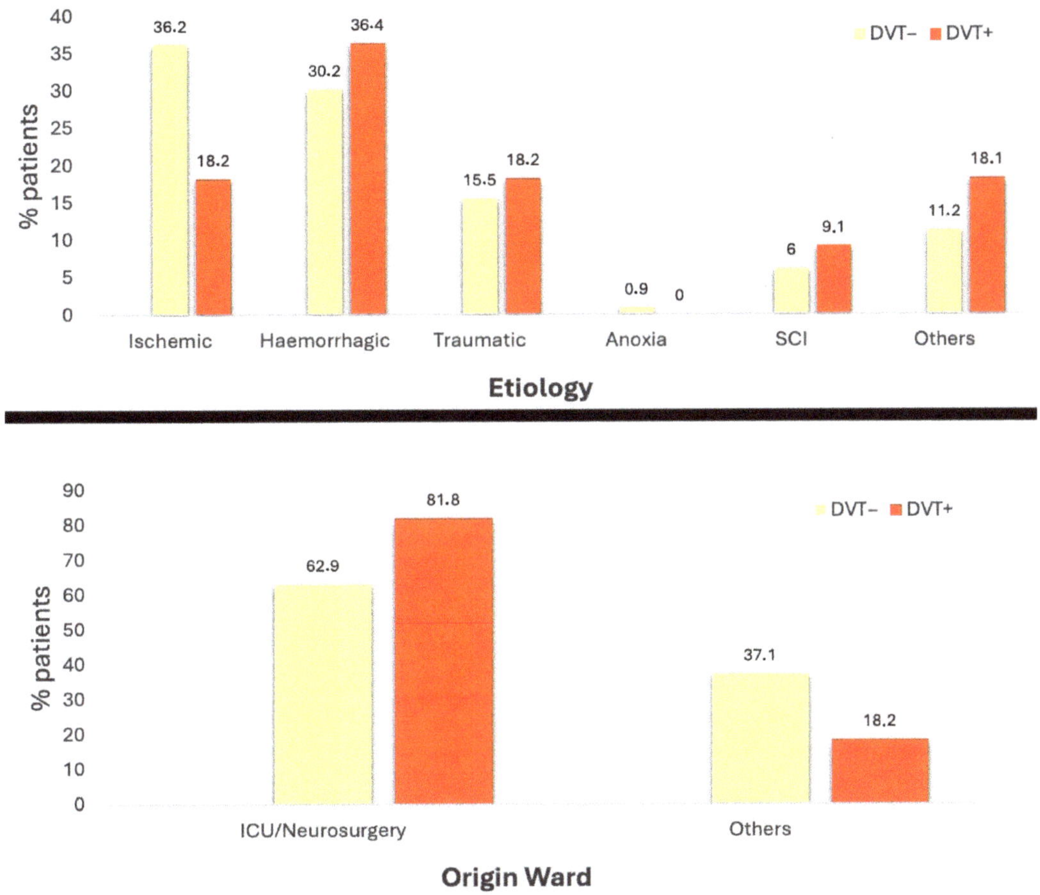


**Figure 2.** Etiology and origin ward prevalence in the ABI population based on DVT diagnosis. SCI: spinal cord injury; Others for Etiology: infections/benign tumor; Others for Origin Ward: Neurology, Psychiatry, and Geriatric.

**Table 1.** Demographic and clinical characteristics of ABI patients on admission to IRU.

| | **DVT−** **(n° 116)** | **DVT+** **(n° 11)** | ***p*-Level** |
|---|---|---|---|
| Age | 60.02 ± 17.8 | 61.45 ± 15.9 | 0.94 |
| Male Sex, n (%) | 72 (62.1%) | 8 (72.7%) | 0.48 |
| Time from event (days) | 30.8 ± 22.8 | 28.2 ± 11.8 | 0.72 |
| **Risk Factors (before IRU admission)** | | | |
| Previous Motor Disability (% yes) | 12 (10.3%) | 0 (0%) | 0.6 |
| SEPSI (<1 month) (% yes) | 29 (25%) | 5 (45.5%) | 0.16 |
| Fractures (<3 months) (% yes) | 21 (18.1%) | 1 (9.1%) | 0.69 |
| Important Surgical Interventions (<3 months) (% yes) | 51 (44%) | 5 (45.4%) | 1 |

**Table 1.** *Cont.*

| | DVT− (n° 116) | DVT+ (n° 11) | *p*-Level |
|---|---|---|---|
| | **Clinical Evaluation** | | |
| PADUA SCORE | 4.7 ± 1.3 | 4.8 ± 1.07 | 0.54 |
| Improve Bleeding Score | 5.42 ± 2.66 | 6.4 ± 2.21 | 0.25 |
| Improve Associative Score for VTE | 4.21 ± 0.7 | 4.2 ± 0.6 | 0.86 |
| Improve DD | 5.6 ± 1.3 | 6 ± 0.9 | 0.27 |
| Barthel Index | 9 [0–75] | 4 [0–20] | 0.48 |
| | **Biochemical Data** | | |
| D-Dimer | 1.97 ± 1.61 | 6 ± 0.9 | **0.001** |
| INR | 1.24± 0.18 | 1.2 ± 0.09 | 0.96 |
| PCR | 3.31 ± 3.8 | 5.5 ± 4.2 | **0.032** |
| PCT | 0.5 ± 2.3 | 0.4 ± 0.6 | 0.94 |
| VES | 47.8 ± 34.7 | 66.7 ± 38.9 | 0.21 |
| HB | 11.7 ± 2. | 11.7 ± 1.9 | 0.96 |
| Leukocyte Count | 8.9 ± 3.6 | 9.4 ± 2.8 | 0.44 |
| PLT | 291.9 ± 127.1 | 289.4 ± 76.6 | 0.56 |

Data are reported as %, median, or mean values accordingly. DVT: deep vein thrombosis. ICU: Intensive Care Unit. IRU: intensive rehabilitation unit. SCI: spinal cord injury. CNS: central nervous system. BOLD value means significant differences between groups at *p*-level < 0.05.

Concerning medication, the totality of DVT-positive patients received VTE prophylaxis on rehabilitation admission. On admission, all DVT patients received anticoagulation medication; however, around 10% (n = 11) had full-dose anticoagulation for atrial fibrillation, and the rest of the patients received EBPM or fondaparinux for DVT prophylaxis. Overall, the pharmacological treatment for DVT+ patients differed from that of DVT− patients since they were more frequently prescribed nadroparin at 0.3 mL for thrombosis prophylaxis (27.3% vs. 1.7%, *p* value = 0.04) (Table 2).

**Table 2.** Pharmacological treatment of ABI patients after admission to IRU.

| | DVT− (n° 116) | DVT+ (n° 11) | *p*-Level |
|---|---|---|---|
| Antiplatelet agents (% Yes) | 30 (25.8%) | 3 (27.3%) | 0.91 |
| Anticoagulation (% Yes) | 11 (9.5%) | 0 (0%) | 0.97 |
| TVB drug prevention | | | **0.04** |
| • None | • 11 (9.5%) | • 0 (0%) | |
| • ENOXAPARIN 2000 UI | • 1 (0.9%) | • 0 (0%) | |
| • ENOXAPARIN 4000 UI | • 72 (62.1%) | • 5 (45.5%) | |
| • ENOXAPARIN 6000 UI | • 16 (13.8%) | • 2 (18.2%) | |
| • NADROPARIN 0.3 ML | • 2 (1.7%) | • 3 (27.3%) | |
| • NADROPARIN 0.4 ML | • 7 (6%) | • 0 (0%) | |
| • NADROPARIN 0.6 ML | • 4 (3.4%) | • 1 (9.1%) | |
| • FONDAPARINUX 1.5 MG | • 0 (0%) | • 0 (0%) | |
| • FONDAPARINUX 2.5 MG | • 3 (2.6%) | • 0 (0%) | |

During the patients' rehabilitation stay, no additional cases of DVT were detected. At discharge, a general clinical worsening was detected in ABI patients with DVT, with a prevalence of transfer to critical awards, while no differences were observed in mortality rate and length of stay (Table 3).

**Table 3.** Clinical evolution during IRU period.

| | DVT− (n° 116) | DVT+ (n° 11) | *p*-Level |
|---|---|---|---|
| N° | 116 | 11 | |
| Length of stay (days) | 84.7 ± 58.4 | 96 ± 38.6 | 0.19 |
| % of death during recovery | 3/116 (2.5%) | 1/11 (9%) | 0.23 |
| % of transfer to critical wards (yes) | 17 (9.5%) | 4 (36%) | 0.058 |
| Barthel Index at discharge | 20 [0–95] | 30 [0–100] | 0.38 |

## 4. Discussion

There are various spectrums of DVT and PE, from asymptomatic to cardiopulmonary dysfunction. Neurorehabilitation patients may under-report symptoms of DVT because of cognitive impairment, aphasia, neglect, or altered conscious states [31]. Consequently, thromboembolism is often underdiagnosed in rehabilitation settings. Early detection is essential because DVT therapy, with the aim of thrombus resolution, can save lives. Clinical PE occurs in 26% to 67% of untreated proximal DVT patients and is associated with an 11% to 23% rate of mortality. If treated, these numbers decrease to 5% and 1%, respectively [32]. A leg duplex ultrasound screening conducted upon IRU admission in 26% of ABI patients may require repeat duplex examinations or anticoagulation, changing the course of treatment. [33].

In this prospective study, we evaluated the prevalence of DVT symptoms in a large population of ABI patients and the clinical outcome. For the screening of DVT, we combined leg duplex ultrasound with D-dimer quantification and included them in the diagnostic algorithm of "Guidelines for the Diagnosis, Treatment and Prevention of Pulmonary Thromboembolism and Deep Vein Thrombosis" [34,35]. Our findings showed that the overall incidence of thromboembolism in rehabilitation patients on admission after acute brain injury was 8.6%, with only two patients with clinical signs of DVT (1.45%). These results are similar to those of previous studies of patients with ABI in neurorehabilitation settings that reported incidences ranging from 8.5 to 18% when asymptomatic screening was employed vs. only 1.6% for patients with symptomatic DVT [22,29]. In agreement with previous studies, D-dimer test sensitivity and NPV were 100% when using a cut-off value of 0.5 mL/L [36,37]. Notably, the D-dimer value can rise in several circumstances, including infections, pressure ulcers, inflammation/trauma, and post-surgery [38], which is more prevalent in patients with ABI undertaking neurorehabilitation. Therefore, because of its low specificity and positive predictive value, the D-dimer test is not advised for DTV rule-in. In our sample, the PPV (10.25%) and specificity (9.48%) were both extremely low. Again, an optimized cut-off value of 2.5 mg/L increased specificity to 75% for the diagnosis of deep vein thrombosis, at the cost of a modest loss in sensitivity (81%). In agreement with Akman et al.'s [39] findings, the mean D-dimer level in our DVT+ patients was considerably higher than the mean level in patients without DVT (6 ± 0.9 vs. 1.97 ± 1.61, *p*-values = 0.0001). Acute brain injury patients with DVT were also characterized by higher values in the PCR test (5.5 ± 4.2) with respect to ABI patients without DVT (3.31 ± 3.8) (*p*-values 0.03). This result is consistent with a previous case-control study that examined inflammatory markers and found that DVT patients had considerably higher levels of inflammatory markers—like CRP—compared to controls [40].

The second main finding of this study refers to the clinical course of ABI patients with DVT. The 30-day mortality rate for DVT patients not receiving anticoagulation exceeds 3%, and the risk of death increases ten-fold in patients who develop PE [41]. In our cohort, the death rate was the same for both groups. DVT+ patients tended to require more urgent transfers to crucial wards for surgical or medical difficulties (*p*-level = 0.058), thus confirming the importance of early diagnosis in reducing critical clinical complications. Furthermore, a DVT diagnosis can also be regarded as a clinician alert since it indicates a subset of complicated patients who have a high risk of internal problems.

At the pharmacological level, no significant risk factors were identified, except the use of seleparine at 0.3 mL as DVT prophylaxis in 27% of DVT-positive patients compared to 1.7% of the DVT-negative group ($p$ value = 0.04), where enoxaparin 4000 UI was more frequently used (65%). This information is in line with the results of a randomized experiment [42], which compared enoxaparin 4000 UI with nadroparin at 0.3 mL in terms of preventing venous thromboembolism. While all patients diagnosed with DVT were receiving medical prophylaxis at the time of admission, 90% of patients who tested negative for DVT started receiving it before admission to rehabilitation. While this result may seem contradictory, it should be remembered that eleven DVT− patients were treated for atrial fibrillation and so received full doses of direct oral anticoagulants. Again, no differences were noticed between the two groups regarding the length of stay in neurorehabilitation and functional impairment measured with the Barthel Index on admission and at discharge. The evaluation of risk scores for thrombosis and hemorrhagic bleeding, such as the Padua score, improve associative score for DVT, improve DD score, and improve bleeding score, revealed a population with extremely high risk for both thrombosis and bleeding, with no discernible differences between patients who were positive and negative for DVT. Finally, ABI patients with DVT tended to be more hemorrhagic and came from the ICU/Neurosurgery ward, although a significant difference with other patients was not revealed.

## 5. Conclusions

DVT is a frequent complication in neurologic patients entering neurorehabilitation. It is difficult to identify because it is often asymptomatic. Few studies have assessed the results of monitoring the prevalence of DVT in rehabilitation, even though it is notably linked to substantial morbidity in ABI patients. According to our findings, a routine screening using compressive leg ultrasonography and the D-dimer assay at the time of rehabilitation admission can help identify patients with asymptomatic DVT early on and treat them appropriately, potentially improving their prognosis. We advocate the use of ultrasound at the time of neurorehabilitation patient admission because it is a quick, safe, and readily available diagnostic procedure. Nevertheless, a stratified screening program based on an individual patient's risk has merit. To lower the risk of life-threatening complications and ascertain the incidence of DVT during a rehabilitation stay, more research is required to evaluate the optimal screening approach, saving resources without increasing patient risk. Since it has been demonstrated that patients who developed VTE are more likely to have undergone placement of invasive intracranial monitoring or neurosurgical intervention compared to their counterparts who did not develop VTE [43], in this study, we only reported the number of patients requiring more urgent transfers to crucial areas for surgical or medical difficulties. Therefore, it remains uncertain which repeated medical/neurosurgical interventions were required for DVT+ patients during the neurorehabilitation stay. Next, it remains to be established which risk factors are associated with clinical outcomes in ABI patients with VTE. In agreement with Jacob et al. [44], while early VTE prophylaxis and low molecular weight heparin compared to heparin were found to be protective factors, penetrating injury mechanism, increasing age, male gender, obesity, tachycardia, neurosurgical procedures (craniectomy/craniotomy), and pre-existing hypertension were linked to an increased risk of VTE. In our study, the lack of a regression statistical model did not allow us to evaluate which demographical, clinical, and biological features could be considered a risk factor for VTE in ABI patients. Indeed, small sample sizes (n = 11) can lead to unstable parameter estimates. However, the prevalence of well-known clinical risk factors for DVT was not different between the two groups (Table 1).

Notwithstanding these limitations, our research emphasizes the importance of monitoring the occurrence of DVT in clinical neurorehabilitation units. The importance of these clinical symptoms is supported by the high frequency on admission of hemorrhagic strokes and of patients coming from the Intensive Care Unit and Neurosurgery wards, as well as the greater number of transfers to critical awards throughout rehabilitation stays in

DVT+ patients. Our findings could provide valuable knowledge for healthcare professionals, enabling the development of tailored preventive strategies [45], early detection methods [46], and effective management protocols to reduce the burden of DVT during the neurorehabilitation period.

**Author Contributions:** Conceptualization R.B. and M.E.P.; methodology, A.C. and M.V.; formal analysis, R.B., M.E.P. and A.C.; investigation, L.F.L. and M.U.; resources, P.T.; data curation, R.B.; writing—original draft preparation, A.C.; writing—review and editing, R.B., M.E.P. and P.T.; supervision, P.T. and M.Q.; project administration, P.T.; and funding acquisition, P.T. All authors have read and agreed to the published version of the manuscript.

**Funding:** This research received no external funding.

**Institutional Review Board Statement:** This study was conducted in accordance with the Declaration of Helsinki and approved by the Review Board of the local ethics committee of "Regione Calabria". (n.320, 21 December 2017).

**Informed Consent Statement:** This study was approved by the local ethics committee of "Regione Calabria Comitato Etico Sezione Area Centro", n.320, 21 December 2017.

**Data Availability Statement:** The datasets associated with the present study are available upon reasonable request by interested researchers.

**Conflicts of Interest:** The authors declare no conflicts of interest.

## References

1. Raskob, G.E.; Angchaisuksiri, P.; Blanco, A.N.; Buller, H.; Gallus, A.; Hunt, B.J.; Hylek, E.M.; Kakkar, A.; Konstantinides, S.V.; McCumber, M.; et al. Thrombosis: A major contributor to global disease burden. *Arterioscler. Thromb. Vasc. Biol.* **2014**, *34*, 23632371. [CrossRef]
2. Torbicki, A.; Perrier, A.; Konstantidines, S.; Agnelli, G.; Galiè, N.; Pruszczyk, P.; Bengel, F.; Brady, A.J.; Ferreira, D.; Janssens, U.; et al. Guidelines on the diagnosis and management of acute pulmonary embolism. *Eur. Heart J.* **2008**, *29*, 2276–2315. [CrossRef]
3. Lu, V.M.; Alvi, M.A.; Rovin, R.A.; Kasper, E.M. Clinical outcomes following early versus late pharmacologic thromboprophylaxis in patients with traumatic intracranial hemorrhage: A systematic review and meta-analysis. *Neurosurg. Rev.* **2020**, *43*, 861–872. [CrossRef]
4. Dentali, F.; Douketis, J.D.; Gianni, M.; Lim, W.; Crowther, M.A. Meta-analysis: Anticoagulant prophylaxis to prevent symptomatic venous thromboembolism in hospitalized medical patients. *Ann. Intern. Med.* **2007**, *146*, 278–288. [CrossRef]
5. Luo, J.; Chen, D.; Tang, L.; Deng, H.; Zhang, C.; Chen, S.; Chang, T.; Dong, L.; Wang, W.; Xu, H.; et al. Multifactorial Shock: A Neglected Situation in Polytrauma Patients. *J. Clin. Med.* **2022**, *11*, 6829. [CrossRef]
6. Geerts, W.H.; Code, K.I.; Jay, R.M.; Chen, E.; Szalai, J.P. A prospective study of venous thromboembolism after major trauma. *N. Engl. J. Med.* **1994**, *331*, 1601–1606. [CrossRef]
7. Ruskin, K.J. Deep vein thrombosis and venous thromboembolism in trauma. *Curr. Opin. Anaesthesiol.* **2018**, *31*, 215–218. [CrossRef]
8. Heit, J.A.; O'Fallon, W.M.; Petterson, T.M.; Lohse, C.M.; Silverstein, D.N.; Mohr, D.N.; Melton, L.J. Relative impact of risk factors for deep venous thrombosis and pulmonary embolism. *Arch. Intern. Med.* **2002**, *162*, 1245–1248. [CrossRef]
9. Chen, D.; Luo, J.; Zhang, C.; Tang, L.; Deng, H.; Chang, T.; Xu, H.; He, M.; Wan, D.; Zhang, F.; et al. Venous Thrombus Embolism in Polytrauma: Special Attention to Patients with Traumatic Brain Injury. *J. Clin. Med.* **2023**, *12*, 1716. [CrossRef]
10. Valle, E.J.; Van Haren, R.M.; Allen, C.J.; Jouria, J.M.; Bullock, M.R.; Schulman, C.I.; Namias, N.; Livingstone, A.S.; Proctor, K.G. Does traumatic brain injury increase the risk for venous thromboembolism in polytrauma patients? *J. Trauma Acute Care Surg.* **2014**, *77*, 243–250. [CrossRef]
11. Pottier, P.; Hardouin, J.B.; Lejeune, S.; Jolliet, P.; Gillet, B.; Planchon, B. Immobilization and the risk of venous thromboembolism. A meta-analysis on epidemiological studies. *Thromb. Res.* **2009**, *124*, 468–476. [CrossRef]
12. Teasell, R.W.; Hsieh, J.T.; Aubut, J.A.; Eng, J.J.; Krassioukov, A.; Tu, L. Venous thromboembolism after spinal cord injury. *Arch. Phys. Med. Rehabil.* **2009**, *90*, 232–245. [CrossRef]
13. Green, D.; Hartwig, D.; Chen, D.; Soltysik, R.C.; Yarnold, P.R. Spinal cord injury risk assessment for thromboembolism (SPIRATE Study). *Am. J. Phys. Med. Rehabil.* **2003**, *82*, 950–956. [CrossRef]
14. Ratnasekera, A.; Seng, S.S.; Ciarmella, M.; Gallagher, A.; Poirier, K.; Harding, E.S.; Haut, E.R.; Geerts, W.; Murphy, P. Thromboprophylaxis in hospitalized trauma patients: A systematic review and meta-analysis of implementation strategies. *Trauma Surg. Acute Care Open* **2024**, *9*, e001420. [CrossRef]
15. Khan, M.T.; Ikram, A.; Saeed, O.; Afridi, T.; Sila, C.A.; Smith, M.S.; Irshad, K.; Shuaib, A. Deep Vein Thrombosis in Acute Stroke—A Systemic Review of the Literature. *Cureus* **2017**, *9*, e1982. [CrossRef]

16. Rousseau, M.C.; Guillotel, B. Risk factors for deep venous thrombosis in tetraparesic mental retarded patients. *Brain Inj.* **2001**, *15*, 1041–1044. [CrossRef]
17. Burbridge, B.E.; Wallace, J.K.; Rajput, A.; McCulloch, L. Doppler ultrasonographic examination of the leg veins of patients with Parkinson disease. *J. Psychiatry Neurosci.* **1999**, *24*, 338–340.
18. Barbar, S.; Noventa, F.; Rossetto, V.; Ferrari, A.; Brandolin, B.; Perlati, M.; De Bon, E.; Tormene, D.; Pagnan, A.; Prandoni, P. A risk assessment model for the identification of hospitalized medical patients at risk for venous thromboembolism: The Padua Prediction Score. *J. Thromb. Haemost.* **2010**, *8*, 2450–2457. [CrossRef]
19. Woller, S.C.; Stevens, S.M.; Jones, J.P.; Lloyd, J.F.; Evans, R.S.; Aston, V.T.; Elliott, C.G. Derivation and validation of a simple model to identify venous thromboembolism risk in medical patients. *Am. J. Med.* **2011**, *124*, 947–954.e2. [CrossRef]
20. Engbers, M.J.; Blom, J.W.; Cushman, M.; Rosendaal, F.R.; van Hylckama Vlieg, A. The contribution of immobility risk factors to the incidence of venous thrombosis in an older population. *J. Thromb. Haemost.* **2014**, *12*, 290–296. [CrossRef]
21. Sartori, M.; Favaretto, E.; Cosmi, B. Relevance of immobility as a risk factor for symptomatic proximal and isolated distal deep vein thrombosis in acutely ill medical inpatients. *Vasc. Med.* **2021**, *26*, 542–548. [CrossRef]
22. Meythaler, J.M.; DeVivo, M.J.; Hayne, J.B. Cost-effectiveness of routine screening for proximal deep venous thrombosis in acquired brain injury patients admitted to rehabilitation. *Arch. Phys. Med. Rehabil.* **1996**, *77*, 1–5. [CrossRef]
23. Greenwald, B.D.; Park, M.J.; Levine, J.M.; Watanabe, T.K. The utility of routine screening for deep vein thrombosis upon admission to an inpatient brain injury rehabilitation unit. *PM R* **2013**, *5*, 340–347. [CrossRef]
24. Rogers, F.B.; Cipolle, M.D.; Velmahos, G.; Rozycki, G.; Luchette, F.A. Practice management guidelines for the prevention of venous thromboembo- lism in trauma patients: The EAST practice management guidelines work group. *J. Trauma* **2002**, *53*, 142–164. [CrossRef]
25. Righini, M.; Perrier, A.; De Moerloose, P.; Bounameaux, H. D-dimer for venous thromboembolism diagnosis: 20 years later. *J. Thromb. Haemost.* **2008**, *6*, 1059–1071. [CrossRef]
26. Taira, T.; Taira, B.R.; Carmen, M.; Chohan, J.; Singer, A.J. Risk of venous thromboembolism in patients with borderline quantitative D-dimer levels. *Am. J. Emerg. Med.* **2010**, *28*, 450–453. [CrossRef]
27. Konstantinides, S.V.; Meyer, G.; Becattini, C.; Bueno, H.; Geersing, G.J.; Harjola, V.-P.; Huisman, M.V.; Humbert, M.; Jennings, C.S.; Jiménez, D.; et al. 2019 ESC Guidelines for the diagnosis and management of acute pulmonary embolism developed in collaboration with the European Respiratory Society (ERS). *Eur. Heart J.* **2020**, *41*, 543–603. [CrossRef] [PubMed]
28. Legnani, C.; Cini, M.; Scarvelis, D.; Toulon, P.; Wu, J.R.; Palareti, G. Multicenter evaluation of a new quantitative highly sensitive D-dimer assay, the Hemosil D-dimer HS 500, in patients with clinically suspected venous thromboembolism. *Thromb. Res.* **2010**, *125*, 398–401. [CrossRef]
29. Wang, L.; Zhao, L.; Li, F.; Liu, J.; Zhang, L.; Li, Q.; Gu, J.; Liang, S.; Zhao, Q.; Liu, J.; et al. Risk assessment of venous thromboembolism and bleeding in COVID-19 patients. *Clin. Respir. J.* **2022**, *16*, 182–189. [CrossRef]
30. Spyropoulos, A.C.; Anderson, F.A., Jr.; FitzGerald, G.; Decousus, H.; Pini, M.; Chong, B.H.; Zotz, R.B.; Bergmann, J.F.; Tapson, V.; Froehlich, J.B.; et al. Predictive and associative models to identify hospitalized medical patients at risk for VTE. *Chest* **2011**, *140*, 706–714. [CrossRef]
31. Partsch, H.; Blattler, W. Compression and walking versus bed rest in the treatment of proximal deep venous thrombosis with low molecular weight heparin. *J. Vasc. Surg.* **2000**, *32*, 861–869. [CrossRef] [PubMed]
32. Merkel, A. Origin and natural history of deep vein thrombosis of the legs. *Sem. Vasc. Med.* **2005**, *5*, 10. [CrossRef] [PubMed]
33. Sachdev, U.; Teodorescu, V.J.; Shao, M.; Russo, T.; Jacobs, T.S.; Silverberg, D.; Carroccio, A.; Ellozy, S.H.; Marin, M.L. Incidence and distribution of lower extremity deep vein thrombosis in rehabilitation patients: Implications for screening. *Vasc. Endovascular. Surg.* **2006**, *40*, 205–211. [CrossRef]
34. Matsuo, H.; Nakajima, Y.; Ogawa, T.; Mo, M.; Tazaki, J.; Doi, T.; Yamada, N.; Suzuki, T.; Nakajima, H. Evaluation of D-Dimer in Screening Deep Vein Thrombosis in Hospitalized Japanese Patients with Acute Medical Diseases/Episodes. *Ann. Vasc. Dis.* **2016**, *9*, 193–200. [CrossRef] [PubMed]
35. JCS Joint Working Group. Guidelines for the diagnosis, treatment and prevention of pulmonary thromboembo- lism and deep vein thrombosis (JCS 2009). *Circ. J.* **2011**, *75*, 1258–1281. [CrossRef] [PubMed]
36. Janssen, M.C.; Wollesheim, H.; Verbruggen, B.; Novakova, I.R. Rapid D-dimer assays to exclude deep venous thrombosis and pulmonary embolism: Current status and new developments. *Semin. Thromb. Hemostas.* **1998**, *24*, 393–400. [CrossRef] [PubMed]
37. Pulivarthi, S.; Gurram, M.K. Effectiveness of d-dimer as a screening test for venous thromboembolism: An update. *N. Am. J. Med. Sci.* **2014**, *6*, 491–499. [CrossRef]
38. Konstantinides, S.V.; Torbicki, A.; Agnelli, G.; Danchin, N.; Fitzmaurice, D.; Galiè, N.; Gibbs, J.S.R.; Huisman, M.V.; Humbert, M.; Kucher, N.; et al. 2014 ESC Guidelines on the diagnosis and management of acute pulmonary embolism. *Eur. Heart J.* **2014**, *35*, 3033–3069. [CrossRef] [PubMed]
39. Akman, M.N.; Cetin, N.; Bayramoglu, M.; Isiklar, I.; Kilinc, S. Value of the D-dimer test in diagnosing deep vein thrombosis in rehabilitation inpatients. *Arch. Phys. Med. Rehabil.* **2004**, *85*, 1091–1094. [CrossRef]
40. Roumen-Klappe, E.M.; den Heijer, M.; van Uum, S.H.; van der Ven-Jongekrijg, J.; van der Graaf, F.; Wollersheim, H. Inflammatory response in the acute phase of deep vein thrombosis. *J. Vasc. Surg.* **2002**, *35*, 701–706. [CrossRef]

41. Simonneau, G.; Laporte, S.; Mismetti, P.; Derlon, A.; Samii, K.; Samama, C.M.; Bergman, J.F.; FX140 Study Investigators. A randomized study comparing the efficacy and safety of nadroparin 2850 IU (0.3 mL) vs. enoxaparin 4000 IU (40 mg) in the prevention of venous thromboembolism after colorectal surgery for cancer. *J. Thromb. Haemost.* **2006**, *4*, 1693–1700. [CrossRef] [PubMed]
42. Søgaard, K.K.; Schmidt, M.; Pedersen, L.; Horváth–Puhó, E.; Sørensen, H.T. 30-year mortality after venous thromboembolism: A population-based cohort study. *Circulation* **2014**, *130*, 829–836. [CrossRef] [PubMed]
43. Cole, K.L.; Nguyen, S.; Gelhard, S.; Hardy, J.; Cortez, J.; Nunez, J.M.; Menacho, S.T.; Grandhi, R. Factors Associated with Venous Thromboembolism Development in Patients with Traumatic Brain Injury. *Neurocrit. Care* **2024**, *40*, 568–576. [CrossRef] [PubMed]
44. Jakob, D.A.; Müller, M.; Lewis, M.; Wong, M.D.; Exadaktylos, A.K.; Demetriades, D. Risk factors for thromboembolic complications in isolated severe head injury. *Eur. J. Trauma Emerg. Surg.* **2024**, *50*, 185–195. [CrossRef] [PubMed]
45. Al Tannir, A.H.; Golestani, S.; Tentis, M.; Murphy, P.B.; Schramm, A.T.; Peschman, J.; Dodgion, C.; Holena, D.; Miranda, S.; Carver, T.W.; et al. Early venous thromboembolism chemoprophylaxis in traumatic brain injury requiring neurosurgical intervention: Safe and effective. *Surgery* **2024**, *175*, 1439–1444. [CrossRef]
46. Hou, T.; Qiao, W.; Song, S.; Guan, Y.; Zhu, C.; Yang, Q.; Gu, Q.; Sun, L.; Liu, S. The Use of Machine Learning Techniques to Predict Deep Vein Thrombosis in Rehabilitation Inpatients. *Clin. Appl. Thromb./Hemost.* **2023**, *29*, 340–347. [CrossRef]

*healthcare*

MDPI

*Technical Note*

# Sexual Disability in Low Back Pain: Diagnostic and Therapeutic Framework for Physical Therapists

**Carla Vanti [1], Silvano Ferrari [2], Marco Chiodini [3], Cesare Olivoni [4], Arianna Bortolami [5,*] and Paolo Pillastrini [1,6]**

1 Department of Biomedical and Neuromotor Sciences (DIBINEM), Alma Mater University of Bologna, Via Massarenti 9, 40138 Bologna, Italy; carla.vanti@unibo.it (C.V.); paolo.pillastrini@unibo.it (P.P.)
2 Studio Arcobaleno, Via Ramazzini, 7, 20129 Milano, Italy; silvano.ferrari@fastwebnet.it
3 Poliambulatorio Medico Associato, Via Monsignor Bertazzoni, 1, 46027 San Benedetto Po, Italy; chiodini_m@hotmail.it
4 Studio Associato Fisioterapico Gallinucci Olivoni, Piazzale Marconi, 3/4, 48025 Riolo Terme, Italy; cesare.olivoni@gmail.com
5 Studio Pelvic Floor, Via Gattamelata, 134/C, 35128 Padova, Italy
6 Unit of Occupational Medicine, IRCCS Azienda Ospedaliero-Universitaria di Bologna, Via Pelagio Palagi 9, 40138 Bologna, Italy
* Correspondence: arianna.bortolami@gmail.com

**Abstract:** Background: The literature shows a relationship between sexual activity and low back pain (LBP). The aim of this work is to provide a theoretical framework and practical proposal for the management of sexual disability in individuals with LBP. Methods: Based on a literature review, a team of specialized physical therapists developed a pattern for the management of LBP-related sexual disability. Results: A patient reporting LBP-related sexual disability may be included in one of four clinical decision-making pathways corresponding to one of the following: #1 standard physical therapy (PT); #2 psychologically informed physical therapy (PIPT); #3 PIPT with referral; or #4 immediate referral. Standard PT concerns the management of LBP-related sexual disability in the absence of psychosocial or pathological issues. It includes strategies for pain modulation, stiffness management, motor control, stabilization, functional training, pacing activities comprising education, and stay-active advice. PIPT refers to patients with yellow flags or concerns about their relationship with partners; this treatment is oriented towards a specific psychological approach. "PIPT with referral" and "Immediate referral" pathways concern patients needing to be referred to specialists in other fields due to relationship problems or conditions requiring medical management or pelvic floor or sexual rehabilitation. Conclusions: The proposed framework can help clinicians properly manage patients with LBP-related sexual disability.

**Keywords:** low back pain; sexual behavior; disability; physical therapy; referral; consultation

**Citation:** Vanti, C.; Ferrari, S.; Chiodini, M.; Olivoni, C.; Bortolami, A.; Pillastrini, P. Sexual Disability in Low Back Pain: Diagnostic and Therapeutic Framework for Physical Therapists. *Healthcare* **2024**, *12*, 80. https://doi.org/10.3390/healthcare12010080

Academic Editor: Philippe Gorce

Received: 17 November 2023
Revised: 18 December 2023
Accepted: 26 December 2023
Published: 29 December 2023



## 1. Introduction

According to a biopsychosocial model, sexual health is defined as a state of physical, emotional, mental, and social well-being in relation to sexuality [1], and it should be protected and promoted also in disabled people [2]. Low back pain (LBP) describes pain between the lower edge of the ribs and the buttock. It can last for a short time (acute), a little longer (subacute), or a long time (chronic) [3]. Different authors observed some alterations of sexual life in patients complained of acute [4] and chronic [5] LBP. Decreasing frequency, arousal, and/or quality of sexual activity were reported by patients treated with conservative or surgical management [6,7]. The prevalence of sexual disability in diverse populations complaining of LBP ranges from 37% to 81% of subjects [6,8–13].

Patients suffering from chronic LBP appear more at risk of developing sexual disability, with some risk factors such as higher age, BMI, levels of depression/anxiety, lower educational level, family income, functional status, physical activity level, being unemployed, irregular menstruation, and prolonged duration of pain [12]. In addition, patients with spinal deformity are likely to have reduced sexual function related to older age, increased LBP, and increased sagittal vertical axis, with a link between sexual activity and lumbar stiffness [14]. However, no association between the severity of degenerative/disc changes and the quality of sex life in patients with LBP was observed [15].

Sexual disability in chronic conditions is related not only to pain but also to psychological dysfunctions [16], such as depression [17], activity avoidance, and rumination [10]. Moreover, a correlation between sexual functioning and relationship satisfaction (e.g., emotional intimacy, sexual intimacy, and mental health) appears. Therefore, an emerging key factor for sexual disability is the level of empathy of the couple, especially the presence of a supportive partner [18]. Patients with LBP report struggling to enable sexual activity, suffering from loss of pleasure and sexual identity, and needing support from partners and professionals to maintain their sex life [19].

In older people, the role of physical health as a predictor of sexual function is conflicting [20,21], even if the reported poor sexual function can be also attributable to the lack of a partner. Steckenrider [22] noted that as people get older, penetrative sex becomes less important. The hierarchy shifts to include more emotional intimacy like touching and fondling. This fact could help in having a different approach when comparing older people to adults with LBP-related sexual dysfunction.

All the cited studies mainly refer to heterosexual couples, but sexual disability should be considered also for nonheterosexual couples and alternative practices to vaginal sex. When examining sex life satisfaction, other sexual practices should be included, such as petting, fondling, masturbation, etc. The acronym KITOMI can be useful to properly describe all sexual activities. KITOMI is composed of the words kissing (Ki), touching (T), oral (O) stimulation of genitalia, masturbation (M), and intercourse (I) [21]. This acronym may help professionals and patients discuss sexual disability related to LBP and its management.

Sexual function is often overlooked by clinicians [10], also due to the influence of cultural and/or religious beliefs; despite this, patients would like to talk more about sexual disability, especially with their own physical therapist (PT) [19], and require indication on how to manage it properly [23–25]. As suggested by Korse and colleagues [26], sexual health counseling skills should be improved among professionals to enhance their abilities in managing these patients. PTs are among the professionals more involved in treating people with LBP [19], but the strategies to manage LBP-related disability are still under debate. For this reasons, the aim of this perspective manuscript is to provide a comprehensive theoretical framework and a practical proposal for the management of sexual disability in individuals with LBP.

## 2. Materials and Methods

A team comprising orthopedic manipulative physical therapists (OMPTs), experts in musculoskeletal (MC, CO) physical therapy and psychologically informed physical therapy (PIPT (SF, CV)), a PT specialized in pelvic floor rehabilitation and sexology consultant (AB), and a full professor of physical therapy (PP) was formed to review the literature and develop a proposal for the management of LBP-related sexual disability. More specifically, MC and CO performed a literature search and the selection of studies and data; SF and CV contributed to proposals relating to intervention on yellow-flag conditions; AB integrated assessment and treatment into clinical conditions requiring referral; and PP constantly supervised the proposals in light of the most recent concepts and procedures of physical therapy.

Each piece of information was accessible in an online document folder shared by all team members, organized and summarized by SF and CV, and the whole team constantly developed, discussed and implemented this project through eight online meetings, from February 2022 to November 2023. All the authors participated in writing this manuscript.

Since this study had no human participants, it was not necessary to obtain approval from any ethics committee.

From February 2022 to November 2022, a narrative literature review was conducted on the main databases and team members' personal libraries. The details of this review are presented in Appendix A. Based on the results of the literature review and the emerging lack of a comprehensive approach on this topic, the team identified and discussed the following four key concepts:

Item #1—How can sexual disability emerge in a patient undergoing physical therapy treatment for LBP?

Item #2—How can PTs classify patients with LBP regarding their sexual disability?

Item #3—What decision-making process can PTs adopt in the case of LBP and sexual disability?

Item #4—How can the practical adoption of this decision-making process by PTs by facilitated?

The results of the teamwork were discussed in a 4 h online course on "LBP and sexual disability" which took place in October 2023 and was attended by 36 PTs. The participants evaluated this proposal and judged both the framework and the indications for assessing and treating this condition to be clear and practically useful but suggested that we better explore the aspects related to PIPT. Then in November 2023, an assistant professor of physical therapy external to this research group assessed the framework by revising the manuscript, Appendix A, and Supplementary Files (see Figure 1).

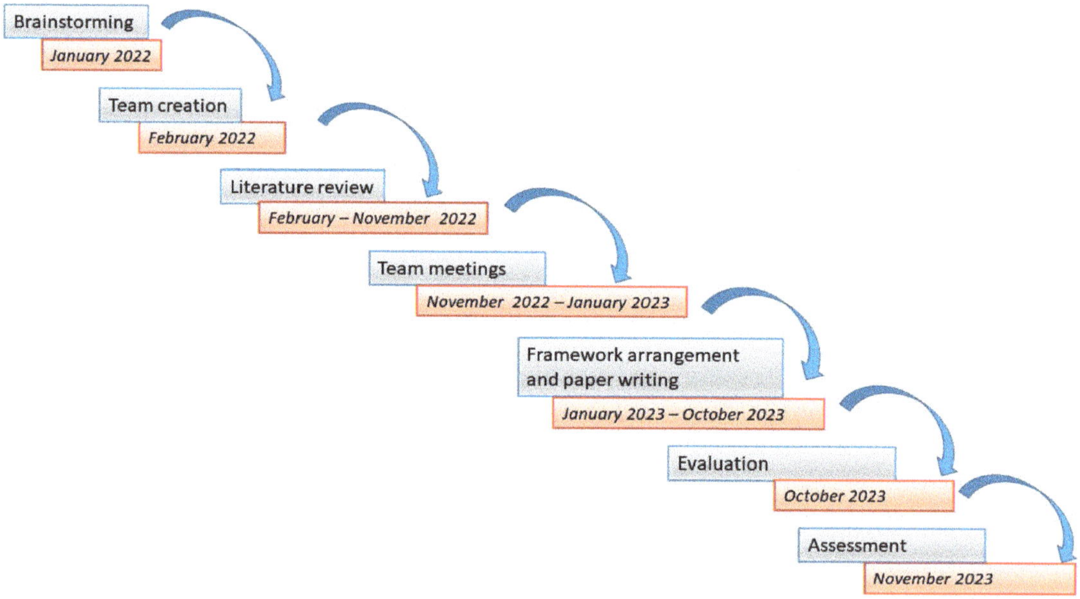


**Figure 1.** Flowchart showing the timeline of the entire project.

## 3. Results

### 3.1. Literature Review

Patient Reported Outcome Measures (PROMs) can be administered by PTs for LBP-related sexual disability. The Oswestry Disability Index was indicated as a PROM for the disability, which includes a specific and optional item related to sexual life (ODI-8) [10,19]. The Fear-Avoidance Beliefs Questionnaire (FABQ) [27]; the Pain Catastrophizing Scale (PCS) [28] for psychosocial aspects; the Zung Depression Scale (ZDS), which contains an item related to sexual enjoyment (ZDS-6) [29]; the Beck Depression Inventory-II (BDI-II), which includes an item on the interest in sex (BDI-II-21) [30]; and the Hospital Anxiety and Depression Scale (HADS) [31] were also indicated.

Two instruments were reported to assess patients' sexual functioning: for females, the Female Sexual Function Index (FSFI) [32], and for males, the International Index of Erectile Function (IIEF) [33].

Most therapeutic indications concern education based on biomechanical data. Concerning the relationship between sexual activity and spinal movements, two studies by Sidorkewicz and McGill [34,35] on motion capture of coitus provided indications of lumbar spine motion for males and females during sexual intercourse. Five different positions were examined: side-lying; quadruped in two variations (with female supporting on elbow; with female supporting on hands); and missionary in two variations (with male supporting on hands and female with hips and knees slightly flexed; with male supporting on elbows and female with hips and knees flexed). The results of these studies showed the amount of lumbar flexion and extension in each position and the overall amount of spinal motion during sexual intercourse.

Through these data, the same authors elaborated an ergonomic strategy, based on a classification of the five positions in three categories: flexion-intolerant, extension-intolerant, and motion-intolerant. The rationale is to inform the patient that certain positions, for males or females, may exacerbate lumbar flexion or extension and provoke or worsen symptoms, according to anamnesis and physical examination. About the "motion-intolerant" category, these authors found that all positions for males need some movement of the lumbar spine, so there is no indication in choosing one or another position; for females instead, some positions require less movement than others. Each patient should be educated to avoid positions based on which movement worsens symptoms (flexion or extension) or, for females, on how much lumbar motion they can engage in during sexual intercourse. Another strategy proposed is the use of lumbar support to decrease spinal load [34,35].

There is emerging evidence about measuring spinal movements during coitus with new tools such as an inertial device [36], which could explore better biomechanics of sexual intercourse also in LBP. We can observe that only healthy subjects were enrolled in these biomechanical studies, whereas the presence of pain during sexual intercourse could modify movement patterns and spinal range of motion (ROM). Moreover, the cited biomechanical studies are related to intercourse positions, in which it is the man who moves, whereas we did not find any study on LBP in the woman's position on top, controlling the movement of her intercourse.

A measurement of male and female hip range of motion (ROM) during different sexual positions was also performed [37]. Intercourse positions for women require flexion (95°), abduction (32°) and mostly external rotation. For men, external rotation is dominant in all positions (40°); flexion and abduction remain in a normal ROM. Considering the regional interdependence between the lumbar spine and pelvis, a screening of hip mobility should be considered to assess the ability of the patient to reach and maintain different positions without discomfort or pain. In addition, restrictions of the hip ROM may interfere with lumbar spine motion and function in patients with LBP-related sexual disability [38].

Out of the cited ergonomic advice, the current literature lacks specific indication on rehabilitation of LBP-related sexual disability, since only suggestions based on clinical practice or common sense are proposed. For example, Nikoobath and colleagues [12] recommend avoiding painful positions or increasing physical activity in order to improve the quality of the sex life. Similar advice was reported in studies on knee, hip, or shoulder joints [39,40].

Finally, some suggestions for managing sexual disability are derived from studies on the rehabilitation of other clinical conditions. More comfortable positions [41], pillows and muscle-relaxing activities [42], pelvic floor training and sex education [43], walking [44], yoga [45], and increasing exercise capacity and self-confidence are suggested [46]. Physical exercise, both strength training and aerobic/cardiovascular training, appears an effective treatment for many aspects of sexual life: body image and self-esteem [47], sexual desire [48], sexual activity [49,50], erectile dysfunction [51], premature ejaculation [52], and depression [53]. Therefore, physical activity seems to have a positive effect on sexual function and may be considered in patients with LBP-related sexual disability.

The literature review showed the lack of a framework providing a comprehensive plan of assessment and treatment in this field for PTs. Therefore, the team elaborated and proposed an original framework for the management of LBP-related sexual disability inspired by the four pathways for decision making concerning yellow-flag management in orthopedic conditions [54]. The framework proposed by our team takes into consideration the characteristics of LBP-related sexual disability, the presence of yellow flags (e.g., fear-avoidance behavior, pain catastrophizing, kinesiophobia, or poor pain self-efficacy), the concerns about the relationship with one's own partner, and the presence of red flags or other conditions related to specific pathologies/dysfunctions. The purpose of this algorithm is to help PTs to frame the clinical profile of each patient complaining of LBP and sexual disability and to manage sexual disability in different clinical conditions through specific assessment and treatment procedures.

### *3.2. How Can Sexual Disability Emerge in a Patient Undergoing Physical Therapy Treatment for LBP?*

LBP-related sexual disability may emerge during both assessment and treatment. The PT can ask a specific question (e.g., "Does your LBP affect your sex life?"), or a patient may spontaneously report problems in his/her sex life. The administration of the Oswestry Disability Index (ODI) [55] or the Aberdeen Low Back Pain Scale (ALBPS) [56] may be another option, with particular reference to items related to sexual disability (ODI #8, ALBPS #17). After PROM completion, the PT may discuss the results of these items with both the patients who did not complete them and the patients reporting sexual disability [10].

To respect the patient's privacy and in considering the sensitivity of the topic, the PT could introduce the discussion on sexual disability in this way: "Would you like us to talk about this?" and "I'm trying to figure out if I can help you…".

### *3.3. How Can PTs Classify Patients with LBP Regarding Their Sexual Disability?*

According to Holmberg and colleagues [11], patients with LBP can be divided into three subgroups: #1 normal sex life, without pain; #2 pain preventing any type of sexual activity; and #3 pain during sexual activity. Therefore, two symptomatic conditions may be considered: patients unable to perform sexual life because of pain, and patients reporting pain during sexual activity. The team investigated this last condition, highlighting that pain could be mainly provoked/worsened by a specific position or by changing position during sexual activity. In addition, another scenario was included, that is, when LBP emerges not during but after sexual activity. Furthermore, the team included other clinical pictures, in which pain related to sexual activity can be also referred to as yellow flags, problems in the couple's relationship, and specific urologic, gynecologic, or andrologic pathologies.

### *3.4. What Decision-Making Process Can PTs Adopt in the Case of LBP and Sexual Disability?*

The framework proposed by our team is composed of four clinical decision-making pathways corresponding to the following: #1 standard physical therapy; #2 psychologically informed physical therapy (PIPT); #3 PIPT with referral; and #4 immediate referral (see Table 1).

**Table 1.** Four pathways of the decision-making process for the management of LBP-related sexual disability. Different colors refer to the usual meaning of green, yellow, orange, and red flags.

**LOW BACK PAIN-RELATED SEXUAL DISABILITY EMERGED THROUGH THE FOLLOWING:**

- A question asked by physical therapist: "Does your low back pain affect your sex life?"
- The Oswestry Disability Index (ODI) questionnaire—item #8.
- The Aberdeen Low Back Pain Scale (ALBPS)—item #17.
- Spontaneous reporting of problems in sexual life by patient.

| STANDARD PHYSICAL THERAPY | PSYCHOLOGICALLY INFORMED PHYSICAL THERAPY (PIPT) | PIPT WITH REFERRAL | IMMEDIATE REFERRAL |
|---|---|---|---|
| **Screening**<br>LBP that prevents intercourse.<br>LBP that does not prevent intercourse, but that appears as follows:<br>- During intercourse (changing position; maintaining a position; during movement).<br>- After intercourse. | **Screening**<br>Fear of LBP (fear-avoidance behaviors).<br>Fear of aggravating one's condition (catastrophizing, kinesiophobia).<br>Fear of influencing the relationship with one's partner. | **Screening**<br>Dissatisfaction with sexual life not related to low back pain (quality or frequency of sexual intercourse).<br>Problems in the relationship with one's partner.<br>Aspects related to one's role in the couple. | **Screening**<br>Urological pathologies.<br>Gynecological pathologies.<br>Andrological pathologies.<br>Sexual dysfunctions already diagnosed. |
| **Outcome Measures**<br>- ODI (item #8)<br>- ALBPS (item #17)<br>- PSEQ | **Outcome Measures**<br>- ODI (item #8)<br>- ALBPS (item #17)<br>- OSPRO—YF<br>- PSEQ<br>- TSK<br>- PCS<br>- FABQ | **Outcome Measures**<br>- ZDS (item #6)<br>- BDI-II (item #21)<br>- HADS<br>- CSFQ<br>- FSFI (females)<br>- IIEF (males)<br>- DAS | **Outcome Measures**<br>- CSFQ<br>- FSFI (females)<br>- IIEF (males) |
| **Therapeutic Goals**<br>- Pain modulation.<br>- Stability increasing.<br>- Endurance increasing.<br>- Information/education.<br>- Pain self-efficacy and self-management enhancement. | **Therapeutic Goals**<br>- Information/education.<br>- Pain self-efficacy and self-management enhancement. | **Therapeutic Goals**<br>Check if the PIPT can proceed together with the care plan of the professional to whom the patient was referred. | **Therapeutic Goals**<br>- Identified by the professional to whom the patient was referred.<br>- Verification of a possible return to condition as pathways #3 or #2. |
| **Plan of Care**<br>- Pain relief therapies (manual therapy, physical agents, exercise).<br>- Motor control training.<br>- Specific graded activity.<br>- Pacing activity.<br>- Stay-active advice. | **Plan of Care**<br>PIPT: physical therapy procedures together with the following;<br>- Pain neuroscience education.<br>- Cognitive behavioral therapy. | **Plan of Care**<br>- Referral to other healthcare professionals (clinical sexologist, pelvic floor physical therapist, etc.).<br>- PIPT strategy (see pathway #2). | **Plan of Care**<br>Referral to other healthcare professionals (specialized doctor, clinical sexologist, pelvic floor physical therapist, etc.). |

ALBPS = Aberdeen Low Back Pain Scale; BDI-II Beck Depression Inventory-II; CSFQ = Changes in Sexual Functioning Questionnaire; DAS = Dyadic Adjustment Scale (revised); FABQ = Fear-Avoidance Beliefs Questionnaire; FSFI = Female Sexual Function Index; HADS = Hospital Anxiety and Depression Scale; IIEF = International Index of Erectile Function; LBP = low back pain; ODI = Oswestry Disability Index; OSPRO—YF = Optimal Screening for Referral and Outcome Yellow Flags; PCS = Pain Catastrophizing Scale; PIPT = psychologically informed physical therapy; PSEQ = Pain Self-Efficacy Questionnaire; TSK = Tampa Scale of Kinesiophobia: ZDS = Zung Depression Scale. Adapted from Stearns ZR et al. [54].

### 3.4.1. "Standard Physical Therapy" Pathway

This pathway concerns the management of LBP-related sexual disability in the absence of relevant psychosocial or pathological issues. Therefore, this category includes symptomatic conditions linked to sexual activity without any presence of yellow or red flags and without any relevant influence by the relationship with one's partner.

The Patient Reported Outcome Measures (PROMs) suggested to identify this condition and measure clinical outcomes are the ODI [55] or ALBPS [56] for disability and the Pain

Self-Efficacy Questionnaire (PSEQ) [57] for predicting the patient adherence towards an active approach.

According to anamnestic collection and outcomes, different steps of rehabilitation are proposed: pain modulation, motor control training, stiffness or stabilization training, and functional training. Pacing activity and stay-active advice complete this program (see Figure 2).

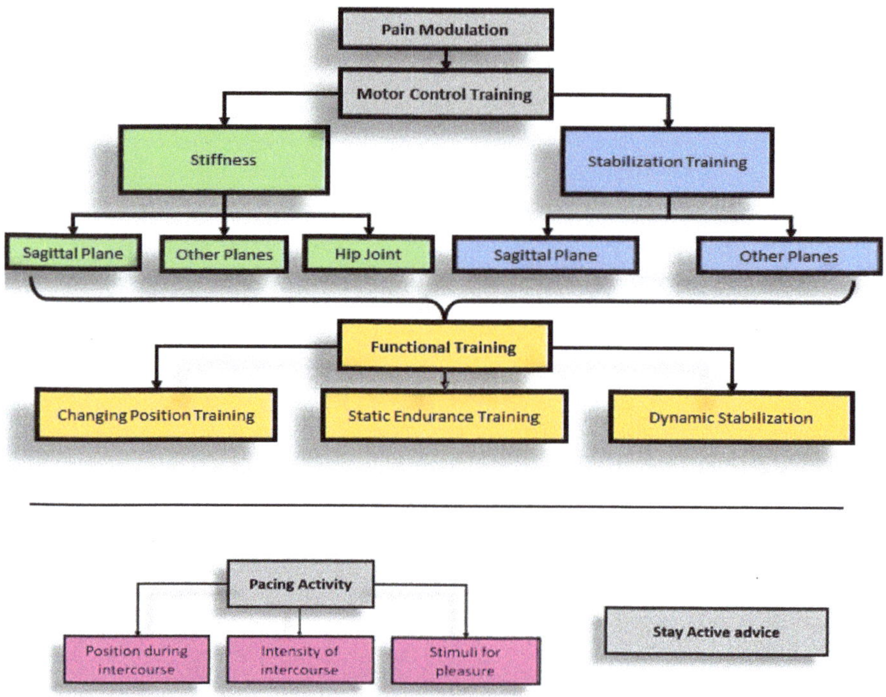


**Figure 2.** Therapeutic algorithm for standard physical therapy.

Many patients report that pain prevents sexual intercourse. In this situation, pain should be reduced to enable sexual activity by using manual therapy [58,59], physical agents (e.g., transcutaneous electrical nerve stimulation) [60,61], and midrange low-load exercises. When pain is no longer inhibiting sexual activity, a PT may proceed with other steps of the therapeutic algorithm; if a patient reports no avoidance of sex because of pain, this therapeutic section can be skipped [62].

A key element of the rehabilitation program is lumbar motor control [63]. According to the studies on motion capture during coitus, through-range motor control of pelvic anti-/retroversion should be trained in the most frequent positions of sexual intercourse (e.g., supine, quadruped, prone, kneeling, seated, and standing) to allow patients to control complete lumbar ROM and increase spinal perception. The PT may use specific positions according to the patient's evaluation [64].

Lumbar or hip stiffness could interfere with sexual intercourse and provoke/worsen pain in any position. For lumbar stiffness on the sagittal plane, flexion/extension movements are suggested; the progression may be from midrange to end-range movements and from low load (e.g., supine, prone) to half load (e.g., seated position) and full load (e.g., standing position). For lumbar stiffness in other planes, a PT may propose single-plane movements (e.g., rotation, side bending, and lateral shift), or multiplane movements. A little amount of pain should be tolerated, and the patient is encouraged to explore progressively wider ROM.

For hip stiffness, the program addresses the movements more involved in sexual activity: flexion, abduction, and external rotation [37].

Other patients need to improve spinal stabilization on the sagittal plane and/or other planes (e.g., coronal, transverse). Stabilization training is more than core muscle strengthening, involving both coordination among core muscles and motor relearning of inhibited muscles. Stabilization training in this field is an evolution of motor control training and should be performed in different intercourse positions, with the specific goal being to improve the quality of sex life [65].

The final step of this program should be functional training, which can be divided in three categories based on anamnesis: #1 "position change" (for patients reporting pain during position changing), #2 "static endurance" (for patients reporting pain while maintaining a position), and #3 "dynamic stabilization" (for patients reporting pain during/after sexual intercourse).

"Position change" training focuses on the ability to assume different positions, as usual during sexual activity, and can be trained by specific sequences of different positions with the aim of achieving pain-free movements between different sequences. "Static endurance" training is the completion of stabilization training but is more specific and progressive with regard to time and difficulty of sustained positions, with the aim of increasing the ability to stay in a position for a long time. "Dynamic stabilization" training aims to reproduce in the clinical setting the movements of sexual intercourse. Using bands, a PT can increase the force needed to complete these movements both in concentric and eccentric phases.

Pacing activity in this field is the patient's education on how to manage symptoms during and after sexual activity. Patients can modulate sexual activity in three ways: the intercourse position, the intercourse intensity, and the stimuli for pleasure.

Figures 3 and 4 show male and female intercourse positions from different studies [34,35,37,66], divided in supine, side-lying, prone, kneeling, seated, and standing.

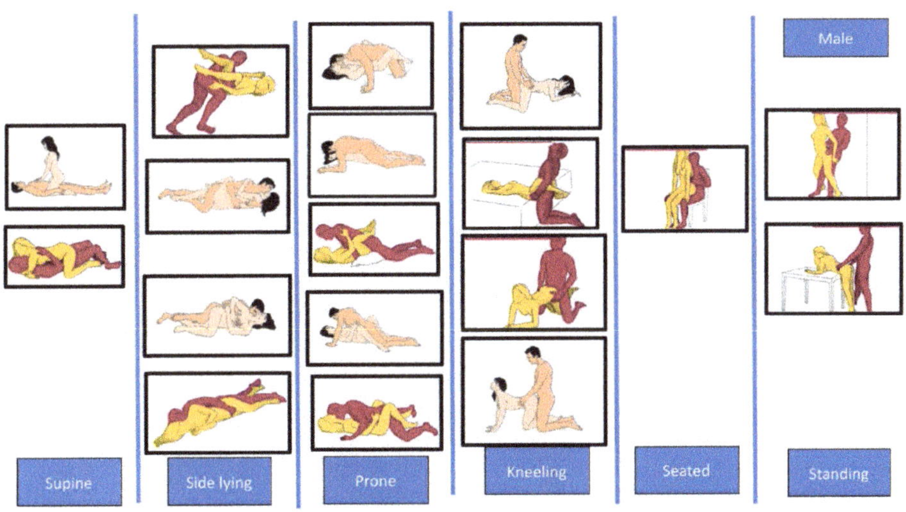


**Figure 3.** Different male positions for sexual intercourse. The pictures are taken from the websites https://www.sexualpositionsfree.com (accessed on 22 March 2023) and https://sexpositions.club/positions (accessed on 22 March 2023).

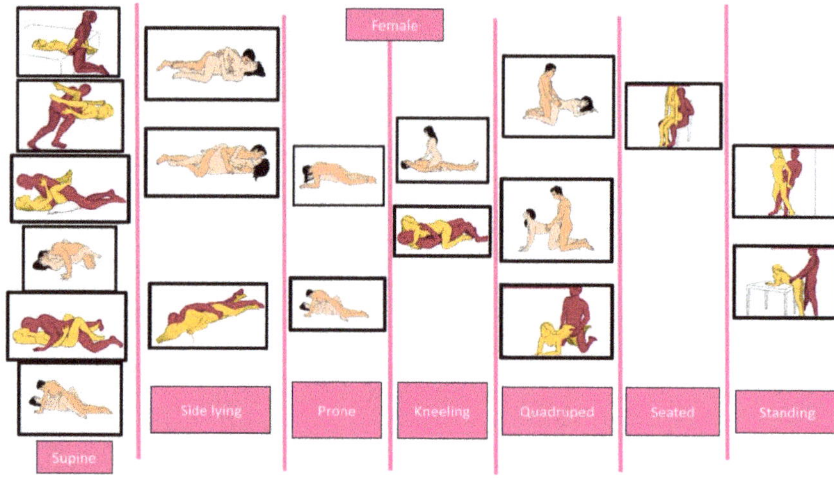


**Figure 4.** Different female positions for sexual intercourse. The pictures are taken from the websites https://www.sexualpositionsfree.com (accessed on 22 March 2023) and https://sexpositions.club/positions (accessed on 22 March 2023).

Figures 5–8 show the suggested positions depending on clinical picture for males and females.

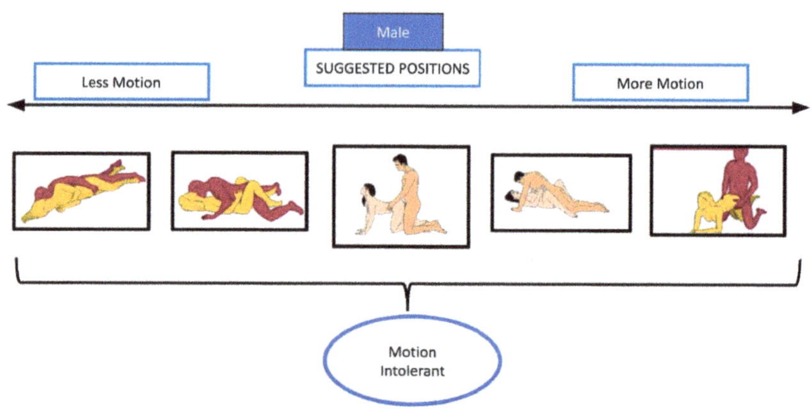


**Figure 5.** Suggested position for motion-intolerant males. The pictures are taken from the websites https://www.sexualpositionsfree.com (accessed on 22 March 2023) and https://sexpositions.club/positions (accessed on 22 March 2023).

First, the PT can advise using the more comfortable position and teach all variations allowed; then, positions that are more difficult may be introduced, for a short time, and alternated with positions that are more comfortable. Another strategy could be using more difficult positions at the beginning of the sexual intercourse and then use pain-free positions. The PT can advise patients on how to manage the onset or worsening of symptoms due to positioning during coitus.

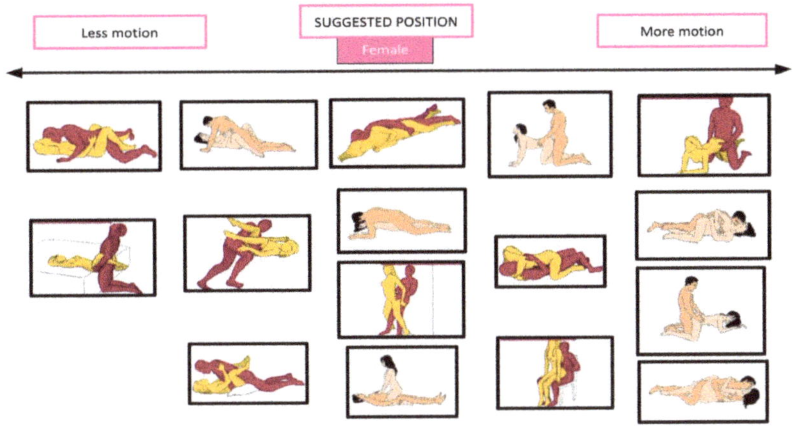


**Figure 6.** Suggested position for motion-intolerant females. The pictures are taken from the websites https://www.sexualpositionsfree.com (accessed on 22 March 2023) and https://sexpositions.club/positions (accessed on 22 March 2023).

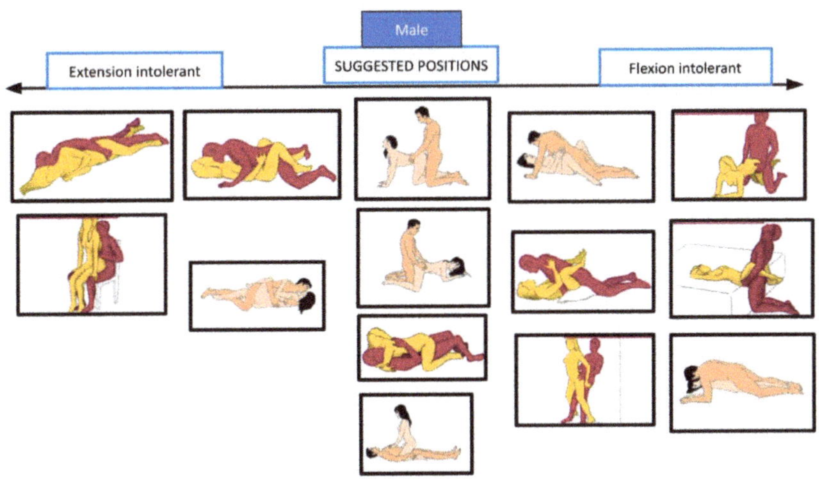


**Figure 7.** Suggested positions depending on the flexion/extension intolerance for males. The pictures are taken from the websites https://www.sexualpositionsfree.com (accessed on 22 March 2023) and https://sexpositions.club/positions (accessed on 22 March 2023).

Finally, stay-active advice means not only maintaining the usual activities of daily living (ADLs) and usual physical activity level but also modifying some risk factors for poor sex life related to habits. A PT can suggest patients increase their level of activity, especially aerobic (e.g., walking, cycling, Nordic walking, running, or swimming) [66–70]; reduce tobacco, alcohol, or drug consumption; manage sleep deprivation; and manage body mass index (BMI) and/or metabolic syndrome [71,72].

Every step of this program is related to a specific issue that may be addressed or not by a PT depending on patients' anamnesis, physical examination, and tests/questionnaires. The focus is a tailored treatment for each single patient, applied with the graded activity and graded exposure concepts, together with stay-active advice, to restore sexual function to the maximum possible level.

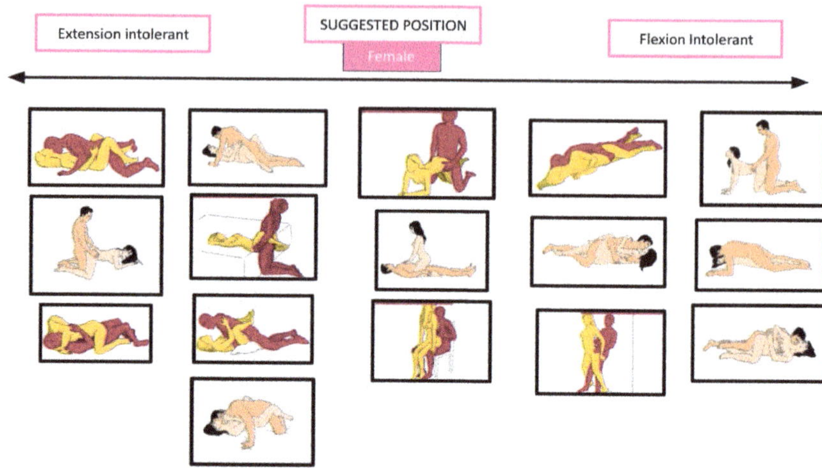


**Figure 8.** Suggested positions depending on the flexion/extension intolerance for females. The pictures are taken from the websites https://www.sexualpositionsfree.com (accessed on 22 March 2023) and https://sexpositions.club/positions (accessed on 22 March 2023).

More details of the therapeutic procedures proposed for this pathway are reported in Supplementary File S1 and Tables S1–S7.

3.4.2. "PIPT" Pathway

This pathway refers to patients with some yellow flags (e.g., kinesiophobia, catastrophizing, fear-avoidance behaviors, and low pain self-efficacy) or concerns about the possible negative influence of sexual life on partnership in absence of evident relationship alterations.

The PROMs suggested for identifying this condition and measuring clinical outcomes are the ODI [55], the ALBPS [56], and the Optimal Screening for Prediction of Referral and Outcome Yellow Flags (OSPRO—YF) [73] as multidimensional tools and the FABQ [27], the PCS [28], the PSEQ [57], and the Tampa Scale of Kinesiophobia (TSK) [74] as unidimensional tools.

PIPT represents the attention and attitude of the PT in exploring and treating the psychosocial aspects of patients complaining of LBP, taking care of sexual disability while improving symptoms and functional limitations. The therapeutic program is similar to the "Standard Physical Therapy" one, with more emphasis on the psychosocial aspects of rehabilitation and less on the mechanical ones.

Managing this situation, it is suggested to proceed with the four steps described in the "Standard Physical Therapy" picture (pain modulation, motor control training, stiffness or stabilization training, and functional training) together with pacing activity and stay-active advice, but the treatment should be oriented towards a specific psychological approach, like pain neuroscience education (PNE) or cognitive behavioral therapy (CBT).

PNE aims to shift from the concept of pain as a portrayal of harm to the concept of pain as an alarm system for tissue protection [75]. There is some growing evidence that it could be combined with usual care in individuals with LBP to reach better outcomes [76,77]. Patients need to know about their pain that pain does not mean hurt; pain experience is multifactorial; and pain overprotective systems can be retrained [78]. For this reason, PNE should be introduced for patients presenting yellow flags.

CBT is one of the nonpharmacological therapies of choice for chronic conditions, with proven effectiveness in the management of individuals complained of LBP [79,80]. It is a psychological approach focused on removing positive reinforcement of pain behaviors and promoting problem-solving behaviors, with an additional focus on changing unhelpful cognitions [81]. This kind of therapy or similar approaches may be useful in the management of sexual disability with psychosocial components.

#### 3.4.3. "PIPT with Referral" Pathway

This pathway concerns patients mainly presenting alterations in the relationship with their partner and needing to be referred to a specialist in other fields. This condition includes patients reporting both LBP and a dissatisfaction with sexual life not necessarily related to that pain. In fact, this condition may be characterized by unsatisfactory quality/frequency of sexual activity, problems in the relationship with one's partner, or aspects related to one's role in the couple.

The PROMs suggested for identifying this condition and measuring clinical outcomes are the ZDS [29], the BDI-II [30], and the HADS [31] for anxiety and depression; the Changes in Sexual Functioning Questionnaire (CSFQ) for sexual dysfunctions [82]; the FSFI [32] and the IIEF [33] for females' and males' sexual dysfunctions, respectively [83]; and finally, the Revised Dyadic Adjustment Scale (DAS) [84] for assessing the quality of the couple's relationship. It is suggested to refer those patients to a clinical sexologist or PT specialized in pelvic floor rehabilitation for better management of these concerns by appropriate professionals. Meanwhile, if agreed with the team and the patient, the PIPT program can proceed as presented in the previous section: like before, the focus is more on the person's needs about sexual disability.

#### 3.4.4. "Immediate Referral" Pathway

This pathway refers to patients needing specialized assessment and treatment or reporting other sexual dysfunctions requiring pelvic floor or sexual rehabilitation.

The PROMs suggested for identifying this condition and measuring clinical outcomes are the CSFQ [82] for sexual dysfunctions and the FSFI [32] and the IIEF [33] for females' and males' sexual dysfunctions, respectively. If a patient reports symptoms/signs of urological, gynecological, or andrological disorders interfering with sexual activity, he/she should be immediately referred for a proper medical evaluation and treatment. In addition, the presence of sexual dysfunctions (e.g., erectile dysfunction, vaginismus, dyspareunia) need specialized assessment on their impact on sexual activity; in this case, a patient may be referred to a doctor, clinical sexologist, and/or PT specialized in pelvic floor rehabilitation. An agreement with those professionals should be sought to decide a possible return to the PIPT rehabilitation program.

### *3.5. How Can the Practical Adoption of this Decision-Making Process by PTs by Facilitated?*

The team decided to elaborate and supply detailed standard physical therapy program and procedures (see Supplementary File S1), complete with images (see Supplementary Tables S1–S7), according to the Consensus on Exercise Reporting Template (CERT) checklist [85]. Four clinical cases were derived from the professional practice of the members, which could practically illustrate the process of managing different clinical conditions of sexual disability in patients treated for LBP, and are reported in Supplementary File S2.

## 4. Discussion

Rehabilitation of LBP has been widely studied; however, counseling and management of LBP-related sexual disability are underestimated. It is confirmed by the current literature, which lacks complete guidance on the assessment and treatment of this condition [86], which the patient does not perceive as an uninteresting or secondary limitation but as an actual disability [87].

It is not certain if lumbar pain reduction and lumbar function enhancement following conservative or surgical procedures will imply an improved sexual life [88,89]. Therefore, health professionals should not avoid this topic and should consider LBP-related sexual disability as a specific field of intervention. A tailored approach to sexual disability can help the patient in transferring motor abilities to a sexual relationship with his/her partner.

On the other hand, a better relationship can reduce the fear of losing sexual identity and the perception of being a disabled person, finally facilitating positive thinking [87].

As recently outlined, people with motor disability require support for recovering and maintaining their sexual life [87], and healthcare professionals need appropriate training on this topic [90]. The barriers that may hinder the management of this condition can be cultural, social, religious, and educational [91], and they can concern both healthcare professionals and patients.

Based on the available evidence and current musculoskeletal approach, this paper presents a diagnostic and therapeutic framework for LBP-related sexual disability. This proposal should be adapted to each single patient and to each single PT by respecting personal beliefs and contextual variables and taking into consideration the sensitivity of this topic.

The strengths of this framework are first linked to the overcoming of a biomechanical approach emerging from the revised literature on LBP-related sexual disability towards a more comprehensive approach to care of patients, because sexual function and the consequent quality of life are closely linked to psychological, relational, and social contexts. Therefore, this framework and therapeutic algorithms move from a mechanical perspective towards a biopsychosocial model by considering all the aspects of sexual life.

This proposal can allow the identification of yellow and red flags and the drafting of a therapeutic program tailored for each patient, which can also be adapted to changes in the clinical picture over time. Moreover, physical therapy programs and education do not follow a negative approach (what a patient must avoid), as highlighted in the past literature, but a positive one (what a patient can do and how he/she can do it).

The main limitations of this study are related to the absence of a systematic literature review before the development of this framework, which may have induced potential bias in the literature search and selection. The suggested proposal may be also biased by our cultural approach to sexual health, which could limit its application in different countries and cultures. Moreover, this theoretical framework was assessed by only one expert instead of a group of experts external to the research team. Future discussion with other experts and updates/revisions are needed to validate this framework and improve its appropriateness and effectiveness.

Some areas of development of this topic may be related to the counseling about specific needs of same-sex couples and nonpenetrative sexual practices. "Sex" and "gender" concepts should be integrated in this framework [91] due to the prevalent studies on males performing vaginal sex. Another area of interest concerns the physical demands of sexual intercourse separate from the kinematic ones (range of motion and penetration circle), e.g., related to energy expenditure, heart rate, blood pressure, and perceived exertion [92]. Further studies on this topic could help to identify the volume or intensity of physical exercise focused on sexual intercourse by considering it as a form of physical activity.

Moreover, we suggest a thorough investigation of the barriers and facilitators for patients and clinicians in addressing and managing LBP-related sexual disability. Future studies could also identify more effective counseling tools (brochures, images, etc.) to be used in a physical therapy setting [90], which may be different from those commonly employed in sexual education addressed to health people.

## 5. Conclusions

Clinicians should include sexual activity within the scope of ADLs and whether a sexual disability emerges, both spontaneously and thanks to a facilitation, they should proceed on the assessment allowing the identification of the specific pathway for each patient and the administration of measures confirming or not the previous hypothesis.

Four pathways for the management of LBP-related sexual disability are proposed, together with useful algorithms for PTs in their clinical practice. It is expected that these four pathways for decision making can help PTs properly assess and treat patients with

LBP-related sexual disability and finally improve the physical and psychological condition of patients through tailored strategies to manage their sexual life.

**Supplementary Materials:** The following supporting information can be downloaded at: https://www.mdpi.com/article/10.3390/healthcare12010080/s1, Supplementary File S1—Standard physical therapy program: detail of the procedures; Supplementary File S2—Clinical cases.

**Author Contributions:** Conceptualization, S.F. and C.V.; methodology, S.F., C.V. and A.B.; software, M.C. and C.O.; validation, S.F., C.V. and P.P.; formal analysis, S.F., C.V., A.B. and P.P.; investigation, M.C. and C.O.; data curation, M.C. and C.O.; writing—original draft preparation, C.V.; writing—review and editing, C.V., S.F., M.C., C.O., A.B. and P.P.; supervision, C.V., S.F., A.B. and P.P. All authors have read and agreed to the published version of the manuscript.

**Funding:** This research received no external funding.

**Institutional Review Board Statement:** Not applicable.

**Informed Consent Statement:** Not applicable.

**Data Availability Statement:** No new data were created or analyzed in this study. Data sharing is not applicable to this article.

**Acknowledgments:** We thank Luca Turone for allowing the inclusion in the Supplementary File of some exercises in which his image is reproduced. We thanks the 36 physical therapists who attended the course on LBP and sexual disability for their observations and proposal. We thank Marco Tramontano for his critical revision of the framework and the manuscript.

**Conflicts of Interest:** The authors declare no conflicts of interest.

## Appendix A. Search Strategy and Results

Key words used for search

- Sexuality, sexual activity, sexual intercourse, sexual health, coital, coitus.
- Rehabilitation, physiotherapy, physical therapy, exercise, physical exercise, physical activity.
- Low back pain, acute low back pain, chronic low back pain.

Inclusion criteria

- Types of studies: any type of study.
- Types of participants: adult population (≥18 years) with nonspecific or specific low back pain.
- Setting: any type of setting.
- Publication date: any year of publication.
- Language: any language.
- State of publication: published study.
- Types of interventions: study on assessment and/or conservative treatment of sexual disability in low back pain.
- Comparison (when applicable): different physical therapy or pharmacological interventions, wait-and-see strategies, placebo, sham, or no intervention.
- Types of outcome measures: PROMs addressing pain, disability, quality of life, sexual function, psychosocial issues.

Exclusion criteria

- Studies on population with systemic pathologies (e.g., infection, fracture, dystonia, cancer, myelopathy, rheumatic disease, fibromyalgia).

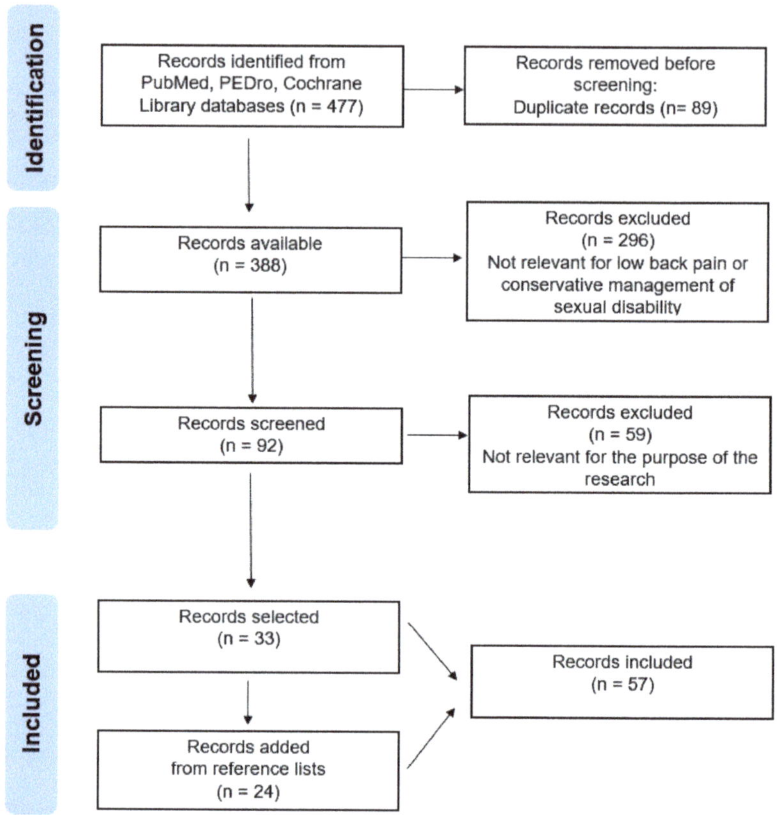


**Figure A1.** Flowchart of studies selection.

## References


1. Giami, A. Sexual health: The emergence, development, and diversity of a concept. *Annu. Rev. Sex Res.* **2002**, *13*, 1–35. [PubMed]
2. World Association for Sexual Health. Declaration of Sexual Rights. 2014. Available online: https://worldsexualhealth.net/wp-content/uploads/2013/08/Declaration-of-Sexual-Rights-2014-plain-text.pdf (accessed on 14 December 2023).
3. World Health Organization. Low Back Pain. Overview. Available online: https://www.who.int/news-room/fact-sheets/detail/low-back-pain (accessed on 14 December 2023).
4. Maigne, J.Y.; Chatellier, G. Assessment of sexual activity in patients with back pain compared with patients with neck pain. *Clin. Orthop.* **2001**, *385*, 82–87. [CrossRef] [PubMed]
5. Panneerselvam, K.; Kanna, R.M.; Shetty, A.P.; Rajasekaran, S. Impact of Acute Lumbar Disk Herniation on Sexual Function in Male Patients. *Asian Spine J.* **2022**, *16*, 510–518. [CrossRef] [PubMed]
6. Bahouq, H.; Fadoua, A.; Hanan, R.; Ihsane, H.; Najia, H.-H. Profile of sexuality in Moroccan chronic low back pain patients. *BMC Musculoskelet. Disord.* **2013**, *14*, 63. [CrossRef] [PubMed]
7. Akbaş, N.B.; Dalbayrak, S.; Külcü, D.G.; Yilmaz, M.; Yilmaz, T.; Naderi, S. Assessment of sexual dysfunction before and after surgery for lumbar disc herniation. *J. Neurosurg. Spine* **2010**, *13*, 581–586. [CrossRef] [PubMed]
8. Berg, S.; Fritzell, P.; Tropp, H. Sex life and sexual function in men and women before and after total disc replacement compared with posterior lumbar fusion. *Spine J. Off. J. North Am. Spine Soc.* **2009**, *9*, 987–994. [CrossRef]
9. Duquesnoy, B.; Allaert, F.A.; Verdoncq, B. Psychosocial and occupational impact of chronic low back pain. *Rev. Rhum. Engl. Ed.* **1998**, *65*, 33–40.
10. Ferrari, S.; Vanti, C.; Frigau, L.; Guccione, A.A.; Mola, F.; Ruggeri, M.; Pillastrini, P.; Monticone, M. Sexual disability in patients with chronic non-specific low back pain-a multicenter retrospective analysis. *J. Phys. Ther. Sci.* **2019**, *31*, 360–365. [CrossRef]
11. Holmberg, S.T.; Salvesen, Ø.O.; Vangen-Lønne, V.; Hara, S.; Fredheim, O.M.; Solberg, T.K.; Jakola, A.S.; Solheim, O.; Nygaard, Ø.P.; Gulati, S. Pain during Sex before and after Surgery for Lumbar Disc Herniation: A Multicenter Observational Study. *Spine* **2020**, *45*, 1751–1757. [CrossRef]

12. Nikoobakht, M.; Fraidouni, N.; Yaghoubidoust, M.; Burri, A.; Pakpour, A.H. Sexual function and associated factors in Iranian patients with chronic low back pain. *Spinal Cord.* **2014**, *52*, 307–312. [CrossRef]
13. Sjögren, K.; Fugl-Meyer, A.R. Chronic back pain and sexuality. *Int. Rehabil. Med.* **1981**, *3*, 19–25. [CrossRef] [PubMed]
14. Daniels, A.H.; Reid, D.; Durand, W.; Disilvestro, K.; Hamilton, D.K.; Passias, P.; Kim, H.J.; Protopsaltis, T.; LaFage, V.; Smith, J.S.; et al. Sexual Dysfunction Secondary to Lumbar Stiffness in Adult Spinal Deformity Patients before and after Long-Segment Spinal Fusion. *World Neurosurg.* **2020**, *139*, e474–e479. [CrossRef] [PubMed]
15. Łabuz-Roszak, B.; Babińska, A.; Skupiński, J.; Czech, E.; Szczygieł, J.; Wawrzynek, W. Sexual quality of life in patients with low back pain and the radiological changes evaluated in magnetic resonance. *Wiad. Lek.* **2018**, *71*, 1039–1045. [PubMed]
16. Katz, H.; Newton-John, T.R.O.; Shires, A. Sexual Difficulties in the Population with Musculoskeletal Chronic Pain: A Systematic Review. *Pain Med.* **2021**, *22*, 1982–1992. [CrossRef]
17. Burri, A.; Hilpert, P.; Williams, F. Pain Catastrophizing, Fear of Pain, and Depression and Their Association with Female Sexual Pain. *J. Sex. Med.* **2020**, *17*, 279–288. [CrossRef] [PubMed]
18. Finn, E.; Morrison, T.G.; McGuire, B.E. Correlates of Sexual Functioning and Relationship Satisfaction among Men and Women Experiencing Chronic Pain. *Pain Med.* **2018**, *19*, 942–954. [CrossRef] [PubMed]
19. Ferrari, S.; Vanti, C.; Giagio, S.; Anesi, M.; Youssef, S.; Bortolami, A.; Cedraschi, C.; Pillastrini, P. Low back pain and sexual disability from the patient's perspective: A qualitative study. *Disabil. Rehabil.* **2022**, *44*, 2011–2019. [CrossRef]
20. Hald, G.M.; Graham, C.; Štulhofer, A.; Carvalheira, A.; Janssen, E.; Træen, B. Prevalence of Sexual Problems and Associated Distress in Aging Men Across 4 European Countries. *J. Sex. Med.* **2019**, *16*, 1212–1225. [CrossRef]
21. Stein, R.; Sardinha, A.; Araújo, C.G.S. Sexual Activity and Heart Patients: A Contemporary Perspective. *Can. J. Cardiol.* **2016**, *32*, 410–420. [CrossRef]
22. Steckenrider, J. Sexual activity of older adults: Let's talk about it. *Lancet Healthy Longev.* **2023**, *4*, e96–e97. [CrossRef]
23. Yoon, B.-H.; Lee, K.-H.; Noh, S.; Ha, Y.-C.; Lee, Y.-K.; Koo, K.-H. Sexual activity after total hip replacement in Korean patients: How they do, what they want, and how to improve. *Clin. Orthop. Surg.* **2013**, *5*, 269–277. [CrossRef] [PubMed]
24. Rougereau, G.; Rabot, C.; de Thomasson, E.; Tourabaly, I.; Mazel, C.; Langlais, T.; Ollat, D. Sexual activity resumption after total hip arthroplasty: A satisfaction survey in 101 patients. *Orthop. Traumatol. Surg. Res.* **2022**, *108*, 103171. [CrossRef] [PubMed]
25. Wang, B.-L.; Yue, D.-B.; Liu, B.X.; Guo, W.-S. Quality of sexual life after total hip arthroplasty in male patients with osteonecrosis of femoral head. *Eur. J. Orthop. Surg. Traumatol.* **2014**, *24*, 1217–1221. [CrossRef] [PubMed]
26. Korse, N.S.; Nicolai, M.P.J.; Both, S.; Vleggeert-Lankamp, C.L.A.; Elzevier, H.W. Discussing sexual health in spinal care. *Eur. Spine J. Off. Publ. Eur. Spine Soc.* **2016**, *25*, 766–773. [CrossRef] [PubMed]
27. Waddell, G.; Newton, M.; Henderson, I.; Somerville, D.; Main, C.J. A Fear-Avoidance Beliefs Questionnaire (FABQ) and the role of fear-avoidance beliefs in chronic low back pain and disability. *Pain* **1993**, *52*, 157–168. [CrossRef] [PubMed]
28. Sullivan, M.J.L.; Bishop, S.R.; Pivik, J. The Pain Catastrophizing Scale: Development and validation. *Psychol. Assess* **1995**, *7*, 524–532. [CrossRef]
29. Zung, W.W. A Self-Rating Depression Scale. *Arch. Gen. Psych* **1965**, *12*, 63–70. [CrossRef]
30. Beck, A.T.; Steer, R.A.; Ball, R.; Ranieri, W. Comparison of Beck Depression Inventories -IA and -II in psychiatric outpatients. *J. Clin. Psychol.* **1996**, *67*, 588–597. [CrossRef]
31. Zigmond, A.S.; Snaith, R.P. The hospital anxiety and depression scale. *Acta Psychiatr. Scand.* **1983**, *67*, 361–370. [CrossRef]
32. Rosen, R.; Brown, C.; Heiman, J.; Leiblum, S.; Meston, C.; Shabsigh, R.; Ferguson, D.; D'Agostino, R. The Female Sexual Function Index (FSFI): A multidimensional self-report instrument for the assessment of female sexual function. *J. Sex. Marital. Ther.* **2000**, *26*, 191–208. [CrossRef]
33. Rosen, R.C.; Riley, A.; Wagner, G.; Osterloh, I.H.; Kirkpatrick, J.; Mishra, A. The international index of erectile function (IIEF): A multidimensional scale for assessment of erectile dysfunction. *Urology* **1997**, *49*, 822–830. [CrossRef] [PubMed]
34. Sidorkewicz, N.; McGill, S.M. Male spine motion during coitus: Implications for the low back pain patient. *Spine* **2014**, *39*, 1633–1639. [CrossRef] [PubMed]
35. Sidorkewicz, N.; McGill, S.M. Documenting female spine motion during coitus with a commentary on the implications for the low back pain patient. *Eur. Spine J.* **2015**, *24*, 513–520. [CrossRef] [PubMed]
36. Oliva-Lozano, J.M.; Martín-Fuentes, I.; Muyor, J.M. Validity and Reliability of a New Inertial Device for Monitoring Range of Motion at the Pelvis during Sexual Intercourse. *Int. J. Environ. Res. Public Health* **2020**, *17*, 2884. [CrossRef] [PubMed]
37. Charbonnier, C.; Chagué, S.; Ponzoni, M.; Bernardoni, M.; Hoffmeyer, P.; Christofilopoulos, P. Sexual activity after total hip arthroplasty: A motion capture study. *J. Arthroplasty* **2014**, *29*, 640–647. [CrossRef] [PubMed]
38. Gómez-Hoyos, J. Editorial Commentary: Hip-Spine Syndrome: When the Hip Does Not Move, the Spine Labors Double. *Arthrosc. J. Arthrosc. Relat. Surg.* **2021**, *37*, 1510–1511. [CrossRef] [PubMed]
39. Lädermann, A.; Cunningham, G.; Chagué, S.; Charbonnier, C. Sexual Activities as Risk Factors of Rotator Cuff Lesions: A Prospective Cohort Study. *Sex. Disabil.* **2018**, *36*, 305–311. [CrossRef] [PubMed]
40. Rodriguez, J.A.; Hobart, S.J.; Deshmukh, A.J.; Menken, L.G.; Ranawat, A.S.; Rathod, P.A. Improved Sexual Function After Total Hip and Knee Arthroplasty for Osteoarthritis. *Orthopedics* **2021**, *44*, 111–116. [CrossRef]
41. Li, V.; Haslam, C.; Pakzad, M.; Brownlee, W.J.; Panicker, J.N. A practical approach to assessing and managing sexual dysfunction in multiple sclerosis. *Pract. Neurol.* **2020**, *20*, 122–131. [CrossRef]

42. Drulovic, J.; Kisic-Tepavcevic, D.; Pekmezovic, T. Epidemiology, diagnosis and management of sexual dysfunction in multiple sclerosis. *Acta Neurol. Belg.* **2020**, *120*, 791–797. [CrossRef]
43. Tirgari, B.; Rafati, F.; Mehdipour Rabori, R. Effect of Sexual Rehabilitation Program on Anxiety, Stress, Depression and Sexual Function among Men with Coronary Artery Disease. *J. Sex. Marital. Ther.* **2019**, *45*, 632–642. [CrossRef] [PubMed]
44. Begot, I.; Peixoto, T.C.A.; Gonzaga, L.R.A.; Bolzan, D.W.; Papa, V.; Carvalho, A.C.C.; Arena, R.; Gomes, W.J.; Guizilini, S. A home-based walking program improves erectile dysfunction in men with an acute myocardial infarction. *Am. J. Cardiol.* **2015**, *115*, 571–575. [CrossRef] [PubMed]
45. Kim, H.-N.; Ryu, J.; Kim, K.-S.; Song, S.-W. Effects of yoga on sexual function in women with metabolic syndrome: A randomized controlled trial. *J. Sex. Med.* **2013**, *10*, 2741–2751. [CrossRef] [PubMed]
46. Schumann, J.; Zellweger, M.J.; Di Valentino, M.; Piazzalonga, S.; Hoffmann, A. Sexual Dysfunction before and after Cardiac Rehabilitation. *Rehabil. Res. Pract.* **2010**, *2010*, 823060. [CrossRef] [PubMed]
47. Stanton, A.M.; Handy, A.B.; Meston, C.M. The Effects of Exercise on Sexual Function in Women. *Sex. Med. Rev.* **2018**, *6*, 548–557. [CrossRef] [PubMed]
48. Lorenz, T.A.; Meston, C.M. Exercise improves sexual function in women taking antidepressants: Results from a randomized crossover trial. *Depress. Anxiety* **2014**, *31*, 188–195. [CrossRef]
49. Cormie, P.; Newton, R.U.; Taaffe, D.R.; Spry, N.; Joseph, D.; Akhlil Hamid, M.; Galvão, D.A. Exercise maintains sexual activity in men undergoing androgen suppression for prostate cancer: A randomized controlled trial. *Prostate Cancer Prostatic Dis.* **2013**, *16*, 170–175. [CrossRef]
50. Zdravkovic, A.; Hasenöhrl, T.; Palma, S.; Crevenna, R. Effects of resistance exercise in prostate cancer patients: A systematic review update as of March 2020. *Wien Klin. Wochenschr.* **2020**, *132*, 452–463. [CrossRef]
51. Fergus, K.B.; Gaither, T.W.; Baradaran, N.; Glidden, D.V.; Cohen, A.J.; Breyer, B.N. Exercise Improves Self-Reported Sexual Function Among Physically Active Adults. *J. Sex. Med.* **2019**, *16*, 1236–1245. [CrossRef]
52. Yildiz, Y.; Kilinc, M.F.; Doluoglu, O.G. Is There Any Association Between Regular Physical Activity and Ejaculation Time? *Urol. J.* **2018**, *15*, 285–289.
53. Pourmousavi, L.; Nikseresht, A. Comparison of the Effect of Aerobic Exercise and Antidepressant Medications on Depression and Sexual Desire of Depressed Middle-Aged Women. *Int. J. Womens Health Reprod. Sci.* **2017**, *5*, 119–122. [CrossRef]
54. Stearns, Z.R.; Carvalho, M.L.; Beneciuk, J.M.; Lentz, T.A. Screening for Yellow Flags in Orthopaedic Physical Therapy: A Clinical Framework. *J. Orthop. Sports Phys. Ther.* **2021**, *51*, 459–469. [CrossRef] [PubMed]
55. Fairbank, J.C.; Couper, J.; Davies, J.B.; O'Brien, J.P. The Oswestry low back pain disability questionnaire. *Physiotherapy* **1980**, *66*, 271–273. [PubMed]
56. Ruta, D.A.; Garratt, A.M.; Wardlaw, D.; Russell, I.T. Developing a valid and reliable measure of health outcome for patients with low back pain. *Spine* **1994**, *19*, 1887–1896. [CrossRef] [PubMed]
57. Nicholas, M.K. The pain self-efficacy questionnaire: Taking pain into account. *Eur. J. Pain* **2007**, *11*, 153–163. [CrossRef] [PubMed]
58. Chen, Z.; Wu, J.; Wang, X.; Wu, J.; Ren, Z. The effects of myofascial release technique for patients with low back pain: A systematic review and meta-analysis. *Complement. Ther. Med.* **2021**, *59*, 102737. [CrossRef] [PubMed]
59. Corp, N.; Mansell, G.; Stynes, S.; Wynne-Jones, G.; Morsø, L.; Hill, J.C.; van der Windt, D.A. Evidence-based treatment recommendations for neck and low back pain across Europe: A systematic review of guidelines. *Eur. J. Pain* **2021**, *25*, 275–295. [CrossRef] [PubMed]
60. Jauregui, J.J.; Cherian, J.J.; Gwam, C.U.; Chughtai, M.; Mistry, J.B.; Elmallah, R.K.; Harwin, S.F.; Bhave, A.; Mont, M.A. A Meta-Analysis of Transcutaneous Electrical Nerve Stimulation for Chronic Low Back Pain. *Surg. Technol. Int.* **2016**, *28*, 296–302.
61. Wu, L.-C.; Weng, P.-W.; Chen, C.-H.; Huang, Y.-Y.; Tsuang, Y.-H.; Chiang, C.-J. Literature Review and Meta-Analysis of Transcutaneous Electrical Nerve Stimulation in Treating Chronic Back Pain. *Reg. Anesth. Pain Med.* **2018**, *43*, 425–433. [CrossRef]
62. Hughes, C.; May, S. A directional preference approach for chronic pelvic pain, bladder dysfunction and concurrent musculoskeletal symptoms: A case series. *J. Man. Manip. Ther.* **2020**, *28*, 170–180. [CrossRef]
63. Niederer, D.; Mueller, J. Sustainability effects of motor control stabilisation exercises on pain and function in chronic nonspecific low back pain patients: A systematic review with meta-analysis and meta-regression. *PLoS ONE* **2020**, *15*, e0227423. [CrossRef] [PubMed]
64. Van Dieën, J.H.; Reeves, N.P.; Kawchuk, G.; van Dillen, L.R.; Hodges, P.W. Analysis of Motor Control in Patients with Low Back Pain: A Key to Personalized Care? *J. Orthop. Sports Phys. Ther.* **2019**, *49*, 380–388. [CrossRef] [PubMed]
65. Aasa, B.; Berglund, L.; Michaelson, P.; Aasa, U. Individualized low-load motor control exercises and education versus a high-load lifting exercise and education to improve activity, pain intensity, and physical performance in patients with low back pain: A randomized controlled trial. *J. Orthop. Sports Phys. Ther.* **2015**, *45*, 77–85. [CrossRef] [PubMed]
66. Dahm, D.L.; Jacofsky, D.; Lewallen, D.G. Surgeons rarely discuss sexual activity with patients after THA: A survey of members of the American Association of Hip and Knee Surgeons. *Clin. Orthop.* **2004**, *428*, 237–240. [CrossRef]
67. Vanti, C.; Andreatta, S.; Borghi, S.; Guccione, A.A.; Pillastrini, P.; Bertozzi, L. The effectiveness of walking versus exercise on pain and function in chronic low back pain: A systematic review and meta-analysis of randomized trials. *Disabil. Rehabil.* **2019**, *41*, 622–632. [CrossRef] [PubMed]

68. Carcelén-Fraile, M.D.C.; Aibar-Almazán, A.; Martínez-Amat, A.; Cruz-Díaz, D.; Díaz-Mohedo, E.; Redecillas-Peiró, M.T.; Hita-Contreras, F. Effects of Physical Exercise on Sexual Function and Quality of Sexual Life Related to Menopausal Symptoms in Peri- and Postmenopausal Women: A Systematic Review. *Int. J. Environ. Res. Public Health* **2020**, *17*, 2680. [CrossRef] [PubMed]
69. Fergus, K.B.; Cohen, A.J.; Cedars, B.E.; Rowen, T.S.; Patino, G.; Breyer, B.N. Risk Factors for Sexual Pain Among Physically Active Women. *Sex. Med.* **2020**, *8*, 501–509. [CrossRef]
70. Lyons, K.S.; Winters-Stone, K.M.; Bennett, J.A.; Beer, T.M. The effects of partnered exercise on physical intimacy in couples coping with prostate cancer. *Health Psychol.* **2016**, *35*, 509–513. [CrossRef]
71. Wekker, V.; Karsten, M.D.A.; Painter, R.C.; van de Beek, C.; Groen, H.; Mol, B.W.J.; Hoek, A.; Laan, E.; Roseboom, T.J. A lifestyle intervention improves sexual function of women with obesity and infertility: A 5 year follow-up of a RCT. *PLoS ONE* **2018**, *13*, e0205934. [CrossRef]
72. Esposito, K.; Giugliano, F.; Di Palo, C.; Giugliano, G.; Marfella, R.; D'Andrea, F.; D'Armiento, M.; Giugliano, D. Effect of lifestyle changes on erectile dysfunction in obese men: A randomized controlled trial. *JAMA* **2004**, *291*, 2978–2984. [CrossRef]
73. Lentz, T.A.; Beneciuk, J.M.; Bialosky, J.E.; Zeppieri, G.; Dai, Y.; Wu, S.S.; George, S.Z. Development of a Yellow Flag Assessment Tool for Orthopaedic Physical Therapists: Results From the Optimal Screening for Prediction of Referral and Outcome (OSPRO) Cohort. *J. Orthop. Sports Phys. Ther.* **2016**, *46*, 327–343. [CrossRef] [PubMed]
74. Vlaeyen, J.W.S.; Kole-Snijders, A.M.J.; Boeren, R.G.B.; van Eek, H. Fear of movement/(re)injury in chronic low back pain and its relation to behavioral performance. *Pain* **1995**, *62*, 363–372. [CrossRef] [PubMed]
75. Wood, L.; Hendrick, P.A. A systematic review and meta-analysis of pain neuroscience education for chronic low back pain: Short-and long-term outcomes of pain and disability. *Eur. J. Pain* **2019**, *23*, 234–249. [CrossRef] [PubMed]
76. Gorji, S.M.; Mohammadi Nia Samakosh, H.; Watt, P.; Henrique Marchetti, P.; Oliveira, R. Pain Neuroscience Education and Motor Control Exercises versus Core Stability Exercises on Pain, Disability, and Balance in Women with Chronic Low Back Pain. *Int. J. Environ. Res. Public Health* **2022**, *19*, 2694. [CrossRef] [PubMed]
77. Malfliet, A.; Kregel, J.; Coppieters, I.; De Pauw, R.; Meeus, M.; Roussel, N.; Cagnie, B.; Danneels, L.; Nijs, J. Effect of Pain Neuroscience Education Combined with Cognition-Targeted Motor Control Training on Chronic Spinal Pain: A Randomized Clinical Trial. *JAMA Neurol.* **2018**, *75*, 808–817. [CrossRef] [PubMed]
78. Leake, H.B.; Moseley, G.L.; Stanton, T.R.; O'Hagan, E.T.; Heathcote, L.C. What do patients value learning about pain? A mixed-methods survey on the relevance of target concepts after pain science education. *Pain* **2021**, *162*, 2558–2568. [CrossRef] [PubMed]
79. Ho, E.K.-Y.; Chen, L.; Simic, M.; Ashton-James, C.E.; Comachio, J.; Wang, D.X.M.; Hayden, J.A.; Ferreira, M.L.; Ferreira, P.H. Psychological interventions for chronic, non-specific low back pain: Systematic review with network meta-analysis. *BMJ* **2022**, *376*, e067718. [CrossRef]
80. O'Sullivan, P.B.; Caneiro, J.P.; O'Keeffe, M.; Smith, A.; Dankaerts, W.; Fersum, K.; O'Sullivan, K. Cognitive Functional Therapy: An Integrated Behavioral Approach for the Targeted Management of Disabling Low Back Pain. *Phys Ther.* **2018**, *98*, 408–423. [CrossRef]
81. Pardos-Gascón, E.M.; Narambuena, L.; Leal-Costa, C.; van-der Hofstadt-Román, C.J. Differential efficacy between cognitive-behavioral therapy and mindfulness-based therapies for chronic pain: Systematic review. *Int. J. Clin. Health Psychol.* **2021**, *21*, 100197. [CrossRef]
82. Clayton, A.H.; McGarvey, E.L.; Clavet, G.J. The Changes in Sexual Functioning Questionnaire (CSFQ): Development, reliability, and validity. *Psychopharmacol. Bull.* **1997**, *33*, 731–745.
83. Daker-White, G. Reliable and valid self-report outcome measures in sexual (dys)function: A systematic review. *Arch. Sex. Behav.* **2002**, *31*, 197–209. [CrossRef] [PubMed]
84. Busby, D.M.; Christensen, C.; Crane, D.R.; Larson, J.H. A revision of the dyadic adjustment scale for use with distressed and nondistressed couples: Construct hierarchy and multidimensional scales. *J. Marital. Fam. Ther.* **1995**, *21*, 289–308. [CrossRef]
85. Slade, S.C.; Finnegan, S.; Dionne, C.E.; Underwood, M.; Buchbinder, R. The Consensus on Exercise Reporting Template (CERT) applied to exercise interventions in musculoskeletal trials demonstrated good rater agreement and incomplete reporting. *J. Clin. Epidemiol.* **2018**, *103*, 120–130. [CrossRef] [PubMed]
86. Thomas, C.M.; Levene, H.B. Lack of Current Recommendations for Resuming Sexual Activity Following Spinal Surgery. *Asian Spine J.* **2019**, *13*, 515–518. [CrossRef] [PubMed]
87. Sologuren-García, G.; Linares, C.L.; Flores, J.R.; Mendoza-Mamani, K.; Pilco, R.M.; Escobar-Bermejo, G.; Sotelo-Gonzales, S.; Palza-Portugal, G. Breaking the taboo: Qualitative analysis of the sexuality in people with acquired motor disability. *BMC Psychol.* **2023**, *11*, 380. [CrossRef] [PubMed]
88. Fasano, F.; Piscitelli, V.; Sicignano, C.; Prudente, M.; Falco, A.; Villa, A.; Lugarà, M.; Pezzullo, G.; D'Agostino, V.; Gatta, G. Sex life and low back pain: The impact of intradiscal ozone therapy in patients with herniated lumbar disc. *Interv. Neuroradiol.* **2023**, 15910199231183108.
89. Shimamura, Y.; Kanayama, M.; Horio, M.; Yamaguchi, A.; Oha, F.; Tsujimoto, T.; Tanaka, M.; Hasegawa, Y.; Endo, T.; Hashimoto, T. Posterior lumbar fusion surgery doesn't change sexual activities in patients with lumbar degenerative disease: An observational study. *BMC Musculoskelet. Disord.* **2023**, *24*, 724. [CrossRef]
90. Prize, N.B.T.; Kanat, S.S.; Wruble, A.C.K.W. Gaps in sexual health content of healthcare professional curriculum: A systematic review of educational interventions. *BMC Med. Educ.* **2023**, *23*, 926. [CrossRef]

91. Khamisy-Farah, R.; Bragazzi, N.L. How to Integrate Sex and Gender Medicine into Medical and Allied Health Profession Undergraduate, Graduate, and Post-Graduate Education: Insights from a Rapid Systematic Literature Review and a Thematic Meta-Synthesis. *J. Pers. Med.* **2022**, *12*, 612. [CrossRef]
92. Oliva-Lozano, J.M.; Alacid, F.; López-Miñarro, P.A.; Muyor, J.M. What are the physical demands of sexual relations? A systematic review of the literature. *Arch. Sex. Behav.* **2022**, *51*, 1397–1417. [CrossRef]

*healthcare*

MDPI

*Article*

# Walking Speed and Risk of Falling Patients Operated for Selected Malignant Tumors

**Anna Latajka [1], Małgorzata Stefańska [2], Marek Woźniewski [2] and Iwona Malicka [2,*]**

[1] Lower Silesian Oncology, Pulmonology, and Hematology Center, 53-413 Wroclaw, Poland; latajka.anna@dco.com.pl

[2] Department of Physiotherapy, Wroclaw University of Health and Sport Sciences, 51-612 Wroclaw, Poland; malgorzata.stefanska@awf.wroc.pl (M.S.); marek.wozniewski@awf.wroc.pl (M.W.)

* Correspondence: iwona.malicka@awf.wroc.pl

**Abstract:** Background: A literature review reveals that studies on walking and fall occurrences in the context of cancer have predominantly centered on geriatric patients. Nonetheless, cancer patients of all ages are susceptible to such risks. Both cancer and its treatments contribute to significant risk factors for disturbances in walking and falls, encompassing muscle weakness, impaired balance, reduced proprioception, cognitive impairment, and functional limitations. Aim: to assess walking speed and the risk of falls among patients undergoing surgery for the most common malignancies: breast (BU), lung (P), colorectal (DS), and reproductive organs (G). Material and Methods: An observational study was conducted using a cohort design. A total of 176 individuals participated in the study, including 139 cancer patients, who were divided into four groups: BU (N = 30), P (N = 35), DS (N = 35), and G (N = 39), as well as 37 healthy volunteers in the control group (C, N = 37). All participants underwent an assessment of walking speed using BTS G-WALK® and an evaluation of the number of falls and the risk of falling using a Fall Control Card. Results: There was a significant decrease in walking speed after surgery compared to the time before surgery, from 2.7% in the BU group, through 9.3% in the P group, and 19.2% in the DS group, to 30.0% in the G group. At the same time, for groups G and DS, the average walking speed fell below 1.0 m/s, amounting to 0.84 m/s and 0.97 m/s, respectively, in the measurement after the surgery and 0.95 m/s and 1.0 m/s in the follow-up measurement. Falling occurred in all the groups except for the BU group. The created logistic regression model showed that increasing the walking speed measured after the procedure (study 2) by 1 m/s reduces the risk of falling by approximately 500 times (OR = 0.002). Limitations in daily activity were observed in the follow-up examination (study 3) in 75% of patients. Conclusions: Surgical intervention has an impact on walking speed, and being part of the study group influences the risk of falling. Further research is needed to determine the precise risk of falls in cancer patients.

**Keywords:** cancer; surgical treatment; walking speed; fall risk

**Citation:** Latajka, A.; Stefańska, M.; Woźniewski, M.; Malicka, I. Walking Speed and Risk of Falling Patients Operated for Selected Malignant Tumors. *Healthcare* **2023**, *11*, 3069. https://doi.org/10.3390/healthcare11233069

Academic Editors: Marco Tramontano and Giovanni Galeoto

Received: 30 October 2023
Revised: 22 November 2023
Accepted: 27 November 2023
Published: 30 November 2023



## 1. Introduction

Malignant tumors are one of the most common groups of diseases in developed countries, causing long-term effects that affect patients' lives, changing their quality in every sphere: personal, professional, and social [1]. In women, the highest incidence of malignant tumors is recorded between the ages of 50 and 74. These include breast (22.9%), lung (9.9%), endometrial (7.0%), colon (5.9%), and ovarian (4.3%) cancer, while in men, between 55 and 79 years of age, they are prostate (20.6%), lung (16.1%), colon (6.8%), bladder (6.4%), rectum (4.2%), and stomach (3.8%) cancer [2].

A literature review reveals that studies on walking and fall occurrences in the context of cancer have predominantly centered on geriatric patients. Nonetheless, cancer patients of all ages are susceptible to such risks. Both cancer and its treatments contribute to significant risk factors for disturbances in walking and falls, encompassing muscle weakness, impaired balance, reduced proprioception, cognitive impairment, and functional limitations [3–6].

Surgery is the leading treatment method for solid tumors in approximately 80% of cancer patients [7]. Injury to the body resulting from surgical procedures can lead to the onset of pain, which, in turn, may cause anxiety. The manifestations of anxiety and pain are physiological patterns that closely resemble each other, making it challenging to interpret them as unique to either pain or anxiety. Dizziness, restlessness, and muscle tremors can be symptoms indicative of both anxiety and pain simultaneously. Prolonged pain can trigger or exacerbate depressive disorders [8,9]. Research suggests that individuals with depression exhibit deviations in their walking [10].

Surgery may cause functional complications within the musculoskeletal system, affecting a reduction in gait efficiency. In addition, as a result of surgical treatment, functional disorders of the musculoskeletal system appear, resulting primarily from aspects related to the formation of scars and adhesions within soft tissues, which cause a limitation of mobility in the joints, pain, and further restriction of physical activity. There are changes in nerve conduction caused by damage to the skin structures, subcutaneous tissue, fascia, and muscles. Body posture disorders may result from increased postoperative pain, changes in joint mechanics, and overloading of muscles and tissues. Changing the mechanics of movement in the joints makes it uneconomical and leads to faster tissue wear and the appearance of degenerative changes [11].

Patients with cancer often use multiple medications simultaneously, and various drug types like opiates, benzodiazepines, steroids, antipsychotics, and sedatives are linked to a substantial risk of falls. Additionally, patients with cancer undergo distinctive forms of treatment, including radiation therapy, chemotherapy, and biologic response modifiers. Those receiving radiotherapy frequently report experiencing weakness and fatigue, and this fatigue can potentially contribute to falls in cancer patients. Chemotherapy also poses a risk for falls in this patient population, with the risk increasing as the cumulative dose of chemotherapy and the use of neurotoxic drugs rise [12].

A disturbed gait pattern may limit not only the efficiency of walking and cause an increase in energy expenditure but also the appearance of secondary, incorrect compensatory reactions that may become permanent [13] and consequently contribute to a greater risk of falls [14]. Lowry et al. [15] indicate that the typical walking speed of healthy adults is in the range of 1.2 to 1.4 m/s and begins to decline naturally between the fifth and sixth decades of life. Maintaining a speed above 1.0 m/s is associated with greater independence in activities of daily living and a lower risk of hospitalization due to adverse events—including falls. Quach et al. [16] and Van Kan et al. [17] showed that the lowest risk of falling occurs at a walking speed of 1–1.3 m/s. The critical value is considered to be 0.6 m/s. Every 0.2 m/s increase in speed from the critical value reduces the risk of requiring personal care by 38% [18].

Therefore, the study aimed to assess the walking speed and risk of falling among patients undergoing surgery for the most common malignancies: breast, lung, colorectal, and reproductive organs.

## 2. Materials and Methods

### *2.1. Participants and Recruitment*

An observational study was conducted using a cohort design (STROBE Statement in the Supplementary Materials).

The study included, from 14 November 2018 to 3 January 2022, 139 cancer patients and 37 healthy volunteers who met the inclusion criteria. Four patient cohorts—breast (BU), reproductive organ (G), pulmonary (P), and digestive system (DS)—were derived from a consecutive series of cancer patients qualified for surgical treatment at the Lower Silesian Oncology, Pulmonology, and Hematology Center in Wroclaw, Poland.

Group 1—BU—breasts (Breast Unit)—30 people were examined: 30 women and 0 men. Surgical procedures in the chest area (simple mastectomy, mastectomy with simultaneous implant reconstruction, mastectomy with lymphadenectomy).

Group 2—G—gynecological—35 people were examined: 35 women and 0 men. Surgical procedures within the pelvic area (gynecological operations—oncological operations of the reproductive organ in women with the opening of the lower abdominal cavity—gynecological laparotomy)

Group 3—P—pulmonary—39 people were examined: 18 women and 21 men. Thoracic surgery with resection of a part of the lung—operator's access to the lung tissue from the intercostal area, VATS lobectomy.

Group 4—DS—digestive system—35 people were examined: 12 women and 23 men. Abdominal surgeries—laparotomy for colorectal cancer.

Group 5—C—control group—37 people were examined: 29 women and 8 men. Healthy people, not suffering from malignant tumors in the past or currently.

The inclusion criteria for the study were as follows:

1. Age: 50–70.
2. BMI 20–35.
3. Independent movement without the use of orthopedic aids.
4. No fall in the last 3 months.
5. Informed consent of the patient to participate in the study.

The criteria for exclusion were as follows:

1. Neoadjuvant chemotherapy and radiotherapy and postoperative complications, e.g., massive hematomas, revisions of postoperative wounds, and wound infections.
2. Orthopedic and traumatological diseases that disturb the normal gait pattern.
3. Diseases of the nervous system.
4. Known balance and coordination disorders.
5. Psychiatric disorders, including a history of diagnosed and treated depression.
6. The use of medicines that affect psychophysical efficiency.
7. Difficult cooperation with the examined person and refusal to participate in the study (at every stage).

Patients were assigned to each group (BU, G, P, DS) using a computer program that randomly selected patients from each patient cohort while considering the inclusion and exclusion criteria as well as the type of surgery.

During the stay in the hospital, each patient was examined twice: before the surgery (study 1) and after the surgery (study 2, when they were able to stand up and move on their own—usually on the second to fourth day after the surgery). In addition, a follow-up examination was conducted four weeks after the end of hospitalization (study 3). Throughout the study, patients were required to maintain their usual lifestyle.

All patients received medical and physiotherapeutic care.

### *2.2. Research Methods*

#### 2.2.1. Walking Speed Measurement

Gait assessment was performed using the BTS G-WALK® accelerometer (BTS Bioengineering, Milan, Italy). A sensor (G-Walk-sensor) was placed on the patient's body using a belt at the level of the lumbar spine (according to the manufacturer's recommendations: in the area of the intervertebral space L4–L5), and then the patient's task was to follow the researcher's command: "start" using your own speed for a distance of 20 m in a straight line one way, and after 20 m, turn back to the starting point. The same footwear was worn during all the examinations of a given patient. Then, the data collected via Bluetooth were sent to a computer and processed using the BTS-WALK software dedicated to the device, and the walking speed was analyzed.

G-Walk is a wireless system consisting of an inertial sensor composed of a triaxial accelerometer, a magnetic sensor, and a triaxial gyroscope. The device calibrates itself automatically each time the walking testing function is activated for a specific patient.

Research indicates that the BTS G-WALK® sensor system is reliable for all measured spatiotemporal parameters. The intraclass correlation coefficient values for walking speed were excellent between consecutive measurements on the same day, with values ranging from 0.83 to 0.96. In terms of validity, the intra-class correlation coefficient values between measurement systems showed excellent levels of agreement for walking speed; range = 0.98 to 0.99 [19].

#### 2.2.2. Fall Control Card

The Fall Control Card allows you to observe falls and subjective feelings related to your daily physical activity for 1 month.

A fall was defined as an event in which an adult unintentionally came to rest on the ground or other lower supporting surfaces, unrelated to a medical incident or to an overwhelming external physical force.

The falls were categorized based on their causes (standing up, sitting down, walking, bending, and turning/turning around), consequences (hospitalization, need for medical assistance, sufficient assistance from others, independent recovery, and resumption of activities), and circumstances (at home/outside the home).

The Fall Control Card was distributed solely to patients in the study group in the form of a self-completed diary.

According to the answers to the questions contained in the card, the researcher's task was to collect information about possible falls and analyze them.

### *2.3. Ethics*

The study received a positive opinion from the Senate Committee on Research Ethics at Wroclaw University of Health and Sport Sciences. Consent number: 28/2018. Approval date: 14 September 2018.

The study was approved and was registered in the Lower Silesian Center of Oncology, Pulmonology, and Hematology in Wroclaw, Poland. Consent number: NDBI-106/18, NDBI 4/18/BN.

### *2.4. Statistical Analysis*

Arithmetic means and standard deviations were calculated for measurable variables. The frequency of their occurrence (percentage) was calculated for categorical variables. The normality of the distribution was checked with the Shapiro–Wilk test, and the homogeneity of the variance was checked with the Levene test. An ANOVA for repeated measures was applied with a post hoc comparison using the Tukey test for quantitative variables. Test power was calculated. The Chi-square ($\chi^2$) test was used for nominal variables. A logistic regression model was performed, and the odds ratio (OR) for the risk of falls was calculated. The effect size of the ANOVA was calculated from Eta-squared ($\eta^2$) and then transformed to Cohen's d value [20]. Values of Cohen's d test $\geq$0.8 indicated great strength of the observed effect, $\geq$0.5 indicated a moderate effect, $\geq$0.2 indicated a weak effect, and <0.02 indicated no effect [21]. Cramer's V coefficient was used to calculate the effect size of the $\chi^2$ test with more than one degree of freedom (categorical variables). Cramer's V value is in the range of 0–1. The closer it is to 0, the weaker the strength of the relationship between the examined features, and the closer it is to +1, the stronger the strength of the studied relationship is [22]. Calculations were made in Statistica 13.3, PQ Stat 1.8.2, and statistical calculators at http://www.psychometrica.de/effect_size (accessed on 26 October 2023). The significance level was taken as $p < 0.05$.

## 3. Results

### *3.1. Participants Characteristics*

The average age of the examined people was 60.56 $\pm$ 5.11 years, the average body height was 166.34 $\pm$ 6.74 cm, and the average body weight was 74.46 $\pm$ 12.85 kg. The BMI index for the examined people was 26.86 $\pm$ 4.08. Detailed results for individual groups are presented in Table 1. The study groups were considered homogeneous regarding age and somatic characteristics. There were no significant differences in the main effect for age and BMI (Table 1).

**Table 1.** Statistical characteristics of age and somatic features.

| Characteristic | G N = 35 | | DS N = 35 | | P N = 39 | | BU N = 30 | | C N = 37 | | ANOVA $p$ | Cohen's d |
|---|---|---|---|---|---|---|---|---|---|---|---|---|
| | **Mean** | **SD** | **Mean** | **SD** | **Mean** | **SD** | **Mean** | **SD** | **Mean** | **SD** | | |
| Age (years) | 60.11 | 4.87 | 61.54 | 5.28 | 60.67 | 5.30 | 61.30 | 4.21 | 59.22 | 5.89 | 0.3307 | 0.35 |
| BMI (kg/m$^2$) | 27.47 | 4.57 | 27.03 | 3.41 | 26.32 | 3.95 | 26.05 | 4.38 | 27.44 | 4.11 | 0.4884 | 0.29 |

Groups: G—gynecological, DS—digestive system, P—pulmonary, BU—breasts, and C—control.

### 3.2. *Walking speed [m/s]*

Table 2 shows the mean values and standard deviation of walking speed for individual groups and subsequent measurements. Significant differences on the level of main effects were found; significant differences were found for the walking speed of the examined groups in relation to the control group and between the individual groups (Table 3); and significant differences were found for subsequent measurements in the study groups (Table 4). A significant decrease in walking speed was found for all the study groups, except BU, in the second measurement compared to the first, and a significant increase in walking speed for group G in the third measurement compared to the second measurement was found (Table 4). Significant differences between measurements 1 and 3 were shown for groups G and DS (Table 4).

**Table 2.** Walking speed and analysis of variance for repeated measurements.

| Walking Speed (m/s) | | | | | | | ANOVA | | | | | |
|---|---|---|---|---|---|---|---|---|---|---|---|---|
| | **Study 1** | | **Study 2** | | **Study 3** | | **Repetition** | | | **Group** | | |
| **Group** | **Mean** | **SD** | **Mean** | **SD** | **Mean** | **SD** | $p$ | **d Cohen's** | **Test Power** | $p$ | **d Cohen's** | **Test Power** |
| All | 1.23 | 0.21 | 1.08 | 0.28 | 1.14 | 0.24 | | | | | | |
| BU | 1.12 | 0.18 | 1.02 | 0.20 | 1.08 | 0.18 | | | | | | |
| G | 1.20 | 0.16 | 0.84 | 0.22 | 0.95 | 0.16 | | | | | | |
| DS | 1.20 | 0.22 | 0.97 | 0.24 | 1.01 | 0.18 | <0.0001 * | 1.22 | 1.00 | <0.0001 * | 1.57 | 1.00 |
| P | 1.29 | 0.23 | 1.17 | 0.23 | 1.26 | 0.19 | | | | | | |
| C | 1.33 | 0.21 | 1.37 | 0.19 | 1.35 | 0.19 | | | | | | |

Groups: G—gynecological, DS—digestive system, P—pulmonary, BU—breasts, and C—control; * $p < 0.05$.

**Table 3.** Evaluation of the differences in average values of walking speed between groups, performed with Tukey's post hoc test.

| Group | | Study 1 | | | | Group | | Study 2 | | | | Group | | Study 3 | | | |
|---|---|---|---|---|---|---|---|---|---|---|---|---|---|---|---|---|---|
| | | **BU** | **G** | **DS** | **P** | | | **BU** | **G** | **DS** | **P** | | | **BU** | **G** | **DS** | **P** |
| Study 1 | G | 0.9728 | | | | Study 2 | G | 0.0270 * | | | | Study 3 | G | 0.4451 | | | |
| | DS | 0.9736 | 1.0000 | | | | DS | 0.9992 | 0.3045 | | | | DS | 0.9902 | 0.9968 | | |
| | P | 0.0512 | 0.7943 | 0.7907 | | | P | 0.2130 | <0.0001 * | 0.0019 | | | P | 0.0398 | <0.0001 * | <0.0001 * | |
| | C | 0.0049 * | 0.2989 | 0.2953 | 1.0000 | | C | <0.0001 * | <0.0001 * | <0.0001 * | 0.0027 * | | C | 0.0001 | <0.0001 * | <0.0001 * | 0.8987 |

Groups: G—gynecological, DS—digestive system, P—pulmonary, BU—breasts, and C—control; * $p < 0.05$.

**Table 4.** Evaluation of the differences in average values of walking speed between successive measurements in the study groups, performed with Tukey's post hoc test.

| Group | Study 1 vs. 2 | Study 1 vs. 3 | Study 2 vs. 3 |
|---|---|---|---|
| G | <0.0001 * | <0.0001 * | 0.0111 * |
| DS | <0.0001 * | <0.0001 * | 0.9785 |
| P | 0.0024 * | 0.9994 | 0.0996 |
| BU | 0.2090 | 0.9994 | 0.8875 |
| C | 0.9904 | 1.0000 | 1.0000 |

Groups: G—gynecological, DS—digestive system, P—pulmonary, BU—breasts, and C—control; * $p < 0.05$.

### 3.3. Risk of Falling

A fall occurred in all groups except for the BU group. It was a statistically significant difference. The number of falls did not differ significantly in the study groups. A detailed analysis of the number of falls is presented in Table 5.

**Table 5.** Analysis of the occurrence of a fall in the study groups (1: yes; 0: no) and the number of falls in the study groups (numerical value from 1 to 3).

| | Fall | | | | Number of Falls | | | | |
|---|---|---|---|---|---|---|---|---|---|
| Group | No | Yes | $\chi^2$ | Cramer's V | 1 | 2 | 3 | $\chi^2$ | Cramer's V |
| BU | 30<br>100% | 0<br>0% | <0.0001 * | 0.39 | 0<br>- | 0<br>- | 0<br>- | 0.5427 | 0.31 |
| G | 24<br>69% | 11<br>31% | | | 4<br>36% | 6<br>55% | 1<br>9% | | |
| DS | 23<br>66% | 12<br>34% | | | 9<br>75% | 3<br>25% | 0<br>0% | | |
| P | 28<br>72% | 11<br>28% | | | 9<br>82% | 2<br>18% | 0<br>0% | | |
| C | 37<br>100% | 0<br>0% | | | 0<br>- | 0<br>- | 0<br>- | | |

Groups: G—gynecological, DS—digestive system, P—pulmonary, BU—breasts, and C—control; $\chi^2$—Chi-square test; * $p < 0.05$.

Most often, a fall occurred in the patient's place of residence. Only for two patients from group G and two from group DS did the fall occur outside their home. In all the study groups, falls were most often observed while standing up, bending down, and turning. No statistically significant differences were found.

In each group, many fell while wearing shoes with an open heel (about 70% of the falls). No statistically significant differences were found. As a consequence of a fall, the help of other people was needed in about 50% of cases. In three quarters of the people who fell, there was no injury, and one quarter reported minor injuries, e.g., epidermal abrasions. No statistically significant differences were found. Limitations in daily activity were observed in the follow-up examination (study 3) in 75% of patients. No statistically significant differences were found between the groups.

The multivariant analysis confirmed a significant impact of walking speed on the risk of falling. The analysis took into consideration belonging to a specific group, age, the BMI of the subjects, and the walking speed measured in study 2 (after surgery) or the difference between the walking speed in studies 1 and 2 (before–after surgery). The created logistic regression model showed that increasing the walking speed measured after the procedure (study 2) by 1 m/s reduces the risk of falling by approximately 500 times (OR = 0.002) (Table 6). It has also been shown that increasing the difference in walking speed measured in studies 1 and 2 by 1 m/s increases the risk of falling by approximately 200 times (OR = 200.36) (Table 7). Both regression models showed a significant effect of surgery on the risk of falls. Belonging to the study group determines an increase in risk by approximately two times.

**Table 6.** Logistic regression model indicating factors that have a significant impact on the risk of falling (walking speed).

| **Dependent Variable: 0—Fall No 1—Fall Yes** | **Coef. B** | **Error B** | **Wald Test** | **OR** | **95% CI** | ***p*** |
|---|---|---|---|---|---|---|
| Group | 6.54 | 3.47 | 3.55 | 2.36 | 1.44–3.87 | 0.0007 * |
| Age (year) | 0.89 | 0.25 | 13.02 | 0.92 | 0.84–1.02 | 0.1157 |
| BMI (kg/m$^2$) | −0.08 | 0.05 | 2.50 | 1.03 | 0.91–1.17 | 0.6656 |
| Walking speed 2 (m/s) | 0.03 | 0.06 | 0.18 | 0.002 | <0.001–0.02 | <0.0001 * |
| *p* | <0.0001 * | | | | | |
| Pseudo R2 | 0.38 | | | | | |

OR—odds ratio; 95%CI—95% confidence interval; Group: 0—control; 1—breasts; 2—gynecological; 3—pulmonary; 4—digestive system; * $p < 0.05$.

**Table 7.** Logistic regression model indicating factors that have a significant impact on the risk of falling (difference in walking speed).

| **Dependent Variable: 0—No Fall 1—Fall** | **Coef. B** | **Error B** | **Wald Test** | **OR** | **95%CI** | ***p*** |
|---|---|---|---|---|---|---|
| Group | 0.81 | 0.23 | 12.03 | 2.25 | 1.42–3.57 | 0.0005 * |
| Age (year) | −0.03 | 0.05 | 0.43 | 0.97 | 0.88–1.06 | 0.4233 |
| BMI (kg/m$^2$) | 0.08 | 0.06 | 1.67 | 1.09 | 0.96–1.23 | 0.1675 |
| Walking speed 1–2 (m/s) | 5.30 | 1.32 | 16.17 | 200.21 | 15.12–2650.36 | 0.0001 * |
| *p* | <0.0001 * | | | | | |
| Pseudo R2 | 0.34 | | | | | |

OR—odds ratio; 95%CI—95% confidence interval; Group: 0—control; 1—breasts; 2—gynecological; 3—pulmonary; 4—digestive system; * $p < 0.05$.

## 4. Discussion

Recovery after surgery is understood as the time when a person strives to regain independence and, consequently, returns to everyday activities. While it is easy to determine the beginning of recovery after a surgical intervention, its end remains uncertain. Several factors influence recovery after surgery. These factors include physical symptoms, emotional disturbances, previous medical history, and its impact on recovery time at that time. Great importance is now also attached to the existence or lack of adequate and regular information and support provided to the patient by their family and/or health professionals. The extent of the surgical procedure also plays a vital role in recovery [23,24].

Gait is considered one of the most reliable parameters reflecting the general condition of a patient and a predisposing factor for safe functioning in everyday life [25]. Walking speed serves as an indicator of frailty, and its evaluation in oncology clinics can significantly enhance patient assessment, prognostication, and the customization of care [26]. In the study groups, a lower walking speed was observed in the initial measurement before surgery for the DS, G and BU groups, and this difference was also maintained in the follow-up measurement. Moreover, in all the examined groups, a significant decrease in walking speed after the surgery was observed in relation to the time before the surgery, from 2.7% in the BU group, through 9.3% in the P group, and 19.2% in the DS group, to 30.0% in the G group. At the same time, for groups G and DS, the average walking speed fell below 1.0 m/s, amounting to 0.84 m/s and 0.97 m/s, respectively, in the measurement after surgery and 0.95 m/s and 1.0 m/s in the follow-up measurement. Hence, the most substantial limitations were observed in patients who underwent surgical procedures for digestive and gynecological cancers. Surgical interventions in the abdominal and lower abdominal regions can lead to limited hip mobility and flexion contracture. Hip flexion contracture results in increased pelvic anteversion during the support phase and, in conjunction with postoperative pain, may lead to crouched walking. Furthermore, a diminished range of hip movement is correlated with a reduction in walking speed [27,28].

Walking speed predicts the length of a hospital stay, readmission, and risk of death [29]. Walking speed below 1.0 m/s is associated with a higher risk of falling [16,17], and below 0.8 m/s is an independent predictor of death in elderly cancer survivors [3]. In connection with the above, it is worth paying particular attention to group G, which seems to be at the highest risk of falling immediately after surgery and worse functioning, which may translate into survival time.

Conversely, it appears that groups P and BU face the lowest level of risk. Although the changes were statistically significant, they were of a smaller magnitude. The damage to anatomical structures during surgery may play a role in dysfunctions of the upper body quadrants. Imbalances in chest wall muscle function and the subsequent disruption of postural muscle balance could lead to increased thoracic kyphosis and subsequent lumbar lordosis, potentially contributing to lower back pain. Lower back pain is frequently accompanied by alterations in walking [28,30]. The walking speed in both groups was, however, above 1.0 m/s, which is consistent with the results obtained by other authors [31,32].

Taking into account the walking speed, Pererai et al. [33] and Middleton et al. [34] further suggest that a change in walking speed of 0.05 m/s, although small, is clinically significant, while a change in walking speed of 0.10 m/s is significant for mobility. Therefore, surgical treatment, especially in the first postoperative period, brings a substantial change in the mobility of cancer patients, indicating the need to introduce physiotherapeutic procedures adequate for existing disorders.

Bluethmann et al. further observed a recurring but varying effect of the history of cancer on patients' mobility. A higher percentage of elderly people with a history of malignancy than those without a history of cancer used mobility aids. At the same time, the use of mobility aids varied depending on the type of cancer, with the highest rates in the group of people who suffered from breast cancer, colorectal cancer, and cancer of the reproductive organs. Cancer patients were also more likely to show signs of mobility impairment [35]. These results suggest the importance of assessing fall risk at follow-up visits and identifying risk factors that appear to be modifiable with appropriate treatment interventions. In our study, a fall occurred in all the study groups except for the BU group. Falls are a multifactorial consequence. Among patients undergoing cancer treatment, there is a deficiency in endurance, muscle weakness, and pain. Pain, as evaluated by Mata et al. [23], is the most critical risk factor for falls compared to other factors. The magnitude and extent of postoperative pain depend on the type of surgery. The most intense pain is experienced following thoracotomies and procedures in the abdominal region [36], which may explain the occurrence of falls in these three study groups (P, DS, G).

It is worth noting that most often, falls occurred in the patient's place of residence. Li et al. emphasize that indoor falls occur more often in frail people who avoid leaving the house [37]. Falls occurred most often while standing up, bending down, or making a turn/turning. Bartoszek et al. indicated that the most common cause of falls is usually everyday activities, such as walking or changing position [38]. Based on the conducted research, it seems crucial to extend the physiotherapeutic procedure for the time after leaving the hospital. It is particularly important that the mean age of the examined patients was 60.56 $\pm$ 5.11 years. This means that gait pattern disorders and a higher risk of falling may occur in patients operated on for the most common malignancies much earlier than indicated by the literature review [39–41]. It is recognized that falls are a serious problem among older people; the incidence of falls increases with age [42]. In patients treated for malignant tumors, the literature review also indicates disorders resulting from combination therapy [43,44]. Our own research indicates that it can be assumed with a high probability that the examined patients were then qualified for adjuvant treatment in the form of chemotherapy, radiotherapy, or hormone therapy.

### 4.1. Strengths and Limitations of This Study

Our own analysis also indicated limitations resulting, among others, from the lack of specification of the time and type of physiotherapy applied immediately after surgery. An analysis with regard to the verticalization day was also not included, which, depending on the surgical procedure, varied from 1 to 3 days. Postoperative rehabilitation may affect the quality of gait in the first postoperative days and, consequently, the risk of falls.

The analysis also did not consider the division into sex, and the impact of gender on the risk of falling was not assessed. Initially, falls are more common in women in early old age, while in late old age, these incidents have the same frequency in both women and men. On the other hand, men are more likely to die from a fall [45]. Perhaps these differences in falls and their consequences would also be observed in the group of patients operated on for selected malignancies.

The analysis also did not take into account the mental state of patients undergoing surgery; anxiety and depression may affect the speed of walking and, thus, the risk of falling.

Despite the indicated limitations, the results presented in the paper may contribute to improving the standards of physiotherapy for patients treated for malignant tumors, along with creating a strategy to minimize the risk of collapse for this population, which has been growing in recent years.

### 4.2. Future Research Directions

The above knowledge of gait speed disorders, depending on the extent of the procedure and the operating site, will help develop rehabilitation methods for patients, emphasizing improving balance and coordination.

Reducing the risk of falls will significantly increase patients' physical activity after surgical procedures due to malignant tumors, which is of particular importance in preventing the adverse effects of oncological treatment. Maintaining physical activity at an appropriate level will allow patients to adopt an active attitude in the fight against cancer and its consequences.

In the future, it is necessary for patients operated on due to malignant tumors to strive for independence. Reducing dependence on the help of others in everyday life will enable oncological patients to use the potential of oncological treatment more optimally. It will also have a positive impact on the prognosis.

Monitoring the level of physical activity and a systematic assessment of the risk of falling during the treatment of malignant tumors and during follow-up examinations after treatment should be a standard of therapeutic management as an element necessary to achieving success and improving the quality of life and functioning in the community of patients with a history of malignant tumor treatment.

## 5. Conclusions

In conclusion, surgical procedures for cancer have an impact on the walking speed of patients being treated for malignant tumors, and the affiliation with the study group determines the risk of falling. Further research is needed to accurately determine the risk of falls among cancer patients.

**Supplementary Materials:** The following supporting information can be downloaded at: https://www.mdpi.com/article/10.3390/healthcare11233069/s1, STROBE Statement.

**Author Contributions:** Conceptualization, A.L., M.W. and I.M.; methodology, A.L., M.W. and I.M.; formal analysis, A.L. and M.S.; investigation, A.L.; data curation, A.L. and I.M.; writing—original draft preparation, A.L., M.S., M.W. and I.M.; writing—review and editing, M.S., M.W. and I.M.; supervision, I.M.; project administration, I.M. All authors have read and agreed to the published version of the manuscript.

**Funding:** This research received no external funding.

**Institutional Review Board Statement:** The study was conducted in accordance with the Declaration of Helsinki and approved by the Local Bioethics Committee Wroclaw University of Health and Sport Sciences. Consent number: 28/2018. Approval date: 14 September 2018. The study was approved and registered in the Lower Silesian Center of Oncology, Pulmonology, and Hematology in Wroclaw, Poland. Consent number: NDBI-106/18, NDBI 4/18/BN.

**Informed Consent Statement:** Informed consent was obtained from all patients for their participation in the study.

**Data Availability Statement:** The data are available upon reasonable request from the corresponding author.

**Conflicts of Interest:** The authors declare no conflict of interest.

## References

1. Wasilewski, P. Comprehensive assessment of the health care system—The most important proposals for changes in the system. *State Control. Supreme Audit. Off.* **2019**, *64*, 38–51.
2. Didkowska, J.; Wojciechowska, U.; Olasek, P.; Caetanodos Santos, F.; Michałek, I. *Malignant neoplasms in Poland*; Krajowy Rejestr Nowotworów: Warsaw, Poland, 2021; pp. 7–13.
3. Pamoukdjian, F.; Lévy, V.; Sebbane, G.; Boubaya, M.; Landre, T.; Bloch-Queyrat, C.; Paillaud, E.; Zelek, L. Slow gait speed is an independent predictor of early death in older cancer outpatients: Results from a prospective cohort study. *J. Nutr. Heal. Aging* **2016**, *21*, 202–206. [CrossRef]
4. Huang, M.H.; Blackwood, J.; Godoshian, M.; Pfalzer, L. Factors associated with self-reported falls, balance or walking difficulty in older survivors of breast, colorectal, lung, or prostate cancer: Results from Surveillance, Epidemiology, and End Results–Medicare Health Outcomes Survey linkage. *PLoS ONE* **2018**, *13*, e0208573. [CrossRef]
5. Huang, M.H.; Lytle, T.; Miller, K.A.; Smith, K.; Fredrickson, K. History of falls, balance performance, and quality of life in older cancer survivors. *Gait Posture* **2014**, *40*, 451–456. [CrossRef]
6. Huang, M.H.; Shilling, T.; Miller, K.; Smith, K.; Fredrickson, K. History of falls, gait, balance, and fall risks in older cancer survivors living in the community. *Clin. Interv. Aging* **2015**, *10*, 1497–1503. [CrossRef]
7. Herman, K. Surgical treatment of cancer in Poland: Today and tomorrow. *Oncol. Clin. Pract.* **2011**, *7*, 311–320.
8. Civilotti, C.; Castelli, L.; Binaschi, L.; Cussino, M.; Tesio, V.; Di Fini, G.; Veglia, F.; Torta, R. Dissociative symptomatology in cancer patients. *Front. Psychol.* **2015**, *6*, 118. [CrossRef]
9. Unseld, M.; Krammer, K.; Lubowitzki, S.; Jachs, M.; Baumann, L.; Vyssoki, B.; Riedel, J.; Puhr, H.; Zehentgruber, S.; Prager, G.; et al. Screening for post-traumatic stress disorders in 1017 cancer patients and correlation with anxiety, depression, and distress. *Psychooncology* **2019**, *28*, 2382–2388. [CrossRef]
10. Zhang, Y.; Folarin, A.A.; Sun, S.; Cummins, N.; Vairavan, S.; Qian, L.; Ranjan, Y.; Rashid, Z.; Conde, P.; Stewart, C.; et al. Associations between depression symptom severity and daily-life gait characteristics derived from long-term acceleration signals in real-world settings: Retrospective analysis. *JMIR Mhealth Uhealth* **2022**, *10*, e40667. [CrossRef]
11. Latajka, A.; Woźniewski, M.; Malicka, M. Influence of surgical treatment of selected malignant tumors on gait kinematics—A pilot study. *Physiother Quart.* **2018**, *26*, 33–39. [CrossRef]
12. Zhao, J.; Wang, G.; Chen, L.; Yu, S.; Li, W. Risk factors for falls in hospitalized patients with cancer: A systematic review and meta-analysis. *Asia-Pac. J. Oncol. Nurs.* **2022**, *9*, 100107. [CrossRef]
13. Drużbicki, M.; Szymczyk, D.; Snela, S.; Dudek, J.; Chuchla, M. Objective, quantitative methods of gait analysis in clinical practice. *Med. Rev. Univ. Rzesz.* **2009**, *4*, 356–362.
14. Zak, M.; Biskup, M.; Macek, P.; Krol, H.; Krupnik, S.; Opuchlik, A. Identifying predictive motor factors for falls in post-menopausal breast cancer survivors. *PLoS ONE* **2017**, *12*, e0173970. [CrossRef]
15. Lowry, K.A.; VanSwearingen, J.M.; Perera, S.; Studenski, S.A.; Brach, J.S. Walking smoothness is associated with self-reported function after accounting for gait speed. *J. Gerontol. Ser. A* **2013**, *68*, 1286–1290. [CrossRef]
16. Quach, L.; Galica, A.M.; Jones, R.N.; Procter-Gray, E.; Manor, B.; Hannan, M.T.; Lipsitz, L.A. The Nonlinear Relationship Between Gait Speed and Falls: The Maintenance of Balance, Independent Living, Intellect, and Zest in the Elderly of Boston Study. *J. Am. Geriatr. Soc.* **2011**, *59*, 1069–1073. [CrossRef]

17. Van Kan, G.A.; Rolland, Y.; Andrieu, S.; Bauer, J.; Beauchet, O.; Bonnefoy, M.; Cesari, M.; Donini, L.; Gillette-Guyonnet, S.; Inzitari, M.; et al. Gait speed at usual pace as a predictor of adverse outcomes in community-dwelling older people an International Academy on Nutrition and Aging (IANA) Task Force. *J. Nutr. Health Aging* **2009**, *13*, 881–889. [CrossRef]
18. Studenski, S.; Perera, S.; Wallace, D.; Chandler, J.M.; Duncan, P.W.; Rooney, E.; Fox, M.; Guralnik, J.M.; Rooney, M.E.; ScD, M.F. Physical Performance Measures in the Clinical Setting. *J. Am. Geriatr. Soc.* **2003**, *51*, 314–322. [CrossRef]
19. De Ridder, R.; Lebleu, J.; Willems, T.; De Blaiser, C.; Detrembleur, C.; Roosen, P. Concurrent Validity of a Commercial Wireless Trunk Triaxial Accelerometer System for Gait Analysis. *J. Sport Rehabil.* **2019**, *28*, 2018-0295. [CrossRef]
20. Lenhard, W.; Lenhard, A. *Calculation of Effect Sizes*; Psychometrica: Dettelbach, Germany, 2016; Available online: https://www.psychometrica.de/effect_size.html (accessed on 26 October 2023).
21. Cohen, J. *Statistical Power Analysis for the Behavioral Sciences*, 2nd ed.; Lawrence Earlbaum Associate: Hillsdale, NJ, USA, 1988.
22. Kearney, M.; Cramer's, V. *The SAGE Encyclopedia of Communication ResearchMethods*; SAGE Publications: New York, NY, USA, 2017.
23. Mata, L.R.F.D.; Azevedo, C.; Policarpo, A.G.; Moraes, J.T. Factors associated with the risk of fall in adults in the postoperative period: A cross-sectional study. *Rev. Lat.-Am. De Enferm.* **2017**, *25*, e2904. [CrossRef]
24. Meneses-Echávez, J.F.; Loaiza-Betancur, A.F.; Díaz-Lopez, V.; Echavarria-Rodriguez, A.M. Prehabilitation programs for cancer patients: A systematic review of randomized controlled trials (protocol). *System. Rev.* **2020**, *9*, 34. [CrossRef]
25. Manikowska, F.; Hojan, K.; Chen, P.-J.; Jóźwiak, M.; Jóźwiak, A. The gait pattern in post-menopausal women. Pilot study. *Ortop. Traumatol. Rehabil.* **2013**, *15*, 575–583. [CrossRef]
26. Liu, M.A.; DuMontier, C.; Murillo, A.; Hshieh, T.T.; Bean, J.F.; Soiffer, R.J.; Stone, R.M.; Abel, G.A.; Driver, J.A. Gait speed, grip strength, and clinical outcomes in older patients with hematologic malignancies. *Blood J. Am. Soc. Hematol.* **2019**, *134*, 374–382. [CrossRef]
27. Nonaka, H.; Mita, K.; Watakabe, M.; Akataki, K.; Suzuki, N.; Okuwa, T.; Yabe, K. Age-related changes in the interactive mobility of the hip and knee joints: A geometrical analysis. *Gait Posture* **2002**, *15*, 236–243. [CrossRef]
28. Lamoth, C.J.C.; Meijer, O.G.; Daffertshofer, A.; Wuisman, P.I.J.M.; Beek, P.J. Effects of chronic low back pain on trunk coordination and back muscle activity during walking: Changes in motor control. *Eur. Spine J.* **2005**, *15*, 23–40. [CrossRef]
29. Dodson, J.A.; Arnold, S.V.; Gosch, K.L.; Gill, T.M.; Spertus, J.A.; Krumholz, H.M.; Rich, M.W.; Chaudhry, S.I.; Forman, D.E.; Masoudi, F.A.; et al. Slow Gait Speed and Risk of Mortality or Hospital Readmission After Myocardial Infarction in the Translational Research Investigating Underlying Disparities in Recovery from Acute Myocardial Infarction: Patients' Health Status Registry. *J. Am. Geriatr. Soc.* **2016**, *64*, 596–601. [CrossRef] [PubMed]
30. Wnuk, D.; Hansdorfer-Korzon, R.; Żuralska-Wnuk, J.; Chwirot, P.; Barna, M. Physiotherapy in patients after lung parenchyma resection. *Adv. Respir. Med.* **2014**, *82*, 46–54. [CrossRef] [PubMed]
31. Blackwood, J.; Rybicki, K. Assessment of Gait Speed and Timed Up and Go Measures as Predictors of Falls in Older Breast Cancer Survivors. *Integr. Cancer Ther.* **2021**, *20*, 15347354211006462. [CrossRef] [PubMed]
32. Tough, D.; Dunning, J.; Robinson, J.; Dixon, J.; Ferguson, J.; Paul, I.; Harrison, S.L. Investigating balance, gait, and physical function in people who have undergone thoracic surgery for a diagnosis of lung cancer: A mixed-methods study. *Chronic Respir. Dis.* **2021**, *18*, 14799731211052299. [CrossRef]
33. Perera, S.; Patel, K.V.; Rosano, C.; Rubin, S.M.; Satterfield, S.; Harris, T.; Ensrud, K.; Orwoll, E.; Lee, C.G.; Chandler, J.M.; et al. Gait Speed Predicts Incident Disability: A Pooled Analysis. *J. Gerontol. A Biol. Sci. Med. Sci.* **2016**, *71*, 63–71. [CrossRef] [PubMed]
34. Middleton, A.; Fritz, S.L.; Lusardi, M. Walking Speed: The Functional Vital Sign. *J. Aging Phys. Ac.t* **2015**, *23*, 314–322. [CrossRef]
35. Bluethmann, S.M.; Flores, E.; Campbell, G.; Klepin, H.D. Mobility Device Use and Mobility Disability in U.S. Medicare Beneficiaries with and Without Cancer History. *J. Am. Geriatr. Soc.* **2020**, *68*, 2872–2880. [CrossRef]
36. Szkutnik-Fiedler, D.; Szałek, E.; Grześkowiak, E. Management of Postoperative Pain. *Farm. Współczesna* **2010**, *3*, 21–29.
37. Li, W.; Keegan, T.H.; Sternfeld, B.; Sidney, S.; Quesenberry, C.P., Jr.; Kelsey, J.L. Outdoor falls among middle-aged and older adults: A neglected public health problem. *Am. J. Public Health* **2006**, *96*, 1192–1200. [CrossRef]
38. Bartoszek, A.; Kocka, K.; Bartoszek, A.; Ślusarska, B.; Dudek, I.; Jamrozik, K. Assessment of the risk, circumstances and consequences of falls and their conditioning among residents of a nursing home. *J. Educ. Health Sport* **2016**, *6*, 257–266.
39. Brown, J.C.; Harhay, M.O.; Harhay, M.N. Walking cadence and mortality among community-dwelling older adults. *J. Gen. Intern Med.* **2014**, *29*, 1263–1269. [CrossRef] [PubMed]
40. Hertzberg, D.; Luksha, Y.; Kus, I.; Eslampia, P.; Pickering, J.W.; Holzmann, M.J. Gait Speed at Discharge and Risk for Readmission or Death: A Prospective Study of an Emergency Ward Population. *Open Access Emerg. Med.* **2020**, *5*, 127–135. [CrossRef] [PubMed]
41. Hsieh, K.L.; Wood, T.A.; An, R.; Trinh, L.; Sosnoff, J.J. Gait and Balance Impairments in Breast Cancer Survivors: A Systematic Review and Meta-analysis of Observational Studies. *Arch. Rehabil. Res. Clin. Transl.* **2019**, *1*, 100001. [CrossRef] [PubMed]
42. Williams, G.R.; Deal, A.M.; Nyrop, K.A.; Pergolotti, M.; Guerard, E.J.; Jolly, T.A.; Muss, H.B. Geriatric assessment as an aide to understanding falls in older adults with cancer. *Support. Care Cancer* **2015**, *23*, 2273–2280. [CrossRef]
43. Ezzatvar, Y.; Ramírez-Vélez, R.; de Asteasu, M.L.S.; Martínez-Velilla, N.; Zambom-Ferraresi, F.; Izquierdo, M.; García-Hermoso, A. Physical Function and All-Cause Mortality in Older Adults Diagnosed with Cancer: A Systematic Review and Meta-Analysis. *J. Gerontol. Ser. A* **2021**, *76*, 1447–1453. [CrossRef] [PubMed]

44. Fino, P.C.; Horak, F.B.; El-Gohary, M.; Guidarelli, C.; Medysky, M.E.; Nagle, S.J. Winters-Stone KM. Postural sway, falls, and self-reported neuropathy in aging female cancer survivors. *Gait Posture* **2019**, *69*, 136–142. [CrossRef] [PubMed]
45. Campbell, G.P.; Wolfe, R.A.M.; Klem, M.L.P. Risk Factors for Falls in Adult Cancer Survivors: An Integrative Review. *Rehabil. Nurs.* **2018**, *43*, 201–213. [CrossRef] [PubMed]

healthcare

MDPI

*Article*

# Arabic Translation and Psychometric Validation of PROMIS General Life Satisfaction Short Form in the General Population

**Hadeel R. Bakhsh, Nouf S. Aldajani, Bodor Bin Sheeha, Monira I. Aldhahi, Atheer A. Alsomali, Ghada K. Alhamrani, Rahaf Z. Alamri and Rehab Alhasani ***

Department of Rehabilitation Sciences, College of Health and Rehabilitation Sciences, Princess Nourah Bint Abdulrahman University (PNU), Riyadh 11671, Saudi Arabia; hrbakhsh@pnu.edu.sa (H.R.B.); bhbinsheeha@pnu.edu.sa (B.B.S.); mialdhahi@pnu.edu.sa (M.I.A.); 438001636@pnu.edu.sa (R.Z.A.)

* Correspondence: rsalhasani@pnu.edu.sa

**Abstract:** This study aimed to translate the Patient-Reported Outcomes Measurement Information System (PROMIS) General Life Satisfaction Short Form (GLS SF5a) into the Arabic language and psychometrically validate the scale in the general population of Saudi Arabia. The translation processes followed the international recommendations of the FACIT Measurement System. The study was a multicentre cross-sectional study conducted in Riyadh, Saudi Arabia. A total of 657 individuals who were above 18 years of age and able to write and comprehend Arabic completed the GLS SF5a. Rasch analysis was used to evaluate item fit, reliability indices, item difficulty, principal component analysis and local item dependency. WINSTEPS (v. 5.6.0) was used for the analysis. The translation process and cognitive defibring were completed with no issues. The rating scale categories had a disordered threshold. All items, except one, demonstrated a satisfactory fit to the Rasch model. The reliability of the person separation was 0.86. The scale was unidimensional, and no items showed local dependency. Overall, this study confirms the psychometric properties of the Arabic version of the PROMIS GLS SF5a, which can be used as an instrument for measuring general life satisfaction in the general population. Further research is required to explore responsiveness, interpretability and feasibility in the clinical setting.

**Keywords:** PROMIS; Arabic; Rasch analysis; outcome measure; psychometrics; quality of life

**Citation:** Bakhsh, H.R.; Aldajani, N.S.; Sheeha, B.B.; Aldhahi, M.I.; Alsomali, A.A.; Alhamrani, G.K.; Alamri, R.Z.; Alhasani, R. Arabic Translation and Psychometric Validation of PROMIS General Life Satisfaction Short Form in the General Population. *Healthcare* **2023**, *11*, 3034. https://doi.org/10.3390/healthcare11233034

Academic Editors: Marco Tramontano and Giovanni Galeoto

Received: 30 October 2023
Revised: 19 November 2023
Accepted: 22 November 2023
Published: 24 November 2023



## 1. Introduction

Life satisfaction is an important element of health that affects different domains of an individual's life [1]. The American Psychological Association defines life satisfaction as the extent to which a person finds life rich, meaningful, full or of high quality [2]. It is a critical component for measuring quality of life (QOL) and an indicator of subjective well-being, which is a key aspect of mental health [3]. A substantial body of evidence has consistently underscored the strong correlation between the evaluation of life satisfaction and a multitude of pivotal factors. These include health status, manifestation of symptoms associated with depression and anxiety, perception of pain, quality of sleep, economic prosperity, and levels of physical activity [1,4–6]. Therefore, assessing and screening life satisfaction aligns with national health policy recommendations, underlining their essential role in comprehensive healthcare evaluations [7].

Patient-reported outcome measures (PROMs) are self-administered questionnaires that assess outcomes and screen for health conditions. The integration of PROMS within the medical sphere yields substantial enhancements in clinician–patient communication and fosters a collaborative environment conducive to shared decision making for treatment processes [8,9]. Consequently, the Patient-Reported Outcome Measurement Information System (PROMIS) was developed to provide valid, reliable and precise PROMs that would outperform traditional instruments and enable improved outcome measures in clinical practice [8,10]. The Patient-Reported Outcome Measurement Information System (PROMIS) has the potential to assess a range of functional abilities in a wide range of patient ages and numerous languages and can be administered in a variety of ways [10]. Furthermore, it facilitates cross-study data comparisons by adapting the item bank for use in multiple countries.

Within the mental health domain, the PROMIS framework offers a set of adult measures designed to evaluate life satisfaction. Specifically, the General Life Satisfaction (GLS) Short Form 5a (SF5a) was used as an assessment tool. Few studies have focused on assessing the construct validity of PROMIS GLS in different populations. Vaughan et al.'s [11] study was the only one that evaluated the psychometric properties of the PROMIS GLS, specifically assessing structural and construct validity among individuals with musculoskeletal pain in Australia. Their study concluded that the GLS SF5 was unidimensional, with acceptable internal consistency and construct validity in this population [11].

Over the last two decades, the use of PROMs in Arab clinical society has progressed, either by developing new PROMs or by translating and adapting existing measures to specific cultural contexts [12–15]. Consequently, numerous studies conducted among different healthcare practitioners in Saudi Arabia indicate that the implementation of PROMs helps with directing the plan of care, improving patient–clinician communication and providing a patient-centred approach [12–14]. All of these facilitate the process of shared decision making, which is considered a key element of patient-centred care [15,16]. In fact, multiple studies have reported improved QOL, better patient and clinician satisfaction and better treatment outcomes through shared decision making [15,17,18].

To the best of our knowledge, no prior studies have translated or assessed the validity and psychometric properties of the PROMIS GLS SF5a in the Arabic language using Rasch analysis. The advantages of the PROMIS tools, and specifically the PROMIS GLS SF5, lie in their efficiency, precision, standardisation and adaptability [19]. Moreover, the adaptive nature of PROMIS assessments helps reduce respondent burden by tailoring the questions to the individual's level of the measured construct, thereby reducing the number of questions required for assessment [19].

Therefore, this study aimed to provide an Arabic translation and cultural adaptation of the PROMIS GLS SF5a and evaluate its psychometric properties in general populations in Saudi Arabia.

## 2. Materials and Methods

### *2.1. Translation and Cultural-Adaptation Process*

#### 2.1.1. Study Team

The Arabic translation team consisted of linguists, translators, proofreaders and cognitive interviewers contracted with FACITtrans (Table 1). The primary focus was to translate items from the FACIT measurement system. All team members were native Arabic speakers, except for the back translator, who was a native English speaker fluent in Arabic. All members of the FACITtrans Arabic translation team met ISO 17100 standards [20] for professional competencies and translation qualifications.

#### 2.1.2. Translation Process

The FACIT translation process included the following stages.

First stage: Forward translations were carried out by two separate professional translators, who were native Arabic speakers and independently translated the source items in English into Arabic. To ensure accuracy and clarity, a third independent translator, who was also a native speaker in Arabic, reviewed and reconciled the two forward translations.

Second stage: Following the reconciliation process, a native English-speaking translator back-translated the provided content. The translator did not have access to the original English sources or item definitions. The purpose of back-translation was to accurately reflect the content of the target language translation without adding or deleting elements. Next, the translation project manager (TPM) performed a thorough comparison between the original and back-translated English versions to identify any discrepancies.

**Table 1.** The FACITtrans Arabic translation team.

| Role | Qualification | Title & Profession |
| --- | --- | --- |
| Translation Account Manager FACITtrans | MBA | Director, PROMIS Lead |
| Translation Project Coordinator FACITtrans | BA | Senior COA Translations Manager—Life Sciences, PROMIS Specialist |
| Translation Project Manager FACITtrans | BA, Spanish Linguistics | Senior COA Translation Project Manager—Life Sciences |
| Forward 1 | BA, Languages and Translation, Simultaneous Interpretation (English < >Arabic) | Senior Translator, Copywriter & Proofreader Professional and Translator Interpreter |
| Forward 2 | MA, Linguistics | Professional Translator and Interpreter |
| Reconciler/Proofreader | Ph.D., Linguistics | Professional Linguist and Translator |
| Back Translator | MA, Diplomacy<br>BA, Medical Technology | Professional Translator<br>16 years full immersion in Arabic public school system and 3.5 years of undergraduate education (nursing) at King Abdul Aziz University, Jeddah Saudi Arabia |
| Reviewer 1 | Ph.D., Linguistics | Linguist and researcher<br>Pragmatics, sociolinguistics, discourse analysis, ideology, identity, and translation studies |
| Reviewer 2 | Ph.D., Linguistics | Professional Linguist and Translator |
| Reviewer 3, Language Coordinator, Proofreader 1 | DDS<br>MA, Biblical Studies | Professional Translator and Interpreter<br>Close to 30 years' experience specializing in medical, legal and religious translation |

Third Stage: Three bilingual translation experts conducted a thorough review of the translation history, carefully selected the most suitable translation for each item and, where needed, offered alternative translations. Prior to finalisation, the translation team at FACITtrans diligently reviewed the reviewers' comments and meticulously analysed their suggested translations for any potential concerns. They subsequently formulated precise questions and comments to aid the Arabic language coordinator in addressing these issues. In addition to providing the final translation, the language coordinator also included a literal back-translation and an improved back-translation.

Fourth and final stage: The comparability of the translated version was assessed by the FACITtrans team in collaboration with the PROMIS Statistical Centre. The quality assurance process included consistency checks with previous translations and between items. If any additional input was needed, the Arabic coordinator was contacted for consultation, and two independent proofreaders meticulously examined all items to identify any spelling and grammatical issues. Subsequently, a reconciliation process was conducted to address and resolve any discrepancies found in the proofreading comments.

#### 2.1.3. Cognitive Debriefing and Pre-Testing

A pilot test was conducted using a convenience sample of 30 native Arabic speakers from the general population to gain an understanding of how individuals comprehend and explain the items. Participants were eligible to participate in the study if they were 18 years or older, native Arabic speakers and were able to provide verbal consent. The questionnaire items were reviewed and tested on at least six individuals from Saudi Arabia, Morocco, Kuwait, Jordan and Egypt. The authors of this study from Princess Nourah University (PNU) in Saudi Arabia conducted the interviews. The authors have extensive knowledge and experience in conducting cognitive interviews and psychometric evaluations of outcome measures. Furthermore, they received training on the study-specific interviewing protocol through teleconferences facilitated by FACITtrans.

Before each administration, the interviewers provided a comprehensive explanation of the study's purpose and details to the participants. The respondents completed the questionnaire independently. Subsequently, a cognitive debriefing interview was conducted following a specific script. Emphasis was placed on scrutinising the wording of each translated item. Participants were asked to restate the items in their own words, define specific terms and phrases and describe their decision making process when selecting their responses. This process allowed for FACITtrans to assess the linguistic validity and acceptability of the Arabic items.

After the interviews were completed, the interviewers took on the task of transcribing them. They carefully compiled all the opinions and suggestions expressed by the interviewees into a comprehensive, cognitive debriefing report. To assess the interviewees' comprehension of each item, the TPM meticulously examined their feedback and identified key issues. In instances where revision suggestions were provided, the TPM, in collaboration with the language coordinator, offered final recommendations for modifications or proposed suitable translation solutions. Finally, the TPM submitted the cognitive debriefing report to the PROMIS Statistical Centre for a quality review.

### 2.2. Study Design and Participants

This was a multicentre cross-sectional study. A convenience sample of participants was recruited between March and May 2023 at the Princess Nourah Bint Abdulrahman University, King Fahad Medical City and King Abdullah bin Abdulaziz University Hospital in Riyadh, Saudi Arabia. The targeted sample size was 729 participants, based on the calculation using C$\alpha$ with a power calculation of 80% and accounting for a 10% drop-out rate [21].

The inclusion criteria were as follows: ability to read and comprehend the Arabic language, healthy 18 years or older, a history of a chronic condition. In this study, the presence of a chronic condition was self-identified by respondents based on the options provided in the first section of the questionnaire. Chronic condition options included metabolic diseases, cardiac diseases, pulmonary diseases, psychological diseases, musculoskeletal diseases, neurological diseases and cancer. The exclusion criteria comprised the presence of cognitive impairments that would interfere with completing the questionnaire and the inability to comprehend the Arabic language.

A total of 729 participants were invited to participate in this study, of whom 29 (4%) declined to participate and 43 (6%) did not meet the inclusion criteria. For the final analysis, 657 participants (90%) were enrolled. A study recruitment flowchart is shown in Figure 1.

### 2.3. Procedure

Participants were approached by the study team, either in the community at college lobbies and libraries (PNU) or patients waiting in the rehabilitation department at the hospitals mentioned above. Once the participants gave consent for participation, a computerised questionnaire was administered using Microsoft Forms during the data collection process in the hospitals, while a paper-and-pencil format was administered across the hospitals.

The authors obtained the required licences and authorisation from the PROMIS Health Organization (PHO) in April 2022 to translate the PROMIS GLS item bank into Arabic. The study was approved by the Institutional Review Board of PNU (KACST, KSA: HAP-01-R-059), KAAUH (RO-2023-P-019) and KFMC (H-01-R-012). This study was conducted in accordance with the Declaration of Helsinki.

### 2.4. Measures

Participants completed a survey that consisted of two parts. The first part asked participants to provide sociodemographic information including age, sex, height, weight, educational level, employment status, marital status and place of residence. The second part consisted of the PROMIS GLS SF5a [21]. The estimated completion time ranged from 5 to 7 min.

The PROMIS GLS SF5 was used to assess life satisfaction, with five items rated on a 7-point Likert scale (1 = strongly disagree, 7 = strongly agree). The stem of the question was 'Indicate how much you agree or disagree'. The lowest raw score was 5, and the highest was 35. The PROMIS uses a *t*-score metric to calculate and interpret responses, which is a standardised measure of the total score for a particular measure with a mean of 50 and a standard deviation (SD) of 10 for a reference population, in which case the US general population is our reference population [22].

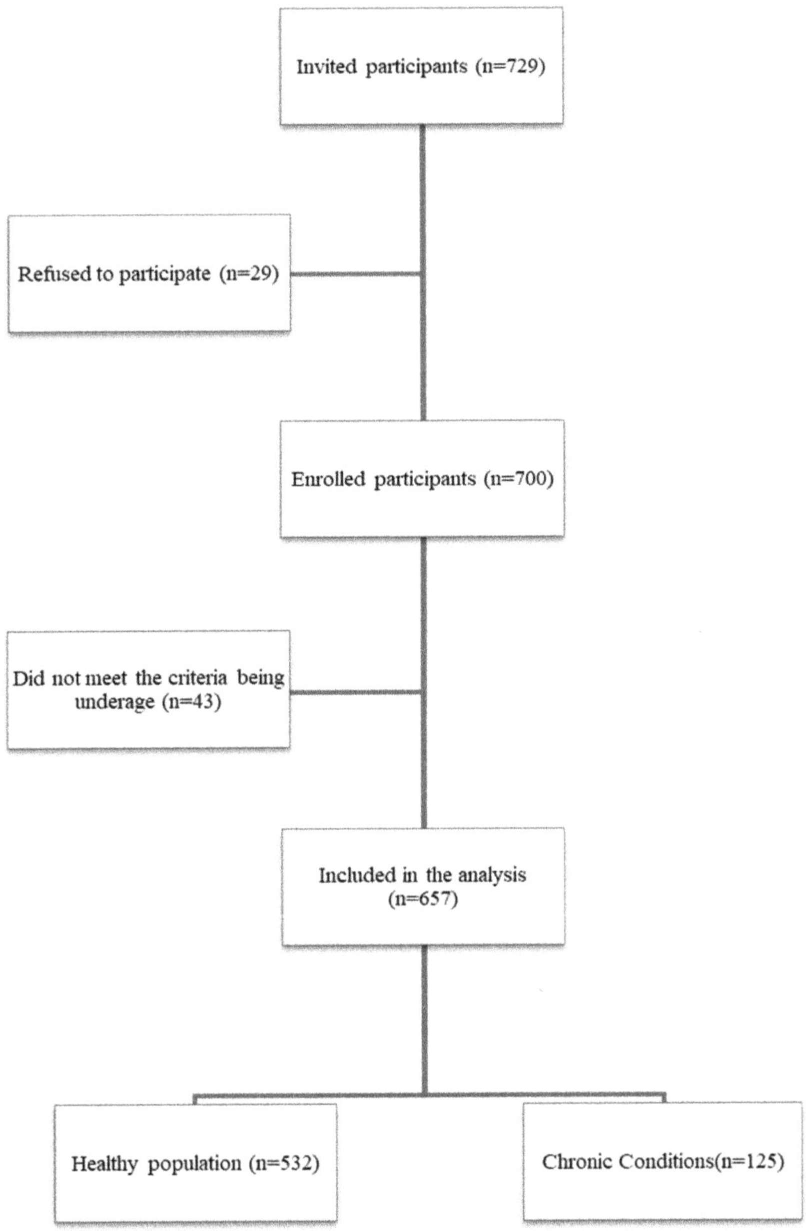


**Figure 1.** Participants recruitment Process.

### 2.5. Data Analysis

Descriptive statistics, including frequency, percentage, mean and standard deviation (SD), were used to identify demographics. Rasch analysis (RA) is a statistical modelling technique that is used primarily to evaluate the relationships between individuals' abilities and the difficulty of items on a scale [23]. It assesses the probability of a person endorsing or succeeding at an item based on their underlying trait or ability and the item's inherent difficulty. This method transforms categorical data into interval-level measurements, facilitating more precise comparisons between individuals and items while ensuring measurement reliability and validity. Its application aids in the development of reliable and valid assessment tools and enhances the understanding of latent traits or abilities within a population [23,24]. The following multistage approach for Rasch analysis was applied to assess the PROMIS GLS SF5a metrics using Winsteps® software (v. 5.6.1) [25] using a rating scale model.

Rating scale category functioning was evaluated using the criteria proposed by Linacre (1999) and Wolfe and Smith (2007) to verify the ordered response thresholds for each question (the threshold being the transition point between adjacent categories) [25–27].

Principal component analysis of the standardised residuals (PCAr) was used to evaluate the following: if other variables are likely to be included in the residuals, the Rasch factor should explain $\geq$ 50% of the variance. If the eigenvalue of the first residual component (first contrast) is greater than 2, additional factors are likely to be present. The presence of local dependency 'correlation' of two items with a correlation greater than 0.30 is regarded as a possible indicator of local dependency.

The internal construct validity of the PROMIS GLS Arabic version was evaluated by assessing how closely the data matched the Rasch model in terms of suitability. For each item on each scale, chi-square fit statistics (expressed as infit and outfit mean-square statistics, MnSq; expectation 1, range 0 to infinity) were calculated. Acceptable fit was defined based on our sample size as mean square values ranging from 0.7 to 1.3, characterised by a standardised $z$-value (ZStd) of less than $\pm$2.0 [26]. To consider an item a misfit, both the MnSq and ZStd values must be outside their specified ranges.

The estimates of item difficulty and subject ability were calculated in logit units, where logit represents the natural logarithm of the odds ratio between mutually exclusive options, such as pass versus fail or higher versus lower responses. Item difficulty refers to the level of difficulty associated with each item, whereas subject ability indicates the location of each individual subject on a common interval scale.

Reliability was evaluated based on both the item and person separation indices, which ranged from 0 to $\infty$. The item separation index (G) provides an estimate of the standard error units of the spread or separation of items. The reliability of the separation indices represents the degree of confidence in the consistency of the estimates and falls within the range of 0 to 1. Coefficients exceeding 0.80 are considered good, while those surpassing 0.90 are regarded as excellent [23].

## 3. Results

### 3.1. Translation and Cultural Adaptation

Thirty adults participated in the cognitive interviews. The participants had an average age of 35.2 years (SD $\pm$ 10.5 years). Among the total participants, 50% ($n$ = 15) were male. Regarding their educational background, 37% ($n$ = 11) had completed high school, 23% ($n$ = 7) possessed a diploma certificate and 40% ($n$ = 12) had an undergraduate degree. The participants hailed from five different Arab countries, with an equal distribution of 20% ($n$ = 5) from Saudi Arabia, Jordan, Egypt, Morocco and Kuwait. All were native Arabic speakers.

The cognitive debriefing report revealed highly positive feedback concerning the clarity and comprehensibility of the item instructions and response options of the PROMIS GLS. All items were culturally suitable, and the same underlying concept as in the original English was measured. All PROMIS GLS item banks were deemed unequivocally clear, with participants accurately restating the items with precise wording when prompted to do so during the interviews.

### 3.2. Descriptive Statistics

The demographic data of the participants are shown in Table 2. A total of 657 participants had a mean age of 28.44 ± 11.36 years, predominantly female (81.28%). More than half were students ($n$ = 287; 43.68%), and the majority were single (70.32%). A total of 125 participants reported having at least one chronic medical condition, with the majority reporting metabolic syndromes (53.60%). The PROMIS GLS SF5a Arabic version had a mean $t$-score of 48.52 ± 10.53 in the general population.

**Table 2.** Characteristics of the sample ($n$ = 657).

| Variables | Total ($n$ = 657) |
|---|---|
| Age in years (Mean ± SD) | 28.44 ± 11.36 |
| BMI (Mean ± SD) | 24.75 ± 5.76 |
| **Sex $n$ (%)** | |
| Female | 534 (81.28%) |
| Male | 123 (18.72%) |
| **Educational level $n$ (%)** | |
| Elementary | 6 (0.91%) |
| Middle School | 3 (0.46%) |
| High School | 90 (13.70%) |
| Diploma | 12 (1.83%) |
| Bachelors | 485 (73.82%) |
| Graduate studies | 61 (9.28%) |
| **Employment status $n$ (%)** | |
| Student | 287 (43.68%) |
| Governmental | 196 (29.83%) |
| Private sector | 21 (3.20%) |
| Military | 3 (0.46%) |
| Retired | 12 (1.83%) |
| Unemployed | 138 (21%) |
| **Marital status $n$ (%)** | |
| Married | 176 (26.79%) |
| Single | 462 (70.32%) |
| Divorced | 16 (2.44%) |
| Widowed | 3 (0.46%) |
| **Presence of chronic condition, $n$ (%)** | |
| Yes | 125 (19.03%) |
| No | 532 (80.97%) |

### 3.3. Rasch Analysis

*Rating scale diagnostics:* The rating scale of the PROMIS GLS SF5a Arabic version did not meet the criteria for category functioning because of disordered thresholds (Table 3 and Figure 2).

**Table 3.** Category functioning for Arabic PROMIS General Life Satisfaction SF5a.

| Category Label | Category Measure | Andrich Threshold | Infit MnSq | Outfit MnSq | Observed Count |
|---|---|---|---|---|---|
| 1. Strongly disagree | −3.34 | None | 1.46 | 1.30 | 332 (10%) |
| 2. Disagree | −1.76 | −2.00 | 0.88 | 1.03 | 364 (11%) |
| 3. Slightly disagree | −0.78 | −1.17 | 0.85 | 0.89 | 472 (14%) |
| 4. Neither agree nor disagree | −0.10 | 0.16 | 0.94 | 0.90 | 313 (10%) |
| 5. Slightly agree | 0.61 | −0.39 | 0.90 | 0.86 | 653 (20%) |
| 6 Agree | 1.82 | 0.93 | 0.93 | 0.93 | 697 (21%) |
| 7. Strongly agree | 3.71 | 2.47 | 1.08 | 1.02 | 454 (14%) |

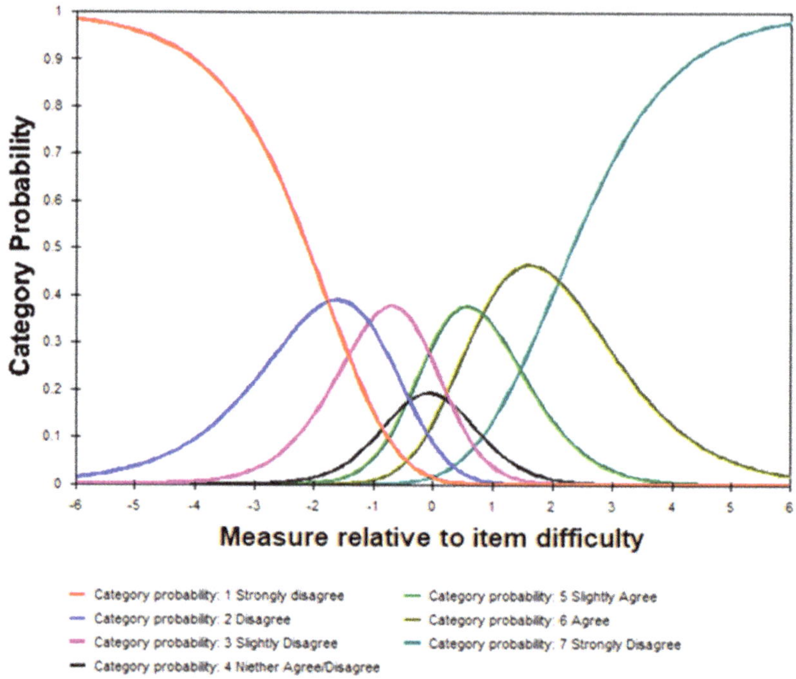


**Figure 2.** ROMIS General Life Satisfaction SF5a Rating Scale Categories functioning.

*Principal component analysis (PCA):* Scale unidimensionality was confirmed by the PCA of standardised residuals, and the variance explained by the Rasch measures was acceptable (72%), whereas that explained by the first contrast in the residuals was low or moderate, with an eigenvalue of 1.4 (8.2%). There was no local dependency on these items ($r > 0.30$).

*Item fit statistics*: Four of the five items fit the Rasch model (see Table 4). Item PA046 ('If I could live my life over, I would change almost nothing') somewhat underfitted the module (Outfit MnSq = 1.33), since it had a few unpredictable answers.

**Table 4.** Item Fit Statistics for PROMIS General Life Satisfaction SF5a.

| Item | Measure (SE) | Infit | | Outfit | |
|---|---|---|---|---|---|
| | | MnSq | Zstd | MnSq | Zstd |
| **If I could live my life over, I would change almost nothing.** | **0.89 (0.04)** | **1.30** | **4.74** | **1.33** | **4.82** |
| So far, I have gotten the important things I want in life. | 0.05 (0.04) | 1.03 | 0.51 | 1.04 | 0.65 |
| In most ways, my life is close to perfect. | 0.18 (0.04) | 0.86 | −2.63 | 0.87 | −2.21 |
| My life situation is excellent. | −0.46 (0.04) | 0.87 | −2.30 | 0.86 | −2.41 |
| My life is just right. | −0.67 (0.04) | 0.84 | −2.02 | 0.78 | −3.88 |

Item fit statistics shows the 4 items that fitted the scale with the underfit item measurement in bold.

*Item difficulty and subject ability*: The range of item difficulty estimates, as demonstrated in Wright's map (Figure 3), was 0.89 logits. Apart from the five maximum scores, the person's ability ranged very evenly from 4.08 to −3.70 logits, with an average of 0.29 logits.

```
MEASURE    Person - MAP - Item
     More Satisfied >|More Difficult to Endorse
   5                +
           .####    |
                    |
                    |
                    |
                    |
             .##    |
   4               T+<--------------------
                    |
                    |
                    |
                    |
            .###    |
                    |
   3                +
                    |
            .###    |
                    |
                    |
          ######    |
                   S|
   2                +
      ##########    |
                    |
      .#########    |
                    |
         #######    |
         .######    |T
   1                +
       .########    |  If I could live my life over, I would change almost nothing.
         .######    |
      .#########    |S
                    |
         ####### M|
       #########    |  In most ways, my life is close to perfect
   0     #######    +M So far, I have gotten the important things I want in life
          .#####    |
       .########    |
           .####    |  My life situation is excellent
             .##    |S
            .###    |  My life is just right
            .###    |
  -1        ####    +
            ####    |T
                    |
          .#### S|
           .####    |
                    |
          .#####    |
  -2                +
             .##    |
                    |
            .###    |
                    |
                    |
                    |
  -3          .#    +
                    |
                   T|
                    |<--------------------
                    |
             .##    |
                    |
  -4         ###    +
    <Less Satisfied>|<Easier to Endorse>
 EACH "#" IS 4: EACH "." IS 1 TO 3
```

**Figure 3.** Wright's Map of participant ability (Satisfaction) and item difficulty Arabic PROMIS General Life Satisfaction SF5a.

*Reliability*: The person separation index and reliability were 2.45 and 0.86, respectively, whereas the item separation index and reliability were 12.97 and 0.99, respectively. The internal consistency of the PROMIS GLS SF5a Arabic version was excellent (Cronbach's $\alpha = 0.90$).

The vertical line signifies the measure of the variable in linear logit units. The left-hand column locates the participant's ability along the variable. Each "#" indicates 4 participants, whereas "." indicates 1–3 participants. The right-hand column locates the items' difficulty measures along the variable. From the bottom, measures indicate "less satisfaction" for participants and "lower difficulty to be endorsed" for items, whereas "higher satisfaction" and "higher difficulty to be endorsed" are located at the top. The mean difficulty of items in the test is set at 0 logits (and indicated with M). Hence, a candidate with mean ability is indicated by M′. The two arrows represent the threshold boundaries for item difficulty.

## 4. Discussion

This study aimed to assess the psychometric properties of the Arabic version of the PROMIS GLS SF5a in general adult populations in Saudi Arabia. The findings showed that the scale exhibited a unidimensional structure with no item dependence; moreover, with the exception of one item, all items demonstrated a favourable fit to the Rasch model. Consequently, the item separation reliability and internal consistency were excellent, and the person separation reliability was deemed good. Internal consistency was rated as excellent.

However, the rating scales did not meet the criteria for category functioning because of item disorder. In the Rasch analysis, 'disordered thresholds' refer to a situation where the response categories (or thresholds) for an item in a measurement instrument do not function as expected [23]. These thresholds represent the points on the measurement scale where respondents change from one response category to the next, indicating increasing levels of the measured trait or ability. When thresholds are disordered, the responses do not follow the expected pattern of increasing difficulty or severity. For instance, respondents may not consistently choose higher response categories (indicating higher levels of trait or ability) as the item becomes more difficult. Instead, they might occasionally choose a lower response category despite having a higher level of the measured trait or vice versa. This can lead to a lack of discrimination between respondents at different ability levels, thereby reducing the reliability and validity of the measurement instrument [23].

The observed disorder in the rating scale categories can be attributed to a combination of factors. One contributing factor may be the presence of too many response options, specifically seven categories. When participants are presented with such a wide range of choices, it can lead to confusion and difficulty in accurately selecting the most appropriate response, resulting in item disordering [28]. Furthermore, the inclusion of response option 4, *neither agree nor disagree*, within the seven-category scale may be indicative of a fundamental problem. This response option suggests that the scale with seven categories might not be the most suitable choice for accurately capturing respondents' perceptions or attitudes. The presence of this midpoint option implies that respondents may often find themselves in a state of ambivalence or uncertainty, which can hinder the precision of the data collected [28]. Therefore, it is crucial to reconsider the quantity of response categories in the rating scale. A more suitable approach might be to simplify the scale to a fewer number of categories, which can enhance respondents' ease of use and improve the overall quality of the data collected.

The unidimensionalityof the GLS SF5a was confirmed via principal component analysis (PCA), which revealed the absence of a second dimension. In addition, the analysis affirmed the local independence of the items. Furthermore, the reliability indices indicated robust performance, with a high person separation index (2.45), substantial person reliability (0.86) and Cronbach's α coefficient of 0.90. Notably, our results (Cα = 0.90) closely aligned with those reported by Vaughan et al. [11], consistent with the reliability of the GLS SF5a English version (Cα = 0.91), underscoring the scale's enhanced precision. In the context of fit statistics analysis, it is noteworthy that item PA046, 'If I could live my life over, I would change almost nothing' slightly underfit the scale. This observation signifies a heightened variability in responses for this particular item. The misfitting values were primarily associated with four healthy participants—despite a substantial agreement about all the other items— who expressed disagreement about their overall satisfaction with how they live their lives.

The item difficulty revealed that the questionnaire's targeting was acceptable, with a person's mean ability of 0.29 logits. Item PA046 "If I could live my life over, I would change almost nothing" was the hardest to endorse, indicating less agreement "satisfaction" with the item and lower scores, while item PA047 "I am satisfied with my life" was the easiest to endorse, indicating a high level of agreement or "satisfaction" with this item, consequently yielding higher scores. It is important to note that direct comparisons with previous studies are not feasible, as no prior research has assessed item difficulty within the context of the GLS SF5.

The Saudi general population had a mean *t*-score of 48.52 ± 10.53, which is comparable to the mean *t*-score of the US GP (50 ± 10), suggesting a similar level of satisfaction between the two populations [22]. Care should be taken when interpreting the results and generalising them to different contexts, as several limitations were observed in the current study. Although data were collected from multiple centres, they were all in the same city; therefore, to improve generalisation, data from multiple cities is recommended. Furthermore, the sex distribution among participants was considered a limitation of this study, as the percentage of female participants was higher than that of male participants (Table 1). It is imperative to acknowledge the disparities observed in the psychological domain, and these findings should be duly recognised as notable limitations. Future studies should evaluate different forms of responses to enhance the options' interpretability and the scale's feasibility. Moreover, we recommend applying the Arabic version of the PROMIS GLS SF5a to specific disease populations to allow for better and more specific comparisons with previous studies.

## 5. Conclusions

The psychometric properties of the Arabic version of the PROMIS GLS SF5a scale are promising for measuring general life satisfaction among Saudi Arabia's general and clinical-based populations. Its application holds promise for efficiently providing high-quality care to patients and for guiding practitioners in tailoring appropriate care plans. Future research should assess its responsiveness, interpretability and feasibility while refining the measures to address the limitations encountered in this study.

**Author Contributions:** Conceptualization, methodology, formal analysis, H.R.B., B.B.S., M.I.A. and R.A.; data curation, N.S.A., A.A.A., G.K.A. and R.Z.A.; writing—original draft preparation, H.R.B. and N.S.A.; writing—review and editing H.R.B., B.B.S., M.I.A. and R.A.; funding acquisition, H.R.B. All authors have read and agreed to the published version of the manuscript.

**Funding:** This research was funded by the Deputyship for Research & Innovation, Ministry of Education in Saudi Arabia for funding this research work through the project number RI-44-0060.

**Institutional Review Board Statement:** The study was conducted according to the guidelines of the Declaration of Helsinki, and approved by the Institutional Review Board of Princess Nourah Bint Abdulrahman University (PNU), Riyadh, Saudi Arabia (KACST, KSA: HAP-01-R-059), KAAUH (RO-2023-P-019) and KFMC (H-01-R-012).

**Informed Consent Statement:** Informed consent was obtained from all subjects involved in the study.

**Data Availability Statement:** The datasets analysed during the current study are available from the corresponding author upon reasonable request.

**Acknowledgments:** The authors extend their appreciation to the Deputyship for Research & Innovation, Ministry of Education in Saudi Arabia for funding this research work through the project number RI-44-0060. Acknowledgements are hereby extended to Ghada Ratah and Rawan AlTurki for their invaluable contributions to the realm of data collection and heart-felt gratitude to the study participants for their essential involvement in this study.

**Conflicts of Interest:** The authors declare no conflict of interest.

## References

1. Fergusson, D.M.; McLeod, G.; Horwood, L.J.; Swain, N.R.; Chapple, S.; Poulton, R. Life satisfaction and mental health problems (18 to 35 years). *Psychol. Med.* **2015**, *45*, 2427–2436. [CrossRef] [PubMed]
2. VandenBos, G.R. *APA Dictionary of Psychology*; American Psychological Association: Washington, DC, USA, 2007.
3. Lombardo, P.; Jones, W.; Wang, L.; Shen, X.; Goldner, E.M. The fundamental association between mental health and life satisfaction: Results from successive waves of a Canadian national survey. *BMC Public Health* **2018**, *18*, 342. [CrossRef] [PubMed]

4. An, H.-Y.; Chen, W.; Wang, C.-W.; Yang, H.-F.; Huang, W.-T.; Fan, S.-Y. The relationships between physical activity and life satisfaction and happiness among young, middle-aged, and older adults. *Int. J. Environ. Res. Public Health* **2020**, *17*, 4817. [CrossRef] [PubMed]
5. Khodabakhsh, S. Factors affecting life satisfaction of older adults in Asia: A systematic review. *J. Happiness Stud.* **2022**, *23*, 1289–1304. [CrossRef]
6. Strine, T.W.; Chapman, D.P.; Balluz, L.S.; Moriarty, D.G.; Mokdad, A.H. The associations between life satisfaction and health-related quality of life, chronic illness, and health behaviors among US community-dwelling adults. *J. Community Health* **2008**, *33*, 40–50. [CrossRef] [PubMed]
7. Duncan, E.A.; Murray, J. The barriers and facilitators to routine outcome measurement by allied health professionals in practice: A systematic review. *BMC Health Serv. Res.* **2012**, *12*, 96. [CrossRef] [PubMed]
8. Fries, J.F.; Bruce, B.; Cella, D. The promise of PROMIS: Using item response theory to improve assessment of patient-reported outcomes. *Clin. Exp. Rheumatol.* **2005**, *23*, S53.
9. Valderas, J.; Kotzeva, A.; Espallargues, M.; Guyatt, G.; Ferrans, C.; Halyard, M.; Revicki, D.; Symonds, T.; Parada, A.; Alonso, J. The impact of measuring patient-reported outcomes in clinical practice: A systematic review of the literature. *Qual. Life Res.* **2008**, *17*, 179–193. [CrossRef]
10. Cella, D.; Riley, W.; Stone, A.; Rothrock, N.; Reeve, B.; Yount, S.; Amtmann, D.; Bode, R.; Buysse, D.; Choi, S. The Patient-Reported Outcomes Measurement Information System (PROMIS) developed and tested its first wave of adult self-reported health outcome item banks: 2005–2008. *J. Clin. Epidemiol.* **2010**, *63*, 1179–1194. [CrossRef]
11. Vaughan, B.; Mulcahy, J.; Fitzgerald, K. PROMIS® General Life Satisfaction scale: Construct validity in musculoskeletal pain patients. *Chiropr. Man. Ther.* **2020**, *28*, 1–7. [CrossRef]
12. Al-Ebrahim, S.Q.; Harrison, J.; Chen, T.F.; Mohammed, M.A. Cross-cultural adaptation and psychometric properties of patient-reported outcome measures in Arabic speaking countries: A scoping review. *Res. Soc. Adm. Pharm.* **2023**, *19*, 989–1006. [CrossRef] [PubMed]
13. Al-Muqiren, T.N.; Al-Eisa, E.S.; Alghadir, A.H.; Anwer, S. Implementation and use of standardized outcome measures by physical therapists in Saudi Arabia: Barriers, facilitators and perceptions. *BMC Health Serv. Res.* **2017**, *17*, 748. [CrossRef] [PubMed]
14. Alaqeel, S.; Alfakhri, A.; Alkherb, Z.; Almeshal, N. Patient-reported outcome measures in Arabic-speaking populations: A systematic review. *Qual. Life Res.* **2022**, *31*, 1309–1320. [CrossRef]
15. Field, J.; Holmes, M.M.; Newell, D. PROMs data: Can it be used to make decisions for individual patients? A narrative review. *Patient Relat. Outcome Meas.* **2019**, *10*, 233–241. [CrossRef] [PubMed]
16. Moore, C.L.; Kaplan, S.L. A framework and resources for shared decision making: Opportunities for improved physical therapy outcomes. *Phys. Ther.* **2018**, *98*, 1022–1036. [CrossRef]
17. Almass, A.; Aljohani, H.M.; Alhaqbani, R.M.; Alromih, A.M.; Hadal, S.; Abozaid, H.S. Patient Satisfaction With Quality of Care at the Kingdom of Saudi Arabia. *Cureus* **2022**, *14*, e32102. [CrossRef]
18. Musella, A.; DeVitto, R.; Anthony, M.; Elliott Mydland, D. The importance of shared decision-making for patients with glioblastoma. *Patient Prefer. Adherence* **2021**, *15*, 2009–2016. [CrossRef]
19. Reeve, B.B.; Hays, R.D.; Bjorner, J.B.; Cook, K.F.; Crane, P.K.; Teresi, J.A.; Thissen, D.; Revicki, D.A.; Weiss, D.J.; Hambleton, R.K. Psychometric evaluation and calibration of health-related quality of life item banks: Plans for the Patient-Reported Outcomes Measurement Information System (PROMIS). *Med. Care* **2007**, *45*, S22–S31. [CrossRef]
20. *ISO 17100*; Translation Services–Requirements for Translation Services. Vernier: ISO. ISO: Geneva, Switzerland, 2015. Available online: https://www.iso.org/standard/59149.html (accessed on 29 October 2023).
21. Arifin, W.N. A Web-based Sample Size Calculator for Reliability Studies. *Educ. Med. J.* **2018**, *10*, 67–76. [CrossRef]
22. Rothrock, N.E.; Amtmann, D.; Cook, K.F. Development and validation of an interpretive guide for PROMIS scores. *Journal of Patient-Reported Outcomes* **2020**, *4*, 16. [CrossRef]
23. Bond, T.; Yan, Z.; Heene, M. *Applying the Rasch Model: Fundamental Measurement in the Human Sciences*; Routledge: London, UK, 2020.
24. Boone, W.J.; Staver, J.R. *Advances in Rasch Analyses in the Human Sciences*; Springer: Berlin/Heidelberg, Germany, 2020.
25. Linacre, J.M. *Winsteps® Rasch Measurement Computer Program User's Guide*; Winsteps.com: Beaverton, OR, USA, 2012.
26. Linacre, J.M. Investigating rating scale category utility. *J. Outcome Meas.* **1999**, *3*, 103–122.
27. Wolfe, E.W.; Smith, E.V., Jr. Instrument development tools and activities for measure validation using Rasch models: Part I-instrument development tools. *J. Appl. Meas.* **2007**, *8*, 97–123.
28. Tesio, L.; Caronni, A.; Kumbhare, D.; Scarano, S. Interpreting results from Rasch analysis 1. The "most likely" measures coming from the model. *Disabil. Rehabil.* **2023**, 1–13. [CrossRef]

healthcare

MDPI

Article

# Complications of Intrathecal Baclofen Pump Therapy: An Institutional Experience from Saudi Arabia

Ahmad Zaheer Qureshi [1,*], Hasan Shacfe [1], Amara Ilyas [2], Saeed Bin Ayaz [3], Khalid Yousef Aljamaan [1,4], Imad Saeed Moukais [1], Mohammed Jameel [1,5], Waqas Sami [6] and Sami Ullah [1,7]

1 Department of Physical Medicine and Rehabilitation, King Fahad Medical City, Riyadh 11525, Saudi Arabia
2 Department of Physical Medicine and Rehabilitation, King Fahad Specialist Hospital, Damam 32553, Saudi Arabia
3 Department of Rehabilitation Medicine, Sheikh Khalifa Bin Zayed Al Nahyan Hospital, Muzaffarabad 13100, Pakistan
4 Medical Rehabilitation Department, King Fahad Hospital, Hofuf 36364, Saudi Arabia
5 Department of Pain Medicine, King Fahad Medical City, Riyadh 11525, Saudi Arabia
6 Department of Pre-Clinical Affairs, College of Nursing, QU Health, Qatar University, Doha P.O. Box 2713, Qatar; waqas@qu.edu.qa
7 Department of Physical Medicine and Rehabilitation, Qatar Rehabilitation Institute, Doha P.O. Box 3050, Qatar
* Correspondence: qureshipmr@gmail.com

**Abstract:** The intrathecal baclofen pump (ITB) is one of the advanced treatment options in the management of spasticity. This retrospective cohort study was conducted to identify the complications of ITB treatment at a tertiary care rehabilitation facility. Various demographic and technical factors were analyzed, which are less often reported in the literature. All patients with ITB who had their refill at the ITB clinic between November 2019 and March 2020 were included. Of 48 patients, 17 patients had 18 (37.5%) ITB-related complications. Catheter-related complications were most common, whereas loss of efficacy (16.7%) and baclofen withdrawal (14.5%) were the most common outcomes of complications. Only catheter occlusion had a significant relationship with the pattern of spastic quadriparesis ($p = 0.001$). Gender, rehabilitation diagnosis, patients' residence, and facility of ITB placement did not have significant association. Similarly, age, distance from hospital, disease onset, ITB therapy duration, and baclofen dose were not statistically significant in relation to ITB-related complications.

**Keywords:** intrathecal baclofen; spasticity; complications; outcomes; Saudi Arabia

**Citation:** Qureshi, A.Z.; Shacfe, H.; Ilyas, A.; Ayaz, S.B.; Aljamaan, K.Y.; Moukais, I.S.; Jameel, M.; Sami, W.; Ullah, S. Complications of Intrathecal Baclofen Pump Therapy: An Institutional Experience from Saudi Arabia. *Healthcare* **2023**, *11*, 2820. https://doi.org/10.3390/healthcare11212820

Academic Editors: Marco Tramontano and Giovanni Galeoto

Received: 24 September 2023
Revised: 16 October 2023
Accepted: 20 October 2023
Published: 25 October 2023



## 1. Introduction

The intrathecal baclofen pump (ITB) is one of the advanced treatment options in the management of spasticity; however, there are various complications associated with it. ITB complications are generally related to operative or technical procedures and device–catheter system malfunction [1–6]. Technical complications may be related to the pump, catheter, surgery, or refill techniques. Pump-related surgeries may be complicated with bleeding, infections, seroma, or cerebrospinal fluid leakage, whereas catheter-related problems can be caused by blockage, kinking, fracture, disconnect, tear, migration, or dislodgement [2,3]. Catheter-related complications are reported to be the highest, whereas pump malfunction is less commonly reported [4]. In addition to device malfunction, human error (such as programming or refill error) can also lead to adverse outcomes [5,6]. Subsequent pharmacological complications, like loss of efficacy, withdrawal, or overdose of baclofen, may impose serious effects on patients [7,8]. Even though the outcomes of ITB complications are reported to be associated with morbidity and mortality, there have been growing trends in the use of ITB across various health systems [9]. ITB management involves a skilled and specialized multidisciplinary team [4]. The requirements of running a safe and effective program are not only limited to clinical expertise. Patient selection, payer system, access to specialized care, support structure, and socioeconomic factors are important considerations in ITB service [10]. Since the clinical expertise, health system, patient population, and institutional practices vary around the globe, it is important to study local practices and outcomes associated with ITB management.

There is a paucity of local data regarding ITB practices [8,11]. Saudi Arabia has a population of approximately 34 million, which is distributed across 13 provinces [12]. Currently, only four hospitals are providing intrathecal baclofen service, out of which three are in the capital city of Riyadh, whereas one is in the Eastern Region. Many patients with ITB are residents of regions with limited or no access to specialized ITB care. Also, it is not uncommon for patients to be placed on ITB in foreign countries without preemptive plans of continued treatment upon their return to Saudi Arabia. Similarly, patient selection and pump placement may be carried out at a facility different than the one handling continued care. Hence, it remains important to analyze the complications associated with ITB management, which can help to identify gaps and facilitate the adaptation of pertinent strategies to improve service delivery.

This study was conducted to identify the complications of ITB treatment at a tertiary care rehabilitation facility and highlight the pertinent challenges involved in ITB care.

## 2. Materials and Methods

### 2.1. Type

This study is a retrospective cohort study.

### 2.2. Setting

The setting is the intrathecal baclofen pump clinic, Rehabilitation Hospital of King Fahad Medical City (KFMC), Riyadh. The Rehabilitation Hospital at KFMC is the largest ministry of health tertiary care rehabilitation facility in the country, receiving referrals from all over the Kingdom and offering comprehensive rehabilitation services. The ITB service involves a multidisciplinary team, including rehabilitation physicians, neurosurgeons, rehabilitation nursing, and therapists as core team members. The ITB clinic at KFMC is a weekly clinic where patients follow-up for review of spasticity and ITB pump management.

### 2.3. Inclusion Criteria

All patients with ITB who had their pump refill at the ITB clinic between November 2019 and March 2020 were included in this study.

### 2.4. Exclusion Criteria

Patients who died during hospital admission or were transferred back to the acute care were excluded.

### 2.5. Procedure

This study was approved by the institutional review board of KFMC, Riyadh. A chart review was carried out for all patients who fulfilled the inclusion criteria. Information was obtained regarding diagnoses, demographics, baclofen dose, device details, and pattern of spasticity. The data regarding complications included pump site infection, programming error, procedural complications, and catheter malfunction. The outcomes were recorded as withdrawal, overdose, or loss of efficacy. Information was collected regarding any pump or catheter-related surgery as a result of complications. Additionally, appointment compliance and follow-up with the primary rehabilitation doctor were reviewed at the last refill clinic visit.

### 2.6. Statistical Analysis

The Statistical Package for Social Sciences (SPSS) version 22 was used for the statistical analysis. A descriptive analysis was carried out by calculating numbers and percentages for the categorical data. The scale data were analyzed for normality using the Shapiro–Wilk test. Means and standard distributions were calculated for the normally distributed scale data, whereas medians and interquartile ranges (IQR) were recorded for the scale data that were not normally distributed. The chi-square/Fischer's Exact tests were used to analyze the relationship between different complications and gender, rehabilitation diagnoses, spasticity pattern, living area of the patients, and place of placement of the ITB. A logistic regression was performed to ascertain the effects of age, distance from Riyadh city (km), time since onset of primary disease (months), duration of ITB placement (months), and baclofen dose (μg/day).

## 3. Results

A total of 48 patients met the criteria for this study. The median age of the patients was 30 years (range: 16–69 years). Out of 48 patients, 36 (75%) were male, and 12 (35%) were female (Table 1). The most common diagnosis was spinal cord injury (SCI) (66.7%, n = 32). All patients were on ITB therapy for the management of spasticity except for one patient with cerebral palsy who had dystonia. A total of 64.6% (n = 31) of the patients with ITB were from outside Riyadh city with most residing at locations 400 km to 1200 km from Riyadh city (Figure 1). The spinal catheter tip was at the thoracic vertebrae level in 23 (47.92%) patients, while in 20 (41.7%) patients, the level of the spinal catheter tip was not known. The other characteristics related to the patients and ITB in our cohort are outlined in Table 1.

**Table 1.** Categorical data related to the patients and intrathecal baclofen pump.

| Variables | n (%) | Variables | n (%) |
|---|---|---|---|
| **Gender** | | **Pump placement** | |
| Male | 36 (75) | King Fahad Medical City | 23 (47.9) |
| Female | 12 (35) | Other Saudi Hospitals | 18 (37.5) |
| | | Outside Saudi Arabia | 7 (14.6) |
| **Regional Distribution** | | | |
| Riyadh | 20 (41.7%) | **Level of spinal catheter tip** | |
| Asir | 7 (14.6%) | Thoracic | 23 (47.9) |
| Jazan | 5 (10.4%) | Lumbar | 5 (10.5) |
| Medina | 4 (8.3%) | Unknown | 20 (41.7) |
| Northern Borders Region | 4 (8.3%) | | |
| Eastern Region | 3 (6.3%) | | |
| Makkah | 2 (4.2%) | **Boluses used for trial** | |
| Najran | 1 (2.1%) | One | 20 (41.7) |
| Al-Qassim | 1 (2.1%) | Two | 5 (10.4) |
| Al-Bahah | 1 (2.1%) | Unknown | 23 (47.9) |
| **Residence of patient** | | **Pump Capacity** | |
| Within Riyadh City | 17 (35.4) | 20 mL | 17 (35.4) |
| Outside Riyadh City | 31 (64.6) | 40 mL | 31 (64.6) |
| **Diagnosis** | | **ITB Related Complication** | |
| Spinal Cord Injury | 32 (66.7) | Yes | 17 (35.4) |
| Stroke | 2 (4.2) | No | 31 (64.6) |
| Traumatic Brain Injury | 2 (4.2) | | |
| Cerebral Palsy | 8 (16.7) | **Primary Rehabilitation Physician** | |
| Demyelinating Disease | 3 (6.3) | Spinal Cord Injury Rehabilitation | 29 (60.4) |
| Anoxic Bain Injury | 1 (2.1) | Neurorehabilitation | 2 (4.2) |
| | | Pediatric Rehabilitation | 2 (4.2) |
| **Pattern of spasticity/dystonia** | | Brain Injury Rehabilitation | 4 (8.33) |
| Spastic Quadriparesis | 24 (50) | None | 11 (22.9) |
| Spastic Paraparesis | 23 (47.9) | | |
| Generalized Dystonia | 1 (2.1) | | |

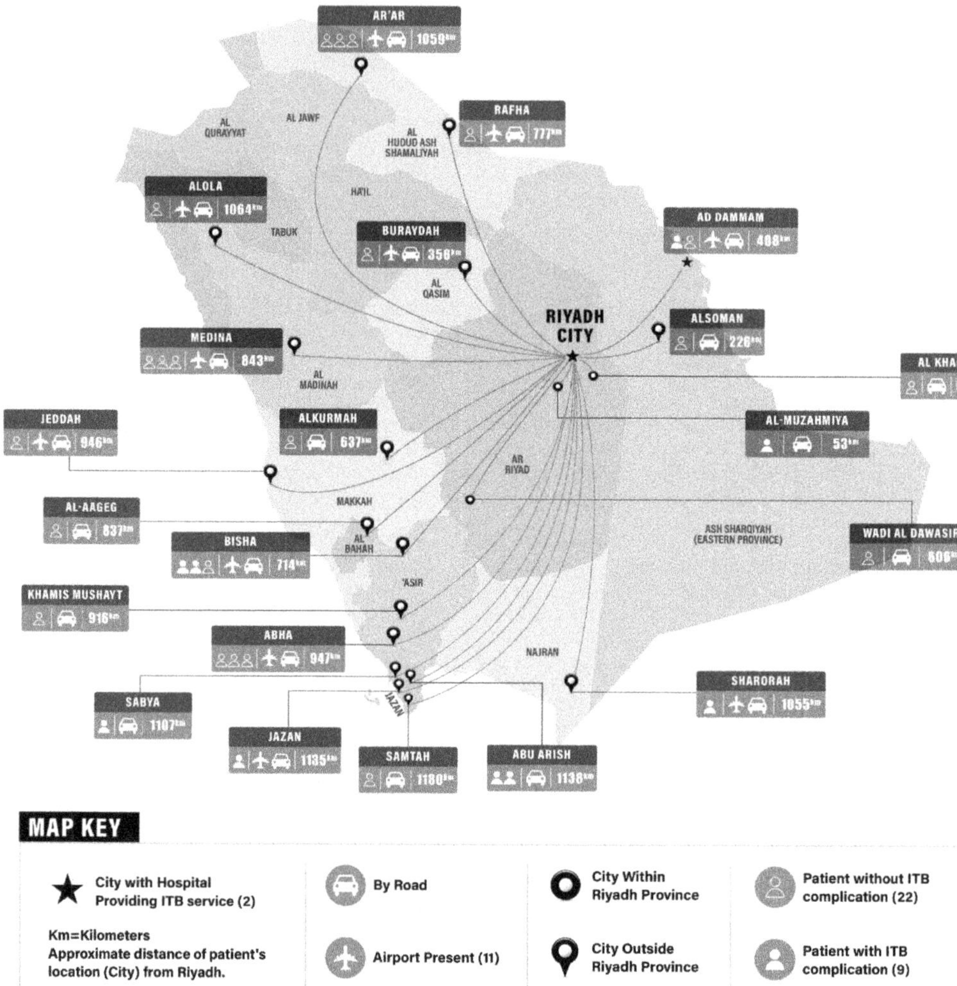


**Figure 1.** Geographic distribution of the patients with an intrathecal baclofen pump outside Riyadh City.

The median daily dose of baclofen at the initial ITB pump placement was 300.2 µg/day with minimum and maximum dosing values of 48.96 µg/day and 661.30 µg/day, respectively; however, at the last clinic visit, there was an increase in the median daily dose to 325.45 µg/day (maximum: 661.30 µg/day; minimum: 48.96 µg/day) (Table 2). The mean time since last refill was approximately 4 months, which approximately remained the same for future refills. The mean time since disease onset was approximately 15 years. The mean time for patients while on ITB therapy was approximately 10 years. The median duration (IQR) of the last appointment with the primary rehabilitation physician (other than the pump manager) was approximately 23 (29) months. Eleven patients did not have a primary rehabilitation physician, and they only followed up with the rehabilitation physician managing the pump.

**Table 2.** Table showing scale data related to the patients and intrathecal baclofen pump.

| Variables | Median (IQR) | Variables | Mean (SD) |
|---|---|---|---|
| Age (years) | 30 (14) | Time since disease onset (months) | 174.64 (60.99) |
| Number of years at King Fahad Medical City | 8 (8) | Duration of ITB (months) since first ITB placement | 119.45 (14.81) |
| Time since ITB trial to ITB placement (months) | 1 (6) | Time since last baclofen pump placement (months) | 38.64 (14.96) |
| Last appointment with primary physician (months) | 23 (29) | Time since last ITB refill (months) | 4.09 (1.45) |
| Baclofen dose (µg/day) | 300.2 (305.45) | Estimated time for future refill (months) | 3.9 (1.45) |

Seventeen patients had 18 ITB-related complications, out of which one patient had complications twice. The frequency of complications was 37.5% (Table 3). Eleven patients with ITB-related complications had been on ITB therapy for more than seven years. The most common complications were catheter-related, which constituted one-third (33.3%) of all the complications, out of which four were catheter occlusions and two were catheter breakages. Programming error occurred in four out of eighteen patients (22.2%). Of all the patients who had ITB-related complications, 11 (64.7%) had their pumps placed at other institutes. Seven out of seventeen patients had ITB withdrawal, out of which four were from outside Riyadh province.

**Table 3.** Complications and outcomes of intrathecal baclofen pump therapy.

| Complications | Outcomes | | | | | Associated Surgery | | |
|---|---|---|---|---|---|---|---|---|
| | Baclofen Withdrawal | Baclofen Overdose | Loss of Efficacy | Local Infection | Total n (%) | Pump Related Surgery | Catheter Related Surgery | Total n (%) |
| Pump infection | 1 | - | - | 1 | 2 (11.1) | 2 | - | 2 (20) |
| Programming error | 3 | 1 | - | | 4 (22.2) | - | - | - |
| Procedural complication (CAP * contrast study) | | 1 | - | - | 1 (11.1) | - | - | - |
| Catheter occlusion | 3 | - | 1 | - | 4 (22.2) | - | 4 | 4 (40) |
| Catheter breakage | - | - | 2 | - | 2 (11.1) | - | 2 | 2 (20) |
| Undetermined loss of efficacy (underwent surgical exploration) | - | - | 2 | - | 2 (11.1) | 2 | - | 2 (20) |
| Undetermined loss of efficacy (no surgical exploration) ** | - | - | 3 | - | 3 (16.6) | - | - | - |
| Total n (%) | 7 (38.8) | 2 (11.1) | 8 (44.4) | 1 (5.5) | 18 (100) | 4 (40) | 6 (60) | 10 (100) |
| (%) of Total patients n = 48 | 14.5% | 4.2% | 16.7% | 2.1% | 37.5% | 8.3% | 12.5% | 20.8% |

* Catheter access port (CAP); ** Patients underwent imaging evaluations, which were non-conclusive.

Overall, the most common adverse outcome in our study population was loss of efficacy (16.7%), which constituted 44.4% of all ITB-related complications. Three patients with loss of efficacy had catheter-related problems for which they underwent catheter replacement. Additionally, two patients underwent ITB exploratory surgery to investigate the loss of efficacy, while the remaining three only required fluoroscopic evaluations, which were non-conclusive. The second most common adverse outcome was baclofen withdrawal (14.5%), which constituted 38.8% of all ITB-related complications. The majority of patients with ITB withdrawal had a diagnosis of SCI (71.4%). Catheter occlusion and programming error were found to be the most common reasons for withdrawal for which catheter replacements were carried out. Three patients had withdrawal due to programming error, while one withdrawal occurred due to a pump malfunction that required pump replacement. Two patients had pump site infections, out of which one was associated with withdrawal, while the other one required pump replacement. One patient had a cerebrospinal fluid culture positive for staphylococcus infection, requiring treatment with cloxacillin. Out of the two cases who had a baclofen overdose, one was due to a programming error, while the other one occurred after fluoroscopic evaluation with contrast through the catheter access port (CAP), requiring intensive care. A total of 10 surgical procedures were carried out, indicating that approximately one in five patients required surgical intervention in our study population. Approximately half (55.5%) of the ITB-related complications required surgical intervention.

Following the chi-square/Fischer's Exact Test analysis, only catheter occlusion showed a significant relationship with spastic quadriparesis ($p$ = 0.001) (Table 4). The rest of the test variables, i.e., gender, rehabilitation diagnoses, spasticity pattern, living area of the patients, and place of placement of ITB pump, did not show any significant correlation with the different ITB-related complications. Moreover, the logistic regression model did not identify age, distance from Riyadh city, time since onset of primary disease, duration of ITB placement, or baclofen dose as possible risk factors for the development of complications (Table 5).

**Table 4.** Correlation of complications of intrathecal baclofen pump with different variables of interest.

| Variable | Pump Infection n (%) | *p*-Value | Programming Error n (%) | *p*-Value | Procedural Complication (CAP * Contrast Study) n (%) | *p*-Value | Catheter Occlusion n (%) | *p*-Value | Catheter Breakage n (%) | *p*-Value | Undetermined Loss of Efficacy n (%) | *p*-Value |
|---|---|---|---|---|---|---|---|---|---|---|---|---|
| **Gender** | | | | | | | | | | | | |
| Male | 2 (5.6) | 0.404 | 3 (8.3) | 1 | 1 (2.8) | 0.560 | 2 (5.6) | 0.228 | 2 (5.6) | 0.404 | 6 (17.1) | 0.937 |
| Female | - | | 1 (8.3) | | - | | 2 (16.7) | | - | | 2 (18.2) | |
| **Rehabilitation diagnoses** | | | | | | | | | | | | |
| Spinal Cord Injury | 2 (6.3) | 0.959 | 3 (6.3) | 0.596 | (3.1) | 0.992 | 2 (6.3) | 0.576 | 2 (6.3) | 0.959 | 4 (12.9) | 0.209 |
| Stroke | - | | - | | - | | - | | - | | - | |
| Cerebral Palsy | - | | - | | - | | 2 (25) | | - | | 2 (18.6) | |
| Demyelinating Disease | - | | 1 (2.1) | | - | | - | | - | | 2 (66.7) | |
| Anoxic Brain Injury | - | | - | | - | | - | | - | | - | |
| Traumatic Brain Injury | - | | - | | - | | - | | - | | - | |
| **Spasticity pattern** | | | | | | | | | | | | |
| Spastic Quadriparesis | - | 0.322 | 3 (12.5) | 0.573 | - | 0.574 | 3 (12.5) | 0.001 | 1 (4.2) | 0.978 | 3 (12.5) | 0.361 |
| Spastic Paraparesis | 2 (8.7) | | 1 (4.3) | | 1 (4.3) | | - | | 1 (4.3) | | 5 (22.7) | |
| Generalized Dystonia | - | | - | | - | | 1 (100) | | - | | - | |

**Table 4.** *Cont.*

| Variable | Pump Infection n (%) | p-Value | Programming Error n (%) | p-Value | Procedural Complication (CAP * Contrast Study) n (%) | p-Value | Catheter Occlusion n (%) | p-Value | Catheter Breakage n (%) | p-Value | Undetermined Loss of Efficacy n (%) | p-Value |
|---|---|---|---|---|---|---|---|---|---|---|---|---|
| **Location of ITB pump placement** | | | | | | | | | | | | |
| KFMC | 1 (4.3) | 0.952 | 1 (4.3) | 0.338 | 1 (4.3) | 0.292 | 2 (8.7) | 0.931 | 1 (4.3) | 0.952 | 5 (21.7) | 0.437 |
| Other Institutes | 1 (4) | | 3 (12) | | - | | 2 (8) | | 1 (4) | | 3 (13) | |
| **Living area of patient** | | | | | | | | | | | | |
| Riyadh City | 2 (11.8) | 0.051 | - | 0.122 | - | 0.454 | 3 (17.6) | 0.084 | - | 0.285 | 3 (20) | 0.745 |
| Outside Riyadh City | - | | 4 (12.9) | | 1 (3.2) | | 1 (3.2) | | 2 (6.5) | | 5 (16.1) | |

* Catheter access port (CAP).

**Table 5.** Logistic regression analysis for possible risk factors for complications of intrathecal baclofen treatment.

| Variables | Programming Error | | Procedural Complication (CAP * Contrast Study) | | Catheter Occlusion | | Catheter Break | | Undetermined Loss of Efficacy | |
|---|---|---|---|---|---|---|---|---|---|---|
| Omnibus Tests of Model Coefficients | $\chi^2 = 10.210$, $p = 0.069$ | | $\chi^2 = 8.835$, $p = 0.116$ | | $\chi^2 = 8.835$, $p = 0.116$ | | $\chi^2 = 5.291$, $p = 0.381$ | | $\chi^2 = 5.488$, $p = 0.359$ | |
| Nagelkerke $R^2$ | 52.3% | | 100% | | 100% | | 41.2% | | 27.7% | |
| Percentage Correct | 90.3% | | 100% | | 100% | | 90.3% | | 80.6% | |
| **Variables in the Equation** | **Exp(B)** | ***p*-value** | **Exp(B)** | ***p*-value** | **Exp(B)** | ***p*-value** | **Exp(B)** | ***p*-value** | **Exp(B)** | ***p*-value** |
| Age (years) | 1.011 | 0.919 | 0.799 | 0.999 | 0.062 | 0.993 | 0.052 | 0.945 | 0.941 | 0.239 |
| Distance from Riyadh (km) | 1.001 | 0.690 | 1.056 | 0.997 | 0.876 | 0.993 | 0.875 | 0.355 | 1 | 0.897 |
| Time since onset of primary disease (days) | 1.065 | 0.371 | 1.173 | 0.998 | 0.966 | 0.995 | 3.277 | 0.392 | 0.986 | 0.162 |
| Duration of ITB pump placement (months) | 0.921 | 0.230 | 1.626 | 0.997 | 0.429 | 0.994 | 0.362 | 0.395 | 1.013 | 0.536 |
| Baclofen dose per day (μg) | 0.993 | 0.257 | 1.284 | 0.996 | 0.761 | 0.995 | 0.768 | 0.807 | 0.995 | 0.240 |

* Catheter access port (CAP).

## 4. Discussion

### 4.1. Patient Characteristics

(a) Pattern of spasticity and functional impairments

All patients in our study population had pump placements for spasticity except one patient with cerebral palsy who had dystonia. Though other institutional studies report the use of ITB in dystonia, ITB is less frequently used in dystonia as compared to spasticity. There may be a lack of studies demonstrating improvements in dystonia with the use of ITB, the need for higher doses, and the risks of a dystonic storm with sudden discontinuation [1,13,14]. On the other hand, the ITB-related complications in patients with dystonia are similar to what is reported in patients with spasticity [15]. It is interesting to note that the patients with ITB in our study had complications that may be expected to be less frequent in patients with controlled spasticity. For example, 87.5% of the patients had bladder and bowel incontinence, while approximately one-third of the patients had pressure ulcers (35.4%) and contractures (33.3%). Though this could be multifactorial, it may be attributed to SCI as the most common diagnosis (66.7%) or because the majority of patients had spastic quadriparesis. This emphasizes the need for multidisciplinary rehabilitation services beyond pump management. It is important for services running ITB programs to ensure that relevant specialties are on board when problems beyond spasticity arise; for example, plastic surgery, orthopedics, and urology are integral services for individuals with long-term disabilities.

(b) Access to continued care

Out of the patients from outside Riyadh, three patients were from the Eastern Region, which has a hospital running its ITB service, but the patient preferred to follow-up at our institute. Since half of the patients who had ITB-related complications were also from outside Riyadh, the potential morbidity or mortality associated with ITB complications brings attention to the need for access to emergency care locally. Currently, only four hospitals are providing ITB services across the country. They include King Fahad Medical City (Riyadh), Prince Sultan Military Medical City (Riyadh), Prince Sultan Bin Abdulaziz Humanitarian City (Riyadh), and King Fahad Specialist Hospital Dammam (Eastern Region). All these hospitals offer inpatient and outpatient comprehensive rehabilitation services and physical medicine, and rehabilitation physicians are involved in the care of patients with ITB. There is no national registry of patients with ITB at present, and patients are observed to shift their care from one hospital to another. Half of the patients with ITB-related complications in our study had their pumps placed at another facility. The reasons for the transfer of care were not analyzed in our study, but to our observation, the usual causes include lack of funding to continue ITB service, closure of ITB service, or ITB placement at a facility outside Saudi Arabia.

(c) Challenges of transfer of care to new institute and its implications

After pump placement at one facility, some patients prefer to establish ITB care with their primary rehabilitation physician at another institute who had been involved in their holistic rehabilitation care previously. Challenges ensue when the primary rehabilitation team may not be aware of the pump placement until notified about it only when the pump has already been placed at another institute. In such situations, there could be insufficient information on the treatment tried for spasticity before pump placement. Similarly, continued treatment at a new facility could be challenging due to lack of clarity on the process of patient selection and appropriateness of ITB therapy for a particular patient. Additionally, there could be deficient information regarding the brand name of baclofen and details of ITB trials. Pump information and most catheter details may be retrievable if it is a Medtronic drug infusion pump; however, the information on catheter tip level may be missing as this information is not auto-retrievable through a programmer. This was a major concern that we identified in our study, since catheter tip level could not be retrieved from chart review in a considerable number (41.7%) of patients. This is primarily because many of the patients who had their pump placements at other institutes established care at our center for routine refills, not requiring imaging for spinal catheters unless there were concerns of complications. Documentation from previous hospitals did not include this information; however, this is an area of improvement. When not known, spinal imaging needs to be included as a part of the initial workup to determine the catheter tip level when a patient with ITB establishes care at a new facility. Knowledge of the catheter tip level is important to know the effectiveness of spasticity treatment. A cervically positioned catheter tip could relieve spasticity in the upper limbs due to a higher cervical concentration of baclofen. At the same time, a bolus or high baclofen doses can affect respiratory function if the catheter tip is high, which could be concerning in patients with impaired ventilation, such as individuals with cervical SCI. Imaging of the catheter can also help to plan safe spinal taps or epidural anesthesia when needed.

Due to the above-mentioned challenges, a pump manager new to the patient who had his or her pump placement elsewhere may not only have to face a cumulative challenge related to patient safety but may also have potential medicolegal implications. This can lead to a clinical dilemma when a rehabilitation physician who had neither been involved in decision-making nor had considered a referral for pump placement may eventually be expected to undertake ITB care post-pump placement carried out at another facility by another provider. So far, we have neither come across a patient with a drug infusion pump other than Medtronic nor is there another brand label currently operating in the country; however, a problematic situation can arise if a patient abroad is placed on an intrathecal drug infusion pump other than Medtronic and returns to Saudi Arabia.

### 4.2. *Importance of Patient Selection in ITB Therapy*

It is of paramount importance to determine appropriate patient selection based on the reliability and capability of the patient and their families to be able to ensure compliance with instructions critical for patient safety [10]. Psychological attributes, socio-economic factors, access to care, support services, and availability of expertise remain important factors in patient selection [16,17]. The treating teams should not only make management decisions on the clinical attributes, but rather non-clinical factors should always be prioritized, given their potential to affect the continuity of safe and effective ITB treatment. For patients opting for ITB management, the statistics regarding expected adverse outcomes published in the literature can help to improve informed decision-making.

### 4.3. *Complications*

The frequency of complications in our study was similar to what has been reported in Japan (37%) [7]. The literature review shows that 20–50% of patients with ITB can have ITB-related complications [18–22].

### 4.4. *Complications—Catheter Related*

Catheter-related complications remain the most common cause of ITB-related problems, which can occur in up to 40% of patients with ITB [18,21,23]. Catheter malfunction constituted 33% of the ITB-related complications in our study, which is similar to what was published (37%) in a meta-analysis of 2264 patients [18]. This raises a high suspicion of catheter-related problems while investigating ITB-related concerns but does not necessitate the need for a catheter workup as the first step during ITB troubleshooting. Various protocols have been recommended to investigate ITB-related problems; however, the approach needs to be individualized for each case [21,23–25]. At the same time, the failure to identify a catheter-related problem does not exclude a catheter malfunction. Plain imaging and fluoroscopic myelography may be non-conclusive, and further evaluations may be required, such as computerized tomography (CT) myelogram, non-contrast CT, magnetic resonance imaging (MRI), lumbar puncture, and isotopic scintigraphy [21,23,24]. The use of catheters other than Ascenda® catheters has been associated with fewer catheter-related complications [22].

### 4.5. Complications—Infection

The incidence of infection related to ITB is reported to be 3.2–27.5% [26]. In our study, two patients had pump site infections, out of which one was associated with withdrawal, while the other one was treated for local infection only. Similarly, two post-surgical pump site infections were reported in 11 years of the observational period in a hospital-based study in Austria [22]. A wide incidence range of infection in the literature may not only be due to procedural or institutional factors but also pump exteriorization may occur long after pump placement due to trauma or pressure injury over the pump site, leading to infection [27]. Hence, factors unrelated to pump, procedures, or spasticity play a crucial role in the successful long-term continuation of ITB therapy.

Approximately one-fifth of the patients with ITB in our study underwent surgical interventions, whereas approximately half of the ITB-related complications required surgical intervention. In a study on 195 patients with ITB, the surgical procedures for complications included 7 pump revisions, 48 catheter revisions, and 41 wound revisions [26]. Since ITB therapy is intended to be a long-term treatment in most cases, the chances of complications persist throughout the treatment period. In our study, 11 out of 17 patients with ITB-related complications had been on ITB therapy for more than 7 years. In a 7-year retrospective study on 243 patients on intrathecal baclofen and opioid therapy, CSF leakage and deep infections were reported in 19% and 5% of patients, respectively, which led to an increase in readmissions and hospital stays [9].

In summary, the infections related to ITB therapy can be attributed to the immediate post-surgical period or delayed infections due to pump exteriorization, pressure injury, or trauma. Peri-operative care has to be optimized for post-operative surgical infections. For patients admitted for pump- or catheter-related surgery, routine screening can be introduced for MRSA *(methicillin-resistant Staphylococcus aureus)* and ESBL *(Extended spectrum beta-lactameses)* producing bacteria. Standard infection control protocols and infectious disease consultations can help to ensure peri-operative care. For delayed infections related to trauma or pressure injury over the pump site, patients and families have to be counselled extensively for pump care at home and should be able to seek immediate care to ensure early intervention. A minor blister, swelling, or bruise over the pump or connector sites should not be ignored and should be brought to the knowledge of the treating physician.

### 4.6. Outcome—Loss of Efficacy

In our study, the most common outcome of ITB-related complication was the loss of baclofen efficacy for which catheter malfunction was identified in three patients. The exact cause of the loss of efficacy could not be determined in the rest of the five patients, out of which three patients underwent fluoroscopic myelography, while two had surgical exploration when fluoroscopic myelography was non-conclusive. Other imaging evaluations were not carried out on these patients. Surgical exploration has its limitations, as it cannot directly visualize the intrathecal component of the catheter for which imaging may still be required. Alternatively, the catheter needs to be replaced in the case of a high suspicion of catheter malfunction. The second most common complication was baclofen withdrawal in our study. Catheter occlusion was found to be the most common reason for withdrawal, for which catheter replacements were carried out. This brings attention to the need for expertise in the radiological evaluation of the pump and catheter systems. Radiologists may not be well-versed in the pump technicalities and operational aspects of the device systems. The dye testing protocol via CAP could potentially lead to a baclofen overdose, as in one of our cases. Baclofen overdose is a rare complication that requires urgent management and intensive care. The detection of the earliest symptoms and signs of baclofen overdose or withdrawal may be challenging in a radiology setting, where staff may not be familiar with emergencies related to ITB. Similarly, clinical expertise across all medical, surgical, nursing, and allied health professionals needs to be ensured at the time of introducing intrathecal drug delivery programs across an institution or health system [16,17]. Feller et al. observed catheter-related complications in 7.1% of patients. They used reinforced catheters, which led to low catheter-related complications as compared to the previous studies [2]. This could be a potential alternate in case catheter replacement is not possible.

The differential diagnosis of withdrawal could be challenging in patients with SCI, as it may mimic autonomic dysreflexia, meningitis, hyperthermia, neuroleptic malignant syndrome, serotonin reuptake syndrome, and sepsis [28,29]. A total of 40% of the patients with ITB complications were reported to be associated with withdrawal and overdose [29]. Watve et al. reviewed 23 articles on ITB withdrawal and reported that 40% of the withdrawal complications were due to catheter-related issues [30]. On the other hand, ITB treatment is commonly used in patients with SCI [5,24,29,31]. Hence, teams managing ITB need to be well-versed with ITB withdrawal as well as the autonomic aspects of SCI. Emergency physicians at institutes managing ITB must be familiar with ITB complications, especially withdrawal. It is imperative that the ITB managing teams are available 24/7, and patients have access to the nearest facility offering specialized ITB care. Of the seventeen patients who had ITB-related complications, nine (53%) had their pumps placed at other institutes. Seven out of eighteen patients had ITB withdrawal, out of which four were from outside Riyadh city. Given that more than half of the patients who had withdrawal were from outside Riyadh city (400–1200 km away), early identification of complications and coordination of their care at a local hospital or the primary pump managing facility remain crucial. This requires a 24/7 helpline or access to a program coordinator, which could be challenging after working hours or on weekends; however, education regarding precautions and withdrawal symptoms needs to be carried out on a regular basis with patients and families. A case study reported that a 31-year-old Saudi male with SCI had baclofen withdrawal twice: once due to missing an appointment, and the second due to the non-availability of his primary pump manager; so, the patient and family decided to wait and did not seek care with another physician or institute as per the case report [8]. This is a classic local example of an ITB-related complication, which merely reflects the tip of an iceberg. The lack of reporting of such cases can result in an inability to determine the actual severity of the problem and its impact. A delay in baclofen refill is a simpler yet preventable problem, the outcomes of which could be disastrous. It can be prevented by proper patient selection, patient and caregiver education, scheduled pump refilling, and timely access to specialized expertise [8].

### 4.7. Factors Associated with ITB Complications and Outcomes

Regarding the relationship of different complications with the variables of this study, only catheter occlusion established a significant association with the spasticity quadriparesis. The remaining variables of gender, rehabilitation diagnoses, location of the patients' home, and place of placement of the ITB pump did not have a significant association. Similarly, age, distance from Riyadh (km), time since onset of primary disease (months), duration of ITB placement (months), and baclofen dose (μg/day) did not prove to be risk factors for the development of any type of ITB-related complication. Other investigations in the literature have also observed similar results. Gender, age, level of ambulation, gastrostomy tube, and pump years were found to have no significant influence on the development of a complication in children by Bonouvrié et al. [3]. Only the type of catheter was identified as a significant risk factor with an odds ratio of 3.75 (95%CI: 1.30–10.83). Another pediatric cohort identified young age, wound dehiscence, and the number of revisions as independent risk factors for infection related to ITB [32]. Potential risk factors described in other studies were the presence of dystonia and age [26,33]. It should be highlighted that the studies on complications in ITB are frequently challenging to compare because of the use of different terminologies to describe the complications and variability of methodology. For example, withdrawal is generally an outcome of an underlying cause, like a catheter break; however, both are described as complications in various studies. To avoid this, we gathered the data discretely to show the cause-and-effect relation for each ITB-related complication (Table 3).

### 4.8. ITB Therapy and Cost Impact—Regional Considerations

Though the clinical effectiveness of ITB treatment has been well established, there are mixed results when it comes to the cost-effectiveness. A study on complications of ITB in children reported an increased hospital length of stay of up to 4 days and an increase in the mean cost from $29,431 to $37,081 [34]. It has also been observed that ITB treatment increases the financial cost as compared to that of other interventions [35,36]. The cost-per-patient up to 1 year of treatment was found to be three times more for patients on ITB treatment as compared to those who underwent selective posterior rhizotomy [37]. ITB treatment was found to be cost-effective as compared to conservative and other surgical interventions in the French population, which reported an ITB complication rate of only 10% [36]. It is important to note that these cost analysis studies were reported from western health systems; however, no such studies have been conducted in health systems in countries like Saudi Arabia, United Arab Emirates, or Qatar, where payer systems are different, and public health is heavily funded by the government. In Saudi Arabia, the additional cost is attributed to support services for a routine clinic visit to alleviate the financial burden of patients visiting the hospital from distant locations. In addition to medical care, various services are offered by the government, which may include travel expenses for appointments. A routine ITB refill may also include the need to address medical concerns that could be otherwise managed at a primary care facility; however, patients generally tend to rely on tertiary care hospitals and may wait for the "all-in-one" visit. The impact of the lack of local specialized ITB care services and subsequent reliance on distant tertiary care specialized hospitals needs to be evaluated to determine the actual cost-effectiveness of ITB therapy in regional health systems. Beyond cost, the burden of travel is an important consideration, especially for patients who are dependent and require full-time assistance of a caregiver. The burden of travel was reported in five out of ten patients in a study from the United States with fatigue as the main contributing factor [35]. Home-based ITB care is an alternate strategy to address these concerns [10,38].

### 4.9. Future Directions and Recommendations

Given that there is a lack of specialized rehabilitation services in the country, hospitals running ITB programs should be able to provide 24/7 ITB services with an on-call ITB team coverage. Improving the expertise at local facilities is of utmost importance, especially for patients from remote areas who have difficult access to urgent care. Measures to ensure the prevention of post-operative infections need to be ascertained. Continual counselling, education, and close follow-up with patients in the community remain a hallmark to prevent or detect problems related to ITB. There could be potential medico-legal complexities in case complications of ITB that are a sequel of recent ITB management or an encounter at another institute. Hence, a patient who undergoes ITB placement at a particular center needs to be facilitated to continue care at the same institute. The criteria for ITB therapy need to be standardized, and a consensual agreement in this regard can be achieved by involving stakeholders from different clinical disciplines at a national level. Payers, device manufacturers, suppliers, and emergency response teams need to be taken onboard in policy making. Specific competencies for clinicians involved in ITB care is important. Currently, there is no standardized process at the level of the Ministry of Health to determine institutional readiness to provide holistic ITB services. Stringent institutional and national policies need to be undertaken to address this challenge. Such initiatives have been undertaken by various national bodies and organizations globally and can be replicated locally after improvisation [10,17,38–40]. The introduction of national policies prior to the approval of intrathecal device programs in healthcare facilities can set standardization and promote safe practices. We recommend creating a panel of experts at the level of the Ministry of Health to review the readiness of a facility interested in establishing ITB services and also to provide the necessary support to facilitate service provision across various regions of the country.

Furthermore, the nomenclature of "complications" and "outcomes" related to ITB therapy has to be standardized. The terms have been interchangeably used in the published literature. This is of utmost importance to generate reliable data and will help in ensuring standardized practice measures.

### *4.10. Limitations*

The retrospective assessment of the data has to be taken into account. Several patients had their ITB pump placed at another facility before establishing care with our institute, limiting access to the data at the other facilities. Patients who had established care at another facility were excluded from this study due to the difficulty in accessing records and documentation. One of the other limitations of this study is the small sample size, which prevents inferential statistics. A multicenter study at the national level can help to determine the extent of problems associated with ITB therapy in the region and facilitate development of strategies and policies.

## 5. Conclusions

A high suspicion for catheter-related problems needs to be considered while investigating ITB-related problems, as catheter malfunction was the most common complication in our study. This could be of particular importance in patients with spastic quadriparesis. To investigate the loss of efficacy, advanced radiological techniques need to be incorporated in addition to fluoroscopy. Though pump placements at other facilities and the distance of the patient from the hospital providing ITB services are obvious challenges, especially in the case of emergency situations, our study did not demonstrate any significant statistical correlation with ITB-related complications. National strategies need to be adapted to establish uniform policies across various institutes offering ITB services.

**Author Contributions:** Conceptualization, A.Z.Q. and H.S.; methodology, A.Z.Q., W.S., S.U. and S.B.A.; software, S.B.A. and W.S.; validation, S.B.A.; data curation, K.Y.A., I.S.M. and M.J.; writing—original draft preparation, A.Z.Q., A.I. and S.B.A.; writing—review and editing, A.Z.Q., A.I., S.U. and H.S. All authors have read and agreed to the published version of the manuscript.

**Funding:** This research received no external funding, and the APC is funded by the Research Center, King Fahad Medical City, Riyadh.

**Institutional Review Board Statement:** This study was conducted in accordance with the Declaration of Helsinki and approved by the Institutional Review Board, King Fahad Medical City, Riyadh (IRB Number 19-036 Dated 24 January 2019).

**Informed Consent Statement:** Not applicable.

**Data Availability Statement:** The data presented in this study are available upon request from the corresponding author.

**Acknowledgments:** We would like to thank the research center at King Fahad Medical City, Riyadh for supporting this study.

**Conflicts of Interest:** The authors declare no conflict of interest.

## References

1. Lake, W.; Shah, H. Intrathecal Baclofen Infusion for the Treatment of Movement Disorders. *Neurosurg. Clin. N. Am.* **2019**, *30*, 203–209. [CrossRef] [PubMed]
2. Feller, C.N.; Awad, A.J.; Nelson, M.E.S.; Ketchum, N.; Pahapill, P.A. Low Rate of Intrathecal Baclofen Pump Catheter-Related Complications: Long-Term Study in over 100 Adult Patients Associated with Reinforced Catheter. *Neuromodulation* **2021**, *24*, 1176–1180. [CrossRef] [PubMed]
3. Bonouvrié, L.A.; Lagendijk, K.E.; Beckerman, H.; Slot, K.M.; van de Pol, L.A.; Buizer, A.I. Surgical complications of intrathecal baclofen in children: A single centre, 20-year retrospective cohort study. *Eur. J. Paediatr. Neurol.* **2022**, *37*, 94–97. [CrossRef] [PubMed]
4. Stetkarova, I.; Yablon, S.A.; Kofler, M.; Stokic, D.S. Procedure- and device-related complications of intrathecal baclofen administration for management of adult muscle hypertonia: A review. *Neurorehabil. Neural Repair.* **2010**, *24*, 609–619. [CrossRef]

5. Delhaas, E.M.; Huygen, F.J.P.M. Complications associated with intrathecal drug delivery systems. *BJA Educ.* **2020**, *20*, 51–57. [CrossRef]
6. Stetkarova, I.; Brabec, K.; Vasko, P.; Mencl, L. Intrathecal Baclofen in Spinal Spasticity: Frequency and Severity of Withdrawal Syndrome. *Pain Physician* **2015**, *18*, E633–E641. [CrossRef]
7. Taira, T.; Ueta, T.; Katayama, Y.; Kimizuka, M.; Nemoto, A.; Mizusawa, H.; Liu, M.; Koito, M.; Hiro, Y.; Tanabe, H. Rate of complications among the recipients of intrathecal baclofen pump in Japan: A multicenter study. *Neuromodulation* **2013**, *16*, 266–272. [CrossRef]
8. Omar, A.M. Is Intrathecal Baclofen Pump Safe as It Thought to Be? *J. Anest. Inten. Care Med.* **2018**, *7*, 555702.
9. Schiess, M.C.; Eldabe, S.; Konrad, P.; Molus, L.; Spencer, R.; Stromberg, K.; Weaver, T.; Plunkett, R. Intrathecal Baclofen for Severe Spasticity: Longitudinal Data from the Product Surveillance Registry. *Neuromodulation* **2020**, *23*, 996–1002. [CrossRef]
10. Goslinga-van der Gaag, S.M.E.; Delhaas, E.M.; Frankema, S.P.G.; Huygen, F.J.P.M. Efficiency and safety of aftercare with intrathecal baclofen on location. *Neuromodulation* **2019**, *22*, 828–833. [CrossRef]
11. Abou Al-Shaar, H.; Alkhani, A. Intrathecal baclofen therapy for spasticity: A compliance-based study to indicate effectiveness. *Surg. Neurol. Int.* **2016**, *7*, S539–S541. [PubMed]
12. General Authority of Statistics, Kingdom of Saudi Arabia. 2021. Available online: https://www.stats.gov.sa/en (accessed on 9 January 2023).
13. Ford, B.; Greene, P.; Louis, E.D.; Petzinger, G.; Bressman, S.B.; Goodman, R.; Brin, M.F.; Sadiq, S.; Fahn, S. Use of intrathecal baclofen in the treatment of patients with dystonia. *Arch. Neurol.* **1996**, *53*, 1241–1246. [CrossRef] [PubMed]
14. Gober, J.; Seymour, M.; Miao, H.; Curry, D.J.; Thomas, S.P. Management of severe spasticity with and without dystonia with intrathecal baclofen in the pediatric population: A cross-sectional study. *World J. Pediatr. Surg.* **2022**, *5*, e000407. [CrossRef] [PubMed]
15. Albright, A.L. Intrathecal baclofen in cerebral palsy movement disorders. *J. Child. Neurol.* **1996**, *11*, S29–S35. [CrossRef]
16. Blue, R.; Shah, P.; Spadola, M.; Lang, S.S.; Yoo, K.; Hampton, S.; Chen, H.I. Instituting an intrathecal baclofen pump program at an academic institution. *PM&R* **2022**, *14*, 395–402.
17. Narendran, R.C.; Duarte, R.V.; Valyi, A.; Eldabe, S. The need for and provision of intrathecal baclofen therapy for the management of spasticity in England: An assessment of the Hospital Episode Statistics database. *BMJ Open.* **2015**, *5*, e007517. [CrossRef]
18. Nuru, M.; Maglinger, B.; Vessell, M.; Simon, J.E.; Daniels, M.W.; Anderson, D.; Mutchnick, I. Infectious Complications and Operative Management of Intrathecal Baclofen Pumps in the Pediatric Population: A Systematic Review and Meta-Analysis of 20 Years of Pooled Experience. *World Neurosurg.* **2022**, *163*, e59–e72. [CrossRef]
19. Follett, K.A.; Burchiel, K.; Deer, T.; DuPen, S.; Prager, J.; Turner, M.S.; Coffey, R.J. Prevention of intrathecal drug delivery catheter-related complications. *Neuromodulation* **2003**, *6*, 32–41. [CrossRef]
20. Teddy, P.; Jamous, A.R.; Gardner, B.; Wang, D.; Silver, J. Complications of intrathecal baclofen delivery. *Br. J. Neurosurg.* **1992**, *6*, 115–118. [CrossRef]
21. Dvorak, E.M.; McGuire, J.R.; Nelson, M.E. Incidence and identification of intrathecal baclofen catheter malfunction. *PM&R* **2010**, *2*, 751–756.
22. Pucks-Faes, E.; Hitzenberger, G.; Matzak, H.; Fava, E.; Verrienti, G.; Laimer, I.; Fritz, J.; Saltuari, L. Eleven years' experience with Intrathecal Baclofen—Complications, risk factors. *Brain Behav.* **2018**, *8*, e00965. [CrossRef] [PubMed]
23. Miracle, A.C.; Fox, M.A.; Ayyangar, R.N.; Vyas, A.; Mukherji, S.K.; Quint, D.J. Imaging evaluation of intrathecal baclofen pump-catheter systems. *AJNR Am. J. Neuroradiol.* **2011**, *32*, 1158–1164. [CrossRef] [PubMed]
24. Boster, A.; Nicholas, J.; Bartoszek, M.P.; O'Connell, C.; Oluigbo, C. Managing loss of intrathecal baclofen efficacy: Review of the literature and proposed troubleshooting algorithm. *Neurol. Clin. Pract.* **2014**, *4*, 123–130. [CrossRef] [PubMed]
25. Ordia, J.; Vaisman, J. Managing loss of intrathecal baclofen efficacy: Review of the literature and proposed troubleshooting algorithm. *Neurol. Clin. Pract.* **2014**, *4*, 371–372. [CrossRef] [PubMed]
26. Vender, J.R.; Hester, S.; Waller, J.L.; Rekito, A.; Lee, M.R. Identification and management of intrathecal baclofen pump complications: A comparison of pediatric and adult patients. *J. Neurosurg.* **2006**, *104*, 9–15. [CrossRef] [PubMed]
27. Reis, P.V.; Vieira, C.R.; Midões, A.C.; Rebelo, V.; Barbosa, P.; Gomes, A. Intrathecal Baclofen Infusion Pumps in the Treatment of Spasticity: A Retrospective Cohort Study in a Portuguese Centre. *Acta Med. Port.* **2019**, *32*, 754–759. [CrossRef]
28. Saulino, M.; Anderson, D.J.; Doble, J.; Farid, R.; Gul, F.; Konrad, P.; Boster, A.L. Best Practices for Intrathecal Baclofen Therapy: Troubleshooting. *Neuromodulation* **2016**, *19*, 632–641. [CrossRef]
29. Watve, S.; Sivan, M.; Raza, W.A.; Jamil, F.F. Management of acute overdose or withdrawal state in intrathecal baclofen therapy. *Spinal Cord.* **2012**, *50*, 107–111. [CrossRef]
30. Penn, R.D.; York, M.M.; Paice, J.A. Catheter systems for intrathecal drug delivery. *J. Neurosurg.* **1995**, *83*, 215–217. [CrossRef]
31. Heetla, H.W.; Staal, M.J.; Kliphuis, C.; van Laar, T. The incidence and management of tolerance in intrathecal baclofen therapy. *Spinal Cord.* **2009**, *47*, 751–756. [CrossRef]
32. Spader, H.S.; Bollo, R.J.; Bowers, C.A.; Riva-Cambrin, J. Risk factors for baclofen pump infection in children: A multivariate analysis. *J. Neurosurg. Pediatr.* **2016**, *17*, 756–762. [CrossRef] [PubMed]
33. Ward, A.; Hayden, S.; Dexter, M.; Scheinberg, A. Continuous intrathecal baclofen for children with spasticity and/or dystonia: Goal attainment and complications associated with treatment. *J. Paediatr. Child Health* **2009**, *45*, 720–726. [CrossRef] [PubMed]

34. Varhabhatla, N.C.; Zuo, Z. Rising complication rates after intrathecal catheter and pump placement in the pediatric population: Analysis of national data between 1997 and 2006. *Pain Physician* **2012**, *15*, 65–74. [PubMed]
35. de Lissovoy, G.; Matza, L.S.; Green, H.; Werner, M.; Edgar, T. Cost-effectiveness of intrathecal baclofen therapy for the treatment of severe spasticity associated with cerebral palsy. *J. Child Neurol.* **2007**, *22*, 49–59. [CrossRef] [PubMed]
36. Bensmail, D.; Ward, A.B.; Wissel, J.; Motta, F.; Saltuari, L.; Lissens, J.; Cros, S.; Beresniak, A. Cost-effectiveness modeling of intrathecal baclofen therapy versus other interventions for disabling spasticity. *Neurorehabil. Neural. Repair.* **2009**, *23*, 546–552. [CrossRef]
37. Steinbok, P.; Daneshvar, H.; Evans, D.; Kestle, J.R. Cost analysis of continuous intrathecal baclofen versus selective functional posterior rhizotomy in the treatment of spastic quadriplegia associated with cerebral palsy. *Pediatr. Neurosurg.* **1995**, *22*, 255–264. [CrossRef]
38. Beersen, N.; Bart de Bruijn, J.H.; Dekkers, M.A.; Ten Have, P.; Hekster, G.B.; Redekop, W.K.; Spincemaille, G.H.; Theuvenet, P.J.; Berg, M.; Klazinga, N.S. Developing a national continuous quality improvement system for neuromodulation treatment in The Netherlands. *Jt. Comm. J. Qual. Saf.* **2004**, *30*, 310–321. [CrossRef]
39. Clinical Commissioning Policy: Intrathecal Baclofen (ITB). Available online: https://www.england.nhs.uk/wp-content/uploads/2013/04/d04-p-c.pdf (accessed on 9 January 2023).
40. National Intrathecal Baclofen Document Revised Consensus Guidelines for Intrathecal Baclofen Therapy. Available online: https://www.bhamcommunity.nhs.uk/EasysiteWeb/getresource.axd?AssetID=2341&type=full&servicetype=Attachment (accessed on 9 January 2023).

healthcare

MDPI

Article

# Feasibility of a Home-Based Mirror Therapy Program in Children with Unilateral Spastic Cerebral Palsy

Anna Ortega-Martínez [1,2], Rocío Palomo-Carrión [3,*], Carlos Varela-Ferro [2,*] and Maria Caritat Bagur-Calafat [1]

1 Physiotherapy Department, Universitat Internacional de Catalunya, 08017 Barcelona, Spain; aortegam@uic.es (A.O.-M.); cbagur@uic.es (M.C.B.-C.)
2 Physiotherapy Department, Fundació Aspace Catalunya, 08038 Barcelona, Spain
3 Physiotherapy Department, Universidad de Castilla-La Mancha, 45071 Toledo, Spain
* Correspondence: rocio.palomo@uclm.es (R.P.-C.); cvarela@aspace.cat (C.V.-F.)

**Abstract:** Children with Unilateral Spastic Cerebral Palsy (US CP) have motor and somatosensory impairments that affect one side of their body, impacting upper limb functioning. These impairments contribute negatively to children's bimanual performance and quality of life. Intensive home-based therapies have been developed and have demonstrated their feasibility for children with US CP and their parents, especially when therapies are designed with the proper coaching of families. Mirror Therapy (MT) is being studied to become an approachable intensive and home-based therapy suitable for children with US CP. The aim of this study is to analyze the feasibility of a five-week home-based program of MT for children with US CP that includes coaching by the therapist. Six children aged 8–12 years old performed the therapy for five days per week, 30 min per day. A minimum of 80% of compliance was required. The feasibility included compliance evaluations, total dosage, perceived difficulty of the exercises, and losses of follow-ups. All children completed the therapy and were included in the analysis. The total accomplishment was 86.47 ± 7.67. The perceived difficulty of the exercises ranged from 2.37 to 4.51 out of 10. In conclusion, a home-based program of Mirror Therapy is a safe, cost-efficient, and feasible therapy for children with US CP when the therapist is involved as a coach during the entire program.

**Keywords:** unilateral spastic cerebral palsy; mirror therapy; feasibility; home-based therapy; intensive therapy

**Citation:** Ortega-Martínez, A.; Palomo-Carrión, R.; Varela-Ferro, C.; Bagur-Calafat, M.C. Feasibility of a Home-Based Mirror Therapy Program in Children with Unilateral Spastic Cerebral Palsy. *Healthcare* **2023**, *11*, 1797. https://doi.org/10.3390/healthcare11121797

Academic Editor: Giorgio Scivoletto

Received: 30 April 2023
Revised: 5 June 2023
Accepted: 16 June 2023
Published: 19 June 2023



## 1. Introduction

Cerebral Palsy (CP) is defined as "a group of permanent disorders of the development of movement and posture, causing activity limitation, that are attributed to non-progressive disturbances that occurred in the developing fetal or infant brain" [1]. Depending on the location and the extent of the brain lesion, motor impairments affect different parts of the body [2].

Unilateral Spastic Cerebral Palsy (US CP) is the second most frequent type of Cerebral Palsy, representing approximately 30% of the total [2,3]. It is caused by a lesion that affects one brain hemisphere, conditioning functional impairments. Even though these impairments are mostly observed in the contralateral side of the body, affecting both the upper and the lower limbs, the ipsilateral side can also suffer some movement limitations [4,5].

The most affected upper limb (AUL) suffers from different impairments in the areas highlighted by the International Classification of Functioning, Disability, and Health: body functions and structures, activities, and participation [6].

Even though spasticity is the main characteristic, especially in flexor muscles, problems related to limitations in the range of movement and low muscle strength are also present. These structural impairments mostly affect the distal parts of the AUL [7]. The somatosensory function of the hand is also affected, but the exact extent of the problem remains unclear [7]. In different studies, the percentage of children with these impairments ranges from 50% to 86% [7–10].

Both motor and sensory impairments have been demonstrated to be partly responsible for the functional limitations of the AUL. The unimanual capacity of the AUL is determined by these functional limitations. Those may include poor grip strength and dexterity, decreased velocity, and others [9,11,12]. Kinematic abnormalities, including mirror movements and movement deviations, are usually observed, especially at the distal parts of the AUL [8,13–15]. Recent investigations suggest that a wide extent of the unimanual lack of movement control relapses in the presence of mirror movements, which may be related to the corticospinal tract reorganization [15,16].

A poorer unimanual capacity of the AUL is related to poorer bimanual performance of children with US CP. This relationship may explain the fact that children with US CP show low performance in the activities of daily living that require performance and coordination of both hands [17]. This finding is also correlated with the functional level in the Manual Ability Classification System (MACS) [7,13]. Usually, children with US CP are classified in the first three levels of MACS, mostly in level II [18].

Some therapies have been highly recommended to improve both unimanual capacity and bimanual performance in children with US CP, especially for those classified in MACS levels I and II. Nevertheless, although the combination of Constraint Induced Movement Therapy and bimanual training seems to be a suitable approach, different strategies and other approaches have also been used and have demonstrated their effectiveness [19–22].

Considering that intensity is an important predictor for the success of the treatment, it can be assumed that in the last two decades, the literature recommending intensive approaches for improving motor activities and function in children with CP has increased [21,22]. Intensity, meaning the duration of the intervention and the distribution of the total dosage of the targeted therapy, may play a key role in all these approaches. That fact is especially crucial when considering the best therapy and its suitability for responding to parents and children's goals [23].

Another key factor when considering the best approach is the setting of the therapy. A natural environment offers the possibility to increase the intensity and repetition, especially when compared to interventions completely set in a clinical environment [20].

In general, family-centered care is correlated with improvements in the well-being of children with disabilities and their families, as it enhances the participation of parents in the interventions and focuses on real context approaches [24]. Moreover, therapies performed at home with the supervision of parents have been demonstrated to increase the enjoyment and positivity of families about their children, as they are capable of experiencing the improvements in a real context [25].

However, families can sometimes find it difficult to follow home-based programs. The most identified difficulties are related to the insights of the home-based approach, as fitting the therapy into the daily routines may become an issue. This difficulty increases when the designed program is too demanding or requires many hours of therapy. Other difficulties have been described, for example, when the therapies are extremely difficult for children and require working memory. In these cases, parents can feel overwhelmed trying to make their children follow them [25].

Some strategies may help to improve and facilitate the adaptation to follow a home-based intervention [25]. Among them, coaching models are recommended. In these models, the communication between therapists and families forms the basis of the clinical approach [24,25]. Tele-rehabilitation and video monitoring have recently been incorporated to improve the participation and achievement of goals in home-based therapies [26]. Thus, designing proper coaching strategies may be crucial to ensure high compliance in any home-based intervention. This design should also consider the type of coaching and its frequency to avoid burning out families. When parents act as either the providers or the supervisors for the therapies, compliance with the treatment is high [25].

Different home-based approaches for children with US CP have demonstrated their feasibility in terms of acceptability and safety [20,26–29].

Studies analyzing the effectiveness of Mirror Therapy (MT) have recently emerged. MT is a non-invasive therapy that consists of placing a mirror in the sagittal plane of a patient suffering from a unilateral condition affecting upper or lower limbs in such a manner that the view of the non-affected limb is superimposed on the image of the affected limb. This positioning results in an illusion of the movement of the affected limb [30].

In the last decade, research on MT for children with US CP has increased. The specific neurological mechanisms that underlie the effects of the mirror illusion in children with US CP remain unclear. Nevertheless, MT has been proven to be capable of increasing the excitability of the primary motor cortex of the brain hemisphere related to the AUL, especially when a bimanual task is performed [31,32].

MT has been studied as part of the therapeutic approach for children with US CP alone or combined with other interventions. Some of the benefits shown in different studies include the improvement of pinch and grasp strength [33,34], dexterity [35], upper limb function [33,36], gross motor skills [37], bimanual skills [36,38], and activity performance [38], but to a limited extent. The repercussion of MT on other aspects defined by ICF-CY as quality of life still remains uncertain. [34,38–41].

From the different studies about MT, discrepancies can be found in the application, such as intensity, dosage, and the setting of the therapy. Some authors have studied MT or mirror conditions in a clinical environment [35,37,38,40,41]. Nevertheless, it is a suitable therapy to be performed at home [33,36,39] as it is a cost-efficient, easy, and approachable therapy. Thus, although there is some evidence supporting the benefits of this therapeutic approach, more research is needed to compare its effectiveness to other therapies that are currently strongly recommended. Moreover, identifying the main requirements for its implementation and a protocolization of the intervention is essential in order to recommend the implementation of MT in therapeutic strategies for children with US CP [21,22,29,34,42,43].

This study aims to evaluate the feasibility and effectiveness of a five-week home-based Mirror Therapy (MT) program for children with Unilateral Spastic Cerebral Palsy. Specifically, we aim to determine the necessary compliance and total dosage of the MT home-based therapy, assess the perceived difficulty of the exercises, analyze potential learning effects, and gauge overall program accomplishment.

## 2. Materials and Methods

### 2.1. Study Design

This is a feasibility study and includes the feasibility analysis of a group of children performing a five-week home-based Mirror Therapy program. This analysis is prior to a full single-blinded Randomized Clinical Trial (RCT) (NCT05244083). The RCT has been approved by the Ethics Committee of FIDMAG Germanes Hospitalàries (PR-2021-18) and the Ethics Committee of the International University of Catalonia (FIS-2021-07).

This study has followed the recommendations of the CONSORT 2010 statement for randomized pilot and feasibility trials [44,45].

### 2.2. Participants

The participants included six children between 8 and 12 years old diagnosed with Unilateral Spastic Cerebral Palsy and classified in levels I and II in MACS. The exclusion criteria were (a) botulinum toxin injections and/or extracorporeal shock waves applied in the affected upper limb in less than three months prior to enrollment; (b) surgeries in the affected upper limb six months prior to enrollment; (c) performing any intensive therapy for the affected upper limb; (d) moderate and severe intellectual disabilities; (e) existing comorbidities affecting attention or behavior; (f) non-corrected visual impairments; and (g) non-controlled epilepsies.

Two more exclusion criteria were applied for the families: at least one of the parents should be capable of answering questionnaires in Spanish, and they should have a table and a chair at home to perform the therapy.

All the participants were recruited from Fundació Aspace Catalunya (Barcelona, Spain) between January and September 2022. Once they were identified as potential participants who met the eligibility criteria, the principal investigator (A.O.-M.) sent an email inviting them to participate. Those who showed interest in participating were contacted by phone to set the training day. Previously to the training, informed consent was obtained from the parents of the participants.

### 2.3. Sample Size

As this was a feasibility study, a formal sample size calculation was not required [44]. Nevertheless, we aimed to recruit 20% of the total sample size of the RCT ($n$ = 22). Finally, a total of six children were included in this feasibility study, representing 27.27% of the RCT sample size.

### 2.4. Intervention

The intervention consisted of a home-based program of Mirror Therapy that was designed to be performed for five weeks, five days a week, 30 min a day. A 5-min rest could be done in the middle of the therapy. All exercises were designed to be performed by the children themselves, while parents were involved in the supervision and maintenance of the concentration of their children. The MT program included four bimanual exercises (forearm pronosupination, sponge squeezing, finger-by-finger modeling clay pressing, and clockwise and anti-clockwise wrist spins), following exercises recommended by other authors [33,35,38,39,46] (see Figure 1). When doing the therapy, children were asked to insert the affected upper limb in a Mirror Box [47] (available from: www.noigroup.com, accessed on 1 January 2022) that was placed at their sagittal plane. All the exercises had to be done bimanually and symmetrically, highlighting the intention to move the AUL over the quality of the movement of the hand.

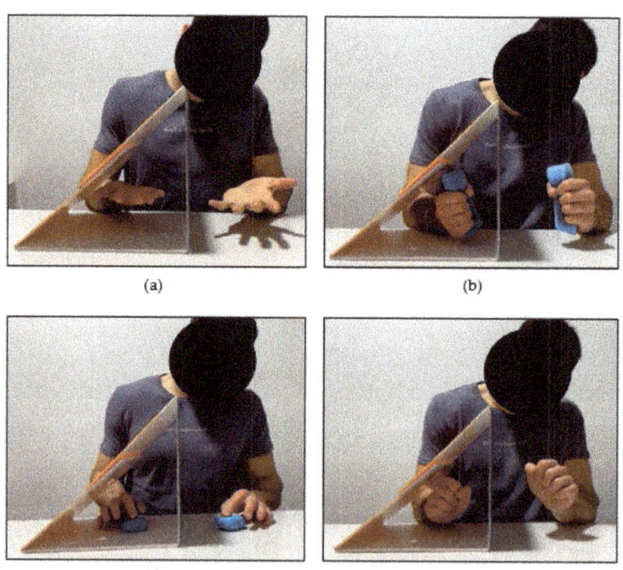

**Figure 1.** Mirror Therapy exercises. (**a**) Forearm pronosupination; (**b**) sponge squeezing; (**c**) finger-by-finger modeling clay pressing; (**d**) clockwise and anti-clockwise wrist spins.

In order to increase motivation, children were told to do at least two of the four exercises suggested each day, letting them choose which exercises they wanted to practice and their order. Families were not told when they should do the therapy to increase the adaptability for the intervention at home. A minimum of 80% compliance with the total dosage (600 out of the total 750 min) was required.

The material needed for the MT intervention was provided to all the families. It included a Mirror Box [47], two cubes of modelling clay, and two sponges. The total cost of the material was lower than 70 € per child. Thus, the study created no cost for the families.

### 2.5. Follow-Up and Monitoring

Regarding the follow-up to the home-based intervention, a mobile health application was used. Each family was logged into the app, where they could find a video of each of the exercises. Every day, families were told to mark which exercises they performed, the exact amount of time they spent doing the exercises, and the child's perceived difficulty performing the exercises. Nevertheless, in order to avoid difficulties with the usage of the app, a registration form was also given to all the families, allowing them to write down the same information that was requested in the app. A printed version of the explanation of the exercises was also given, replacing the videos in the app.

Moreover, the principal investigator (A.O.-M.) set up a weekly video call with each family to encourage and help them. When the video call could not be made, families were asked to send videos to the principal investigator doing the therapy.

A training day was scheduled before the beginning of the intervention in which both the child and the family were instructed by the principal investigator about the procedure of the intervention and the functioning of the app.

### 2.6. Variables and Measurement Instruments

During the entire duration of the study, three evaluations were established: at baseline, at the end of the intervention, and at the one-month follow-up. In these, the bimanual performance, the somatosensory function of the affected upper limb, and quality of life were assessed.

First, bimanual performance was assessed with the Children's Hand-use Experience Questionnaire 2.0 (CHEQ 2.0) [48–50]. The CHEQ 2.0 is a valid and reliable questionnaire designed to assess the quality of the bimanual performance of children with Unilateral Cerebral Palsy from 6 to 18 years old. The Spanish version was used for this study available online (www.cheq.se, accessed on 1 January 2022). It analyzes grasp efficacy, the time taken, and the discomfort that children and/or parents perceive when performing 27 different daily activities, rating on a four-category scale. Then, the score was transferred to a 0–100 scale. CHEQ 2.0 can be answered by children or by parents. Nevertheless, the recommendation for children under 12 years old is for it to be answered by children helped by parents or only by parents as a proxy [49,50]. In this study, parents were the responders to the CHEQ 2.0.

Second, the somatosensory function assessment was performed according to six tests described and recommended by Auld et al. [51,52]. The assessment was done by a physiotherapist. A newly calibrated 20-item Semmes Weinstein Monofilaments (SWM) was used to test tactile registration [53], as well as for the single-point localization (SPL) and the double simultaneous (DS). The two-point discrimination tests, both static (s2PD) and moving (m2PD), were performed using a Disk-Criminator [54]. Of all these tests, SWM, s2PD, m2PD, and SPL are considered the most reliable in terms of detecting changes over time [51]. Finally, stereognosis was assessed with nine common objects [51,52]. The procedure of these tests can be found in the study of Auld et al. [51,52].

Third, quality of life was assessed with the Spanish version of Child and Parent Reports of the Pediatric Inventory of Quality of Life for Cerebral Palsy (PedsQL 3.0 ™), Cerebral Palsy module for children aged 8–12 [55]. PedsQL™ are valid and reliable questionnaires to assess the quality of life of children with Cerebral Palsy. For the range of age to which this study was addressed, the tool offers two questionnaires to be answered by the children and by the parents, respectively. Both are five-point Likert scale questionnaires that include 35 items regarding the areas of daily activities, school activities, movement and balance, pain and hurt, fatigue, eating activities, and speech and communication. After completing the questionnaires, the obtained score is transferred to a 0–100 point scale [55].

Due to the structure of the evaluations, the evaluator could only be blinded for the somatosensory function assessment. C.V-F acted as the blinded evaluator.

Apart from these assessments, age, sex, MACS level, and impaired side were recorded for all participants at the baseline evaluation.

### *2.7. Feasibility Evaluation*

To evaluate the feasibility of the MT program, data regarding compliance, total dosage, perceived difficulty of the exercises, and accomplishment of the follow-up and evaluations were recorded. The appearance of side effects or contraindications was also recorded.

Regarding the recording of compliance with the intervention, as previously stated, the application allowed families and children to use a chronometer to quantify the total daily amount of time for the duration of the intervention. Therefore, the recording of the completed time was performed automatically. In addition, the application also allowed reporting of the exercises performed each day, as well as their perceived difficulty, through a very simple visual scale. It was rated from 0 (no perceived difficulty) to 10 (extremely difficult).

Finally, the accomplishment of the follow-ups was recorded weekly by the principal investigator in an Excel form. The completed evaluations were recorded using the same strategy.

Regarding the side effects or contraindications, all families were asked to document any problem detected during the entire intervention.

### *2.8. Statistical Analysis*

For the analysis of the feasibility outcomes, descriptive statistics were used to show general characteristics, with means (standard deviation) for quantitative data and percentages for qualitative data.

Statistical analysis was only performed for the perceived difficulty outcome. In this, the Kolmogorov-Smirnov test was used to test normality. The Mann-Whitney U test was used to analyze intra-group effect differences. The significance level was set at $\alpha = 0.05$. All analyses were performed by using the v.29 SPSS software package.

Due to the nature of this feasibility study, it was decided not to perform an effectiveness analysis on the bimanual performance, somatosensory function, and quality of life data. The same reasoning was used to decide not to perform statistical analysis regarding other relationships between age, sex, MACS level, impaired side, and feasibility outcomes [44].

## 3. Results

### *3.1. Participants*

Six participants were included in this feasibility study. The mean age was $10.37 \pm 2.05$. Table 1 shows the main characteristics of the whole group.

**Table 1.** Characteristics of the MT group.

| Participants Characteristics | MT Group (*n* = 6) | |
|---|---|---|
| | n | % |
| **Sex** | | |
| Male | 2 | 33.3 |
| Female | 4 | 66.7 |
| **MACS [1] level** | | |
| I | 3 | 50.0 |
| II | 3 | 50.0 |
| **Affected Side** | | |
| Left | 1 | 16.7 |
| Right | 5 | 83.3 |

[1] MACS: Manual Ability Classification System.

### 3.2. Compliance and Total Dosage

All the participants acquired the minimum compliance required (80% of the total therapy), ranging from 80.0% to 96.0%. The mean percentage of compliance was 86.47 ± 7.67. When considering the total minutes of therapy performed, the mean was 648.55 ± 57.55. Table 2 shows the total minutes of MT performed by each child, and Figure 1 shows individual compliance.

**Table 2.** Compliance and total dosage of MT.

| Participant | Total Minutes of MT |
|---|---|
| 1 | 600.0 |
| 2 | 651.0 |
| 3 | 717.0 |
| 4 | 720.0 |
| 5 | 603.3 |
| 6 | 600.0 |

### 3.3. Perceived Difficulty of the Exercises

The data extraction of the perceived difficulty of the exercises was performed considering $n = 5$ because one child participant did not complete this recording. This child was given a paper form registration for recording the therapy, as the family had problems with using the app. She did not record the difficulty due to the fact that she did not have the visual scale.

All the children rated the four included exercises in the MT program (forearm pronosupination, sponge squeezing, finger-by-finger modeling clay pressing, and clockwise and anti-clockwise wrist spins) below 8 when scoring their perceived difficulty. The forearm pronosupination and the sponge squeezing exercises were considered the easiest, with a weekly individual mean ranging from 2.37 to 3.17 and from 2.56 to 3.19, respectively.

No differences in the perceived difficulty were shown regarding age, sex, or MACS level of the participants ($p > 0.05$).

Table 3 shows the weekly mean (standard deviation) of the perceived difficulty of all exercises. No statistical differences were shown when comparing the evolution of the perceived difficulty of any exercise. These results may be affected by the loss of the complete registration of one child.

**Table 3.** Weekly perceived difficulty.

| Data ($n$ = 5) | Forearm Pronosupination | Sponge Squeezing | Finger-by-Finger Pressing | Wrist Spins |
|---|---|---|---|---|
| Week 1 | 3.17 (2.51) | 2.91 (1.44) | 4.41 (2.49) | 4.51 (1.81) |
| Week 2 | 2.38 (2.23) | 3.19 (2.24) | 4.46 (2.57) | 4.32 (1.62) |
| Week 3 | 2.55 (2.32) | 2.56 (2.38) | 3.66 (2.59) | 3.80 (1.41) |
| Week 4 | 2.37 (2.15) | 2.82 (1.91) | 3.23 (2.04) | 4.07 (1.71) |
| Week 5 | 2.60 (2.71) | 2.68 (1.90) | 2.94 (2.04) | 3.91 (1.98) |
| Differences between Week 1 and Week 5 ($p$-value) | 0.345 | 0.715 | 0.225 | 0.068 |

### 3.4. Losses of Follow-Ups and Evaluations

There was no loss of follow-ups in this study. All six children completed the entire therapy. Only one participant needed the paper form registration, as the family had difficulties with the app functioning. Although one child did not use the app, all six children recorded the daily therapy. The six families were available weekly either for a video call with A.O-M or to send videos performing the therapy.

All evaluations were completed at baseline and at the end of the intervention. Only one child did not entirely complete the PedsQL 3.0 ™ at the one-month follow-up evaluation.

### 3.5. *Adverse Events or Contraindications*

No adverse events or contraindications were observed. Families reported some fatigue only in the last minutes of the therapy, but this cannot be considered as an adverse event.

## 4. Discussion

This study aimed to analyze the feasibility of a home-based program of Mirror Therapy designed for improving motor and somatosensory impairments, as well as the quality of life of children with Unilateral Spastic Cerebral Palsy. Concretely, this study analyzes the compliance, the total dosage, the children's perceived difficulty with the included exercises, and losses of follow-ups and evaluations.

Completing this feasibility study, previous to an RCT, has demonstrated that a five-week home-based program of MT is feasible for children with US CP and their families, as a high compliance rate and total dosages have been shown. Moreover, it has been stated that the included exercises were not considered to be very difficult, nor were they too easy. Last, this home-based MT program proved its feasibility, as there were no follow-ups were lost.

Other authors have previously studied MT in the same population. Bruchez et al. [39], designed a home-based protocol that included seven exercises comprising symmetrical movements of both distal and proximal parts of the upper limbs (finger-by-finger modeling clay pressing, thumb-index pinch-extension, palmar squeezing, wrist rotations, pronation and supination of the forearms, shoulder antepulsion and retropulsion, and shoulder abduction and adduction). Narimani et al. [35] designed a six-week clinical-based program of MT that included flexion and extension of the fingers and wrists, supination and pronation, and functional movements. The pilot study of Gygax et al. [33] described an MT intervention of three weeks that included three bilateral exercises (two regarding thumb-finger pinch and one of forearm pronosupination). Kara et al. [38], proposed a combination of MT and upper limb strength and power exercises. The MT was performed by doing four exercises (two of thumb-finger pinch, one of grasping a ball, and one of forearm pronosupination) for 30 min, 3 days a week, for 12 weeks. Auld et al. [40] designed an MT intervention that combined motor and tactile exercises, during 1.5 h in two sessions. Farzamfar et al. [37] included several exercises that involved the whole upper limb. Palomo-Carrión et al. [36] designed a four-week intervention with MT combined with Action-Observation Therapy. In this last study, MT was performed for 15 min per day and included six exercises.

In our study, the intervention was designed to comprise 750 min of MT distributed for 30 min daily for five weeks. This routine is consistent with other studies implementing MT where the designed total dosage ranged between 94 and 1080 min [33,35–40]. The distribution of the therapy is not inconsistent among studies. While other studies distributed the therapy between 2 days and 12 weeks, our study designed a five-week therapy. Moreover, the duration of the sessions varied between 15 min and 90 min [33,35–40]. Nevertheless, a duration of 30 min for each session, as our study proposed, was the most designed intervention [35,37,38]. A systematic review showed that different home-based programs for children with US CP lasted between two weeks and six months, with an intensity between 70 min and 56 h a week [25]. In these terms, our study was designed like these recommendations with regard to the total dosage and the distribution of the therapy. A five-week duration was the minimum duration for an intensive program for Myrhaug et al. [20]. This study also accomplished that specification, as all children completed the five-week program. For Beckers et al. [56], a duration of 12 weeks was considered too difficult for families and children.

Compliance of more than 85% was shown in this study. This result agrees with other studies analyzing the feasibility of different home-based programs, where compliance from 56% to 99% was shown [25,36,57,58]. The compliance in an MT intervention was only reported by Palomo-Carrión et al. [36], where 96% of the total dosage of the intervention was completed by all participants.

Our high compliance rates could be explained by many factors. First of all, the fact that parents acted as providers of the therapy could engage families to participate and continue until the end of the intervention. It has been stated that home-based therapies provided by parents are the most common home-based approach, as it increases confidence and satisfaction of families with the therapies without giving a therapist role to parents [24,25,56,59]. The family-provider approach has been studied and recommended as a key aspect of treating children with CP. Nevertheless, there is a lack of consensus in some terms regarding the relationship between the therapist and the family [24]. Although having coaching parents who act as providers of the therapy seems to be an important factor that may influence participation and compliance, most of the studies do not provide or report it specifically. Considering different studies that showed results of a home-based MT intervention, only those by Bruchez et al. [39] and Palomo-Carrión et al. [36] were provided by parents and coached by the therapist. Bruchez et al. [39] gave a DVD with instructions and the training regimen to the families, as well as the contact of the coordinator. In the same way, the families of the study by Palomo et al. [36] received a weekly online follow-up. Gygax et al. [33] also proposed a home-based intervention, but no coaching was described. Finally, the study from Auld et al. [40] varied from others, as the home-based intervention was provided by the therapist. None of these studies reported a rate of compliance, although we could expect high compliance in the study of Auld et al. [40], as it was therapist-delivered. Other studies with different home-based interventions used other ways to coach families. Some of them used webcam-monitoring during the performance of the intervention [60], while others maintained weekly phone calls and home visits [27,28].

In order to give complete coaching, an online follow-up with an app (that contained specific videos of each of the exercises), a weekly video call, and/or sending videos were required in this study. This coaching approach is similar to that used by Beckers et al. [56], where parents were asked to record the daily intervention and to send a video every week. Moreover, they utilized more strategies to resolve issues during the implementation of the home-based program, including home visits. Telemedicine has experienced an exponential increase since the COVID-19 pandemic. It has demonstrated that it can be an opportunity for reducing travels to clinics, and maintaining continuity and accessibility of treatments for children with CP [61]. The systematic review from Beckers et al. [25] described these strategies and others to coach families involved in home-based programs. Finding a balance between sufficient and excessive coaching for families involved in home-based therapy seems to be crucial. Parents sometimes reported the coaching received to be useful and valuable for them during the entire intervention, but having too much follow-up (e.g., too many phone calls or home visits) can put extra pressure on families [56].

When designing our therapeutic approach, we tried to include all these main ingredients to ensure good coaching during the five-week program, as we included the direct coaching of the therapist with online video calls and the video instructions of the therapy in the app. Moreover, we instructed the families to perform the intervention when they considered that it best fit their daily routine. All these factors may have been crucial for the great compliance and total dosage rates.

Other strategies for improving the preparation and confidence of the families included training sessions. In this study, a training session was set with every family in order to explain the therapy and the functioning of the app. Other authors have also implemented this strategy [57]. Apart from the training day and the video calls, all families could perform the entire intervention without reporting difficulties or the need for extra coaching.

Another remarkable strategy that we believe increased compliance and motivation of children was that we let them choose which exercises they wanted to practice every day. Other studies, like those by Bruchez et al. [39], Narimani et al. [35], and Kara et al. [38], described concrete protocols for intervention, where the number of repetitions and the order of the exercises were determined by the therapist or the coordinator. A different approach was utilized by Auld et al. [40] where motor and tactile exercises were included. They distributed a total amount of time for each stimulation but did not describe a specific order for the motor exercises. Other authors did not describe the distribution of the exercises during the intervention [33,37,46]. Engaging and motivating children seems to be a key factor when considering the benefits and the achievement of outcomes in family-centered approaches; it also may be increased when both children and parents are active subjects in the decision-making process of the intervention [24,56]. To our knowledge, this is the first MT program that allows children to choose the exercises performed in order to increase motivation. For us, this may be one of the reasons for having obtained no losses of follow-ups during the entire intervention, as well as at the last evaluation.

In this study, children were required to score the perceived difficulty of the exercises performed daily. Even though one child did not complete the difficulty assessment, we found that none of the exercises were considered very difficult, as all children scored them below 8. Gygax et al. [33] reported that half of the children reported difficulty maintaining concentration during the entire intervention but did not specifically find a correlation with a difficulty with the exercises. Palomo-Carrión et al. [36] reported that one family had trouble with the intervention. In our study, we decided not to increase the difficulty of the exercises, as MT itself can sometimes become quite difficult to perform or require children to focus on the performing. Other authors also decided not to increase the difficulty nor to change the exercises during the entire intervention [33,35,37,39,40,46]. Contrarily, Kara, et al. [38] reported an increase in the number of repetitions of the exercises and the level of difficulty when children were more capable of performing the exercises. Our results suggest that the difficulty of the exercises does not necessarily have to be increased, as we found no statistical differences in children's perceived difficulty. Thus, children performing MT find the same difficulty in the exercises during the entire intervention, meaning that the exercises do not grow easier. As far as we are concerned, this is the first study of MT in children with US CP that includes the assessment of the perceived difficulty of the exercises. Our results in this area may also explain the fact that children did not fail to accomplish the entire intervention, as they did not find it too difficult or frustrating.

In terms of the acceptability of the intervention, all families accomplished these requirements and completed the registration every day. Only one family had difficulties with the usage of the app, so they were given a paper form for registration and a paper copy of the exercises.

Moreover, all families could perform the entire intervention with the initial kit of material they were given during the training day. Thus, participation in the study cost the families nothing. The total cost of the intervention was lower than 70 euros per child, meaning that the MT intervention was cost-efficient. A recent study in the Spanish population showed that children with CP attend around 22 consultations per year at the health services, with 14.6% of those in rehabilitation care [62]. Moreover, it is important to consider that the individual average cost of home-based care in children with CP is considerably lower than center-based care [63]. Family-centered care is still an approach that needs to be implemented more in healthcare services and requires further investment from different institutions. The low cost of the implementation of these therapies, considering the reduction of total costs and displacements, could be important arguments in favor of implementing them for both the healthcare providers and accessibility for all families [24,64].

None of the families reported any adverse events. During the video calls, some families only reported some fatigue in children when performing the therapy. Other studies also found no adverse events in MT or home-based programs for children with US CP [28,36,38].

All children included in this study completed the entire intervention. Thus, we obtained no losses of follow-ups. Nevertheless, one child did not fully complete one questionnaire for the last evaluation. Therefore, it was excluded. In other studies of MT, losses of follow-ups were related to failures in the execution of the intervention or evaluations [36,39], lack of cooperation of the children, or difficulties with transportation when the therapy was not set at home [38]. Our results align with those of other studies that did not report losses of follow-ups [33,35,37,40]. However, only one of the last studies was set at home, with parents delivering the intervention [33]. Comparing our results with other studies with the same population, other difficulties were described regarding the personal issues of the families [56].

This study has some limitations. First, a limitation has been identified regarding the nature of the MT. This therapy needs children to concentrate and focus on the mirror. Gygax et al. [33] reported this as an issue for their pilot study. However, we planned different strategies to enhance engagement, including the mobile health application following. As the mean compliance was high and all the participants acquired the minimum required, we could assume that this issue was not sufficiently remarkable to withdraw the study.

Another limitation has been identified regarding the recording of the difficulty of the exercises, as one child did not complete it. Even though the app functioned easily, using technologies may be difficult for some families. Given that we consider the app useful for most families, a more complete and detailed training session could be performed to avoid difficulties in this area.

To our knowledge, this is the first study to analyze the feasibility of a home-based MT program that includes specific and structured coaching for parents and evaluates the difficulty that children perceive of the therapy.

Proving the feasibility of this home-based program highlights the importance of implementing family-friendly therapies suitable to perform in a home-based context, facilitating its fitting into the daily routines of the families. The success of home-based therapies relapses partly in the support and coaching that families receive. Our results also highlight the importance of coaching parents during the entire intervention as they become providers.

Further studies comparing different coaching approaches for families and the suitability of this coaching in home-based therapies are needed to define an optimum follow-up for them.

Further research on MT is still needed in order to identify its effectiveness, as it has already demonstrated its safety, cost-efficiency, and feasibility when provided in a home setting with the coaching of the therapist.

Given the results of this study, we consider that the designed five-week home-based MT program has proved its feasibility. For this reason, we expect promising results in further RCT, where we will be able to analyze the effectiveness of this therapy in bimanual performance, somatosensory function, and quality of life of children with US CP.

## 5. Conclusions

A five-week home-based Mirror Therapy program is a feasible intervention for children with Unilateral Spastic Cerebral Palsy, demonstrating high compliance rates and no losses of follow-ups. Factors such as encouraging and coaching families during the entire home-based therapy may be crucial for maintaining and increasing motivation and obtaining high rates of compliance.

Designing comprehensive interventions that allow families to fit the therapies into their daily routines ease the follow-up of these type of approaches.

More research is needed to determine the effectiveness of Mirror Therapy in children with US CP to indicate its suitability in the therapeutic opportunities of these children.

**Author Contributions:** Conceptualization, A.O.-M., M.C.B.-C., R.P.-C. and C.V.-F.; methodology, A.O.-M., M.C.B.-C. and R.P.-C.; software, A.O.-M.; validation, A.O.-M., M.C.B.-C., R.P.-C. and C.V.-F.; formal analysis, A.O.-M., M.C.B.-C., R.P.-C. and C.V-F; investigation, A.O.-M. and C.V.-F.; resources, A.O.-M., M.C.B.-C., R.P.-C. and C.V.-F.; data curation, A.O.-M.; writing—original draft preparation, A.O.-M.; writing—review and editing, A.O.-M., M.C.B.-C., R.P.-C. and C.V.-F.; visualization, A.O.-M.; supervision, M.C.B.-C. and R.P.-C.; project administration, M.C.B.-C. and R.P.-C.; funding acquisition, A.O.-M., M.C.B.-C., R.P.-C. and C.V.-F. All authors have read and agreed to the published version of the manuscript.

**Funding:** This research was funded by the X Award for Research of the Societat Catalano-Balear de Fisioteràpia.

**Institutional Review Board Statement:** The study was conducted in accordance with the Declaration of Helsinki and approved by the Ethics Committee of FIDMAG Germanes Hospitalàries (PR-2021-18) and the Ethics Committee of the International University of Catalonia (FIS-2021-07).

**Informed Consent Statement:** Informed consent was obtained from all subjects involved in the study.

**Data Availability Statement:** Not applicable.

**Acknowledgments:** We acknowledge the support of Fundació Aspace Catalunya for their administrative and technical support in this study. We also acknowledge Societat Catalano-Balear de Fisioteràpia for having awarded this project and Universitat International de Catalunya for making available the material needed to complete this study.

**Conflicts of Interest:** The authors declare no conflict of interest. The funders had no role in the design of the study; in the collection, analyses, or interpretation of data; in the writing of the manuscript; or in the decision to publish the results.

## References

1. Rosenbaum, P.; Baxter, P.; Morris, C.; Paneth, N.; Leviton, A.; Goldstein, M.; Bax, M.; Colver, A.; Damiano, D.; Graham, H.K.; et al. The Definition and Classification of Cerebral Palsy Contents Foreword Historical Perspective Definition and Classification Document. *Dev. Med. Child Neurol.* **2007**, *48*, 1–44. [CrossRef]
2. Wimalasundera, N.; Stevenson, V.L. Cerebral palsy. *Pract. Neurol.* **2016**, *16*, 184–194. [CrossRef] [PubMed]
3. National Institute for Health and Care Excellence. *Cerebral Palsy in under 25s: Assessment and Management*; National Institute for Health and Care Excellence: London, UK, 2017; Volume 47.
4. Waikato District Health Board. *Cerebral Palsy Clinical Practice Guideline*; Waikato District Health Board: Hamilton, New Zealand, 2014.
5. Souto, D.O.; Cruz, T.K.F.; Fontes, P.L.B.; Moeller, K.; Haase, V.G. Neuromotor examination in unilateral cerebral palsy: Bilateral impairments in different levels of motor integration. *Appl. Neuropsychol. Child* **2022**, *11*, 658–668. [CrossRef]
6. World Health Organization. *International Classification of Functioning, Disability, and Health: Children & Youth Version: ICF-CY*; World Health Organization: Geneve, Switzerland, 2017; Volume 91, pp. 399–404.
7. Klingels, K.; Demeyere, I.; Jaspers, E.; De Cock, P.; Molenaers, G.; Boyd, R.; Feys, H. Upper limb impairments and their impact on activity measures in children with unilateral cerebral palsy. *Eur. J. Paediatr. Neurol.* **2012**, *16*, 475–484. [CrossRef]
8. Chaleat-Valayer, E.; Bard-Pondarre, R.; Ganne, C.; Roumenoff, F.; Combey, A.; Bernard, J.C. Relation between unimanual capacities and bimanual performance in hemiplegic cerebral-palsied children: Impact of synkinesis. *Eur. J. Paediatr. Neurol.* **2015**, *19*, 193–201. [CrossRef] [PubMed]
9. Sakzewski, L.; Ziviani, J.; Boyd, R.N. The relationship between unimanual capacity and bimanual performance in children with congenital hemiplegia. *Dev. Med. Child Neurol.* **2010**, *52*, 811–816. [CrossRef]
10. Auld, M.L.; Boyd, R.N.; Moseley, G.L.; Ware, R.S.; Johnston, L.M. Tactile function in children with unilateral cerebral palsy compared to typically developing children. *Disabil. Rehabil.* **2012**, *34*, 1488–1494. [CrossRef]
11. Auld, M.L.; Boyd, R.N.; Moseley, G.L.; Ware, R.S.; Johnston, L.M. Impact of tactile dysfunction on upper-limb motor performance in children with unilateral cerebral palsy. *Arch. Phys. Med. Rehabil.* **2012**, *93*, 696–702. [CrossRef]
12. Arnould, C.; Bleyenheuft, Y.; Thonnard, J.L. Hand functioning in children with cerebral palsy. *Front. Neurol.* **2014**, *5*, 48. [CrossRef]
13. Gaillard, F.; Cretual, A.; Cordillet, S.; Le Cornec, C.; Gonthier, C.; Bouvier, B.; Heyman, R.; Marleix, S.; Bonan, I.; Rauscent, H. Kinematic motion abnormalities and bimanual performance in children with unilateral cerebral palsy. *Dev. Med. Child Neurol.* **2018**, *60*, 839–845. [CrossRef]
14. Cacioppo, M.; Lempereur, M.; Marin, A.; Rauscent, H.; Créutal, A.; Brochard, S.; Bonan, I. Motor patterns of the impaired upper limb in children with unilateral cerebral palsy performing bimanual tasks. *Clin. Biomech.* **2022**, *97*, 105710. [CrossRef] [PubMed]
15. Sukal-Moulton, T.; Gaebler-Spira, D.; Krosschell, K.J. Clinical Characteristics Associated with Reduced Selective Voluntary Motor Control in the Upper Extremity of Individuals with Spastic Cerebral Palsy. *Dev. Neurorehabil.* **2021**, *24*, 215–221. [CrossRef] [PubMed]
16. Nardone, R.; Sebastianelli, L.; Ferrazzoli, D.; Brigo, F.; Lochner, P.; Saltuari, L.; Trinka, E.; Versace, V. Brain functional reorganization in children with hemiplegic cerebral palsy: Assessment with TMS and therapeutic perspectives. *Neurophysiol. Clin.* **2021**, *51*, 391–408. [CrossRef] [PubMed]
17. James, S.; Ziviani, J.; Ware, R.S.; Boyd, R.N. Relationships between activities of daily living, upper limb function, and visual perception in children and adolescents with unilateral cerebral palsy. *Dev. Med. Child Neurol.* **2015**, *57*, 852–857. [CrossRef]
18. Park, E.S.; Rha, D.W.; Park, J.H.; Park, D.H.; Sim, E.G. Relation among the gross motor function, manual performance and upper limb functional measures in children with spastic cerebral palsy. *Yonsei Med. J.* **2013**, *54*, 516–522. [CrossRef]
19. Klevberg, G.L.; Østensjø, S.; Elkjær, S.; Kjeken, I.; Jahnsen, R.B. Hand Function in Young Children with Cerebral Palsy: Current Practice and Parent-Reported Benefits. *Phys. Occup. Ther. Pediatr.* **2017**, *37*, 222–237. [CrossRef]
20. Myrhaug, H.T.; ØstensjØ, S.; Larun, L.; Odgaard-Jensen, J.; Jahnsen, R.B. Intensive training of motor function and functional skills among young children with cerebral palsy: A systematic review and meta-analysis. *BMC Pediatr.* **2014**, *14*, 292. [CrossRef]
21. Novak, I.; Morgan, C.; Fahey, M.; Finch-Edmondson, M.; Galea, C.; Hines, A.; Langdon, K.; Namara, M.M.; Paton, M.C.; Popat, H.; et al. State of the Evidence Traffic Lights 2019: Systematic Review of Interventions for Preventing and Treating Children with Cerebral Palsy. *Curr. Neurol. Neurosci. Rep.* **2020**, *20*, 3. [CrossRef]

22. Shierk, A.; Lake, A.; Haas, T. Review of Therapeutic Interventions for the Upper Limb Classified by Manual Ability in Children with Cerebral Palsy. *Semin. Plast. Surg.* **2016**, *30*, 14–23. [CrossRef]
23. Klepper, S.E.; Clayton, D.; Gilb, M.C.; Khalil, N. Comparing Unimanual and Bimanual Training in Upper Extremity Function in Children with Unilateral Cerebral Palsy. *Pediatr. Phys. Ther.* **2017**, *29*, 288–306. [CrossRef]
24. King, G.; Chiarello, L. Family-centered care for children with cerebral palsy: Conceptual and practical considerations to advance care and practice. *J. Child Neurol.* **2014**, *29*, 1046–1054. [CrossRef] [PubMed]
25. Beckers, L.W.M.E.; Geijen, M.M.E.; Kleijnen, J.; Rameckers, E.A.A.; Schnackers, M.L.A.P.; Smeets, R.J.E.M.; Janssen-Potten, Y.J.M. Feasibility and effectiveness of home-based therapy programmes for children with cerebral palsy: A systematic review. *BMJ Open* **2020**, *10*, e035454. [CrossRef] [PubMed]
26. Agarwal, S.; Scher, M.S.; Tilton, A. Cerebral Palsy and Rehabilitative Care: The Role of Home-Based Care and Family-Centered Approach. *Indian Pediatr.* **2021**, *58*, 813–814. [CrossRef]
27. Schnackers, M.; Beckers, L.; Janssen-Potten, Y.; Aarts, P.; Rameckers, E.; van der Burg, J.; de Groot, I.; Smeets, R.; Geurts, S.; Steenbergen, B.; et al. Home-based bimanual training based on motor learning principles in children with unilateral cerebral palsy and their parents (the COAD-study): Rationale and protocols. *BMC Pediatr.* **2018**, *18*, 139. [CrossRef]
28. Beckers, L.W.M.E.; Rameckers, E.A.A.; Aarts, P.B.M.; van der Burg, J.J.W.; Smeets, R.J.E.M.; Schnackers, M.L.A.P.; Steenbergen, B.; de Groot, I.J.M.; Geurts, A.C.H.; Janssen-Potten, Y.J.M.; et al. Effect of Home-based Bimanual Training in Children with Unilateral Cerebral Palsy (The COAD-study): A Case Series. *Dev. Neurorehabil.* **2021**, *24*, 311–322. [CrossRef] [PubMed]
29. Sakzewski, L.; Ziviani, J.; Boyd, R.N. Efficacy of Upper Limb Therapies for Unilateral Cerebral Palsy: A Meta-analysis. *Pediatrics* **2014**, *133*, e175–e204. [CrossRef]
30. Thieme, H.; Mehrholz, J.; Pohl, M.; Behrens, J.; Dohle, C. Mirror therapy for improving motor function after stroke. *Cochrane Database Syst. Rev.* **2012**, *7*, CD008449. [CrossRef]
31. Weisstanner, C.; Saxer, S.; Wiest, R.; Kaelin-Lang, A.; Newman, C.J.; Steinlin, M.; Grunt, S. The neuronal correlates of mirror illusion in children with spastic hemiparesis: A study with functional magnetic resonance imaging. *Swiss Med. Wkly.* **2017**, *147*, w14415. [CrossRef]
32. Grunt, S.; Newman, C.J.; Saxer, S.; Steinlin, M.; Weisstanner, C.; Kaelin-Lang, A. The Mirror Illusion Increases Motor Cortex Excitability in Children with and Without Hemiparesis. *Neurorehabil. Neural Repair* **2017**, *31*, 280–289. [CrossRef]
33. Gygax, M.J.; Schneider, P.; Newman, C.J. Mirror therapy in children with hemiplegia: A pilot study. *Dev. Med. Child Neurol.* **2011**, *53*, 473–476. [CrossRef]
34. Oliva-Sierra, M.; Ríos-León, M.; Abuín-Porras, V.; Martín-Casas, P. Effectiveness of mirror therapy and action observation therapy in infantile cerebral palsy: A systematic review. *An. Sist. Sanit. Navar.* **2022**, *45*, e1003. [CrossRef] [PubMed]
35. Narimani, A.; Kalantari, M.; Dalvand, H.; Tabatabaee, S.M. Effect of Mirror Therapy on Dexterity and Hand Grasp in Children Aged 9-14 Years with Hemiplegic Cerebral Palsy. *Iran. J. Child Neurol.* **2019**, *13*, 135–142. [PubMed]
36. Palomo-Carrión, R.; Zuil-Escobar, J.C.; Cabrera-Guerra, M.; Barreda-Martínez, P.; Martínez-Cepa, C.B. Terapia en espejo y de observación de la acción en niños con parálisis cerebral espástica unilateral: Estudio de viabilidad. *Rev. Neurol.* **2022**, *75*, 325–332. [CrossRef] [PubMed]
37. Farzamfar, P.; Heirani, A.; Sedighi, M. The effect of motor training in mirror therapy on gross motor skills of the affected hand in children with hemiplegia. *Iran. Rehabil. J.* **2017**, *15*, 243–248. [CrossRef]
38. Kara, O.K.; Yardimci, B.N.; Sahin, S.; Orhan, C.; Livanelioglu, A.; Soylu, A.R. Combined Effects of Mirror Therapy and Exercises on the Upper Extremities in Children with Unilateral Cerebral Palsy: A Randomized Controlled Trial. *Dev. Neurorehabil.* **2020**, *23*, 253–264. [CrossRef] [PubMed]
39. Bruchez, R.; Jequier Gygax, M.; Roches, S.; Fluss, J.; Jacquier, D.; Ballabeni, P.; Grunt, S.; Newman, C.J. Mirror therapy in children with hemiparesis: A randomized observer-blinded trial. *Dev. Med. Child Neurol.* **2016**, *58*, 970–978. [CrossRef]
40. Auld, M.L.; Johnston, L.M.; Russo, R.N.; Moseley, G.L. A Single Session of Mirror-based Tactile and Motor Training Improves Tactile Dysfunction in Children with Unilateral Cerebral Palsy: A Replicated Randomized Controlled Case Series. *Physiother. Res. Int. J. Res. Clin. Phys. Ther.* **2017**, *22*, e1674. [CrossRef]
41. Smorenburg, A.R.P.P.; Ledebt, A.; Deconinck, F.J.A.A.; Savelsbergh, G.J.P.P. Matching accuracy in hemiparetic cerebral palsy during unimanual and bimanual movements with (mirror) visual feedback. *Res. Dev. Disabil.* **2012**, *33*, 2088–2098. [CrossRef]
42. Auld, M.L.; Johnston, L.M. Perspectives on tactile intervention for children with cerebral palsy: A framework to guide clinical reasoning and future research. *Disabil. Rehabil.* **2018**, *40*, 1849–1854. [CrossRef]
43. Auld, M.L.; Russo, R.N.; Moseley, G.L.; Johnston, L.M. Determination of interventions for upper extremity tactile impairment in children with cerebral palsy: A systematic review. *Dev. Med. Child Neurol.* **2014**, *56*, 815–832. [CrossRef]
44. Eldridge, S.M.; Chan, C.L.; Campbell, M.J.; Bond, C.M.; Hopewell, S.; Thabane, L.; Lancaster, G.A.; Altman, D.; Bretz, F.; Campbell, M.; et al. CONSORT 2010 statement: Extension to randomised pilot and feasibility trials. *BMJ* **2016**, *355*. [CrossRef]
45. O'Cathain, A.; Hoddinott, P.; Lewin, S.; Thomas, K.J.; Young, B.; Adamson, J.; Jansen, Y.J.F.M.; Mills, N.; Moore, G.; Donovan, J.L. Maximising the impact of qualitative research in feasibility studies for randomised controlled trials: Guidance for researchers. *Pilot Feasibility Stud.* **2015**, *1*, 32. [CrossRef]

46. Palomo-Carrión, R.; Zuil-Escobar, J.C.; Cabrera-Guerra, M.; Barreda-Martínez, P.; Martínez-Cepa, C.B.; Palomo-Carrion, R.; Zuil-Escobar, J.C.; Cabrera-Guerra, M.; Barreda-Martinez, P.; Martinez-Cepa, C.B.; et al. Mirror Therapy and Action Observation Therapy to Increase the Affected Upper Limb Functionality in Children with Hemiplegia: A Randomized Controlled Trial Protocol. *Int. J. Environ. Res. Public Health* **2021**, *18*, 1051. [CrossRef]
47. Neuro Orthopaedic Institute. NOI Group. 2023. Available online: https://www.noigroup.com/ (accessed on 1 January 2022).
48. Karolinska Institutet Children's Hand-Use Experience Questionnaire 2.0. 2011. Available online: https://www.cheq.se/questionnaire (accessed on 1 January 2022).
49. Amer, A.; Eliasson, A.C.; Peny-Dahlstrand, M.; Hermansson, L. Validity and test–retest reliability of Children's Hand-use Experience Questionnaire in children with unilateral cerebral palsy. *Dev. Med. Child Neurol.* **2016**, *58*, 743–749. [CrossRef]
50. Sköld, A.; Hermansson, L.N.; Krumlinde-Sundholm, L.; Eliasson, A.C. Development and evidence of validity for the Children's Hand-use Experience Questionnaire (CHEQ). *Dev. Med. Child Neurol.* **2011**, *53*, 436–442. [CrossRef]
51. Auld, M.L.; Ware, R.S.; Boyd, R.N.; Moseley, G.L.; Johnston, L.M. Reproducibility of tactile assessments for children with unilateral cerebral palsy. *Phys. Occup. Ther. Pediatr.* **2012**, *32*, 151–166. [CrossRef]
52. Auld, M.L.; Boyd, R.N.; Moseley, G.L.; Johnston, L.M. Tactile assessment in children with cerebral palsy: A clinimetric review. *Phys. Occup. Ther. Pediatr.* **2011**, *31*, 413–439. [CrossRef] [PubMed]
53. Bell-Krotoski, J.; Tomancik, E. The repeatability of testing with Semmes-Weinstein monofilaments. *J. Hand Surg. Am.* **1987**, *12*, 155–161. [CrossRef] [PubMed]
54. Dellon, A.L.; Mackinnon, S.E.; Crosby, P.M.D. Reliability of two-point discrimination measurements. *J. Hand Surg. Am.* **1987**, *12*, 693–696. [CrossRef]
55. Varni, J.W.; Burwinkle, T.M.; Berrin, S.J.; Sherman, S.A.; Artavia, K.; Malcarne, V.L.; Chambers, H.G. The PedsQL in pediatric cerebral palsy: Reliability, validity, and sensitivity of the Generic Core Scales and Cerebral Palsy Module. *Dev. Med. Child Neurol.* **2006**, *48*, 442–449. [CrossRef]
56. Beckers, L.; van der Burg, J.; Janssen-Potten, Y.; Rameckers, E.; Aarts, P.B.M.; Smeets, R. Process evaluation of two home-based bimanual training programs in children with unilateral cerebral palsy (the COAD-study): Protocol for a mixed methods study. *BMC Pediatr.* **2018**, *18*, 141. [CrossRef]
57. Palomo-Carrión, R.; Romay-Barrero, H.; Lirio-Romero, C.; Arroyo-Fernádez, R.; M-Guijarro-Herraiz, M.; Ferri-Morales, A. Feasibility of family-directed home-based bimanual intensive therapy combined with modified constraint induced movement therapy (h-BITmCI) in very low and low bimanual functional level: A brief report. *Dev. Neurorehabil.* **2023**, *26*, 63–70. [CrossRef]
58. Beani, E.; Menici, V.; Ferrari, A.; Cioni, G.; Sgandurra, G. Feasibility of a Home-Based Action Observation Training for Children With Unilateral Cerebral Palsy: An Explorative Study. *Front. Neurol.* **2020**, *11*, 16. [CrossRef] [PubMed]
59. Almasri, N.A.; An, M.; Palisano, R.J. Parents' Perception of Receiving Family-Centered Care for Their Children with Physical Disabilities: A Meta-Analysis. *Phys. Occup. Ther. Pediatr.* **2018**, *38*, 427–443. [CrossRef] [PubMed]
60. Ferre, C.L.; Brandão, M.; Surana, B.; Dew, A.P.; Moreau, N.G.; Gordon, A.M. Caregiver-directed home-based intensive bimanual training in young children with unilateral spastic cerebral palsy: A randomized trial. *Dev. Med. Child Neurol.* **2017**, *59*, 497–504. [CrossRef]
61. Ben-Pazi, H.; Beni-Adani, L.; Lamdan, R. Accelerating Telemedicine for Cerebral Palsy During the COVID-19 Pandemic and Beyond. *Front. Neurol.* **2020**, *11*, 746. [CrossRef] [PubMed]
62. Pérez-Ardanaz, B.; Morales-Asencio, J.M.; León-Campos, Á.; Kaknani-Uttumchandani, S.; López-Leiva, I.; Garcia-Piñero, J.M.; Martí-García, C.; García-Mayor, S. Quality of Life and Health Services Utilization for Spanish Children With Cerebral Palsy. *J. Pediatr. Nurs.* **2020**, *53*, e121–e128. [CrossRef] [PubMed]
63. Sharif Azar, E.; Ravanbakhsh, M.; Torabipour, A.; Amiri, E.; Haghighyzade, M. Home-based versus center-based care in children with cerebral palsy: A cost-effectiveness analysis. *J. Med. Life* **2015**, *8*, 245–251.
64. Majnemer, A.; Shikako-Thomas, K.; Lach, L.; Shevell, M.; Law, M.; Schmitz, N.; Poulin, C.; Gardiner, M.; Guimond, D.; Lepage, C.; et al. Rehabilitation service utilization in children and youth with cerebral palsy. *Child. Care. Health Dev.* **2014**, *40*, 275–282. [CrossRef]

healthcare

MDPI

*Systematic Review*

# Effectiveness of Respiratory Rehabilitation in COVID-19's Post-Acute Phase: A Systematic Review

**Matteo Tamburlani [1], Rossana Cuscito [2], Annamaria Servadio [1] and Giovanni Galeoto [3,4,*]**

1 Local Health Board Roma 2, 00145 Rome, Italy
2 Master's Degree Course in Rehabilitation Sciences of the Health Professions, University of Rome Tor Vergata, 00133 Roma, Italy
3 Departement of Human Neurosciences, Sapienza University of Rome, 00185 Rome, Italy
4 Neuromed, IRCCS, 86077 Pozzilli, Italy
* Correspondence: giovanni.galeoto@uniroma1.it

**Abstract:** Background: The COVID-19 pandemic, caused by the new grave and acute respiratory syndrome Coronavirus-2 (SARS-CoV-2), generated an unprecedented danger to public health. This condition may impact survivors' quality of life and includes extensive pulmonary and respiratory outcomes. Respiratory rehabilitation is known for its effects in improving dyspnea, alleviating anxiety and depression, reducing complications, preventing and ameliorating dysfunctions, reducing morbidity, preserving functions and improving subjects' quality of life. For this reason, respiratory rehabilitation may be recommended for this category of patients. Objective: Our objective was to evaluate the effectiveness and benefits produced by the adoption of pulmonary rehabilitation (PR) programs in COVID-19's post-acute phase. Material and Methods: A search of relevant publications was conducted using the following electronic databases: PubMed, Scopus, PEDro, and Cochrane Library. A single reviser selected pertinent articles that studied the effects of pulmonary rehabilitation during COVID-19's post-acute phase in improving the respiratory function, physical performance, autonomy and quality of life (QoL). Results: After an initial selection, 18 studies were included in this systematic review, of which 14 concern respiratory rehabilitation delivered in conventional form and 4 concern respiratory rehabilitation provided in telehealth. Conclusions: Pulmonary rehabilitation combining different types of training—breathing, aerobic, fitness and strength—and not bypassing the neuropsychological aspects revealed itself to be capable of improving pulmonary and muscular functions, general health and quality of life in post-acute COVID-19 patients, besides increasing workout capacity and muscle strength, improving fatigue states and reducing anxiety and depression.

**Keywords:** COVID-19; Coronavirus; post-acute; pulmonary rehabilitation; pulmonary function; respiratory physiotherapy; telerehabilitation

**Citation:** Tamburlani, M.; Cuscito, R.; Servadio, A.; Galeoto, G. Effectiveness of Respiratory Rehabilitation in COVID-19's Post-Acute Phase: A Systematic Review. *Healthcare* **2023**, *11*, 1071. https://doi.org/10.3390/healthcare11081071

Academic Editor: Federico Longhini

Received: 3 January 2023
Revised: 29 March 2023
Accepted: 3 April 2023
Published: 8 April 2023



## 1. Introduction

The COVID-19 pandemic, caused by the new grave and acute respiratory syndrome Coronavirus-2 (SARS-CoV-2), identified for the first time in December 2019, generated an unprecedented danger to public health and still represents an extraordinarily impactful event that continues to negatively affect people's health across the globe. Since the beginning of the pandemic, 640,395,651 confirmed cases worldwide have been registered and 6,618,579 deaths have been recorded so far [1], even though the number of new infections has significantly decreased in the past few months thanks to the ample vaccine campaign conducted by all countries globally. The infection's clinical spectrum is wide and varied, ranging from asymptomatic infection to a slight sickness of the higher respiratory tract, a moderate illness to a critical one, which can be described as a serious viral pneumonia with respiratory distress, septic shock and/or multiple organ failure [2]. A total of 41.8% of infected subjects developed ARDS and 52.4% of these died [3]. The American-European

Consensus Conference on ARDS defined the acute respiratory distress syndrome (ARDS) as a process of nonhydrostatic pulmonary edema and hypoxemia associated with a variety of etiologies and carries a high morbidity and mortality (10 to 90%) [4].

A considerable pulmonary concern has characterized this condition; indeed, only 25.8% of patients had lesions affecting a single lung, whereas 75.7% of patients had lesions affecting both lungs bilaterally [5]. Respiratory damage plays a crucial role within patients who have passed COVID-19, since the removal of the cause of lung damage does not hinder the development of fibrotic and progressive interstitial lung disease. Pulmonary fibrosis is indeed known to be consequence of ARDS [6]. Not surprisingly, reduced diffusion capacity, restrictive pulmonary physiology, ground glass opacity and fibrotic imaging changes were found at the follow-up of COVID-19 survivors [7].

The issue for the survivors of COVID-19 does not terminate with the end of the pulmonary inflammation, since a significant number of patients continue signaling persistent symptoms way beyond the acute phase of the sickness. According to the Office for National Statistics, one person out of five found positive to COVID-19 shows symptoms for a period of 5 weeks or more, while one person out of ten develops symptoms lasting 12 weeks or longer [8].

These medium- and long-term effects—known as post-COVID-19 syndrome, signs and symptoms that continue for more than 12 weeks, or "Long COVID", including both ongoing symptomatic COVID-19 (from 4 to 12 weeks) and post-COVID-19 syndrome (12 weeks or more)—are extremely varied and extensive [9].

Within 6 months of COVID-19 infection, fatigue and muscular weakness (63%), sleeping difficulties (26%) and anxiety and depression (23%) are the most common symptoms [10].

Data from the UK National Statistical Office suggest that Post-COVID-19 or "Long COVID" syndrome has an incidence rate of 13.7% [11]. This makes rehabilitation measures for the promotion of physical recovery a crucial necessity. Rehabilitation programs play a crucial role in combating the pandemic, in addition to the use of vaccines [12], as they are an effective means of containing the adverse effects of COVID-19 on public health [13].

The National Institute for Health and Care Excellence (NICE) recommends that gradual rehabilitation programs be used within the first 30 days (post-acute phase) to have a maximum impact on recovery [14]. In the literature, there is no unique and officially recognized definition of the post-acute phase; some authors use this expression to indicate the immediate phase after the acute one (after 4 weeks) with persistent symptoms [15].

It thus seems necessary to prepare a multidiscipline and holistic rehabilitation program that considers respiratory rehabilitation tailored on the needs of the single individual to favor complete recovery. Although respiratory rehabilitation was primarily planned for treating chronic lung diseases, numerous reports, guidelines and expert opinions focus on the recommendation of pulmonary rehabilitation in patients recovering from SARS-CoV-2 infection [16,17].

Respiratory rehabilitation aims to ameliorate dyspnea, alleviate anxiety and depression, reduce complications, prevent and ameliorate dysfunctions, reduce morbidity, preserve functions and improve subjects' quality of life as much as possible [16].

The objective of this study is to conduct a systematic review of the scientific literature to assess the efficacy and benefits of pulmonary rehabilitation (PR) programs in the post-acute phase of COVID-19, which is useful in promoting an improvement in the respiratory functions, autonomy and quality of life (QoL) of people affected by COVID-19 and reduce the incidence and severity of lung complications.

## 2. Materials and Methods

### 2.1. Research

This systematic review was conducted following the international guidelines of the Preferred Reporting Items for Systematic Reviews and Meta-Analyses (PRISMA).

A search of relevant publications was conducted with the use of the following electronic databases: Medline (via PubMed), Scopus, PEDro and the Cochrane Library and was carried out between December 2020 and September 2022.

The literature presented has been vetted through the formulation of a search string common to the following databases: Medline, Scopus, PEDro and Cochrane Library containing keywords and Boolean operators AND/OR in combination as follows: (Pulmonary rehabilitation OR post-acute) AND COVID-19.

On the PEDro database, the search was carried out using the following word couples: Pulmonary rehabilitation AND COVID, COVID-19 AND Rehabilitation, COVID-19 AND Physiotherapy, SARS-CoV-2 AND Rehabilitation, SARS-CoV-2 AND Physiotherapy, COVID-19, SARS-CoV-2.

The search terms are shown in Table A1 in the Appendix A.

### 2.2. *Eligibility Criteria*

In alignment with the PRISMA guidelines, inclusion and exclusion criteria were laid out through the definition of the PICO strategy (population, intervention, comparison and outcome), as reported below:

- P (population): patients diagnosed with COVID-19 in the post-acute phase and clinically stable were included. Instead, severe COVID-19 cases or acute-phase cases with clinical instability were excluded.
- I (intervention): respiratory physiotherapy in its different means were included, either delivered in conventional form (in person) or through telemedicine. Other forms of rehabilitation were excluded.
- C (comparison): patients who only receive standard assistance/cure or receive no cure.
- O (outcome): improvement of respiratory function and physical performance, reduction in dyspnea and fatigue and improvement of autonomy and quality of life in patients affected by COVID-19. The Table 1 shows the PICO strategy used.

**Table 1.** PICO strategy.

| | |
|---|---|
| P (population) | Patients diagnosed with COVID-19 in the post-acute phase and clinically stable. Severe COVID-19 cases or acute-phase cases with clinical instability were excluded. |
| I (intervention) | Physiotherapeutic respiratory intervention in its different means, either delivered in conventional form (in person) or through telemedicine. |
| C (comparison) | Patients who only receive standard assistance/cure or receive no cure whatsoever. |
| O (outcome) | Improvement of the respiratory function and physical performance, reduction in dyspnea and fatigue and improvement of autonomy and quality of life in patients affected by COVID-19. |

In addition, the research was limited to the use of the following filters:

- Publication date (year) of the articles: we have included in the revision those articles that had been published in multimedia databases in the time range spanning from the 1 January 2020 to the 27 September 2022.
- Language of publication of the articles: all studies that were not redacted in either Italian or English were excluded.
- Type of study: in the present review, we included randomized controlled trials, cohort studies, declarations of consent and practical guidelines on pulmonary rehabilitation for SARS-CoV-2.

### 2.3. Selection of the Studies

After the deletion of duplicates using the EndNOTE software 20, an editor evaluated the studies taken from the databases based on the title and later the studies' abstract. After this initial selection, we moved on to analyzing the studies' full texts to determine whether they met the required criteria of inclusion/exclusion. Following the full-text analysis, a decision was made as to which articles must be included in the final review. For those articles over which there were some doubts, the decision was taken after another proofreading of the full text.

### 2.4. Data Collection Process

After inclusion, the studies' characteristics, aims and results were extracted and summarized using an extraction table. More specifically, the following data were gathered: name of the first author, publishing date, title of the article, study's design, size and characteristics of the sample (sex, average age of patients), rehabilitation protocol, frequency of intervention, primary and secondary outcome measures, evaluation time and obtained results.

### 2.5. Evaluation of Methodologic Quality

The randomized controlled trials (RCT) included were evaluated using the Physiotherapy Evidence-Based Database (PEDro) scale, considered a reliable instrument allowing critical evaluation of methodologic quality in experimental studies on physical therapy. The final score of the PEDro scale varies from 0 to 10 with each satisfied element contributing 1 point. No score is assigned if one criterion is not described or is unclear.

The Newcastle—Ottawa quality assessment scale evaluated the cohort and observational studies. The NOS scale allows the evaluation of the quality of non-randomized studies (cohort studies and case–control studies) with its design, content and ease of usage allowing for the incorporation of quality evaluation in the interpretation of meta-analytic results. A "star system" was developed in which a study is evaluated based on three outlooks: the quality of the selected cohort, the comparability of cohorts and the obtained results, thus assigning up to a maximum of nine stars.

The Newcastle-Ottawa Scale quality instrument is scored by awarding a point for each answer that is marked with a star symbol ♦. Possible total points are 4 points for Selection, 2 points for Comparability, and 3 points for Outcomes with a maximum of 9 points.

The practical guidelines and declaration of consent were included, as they are relevant for the revision, but not methodologically evaluated.

## 3. Results

### 3.1. Selection of Studies

The total number of articles identified through multimedia database research was 3542, of which 692 articles were duplicates and thus excluded. A total of 2423 articles were also excluded based on their title since it did not fit the required inclusion criteria; subsequently, 320 articles were excluded after their abstract was read and another 87 articles were eliminated after their full text was examined. In the end, 18 articles were deemed useful and relevant: 4 randomized controlled trials (RCT), 7 cohort studies, 5 observational studies, 1 practical guideline and 1 declaration of consent.

The diagram in Figure 1 shows the scheme that was followed to select the articles.

### 3.2. Evaluation of the Methodologic Quality

The evaluation of the randomized controlled trials was carried out with the aid of the PEDro scale. Following the PEDro criteria, the studies' quality can be sorted in low quality (0–3 points), medium quality (4–7 points) and high quality (8–10 points), with 10 being the highest score. A study with a score of at least 6–10 points is of medium-high quality. The final score obtained in the evaluation of the randomized controlled trials included varies from 5 to 7; with an average of 6.3, the included RCTs are of medium-high quality [18–20], and only one RCT is of medium quality [21]. The evaluation of the randomized controlled trials is shown in Table 2.

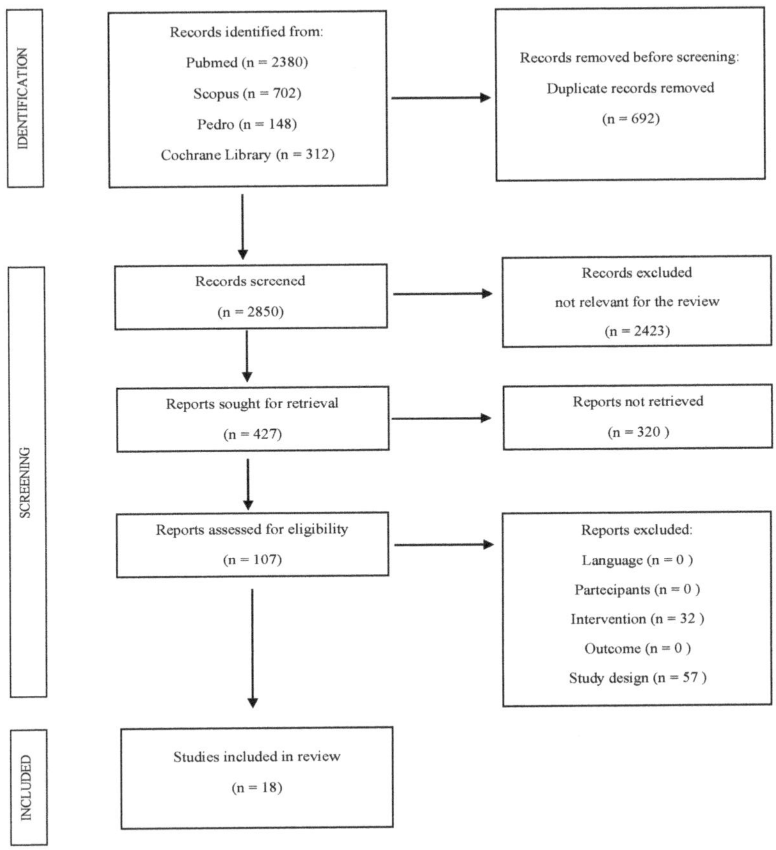


**Figure 1.** Flow chart.

**Table 2.** Pedro scale.

| Autor | Item 1 | Item 2 | Item 3 | Item 4 | Item 5 | Item 6 | Item 7 | Item 8 | Item 9 | Item 10 | Item 11 | Score |
|---|---|---|---|---|---|---|---|---|---|---|---|---|
| Capin 2022 [18] | Y | Y | Y | Y | N | N | Y | Y | N | Y | Y | 7 |
| Li 2021 [19] | Y | Y | Y | Y | N | N | Y | Y | N | Y | Y | 6 |
| Liu 2020 [21] | Y | Y | N | Y | N | N | N | Y | N | Y | Y | 5 |
| Pehlivan 2022 [20] | Y | Y | Y | Y | N | N | N | N | N | Y | Y | 6 |

Y: Yes; N: NO.

The cohort and observational studies were evaluated using the Newcastle—Ottawa scale. The final score obtained in the evaluation of said studies varies from a minimum of 3 to a maximum of 7 points, with an average of 5.1. The 12 evaluated studies [22–33] were of heterogeneous quality with generally low scores. A total of five cohort studies [25,29–32] and two observational studies [24,33] obtained less than 6 points on the NOS scale and were categorized as being of low methodological quality. In this case, the results of these studies should be considered as questionable compared to the others. This significant difference is attributable to certain issues such as the absence of control groups, the application of a rehabilitation protocol on a small cohort made up of a low number of patients and, lastly, a lack of adequate follow-up, which is necessary to better understand the long-term benefits of the variables under scrutiny. The evaluation of the cohort and observational studies is shown in Tables 3 and 4.

**Table 3.** NOS for cohort studies and prospective observational studies.

| Autor | Quality of Selected Cohort | Cohort Comparability | Results Obtained | Score |
|---|---|---|---|---|
| Al Chikhanie 2021 [22] | ♦♦♦♦ | ♦ | ♦ | 6/9 |
| Daynes 2021 [25] | ♦♦♦ | | ♦♦ | 5/9 |
| Dun 2021[26] | ♦♦♦♦ | ♦ | ♦♦ | 7/9 |
| Gloeckl 2021 [27] | ♦♦♦ | ♦ | ♦♦ | 6/9 |
| Hameed 2021 [28] | ♦♦♦♦ | ♦ | ♦♦ | 7/9 |
| Hayden 2021 [29] | ♦♦♦ | ♦ | ♦ | 5/9 |
| Hermann 2020 [30] | ♦♦♦ | ♦ | ♦ | 5/9 |
| Puchner 2021 [31] | ♦♦♦ | | ♦ | 4/9 |
| Spielmanns 2021 [32] | ♦♦♦ | ♦ | ♦ | 5/9 |

**Table 4.** NOS for retrospective observational studies.

| Autor | Selection | Comparability | Exposure | Score |
|---|---|---|---|---|
| Busching 2021 [23] | ♦♦♦ | ♦ | ♦♦ | 6/9 |
| Curci 2021 [24] | ♦♦ | | ♦ | 3/9 |
| Zampogna 2021 [33] | ♦♦ | | ♦ | 3/9 |

### 3.3. Features of Studies

The characteristics of the studies included are given below in the way the data were extracted.

### 3.4. Population

The analyzed studies included an overall population of 1592 subjects affected by COVID-19 in the post-acute phase. The number of patients for studies varies from 23 [19] to 518 [32]. The average age of patients varied from 49.17 [21] to 72.15 years [25]. The average age of the overall population was 58.12 years. Most patients were male. The data related to the overall population included in the analyzed studies are shown in Table 5.

**Table 5.** Data Extraction of Selected Studies.

| Author Year Title | Study Design | Rehabilitation Protocol | Intervention Frequency | Participants | Outcome Measures | Evaluation Time | Results |
|---|---|---|---|---|---|---|---|
| Al Chikhanie et al., 2021 [22] | Cohort study | EG and CG: breathing exercises, muscle strengthening, balance and walking when possible, cycling and gymnastics according to current ATS/ERS recommendations | EG: 27.6 ± 14.2 days<br>CG: 29.9 ± 17.3 days | EG: (n.21)<br>-Mean age: 70.9 ± 10.6<br>-Gender: 14M/7F<br>CG: (n.21)<br>-Mean age: 69.1 ± 9.4<br>-Gender: 13M/8F | Primary: FEV1; CVF: PImax; PEmax; 6MWT; Tinetti Scale; Borg test; Muscle strength; St George Questionnaire: Quality of Life (QoL); Pichot's questionnaire; HADS; PCLS<br>Secondary: N/A | At baseline and at the end of the PR program. 6MWT, also performed weekly during PR. | Extensive and rapid recovery of exercise capacity among COVID-19 patients rehabilitated after admission to intensive care, as well as extensive improvements in muscle strength, balance and psychosocial status. Significant improvement in 6MWT, greater in COVID-19 patients (+205 ± 121 m) compared to non-COVID-19 patients (+93 ± 66 m). |
| Busching et al., 2021 [23] | Retrospective observational study | EG and GC: cardiopulmonary training (cycling, guided walking), strength exercise (free weight, resistance bands), breathing exercises (deep breathing, sputum evacuation), relaxation techniques (progressive muscle relaxation), if indicated psychological, nutritional, speech therapy and occupational therapy. | A minimum of 540 min of patient education and therapy in individual and group settings. | EG: (n.51)<br>-Mean age: 65.8 ± 11.7<br>-Gender: 38M/13F<br>CG: (n.51)<br>-Mean age: 69.8 ± 9.6,<br>-Gender: 23M/28F | Primary: 6 MWT; FIM: Functional Independence Measure; CRQ: chronic respiratory questionnaire<br>Secondary: N/A | At baseline and at the end of the PR program | Both groups achieved significant improvements in 6MWT, CRQ and FIM. At discharge, COVID-19 patients performed better in 6MWT and FIM, but similar CRQ scores compared to the control group. Regression analysis of the 2 subgroups: COVID-19 intensive care versus non-ICU subgroup: no significant difference in 6MWT at discharge. The outcome of physical functioning in the PR program is similar among critical and severe COVID-19 patients. |
| Capin et al., 2022 [18] | RCT | EG: breathing and compensation techniques, high-intensity strength training, aerobic and cardiovascular exercises, balance exercises, functional activities, stretching and lifestyle coaching and motivational interviewing. The Health in Motion application used to facilitate self-directed intervention outside of supervised sessions.<br>CG: exercise education with educational handout and weekly check-in phone calls. | 12 individual and supervised telerehabilitation sessions provided: 3 times a week in the first week, 2 times a week in weeks 2–4 once a week in weeks 5–6 and 1 single "recall" visit session during week 9 or 10. | EG: (n.29)<br>CG: (n.15)<br>-Mean age: 52 aa<br>-Gender: 23M/21F | Primary: Feasibility through safety and adherence (percentage of sessions attended).<br>Secondary: TUG; MRC; ABC; PROMIS-SF; PHQ8; MoCA | At baseline, 6 weeks after baseline and 12 weeks after baseline (week 12). | The informed multi-component and biobehavioral telerehabilitation program for COVID-19 survivors is safe and feasible. Participants in both groups functionally improved from baseline to 6 weeks and 12 weeks after intervention. |

**Table 5.** *Cont.*

| Author Year Title | Study Design | Rehabilitation Protocol | Intervention Frequency | Participants | Outcome Measures | Evaluation Time | Results |
|---|---|---|---|---|---|---|---|
| Curci et al., 2021 [24] | Retrospective observational study | EG: Initially: posture changes, passive mobilization, postural drainage, chest clapping and vibration, breathing control exercises and chest-abdomen coordination. Muscle strengthening exercises of the upper and lower limbs, trunk and gluteal muscles. Breathing exercises with the pep bottle, forced inhalation/exhalation and use of the incentive spirometer. Balance and coordination exercises and train yourself to walk for progressive distances. CG: N/A | 30 min/set, 2 times a day for the duration of hospitalization. (LOS average in the COVID-19 Rehabilitation Unit was 31.97 ± 9.06 days). | EG: (n.41) -Mean age 72.15 ± 11.07 aa -Gender: 25M/16F CG: N/A | Primary: BI Secondary: MRC; 6-MWT; RPE; Type of respiratory support required; Results of arterial blood gas analysis; Serum levels of laboratory markers. | At hospitalization (T0) and at the end of the PR program (T1). | Statistically significant improvement in the Barthel Index (BI) (84.87 ± 15.56 vs. 43.37 ± 26.00), 6-MWT (303.37 ± 112.18 vs. 240.0 ± 81.31 m) and Borg RPE scale (12.23 ± 2.51 vs. 16.03 ± 2.28). Finally, an improvement also in CT scans in 74.4% of cases |
| Daynes et al., 2021 [25] | Cohort study | EG: Aerobic exercises based on walking/treadmill, upper and lower limb strength training. Educational sessions with handouts included: dyspnea, cough, fatigue, fear and anxiety, memory and concentration, managing daily activities and returning to work. CG: N/A | 2 sessions per week for 6 weeks. | EG: (n.32) -Mean age: 58 aa -Gender: 52%M/48%F CG: N/A | Primary: Incremental running and resistance test (ISWT/ESWT); CAT; FACIT; HADS; EQ5D; MoCA. Secondary: N/A | At baseline and at the end of the PR program | PR produced average improvement within the group of 112 m in the Incremental Shuttle Walking Test (ISWT) and 544 s in the Endurance Shuttle Walking Test (ESWT). The FACIT improved by 5 points, the EQ5D improved by 8 points and the MoCA by 2 points. The CAT score improved by 3 points, while for Anxiety and depression: minimal improvement, equal to 1 point. |

**Table 5.** *Cont.*

| Author Year Title | Study Design | Rehabilitation Protocol | Intervention Frequency | Participants | Outcome Measures | Evaluation Time | Results |
|---|---|---|---|---|---|---|---|
| Dun et al., 2021 [26] | Retrospective cohort studies | EG: inspiratory muscle training; 30 sets of ruffled lip breathing techniques and active breathing cycle (ACBT); a series of 30 repetitions of maximum voluntary diaphragmatic contractions in the supine position, placing an average weight (1–3 kg) on the anterior abdominal wall to resist diaphragmatic descent; two high-intensity interval workouts of 4 min via bike or treadmill interspersed with 4 min low-intensity intervals.<br>CG: patients that did not perform any PR during the 6 m of convalescence. | 3 sessions per week for 12 weeks. | EG (n.27)<br>-Mean age: 54 ± 16<br>-Gender: 9M/18FCG (n.71)<br>-Mean age: 44 ± 13<br>-Gender: 36M/35F | Primary: 6-MWT<br>Secondary:<br>-Changes in SARS-CoV-2 specific IgG and IgM immunoglobulins, T lymphocytes and blood chemistry | Baseline, 2 weeks and 6 months. | Patients in the PR group acquired a greater increase in the distance traveled in 6-MWT compared to the control.<br>There were no significant differences between PR and control groups in IgG and IgM specific for SARS-CoV-2, CD3+ T cells, CD8+ cells, CD8+ T cells, CD4+/CD8+ ratio, and all biomarkers. |
| Gloeckl et al., 2021 [27] | Prospective and observational cohort study | EG1 (COVID-19 mild/moderate) and EG2 (COVID-19 severe/critical): Pulmonary rehabilitation program for COVID-19 patients includes resistance training, strength training, patient education sessions, respiratory physiotherapy, daily life training activities and relaxation techniques.<br>CG: N/A | 3 weeks | EG1 (COVID-19 mild/moderate) (n.24)<br>-Mean age: 52<br>-Gender: 4M/20F<br>EG2 (COVID-19-severe/critical) (n.26)<br>-Mean age: 66<br>-Gender: 18M/8F<br>CG: N/A | Primary: 6MWT.<br>Secondary:<br>-Complete effort test (only in the subgroup of patients with severe/critical COVID-19); Shuttle walking test (ESWT); Maximum isometric knee extension force (MicroFET 2 dynamometer) and grip force (Jamar manual dynamometer) evaluated by dynamometry; Test sit-to-stand; FVC; FEV $_1$), TLC; DLCO; MRC; SF-36; GAD-7; PHQ-9 | At baseline and at the end of the PR program | Measures of FVC or FEV1 lung function improved significantly in the range of 7.7–15.7% in both groups.<br>Quality of life improved significantly only in patients with severe/critical COVID-19 in the SF-36 mental sum score (38.5 to 52.9 points; $p < 0.001$). |

**Table 5.** *Cont.*

| Author Year Title | Study Design | Rehabilitation Protocol | Intervention Frequency | Participants | Outcome Measures | Evaluation Time | Results |
|---|---|---|---|---|---|---|---|
| Hameed et al., 2021 [28] | Prospective cohort study | EG1 (MTM): virtual physical therapy via a telemedicine platform.<br>EG2 (HPT): Home Physical Therapy<br>EG3 (IE): independent exercise program<br>CG: No therapy. | 1–2 times a week with sessions of 30–60 min. | EG1 (VPT) (n.44)<br>-Mean age: 60<br>-Gender: 53%M/57%F<br>EG2 (HPT) (n.25)<br>-Mean age: 57<br>-Gender: 86%M/24%F<br>EG3 (IE) (n.17)<br>-Mean age: 59<br>-Gender: 65%M/35%F<br>CG (n.20)<br>-Mean age: 58<br>-Gender: 55%M/55%F | Primary: Change in lower limb strength; sit-to-stand test; 2MWT.<br>Secondary: N/A | At baseline and 2-week follow-up. | At follow-up, 65% of patients in the VPT group and 88% of patients in the HPT group achieved clinically significant difference for improvement in sit-to-stand scores, compared with 50% and 17% of those in the IE group and the non-exercise group ($p = 0.056$).<br>The clinically significant difference for step test improvement was met by 74% of patients in the VPT group and 50% of patients in the HPT, IE and non-exercise groups ($p = 0.12$). |
| Hayden et al., 2021 [29] | Prospective observational study | EG1 (Severe Acute COVID-19);<br>EG2 (Severe COVID-19);<br>EG3 (Mild COVID-19): the program has been adapted to individual needs.<br>Physical training with resistance and strength training, vibratory training for the whole body and inspiratory muscle training.<br>Respiratory physiotherapy with individual training on breathing, seminar on coughing techniques and mucolytic inhalation therapies.<br>General physiotherapy with mobility and gait training.<br>Psychosocial support, nutritional counselling and occupational therapy.<br>CG: N/A | 3 weeks<br>Average duration of PR treatment: 26.3 ± 5.9 days | EG1 (Severe Acute) (n.55)<br>-Mean age: 57.9 ± 10.8<br>-Gender: 34M/21F<br>EG2 (Severe) (n.32)<br>-Mean age: 54.0 ± 9.9<br>-Gender: 21M/11F<br>EG3 (Mild) (n.21)<br>-Mean age: 52.1 ± 6.8<br>-Gender: 4M/17F<br>CG: N/A | Primary: NRS; MRC<br>Secondary:Cardinal symptom: list of symptoms associated with COVID-19;<br>6MWT, FEV1, vital capacity (CV), residual volume (VR), total lung capacity (TLC), total specific airway resistance (sRtot), maximum inspiratory pressure (PImax) and capillary carbon monoxide alveolus diffusion (TLCO)<br>Blood gas analysis,<br>Laboratory blood test,<br>NRS, BFI, EQ-5D-5L, PHQ-9, GAD-7, GROC,<br>Estimation of the overall effectiveness of rehabilitation from the point of view of the patient: 11-point Likert scale | At baseline and at the end of the PR program. | PR was effective after acute COVID-19 in all three groups analyzed.<br>6MWT improved with large effect sizes in all groups, with major changes in subgroups 1 and 2.<br>Groups 1 and 2 showed statistically significant improvements with moderate to high effect sizes in VC%, TLC%, FEV1%, TLCO_SB% and PImax.<br>Significant decrease in fatigue was observed in groups 1 and 2, with large effect sizes.<br>Anxiety values decreased, with moderate to high effect sizes.<br>All groups showed significant improvement with high effect sizes in QoL. |

**Table 5.** *Cont.*

| Author Year Title | Study Design | Rehabilitation Protocol | Intervention Frequency | Participants | Outcome Measures | Evaluation Time | Results |
|---|---|---|---|---|---|---|---|
| Hermann et al., 2020 [30] | Cohort study | EG1 (ventilated), EG2 (unventilated): individualized training including aerobic exercise and strength training. Respiratory physiotherapy consisted of teaching breath control (breathing of ruffled lips, mobilization of secretions and diaphragmatic breathing), energy-saving techniques and controlled cough exercises. Twice a week (1 h each), all patients participated in educational sessions. CG: N/A | 2–4 weeks with 25–30 therapy sessions, which took place on 5–6 days a week. | EG1 (ventilated) (n. 12) -Mean age: 64.3 -Gender: 9M/12F EG2 (not ventilated) (n. 16) -Mean age: 67.4 -Gender: 5M/16F CG: N/A | Primary: 6-MWT, CRQ, FIM, CIRS, HADS -Patients' feelings about their actual well-being: Sensitive thermometer (FT) -Lung function, blood gas analysis and oxygen therapy Secondary: N/A | At baseline and at the end of the PR program. | Significant improvements were observed in 6-MWT (+130 m) and FT (+40 points) for the total cohort with no significant differences in intergroup comparison, between ventilated and unventilated patients. Pulmonary function tests showed persistent obstructed ventilation only in a few cases, however, still a part of the patients had limited ventilation and reduced diffusion capacity with the following results: mean FEV1 56%, mean FEV1% FVC 81%, mean TLC 62%, DLCO 56%. |
| Li et al., 2021 [19] | RCT | EG: via a smartphone application called RehabApp: breathing control and chest expansion, aerobic exercise and LMS exercises specified in a three-level exercise plan with difficulty and intensity programmed to increase over time. CG: Brief Educational Instructions | 3–4 sessions per week for 6 weeks. | EG (TERECO) (n. 59) -Mean age: 49.17 -Gender: 26M/34F CG (n.61) -Mean age: 52.03 -Gender: 27M/32F | Primary: 6MWT Secondary: -Squat time in seconds to evaluate the muscle strength of the lower limbs; -Lung function: spirometry, SF-12, mMRC | At baseline, at 6 weeks (post-treatment) and at 28 weeks (follow-up). | The 6MWT in the TERECO group improved by 80.2 m in the after-treatment period, while in the control group there was a small improvement of 17.1 m. Lower limb muscle strength (SML) improved to a greater extent in the TERECO group, treatment effects were 20.12 sec post-treatment and 22.23 sec at follow-up. Lung function parameters improved in both groups, except for maximal voluntary ventilation (MVV) which improved post-treatment most in the TERECO group. The increase in the physical component of SF-12 was greater in the TERECO group with treatment effects estimated at 3.79 post-treatment and 2.69 following. |

**Table 5.** *Cont.*

| Author Year Title | Study Design | Rehabilitation Protocol | Intervention Frequency | Participants | Outcome Measures | Evaluation Time | Results |
|---|---|---|---|---|---|---|---|
| Liu et al., 2021 [21] | RCT | EG: training of respiratory muscles; exercise for cough; diaphragmatic training; stretching exercise; and exercise at home (ruffled lip breathing and cough training: 30 sets per day).<br>Exercises for upper limb in flexion, horizontal extension, abduction and external rotation.<br>CG: no treatment | 2 sessions per week for 6 weeks. | EG (n. 36)<br>-Mean age: 69.4<br>-Gender: 24M/12F<br>CG (n.36)<br>-Mean age: 68.9<br>-Gender: 25M/11F | Primary: Respiratory function: forced expiratory volume in 1st second forced expiratory volume(FEV1); Forced vital capacity (CVF); capillary alveolus diffusion of carbon monoxide DLCO (%)<br>Secondary:6MWT, FIM, SF-36, SDS, SAS | At baseline and at the end of the PR program. | In the intervention group, significant differences were found in FEV1(L), FVC(L), FEV1/FVC%, DLCO% and 6MWT. SF-36 scores, in 8 dimensions, were statistically significant within the intervention group and between the two groups.<br>SAS and SDS scores in the intervention group decreased after the intervention, but only anxiety had a significant outcome within and between the two groups. |
| Pehlivan et al., 2022 [20] | RCT | EG (TeleGr): patient education, rhythm running/autonomous walking in the corridor, breathing exercises, active cycle of breathing techniques, range of motion exercises and standing squats. The exercises were performed 10 times per session. The number of repetitions has been adjusted according to the fatigue rate.<br>CG: exercise brochures with the same content (patient education, breathing exercises, movement exercises, self-walking and squats) | 3 days a week for 6 weeks. | EG (TeleGr): (n.34)<br>-Mean age: 50.76<br>-Gender: 14M/3F<br>CG: (n.34)<br>-Mean age: 43.24<br>-Gender: 6M/11F | Primary: MRC; VAS, TUG, Short Battery for Physical Performance (SPPB) includes three tasks: a standing balance test (side-by-side, semi-tandem and tandem), a usual gait speed of 4 m and sitting and getting up 5v from a chairSt. George's breathing questionnaire, BDI<br>Secondary: N/A | At baseline and at the end of the PR program. | Significant improvement in EG (TelerGr) in terms of mMRC ($p$ = 0.035), 30STS ($p$ = 0.005), 5 sitting to standing time, which is one of the subtests of SPPB ($p$ = 0.039) and SGRQ scores.<br>A significant improvement was observed only in the pain score in the CG ($p$ = 0.039).<br>Statistically significant difference between groups in SGRQ ($p$ = 0.035) and total ($p$ = 0.042) scores.<br>In addition, a more symptomatic improvement was found in TeleGr. |

**Table 5.** *Cont.*

| Author Year Title | Study Design | Rehabilitation Protocol | Intervention Frequency | Participants | Outcome Measures | Evaluation Time | Results |
|---|---|---|---|---|---|---|---|
| Puchner et al., 2021 [31] | Observational cohort study | EG: Respiratory therapy;<br>Training of respiratory muscles;<br>Mobilization and perception of breath;<br>Endurance and strength training;<br>Speech therapy intervention and swallowing evaluation;<br>Occupational therapy, psychological therapy.<br>CG: N/A | 25–50 min sessions for 3 weeks. | EG (n.23)<br>-Mean age: 57 ± 10<br>-Gender: 16M/7F<br>CG: N/A | Primary:Respiratory function by spirometry: forced vital capacity (FVC), forced vital capacity in one second (FEV1), FEV1/FVC, total lung capacity (TLC), residual volume (RL) and diffusion capacity for carbon monoxide (DLCO) and blood gas analysis pH, pO2 and pCO2, MIP, 6MWT, BI | At baseline and at the end of the PR program. | Significant improvement in lung function: increased forced vital capacity (FVC), forced expiratory volume in one second ($FEV_1$), total lung capacity (TLC) and carbon monoxide diffusion capacity (DLCO).<br>The state of physical performance has improved: average increase of 176 m in 6MWT and significant improvement in the Barthel Index (BI).<br>Lung function is still impaired in 57% of all patients, and 83% of all study participants still had DLCO reduction at the end of the rehabilitation program. |
| Spielmanns et al., 2021 [32] | Prospective observational study | EG and CG:<br>resistance training (cycling and treadmill), 3-level gymnastics, 3-level indoor and outdoor walking and strength training;<br>Respiratory physiotherapy: breathing with wrinkled lips, mobilization of secretions and diaphragmatic breathing), energy-saving techniques and controlled cough exercises;<br>Twice a week (1 h each): educational sessions (self-management, coping skills, self-medication, infection and exacerbation management, dyspnea, oxygen use and nutritional interventions). | 25–30 therapy sessions in 5–6 weekdays for 3 weeks. | EG (n.99)<br>-Mean age: 67.72<br>-Gender: 57M/42F<br>CG: (n.419)<br>-Mean age: 69.28<br>-Gender: 206M/213F | Primary: 6MWT,<br>Pulmonary function test: spirometry and plethysmography and blood gas analysis,CRQ, FIM, HADS, CIRS<br>-Wellness: Sensitive thermometer (FT)<br>Secondary: N/A | At baseline and at the end of the PR program. | Improvements in 6-MWT in pre-post comparison averaged 180 (±101) meters for EG and 102 (±89) meters for CG ($p < 0.001$).<br>FT showed a significant improvement for post-COVID-19 patients (PG) of 21 (±14) points and for patients with other lung disease (LG) of 17 (±16) points ($p < 0.039$), while FIM increased significantly by 11 (±10) points in post-COVID-19 patients (PG) and 7 (±8) points in patients with other lung disease (LG) ($p < 0.001$). |
| Vitacca et al., 2020 [34] | Practical guideline | / | / | / | / | / | / |
| Vitacca et al., 2020 [35] | Declaration of consent | / | / | / | / | / | / |

**Table 5.** *Cont.*

| Author Year Title | Study Design | Rehabilitation Protocol | Intervention Frequency | Participants | Outcome Measures | Evaluation Time | Results |
|---|---|---|---|---|---|---|---|
| Zampogna et al., 2021 [33] | Multicenter retrospective observational study | EG:<br>Level A: SPPB < 6 with a 1:1 physiotherapist/patient ratio with mobilization, active exercises and free walking, peripheral limb muscles, shoulders and upper limb activity.<br>Level B: SPPB ≥ 6 with a 1:4–5 physiotherapist/patient ratio with gymnastics, strengthening, balance exercise, rhythmic walking, and thoracic physiotherapy with bronchial hygiene techniques and lung expansion procedures.<br>CG: N/A | From a minimum of 1 session a day of 20 min up to 2–3 sessions of 30 min a day. | EG (n.140)<br>-Mean age: 71.0<br>-Gender: 95M/45F<br>CG: N/A | Primary:<br>-Exercise tolerance: 6 Minutes Walking Test (6MWT);<br>-Function of the lower limbs: Short Physical Performance Battery (SPPB);<br>-Motor performance: the Barthel Index (BI).<br>Secondary: N/A | At baseline and at the end of the PR program | Improvements in lower limb function in SPPB and motor performance in BI with scores ranging from 55 to 95.<br>81 patients after rehabilitation treatment were able to complete the 6 MWT with an average distance of 285 m.<br>The percentage of patients who at the time of admission were unable to stand, get up from a chair and walk after rehabilitation is significantly reduced. |

FEV1: forced expiratory volume in the 1st second; CVF: forced vital capacity; PImax (cmH2O): inspiratory pressure; PEmax (cmH2O): aspiratory pressure; 6MWT: six minute walking test; Tinetti scale: balance; Borg test: dyspnea; muscle strength; St George questionnaire: quality of life (QoL); Pichot's questionnaire: fatigue; hospital anxiety and depression questionnaire: anxiety and depression; post-traumatic stress disorder checklist scale (PCLS): post-traumatic stress; FIM: functional independence measure; CRQ: chronic respiratory questionnaire; Medical Research Council (MRC); time up and go (TUG); activity-specific balance confidence: activity-specific balance confidence scale (ABC); general self-effectiveness: patient-reported outcomes measurement and information system (PROMIS) short form (SF); clinical frailty scale (self-reported) and patient health questionnaire 8 (PHQ8); cognitive assessment: Montreal cognitive assessment (MoCA)-blind; Barthel index (BI); Borg rating of perceived exertion (RPE scale); COPD assessment test (CAT); functional assessment of chronic illness therapy fatigue scale (FACIT); anxiety and depression: hospital anxiety and depression scale (HADS); EuroQual 5 domains (EQ5D); total lung capacity (TLC) and carbon monoxide diffusion capacity (DLCO); quality of life: related to health (SF-36); anxiety symptoms: generalized anxiety disorder-7 (GAD-7) questionnaire; depressive symptoms: patient health questionnaire (PHQ-9).

### 3.5. Intervention

The different approaches used within the selected studies include respiratory rehabilitation delivered through different protocols and with a varying number of sessions and methods of intervention. The approaches were different for all studies and w described for each one.

Four studies adopted a respiratory physiotherapy program comprising deep breathing, inhaling muscle training and bronchial hygiene techniques [19,23,29,33]. One study kept to the European Respiratory Society and American Thoracic Society's recommendations (ATS/ERS) for that concerning breathing exercises [22].

Another study provided a program of respiratory rehabilitation based on thoracic clapping and vibrations, breathing control and thorax–abdominal coordination exercises, breathing exercises using a pep bottle, forced inhaling/exhaling and the use of incentive spirometers [24]. Three studies envisioned the teaching of breathing control (breathing with pursed lips, secretion mobilization and diaphragmatic breathing) and controlled coughing exercises [20,30,32]. One study combined muscular training with active cycle breathing training (ACBT) [26,31]. Instead, two studies gave a less detailed definition of the respiratory rehabilitation program [25,27].

Four studies envisioned a telerehabilitation program that provided for a virtual and supervised respiratory and muscular rehabilitation program, deployed through a telemedicine platform [18,21,28,31]. Two of these studies (Hameed et al. and Pehlivan et al.) describe a rehabilitation program delivered on a telerehabilitation platform. In Hameed et al. [28], diaphragmatic breathing exercises, spirometry incentive, sit-to-stand, standing gear, shoulder scaption, standing heel lifts, sidestepping and wall flexion are proposed. In Pehlivan et al. [20], patient education, rhythm run/autonomous walk in the corridor, breathing exercises and an active cycle of breathing techniques is proposed, in addition to range of motion exercises and standing squats. Instead, in two of these studies, telerehabilitation program is proposed through a smartphone app. In Capin et al. [18], the program includes breathing and compensation techniques, high-intensity strength training, aerobic and cardiovascular exercises, exercise balance, functional activities, stretching, and lifestyle coaching and motivational talk. In addition, this application is used for facilitating self-directed intervention outside supervised sessions. In Li et al. [19], the use of an application for smartphones called "RehabApp" is described, and this study includes chest breathing and expansion and aerobic exercise in a three-level exercise plan with the difficulty and intensity programmed to increase over time.

All of the studies adopted a rehabilitation protocol in which respiratory physiotherapy is deployed with strength and resistance training of both the upper and lower limbs, balance and coordination exercises, aerobic exercise based on walking/treadmill and cycling and muscular relaxation techniques. Five studies implemented educational sessions, in conjunction with the rehabilitation protocol, which concerned dyspnea, cough, fatigue, fear and anxiety, memory and concentration, self-management of ordinary activities and back-to-office activities [25,27,29,30,32]. Only four studies included psychosocial support with lifestyle and motivational coaching, nutritional consultation and occupational therapy as part and parcel of the rehabilitation protocol [18,19,23,29].

Concerning the length of the interventions, treatment length varies from study to study, from a minimum of one session [28] to a maximum of five–six sessions per week [32], distributed on a time interval spanning a minimum of 3 weeks [27] to a maximum of 12 weeks of treatment [26]. The intensity of the rehabilitation action is also quite heterogeneous and comprises between 20 [32] and 60 min per session [28] (Table 5).

### 3.6. Comparison

Not all the studies included had a control group. One of the studies compares three experimentation groups, each undergoing virtual physical therapy by means of a telemedicine platform, home-delivered physical therapy, an autonomous physical exercise program and one control group that receives no treatment [28].

Three of the included studies made a comparison between cohorts undergoing the same rehabilitation program, which differ in the type of COVID-19 they show: mild/moderate and severe/critical COVID-19 [27], acute/grave/serious/mild COVID-19 [29] and patients on ventilation or not [30].

Three studies compare two cohorts undergoing the same rehabilitation program but draw a distinction between: COVID-19 and non-COVID-19 patients [22], COVID-19 patients and patients with other kinds of pneumonia [23], COVID-19 patients and patients with other types of lung disease [32].

Three studies included a control group which received educational sessions [18,21,31]. Instead, two studies included a control group that received no treatment [20,26].

Lastly, four included studies did not exhibit any control group [19,24,25,32] (Table 5).

### 3.7. Outcome

The analyzed studies show the main results related to two macro-areas: lung function and functional capacity (exercise), which were evaluated in almost all of the studies using different scales and other tools.

The test which was most used to evaluate functional capacity was the six minute walking test (6MWT) [19,21–24,26,29–33]; one study used the shortened version of the test, namely, the two minute walking test [28]; one study used a different test, namely, the incremental shuttle walking test and the endurance shuttle walking test (ISWT and ESWT) [25]; and one study used both the six minute walking test (6MWT) and the endurance shuttle walking test (ESWT) [27]. Apart from the six minute walking test (6MWT), two studies also used as a stress test the 30 s sit-to-stand test [26,28], while two studies evaluated the functioning of lower limbs using the short physical performance battery (SPPB) [28,31].

The patients' physical functional, psychological and social state was mainly evaluated using the functional independence measure (FIM) [20,23,30,32]. Only three studies evaluated autonomy in the activities of daily life (ADL) through the Barthel index (BI) [19,24,33].

Only two of the studies considered did not use the six minute walking test as their functional capacity assessment (6MWT), but rather used the time up and go test (TUG) to evaluate patients' mobility [18,19].

Functional capacity was considered a primary outcome in 11 studies [19,22,23,25–28,30–33] and as a secondary outcome in 3 studies [20,24,29].

Pulmonary function was examined in only seven studies using spirometry and plethysmography, using the following parameters: forced expiratory volume in the 1st second (FEV1), forced vital capacity (FVC), residual volume (VR), maximum and minimum inspiratory pressure (Pi max/min), total lung capacity (TLC) and carbon monoxide alveolar–capillary diffusion (DLCO) [19–22,29,30,32]. In addition to all parameters for pulmonary function above, three studies also included blood gas analysis [19,29,30]. On the other hand, nine studies did not include the evaluation of pulmonary function as an outcome [18,23,26–28,31,33]. The pulmonary function was considered a primary outcome in five studies [19,21,22,30,32] and as a secondary outcome for two studies [21,29].

Dyspnea was considered as an outcome only in seven studies. To assess dyspnea, the widest-spread scale used was the Modified British Medical Research Council Questionnaire (mMRC) [18–20,24,27,29]; only one study assessed dyspnea using the Borg scale [22]. Dyspnea was considered a primary outcome in three studies [22,29,31] and a secondary outcome in four studies [18,21,24,27]. Nine of the selected studies did not assess dyspnea [21,23,25,26,28,30–33].

Within the outcomes that were considered, we also have those related to the quality of life in correlation to health (QoL), which was analyzed in nine studies and evaluated through different scales: St George questionnaire [22,31], chronic respiratory questionnaire [30,32], short form 36 [20,27], short form 12 [21] and Euroquol 5D [25,29].

Anxiety and depression were also evaluated with different scales: the hospital anxiety and depression scale (HADS) [22,25,30,32], the general anxiety disorder-7 (GAD-7) and the patient health questionnaire-9 (PHQ-9) [27–29] and the Beck depression inventory (BDI) [31].

In addition to this, we must also add cognitive function [18,25], fatigue [22,25,29], equilibrium [18], clinic fragility [18], pain [31] and subjective change in health status [29]. (Table 5).

### 3.8. *Summary of Results*

The analysis of the obtained results highlights that, in the post-acute phase of COVID-19, a complete rehabilitation program, which is most frequently adopted, provides for respiratory physiotherapy deployed together with aerobic exercise and both strength and resistance exercise, carried out both in person and remotely through telemedicine platforms.

Indeed, out of the 18 studies considered in this systematic review, 12 provided for a pulmonary rehabilitation program deployed in hospital or outpatient settings, while 4 present a remotely deployed rehabilitation program through telemedicine platforms. To this, a practical guideline and a declaration of consent added, which gives suggestions for the planning of rehabilitation programs for COVID-19 patients in different phases.

Specifically for the post-acute phase, the following actions are suggested: disability recovery, peripheral muscle strengthening, thoracic physiotherapy with respiratory muscle training, dry nonproductive cough management and bronchial clearance techniques with appropriate preventive measures. To this, we must add aerobic exercise < 3.0 MET with progressive intensity increase in patients with no or slight disability (SPPB > 10; Barthel index > 70); a complete pulmonary rehabilitation program is necessary in patients with moderate-to-severe disability (SPPB < 10; Barthel index < 70). During exercise training, the continuous monitoring of essential parameters such as blood pressure, SpO2, dyspnea and perceived effort (Borg scale) is recommended. The use of continuous or temporary positive expiratory pressure devices with or without oscillation (PEP, TPEP and OPEP) is suggested for patients with hypersecretion, either alone or in combination with lung expansion strategies to increase lung volume, better control exhalation and facilitate peripheral and proximal mucus movement [34,35]. Based on the protocols suggested by the studies, we hereby summarize the results obtained for the main outcomes that were examined: In evaluating functional capacity, which is the primary outcome for almost all included studies, we detected improvements in all groups that underwent a complete rehabilitation program; in more detail, three of the studies taken into account detected significant improvements in all groups, which differed for the type of COVID-19 they exhibited: light/moderate COVID-19 and severe/critical COVID-19 undergoing the same rehabilitation program showed a slight difference in favor of the patients with severe/critical COVID-19 [27,29,30].

Three studies noted significantly better improvements in COVID-19 group patients compared to the control group, which received the same rehabilitation program but composed of patients suffering from common pneumonia or other lung diseases [22,23,32].

Four studies analyzed a single cohort of COVID-19 patients without a control group and have noted a significant improvement in functional capacity in terms of an increase in the 6MWT, the ISWT, the ESWT and the SPPB, as well as an improvement in autonomy in daily life activities (ADL), assessed through the Barthel index. [19,24,25,33]. The four studies that comprised a rehabilitation program deployed through telemedicine registered significant improvements not only regarding functional capacity but also in symptoms and quality of life, in favor of the group that received the complete rehabilitation program remotely through a telemedicine platform compared to the control group that received no therapy or brief educational instructions [18,21,28,31].

Lastly, two studies highlighted a considerable improvement in functional capacity including quality of life in favor of the group that received the complete lung rehabilitation program with respect to the control group that received no treatment [20,26].

In evaluating the pulmonary function, another outcome analyzed by most studies considered, the same instruments were used; however, heterogeneous results were obtained. Two of the studies noted statistically significant improvements in pulmonary function in favor of the group that received the complete rehabilitation program concerning the control group which received no therapy [20,21].

Two other studies, which compared two groups constituted by COVID-19 patients and patients affected by other pulmonary disease or respiratory failure, found a sizeable improvement in the lung function of the COVID-19-patient group.

Another study analyzed a single cohort of COVID-19 patients without a control group and registered a considerable improvement in lung function, which is still compromised even after the rehabilitation program [19]. One of the studies traced significant improvements in all groups considered, which underwent the same rehabilitation program. The patients differed for the type of COVID-19 they presented: grave/severe/moderate. The results also show a slightly more favorable outcome for those with grave/severe COVID-19, concerning lung function and quality of life and fatigue [29].

Lastly, only one study did not exhibit any significant differences in pulmonary function between the two groups that underwent the same rehabilitation program but were distinguished between ventilated and unventilated [30].

In the analyzed studies, it was observed that COVID-19 patients underwent a complete respiratory rehabilitation program with breathing, aerobic, strength and endurance exercises, carried out both in hospital and remote with telemedicine, recording a gradual recovery of functional capacity, the operating capacity that translates into an initial increase in the distance traveled to 6MWT. This results in a gradual increase in autonomy and improvement of the quality of life. Some studies have shown that the same rehabilitation program focused on respiratory function could improve functional capacity even in patients with different stages of COVID-19 (Table 5).

## 4. Discussion

Our systematic review was carried out to analyze the role of a multidimensional respiratory rehabilitation program in improving the functional impairments detected in post-acute COVID-19 patients to evaluate the effectiveness and the benefits derived and identify specific protocols that may be included within tailored rehabilitation programs.

The results suggest that a complete rehabilitation protocol comprised of respiratory physiotherapy, aerobic training and strength and resistance training is beneficial to ameliorate the typical fallouts in COVID-19 patients. However, the low number of high-quality studies in the literature does not allow the recognition of an elective protocol. Stemming from the suggestion given in the guidelines, recommendations and declarations of consent [34–36] that have followed one another in these two years of the pandemic, we can see that an aspect in common for almost all of the studies is the centrality of physical exercise, which represents the key aspect in treating pulmonary illnesses. This is because it allows for a progressive improvement of peak absorption of lung oxygen, functional capacity, muscular strength and size, systematic oxidative stress and health-correlated quality of life [37].

Therefore, the studies we analyzed in this review show results related to two macro-areas: lung function and exercise capacity, evaluated by the six minute walking test (6MWT).

The element that distinguishes the rehabilitation protocols is the type of exercise they suggest: some protocols consider deep breathing, training of inspiratory muscles and bronchial hygiene techniques with a positive finding in the functional tests used, significant results and performance improvement in 6MWT, Barthel index, functional independence measure and lung function tests such as FEV1, CV, TLC, TLCO [23,29,31,33]. Only one study proposes thoracic clapping and vibration, breathing control exercises and thoracoabdominal coordination exercises, breathing exercises with the pep bottle, forced inhalation/exhalation and the use of an incentive spirometer with a significant improvement in the main functional test used: 6MWT, Barthel index and perceived effort with the Borg scale [24]. Others planned the teaching of breathing control: breathing with wrinkled lips, mobilization of secretions, diaphragmatic breathing and controlled coughing exercises with a significant improvement in functional abilities and therefore positive results in 6MWT, functional independence measure and positive results on lung function test. This results in a general improvement in the quality of life [21,30,32].

Respiratory physiotherapy is associated with strength and endurance training of the upper and lower limbs, aerobic exercise, muscle relaxation techniques and, in one case, balance and coordination exercises [24] to achieve progressive functional improvement and a reduction in the level of disability. These rehabilitation programs have allowed the achievement of a gradual recovery of exercise capacity and extensive improvements in muscle strength, balance, reduction in dyspnea and its impact on daily life activities [22–24,29,30,32,33].

However, it must be recognized that respiratory rehabilitation does not limit itself to breathing muscle training, but it is indeed, as stated by the American Thoracic Society (ATS) and The European Respiratory Society (ERS), a global approach based on a deep evaluation of the patient eligible for tailored therapy. This therapy must include, but is not limited to, the re-education of physical effort, educational activities aiming at a change in lifestyle and bad behavioral habits and improving lifestyle [38].

To this end, certain studies envisioned coupling the rehabilitation protocol with educational sessions aided by handouts that included: dyspnea, cough, fatigue, fear and anxiety, memory and concentration, self-handling of daily activities and back-to-office activities [25,27,29,30,32].

Only in a few cases was psychosocial support included as part and parcel of the rehabilitation protocol, together with lifestyle coaching and motivational interview [18,23,29,31], to favor the improvement of physical and psychological health, promote therapeutic adherence and ameliorate health in general in patients affected by respiratory disease. In these cases, there was a progressive improvement in the quality of life and a reduction in the symptoms of anxiety and depression, although with minimal dimensions.

Both the educational and the psychosocial components hold key roles in the rehabilitation program; they indeed amount to an important factor that can influence one's perception of the functional condition and one's health status in general. This rehabilitation program can also improve patient compliance and better outcomes in terms of limitations and functionality, as well as rapid return to work and social activities.

A comprehensive and multidimensional respiratory rehabilitation program showed positive outcomes in all examined COVID-19 patients. However, most of the studies in the literature focused more on evaluating the effectiveness of rehabilitation in patients who survived intensive care, and little is known about non-ICU-COVID-19 patients. Some studies report how a comprehensive respiratory rehabilitation program can significantly improve functional outcome measures in patients with severe–critical COVID-19 [27,29]. Only one study reports no significant differences in the functional outcomes analyzed at discharge among patients [23].

The novelty suggested in this review of scientific literature is its focus on remote rehabilitation programs. The studies showed that a remote rehabilitation program deployed through telemedicine and under supervision is safe, feasible and effective. The data obtained reveal how a good efficacy and foremost significant improvements from the functional point of view in patients involved, as shown by the increase in distance walked in the six minute walking test (6MWT), to which we can add the increase in lung function and health correlated quality of life [18,21,28,31].

During the pandemic, there was a high percentage of patients with damage and limitations of physical and lung function, and remote rehabilitation has proved to be a viable alternative that could become a new frontier in rehabilitation, to ensure greater continuity in patient care. Since we have seen the issues healthcare systems experienced in the current pandemic, we consider it more important to assure equity in access to therapy in remote areas, continuity in assistance and support for the management of chronic situations.

Hence, we can state that even though we have the presence in the scientific literature, concerning COVID-19's post-acute phase and heterogeneous pulmonary rehabilitation protocols in terms of suggested exercises, we can still see that a rehabilitation protocol that combines respiratory physiotherapy, aerobic training and strength, without neglecting the neuropsychological aspect, produces a positive effect on exercise capacity, lung function, dyspnea, fatigue, reduction in anxiety and depression and improvement of quality of life (QoL). This goes to show the fundamental importance of starting complete and tailored rehabilitation protocols in the post-acute phase, especially in those patients that exhibited a grave/critical form of pneumonia, to ensure the obtainment of the highest level of physical, functional, social autonomy possible and improve quality of life in COVID-19 survivors, as well as reducing the incidence of serious lung and functional complications, thus producing benefits from the economic–health point of view.

In carrying out this systematic review, we encountered several issues, the largest of which was the selection of the studies, since the pandemic has hit the world with dramatic effects leaving few possibilities to carry out high-quality clinical studies on a wide range of patients. Hence, most of the current protocols are based on preliminary results, observational studies, cohort studies, experts' opinions, consent of professionals and previous experiences derived from the acute respiratory distress virus pandemic (SARS). This aspect has determined the vast array of suggested designs proposed by the studies we considered and their different methodologies and respective quality.

Another relevant limit is the absence, for the most part, of a control group, which did not allow the obtaining of absolute proof regarding the efficacy of the rehabilitation protocol proposed for the treatment of COVID-19 derived functional impairments.

Indeed, most of the studies accounted for that suggested the application of a rehabilitation program on a small cohort comprised of a limited number of patients, which further limits the extensibility of the acquired results over the global population. In addition, many studies did not carry out any adequate follow-up, thus needing further verification to better understand the long-term benefits of the suggested protocols for respiratory rehabilitation in the post-acute COVID-19 phase. Finally, a significant limitation is represented by the lack of a unique definition of post-acute phase in the literature, which creates differences between the different studies that have analyzed this phase.

Despite the limitations found, the quality of the studies included is such that it allows the definition of adequate results to the aim of the research for which they were intended.

## 5. Conclusions

To conclude, the consequences stemming from the COVID-19 pandemic caused a sizeable impact on the entire population's health, producing long-term effects that impair the physical performance and quality of life of COVID-19 survivors. In such a context, pulmonary rehabilitation, in its many facets, holds a primary role by allowing a gradual recovery of lung elasticity and optimal breathing flux, obtaining better alveolar ventilation and increasing oxygenation.

Combining exercises such as aerobic, respiratory, fitness and strength exercises without foregoing the neuropsychological aspect has proven to be apt for ameliorating health status, well-being and quality of life in post-acute COVID-19 patients. It has also increased exercise capacity, improved fatigue levels and inhalator muscle strength and diminished anxiety and depression conditions, which are very frequent aspects that can greatly influence patients' compliance, the latter being key in successfully implementing of a rehabilitation program.

Therefore, it is advisable to increase the implementation of comprehensive and customized rehabilitation protocols for COVID-19 patients, in which a large part is devoted to respiratory rehabilitation to recover overall function and improve in the quality of life.

**Author Contributions:** M.T., R.C. conception of the study, methodology and drafting the work; A.S., G.G. drafting the work and revisiting it critically for important intellectual content. All authors have read and agreed to the published version of the manuscript.

**Funding:** This research received no external funding.

**Institutional Review Board Statement:** Not applicable. Institutional Review Board approval was not required because no interventions nor procedures were performed.

**Informed Consent Statement:** Not applicable.

**Data Availability Statement:** Not applicable.

**Conflicts of Interest:** The authors declare no conflict of interest.

## Appendix A

**Table A1.** Search terms.

| | |
|---|---|
| Medline: Scopus and Cochrane Library | (Pulmonary rehabilitation OR post-acute) AND COVID-19. |
| Pedro | (Pulmonary rehabilitation OR post-acute) AND COVID-19; Pulmonary rehabilitation AND COVID, COVID-19 AND Rehabilitation, COVID-19 AND Physiotherapy, SARS-CoV-2 AND Rehabilitation, SARS-CoV-2 AND Physiotherapy, COVID-19, SARS-CoV-2. |

## References


1. OMS Dashboard Updated to 2/12/2022. Available online: https://covid19.who.int/ (accessed on 2 December 2022).
2. National Institutes of Health. COVID-19 Treatment Guidelines. Management of Persons with COVID-19. Bethesda, MD NIH. 2020. Available online: https://files.covid19treatmentguidelines.nih.gov/guidelines/covid19treatmentguidelines.pdf (accessed on 20 November 2022).
3. Wu, C.; Chen, X.; Cai, Y.; Xia, J.; Zhou, X.; Xu, S.; Huang, H.; Zhang, L.; Zhou, X.; Du, C.; et al. Risk Factors Associated with Acute Respiratory Distress Syndrome and Death in Patients with Coronavirus Disease 2019 Pneumonia in Wuhan, China. *JAMA Intern Med.* **2020**, *180*, 934–943. [CrossRef]
4. Bernard, G.R.; Artigas, A.; Brigham, K.L.; Carlet, J.; Falke, K.; Hudson, L.; Lamy, M.; Legall, J.R.; Morris, A.; Spragg, R. The American-European Consensus Conference on ARDS. Definitions, mechanisms, relevant outcomes, and clinical trial coordination. *Am. J. Respir. Crit. Care. Med.* **1994**, *149*, 818–824. [CrossRef]
5. Zhu, J.; Ji, P.; Pang, J.; Zhong, Z.; Li, H.; He, C.; Zhang, J.; Zhao, C. Clinical characteristics of 3062 COVID-19 patients: A meta-analysis. *J. Med. Virol.* **2020**, *92*, 1902–1914. [CrossRef]
6. Spagnolo, P.; Balestro, E.; Aliberti, S.; Cocconcelli, E.; Biondini, D.; Della Casa, G.; Sverzellati, N.; Maher, T.M. Pulmonary fibrosis secondary to COVID-19: A call to arms? *Respir. Med Hand.* **2020**, *8*, 750–752. [CrossRef]
7. Nalbandian, A.; Sehgal, K.; Gupta, A.; Madhavan, M.V.; McGroder, C.; Stevens, J.S.; Cook, J.R.; Nordvig, A.S.; Shalev, D.; Sehrawat, T.S. Sindrome post-acuta da COVID-19. *Nat. Med.* **2021**, *27*, 601–615. [CrossRef] [PubMed]
8. Office for National Statistics. The Prevalence of Long COVID Symptoms and COVID-19 Complications. 2020. Available online: https://www.ons.gov.uk/news/statementsandletters/theprevalenceoflongcovidsymptomsandcovid19complications (accessed on 10 November 2022).
9. COVID-19 Rapid Guideline: Managing the Longterm Effects of COVID-19 9—NICE, RCGP, and SIGN. 1.20 Published on 3 November 2022. Available online: https://www.nice.org.uk/guidance/ng188/resources/covid19-rapid-guideline-managing-the-longterm-effects-of-covid19-pdf-51035515742 (accessed on 10 November 2022).
10. Huang, C.; Huang, L.; Wang, Y.; Li, X.; Ren, L.; Gu, X.; Kang, L.; Guo, L.; Liu, M.; Zhou, X.; et al. 6-month consequences of COVID-19 in patients discharged from hospital: A cohort study. *Lancet* **2021**, *397*, 220–232. [CrossRef] [PubMed]
11. Cattadori, G.; Di Marco, S.; Baravelli, M.; Picozzi, A.; Ambrosio, G. Training exercise in post-COVID-19 patients: The need for a multifactorial protocol for a multifactorial pathophysiology. *J. Clin. Med.* **2022**, *11*, 2228. [CrossRef]
12. Peng, X.L.; Cheng, J.S.; Gong, H.L.; Yuan, M.D.; Zhao, X.H.; Li, Z.; Wei, D.X. Advances in the design and development of SARS-CoV-2 vaccines. *Mil. Med. Res.* **2021**, *8*, 67. [CrossRef] [PubMed]
13. Nieman, D.C. Exercise Is Medicine for Immune Function: Implication for COVID-19. *Curr. Sports Med. Rep.* **2021**, *20*, 395–401. [CrossRef]
14. NICE. Rehabilitation After Critical Illness in Adults. 2009. Available online: https://www.nice.org.uk/guidance/cg83/resources/rehabilitation-after-critical-illness-in-adults-pdf-975687209413 (accessed on 10 November 2022).
15. Greenhalgh, T.; Knight, M.; A'Court, C.; Buxton, M.; Husain, L. Management of post-acute covid-19 in primary care. *BMJ* **2020**, *370*, m3026. [CrossRef]
16. Zhao, H.M.; Xie, Y.X.; Wang, C.; Chinese Association of Rehabilitation Medicine; Respiratory Rehabilitation Committee of Chinese Association of Rehabilitation Medicine; Cardiopulmonary Rehabilitation Group of Chinese Society of Physical Medicine and Rehabilitation. Recommendations for respiratory rehabilitation in adults with coronavirus disease 2019. *Chin. Med. J. (Engl.)* **2020**, *133*, 1595–1602. [CrossRef] [PubMed]
17. Barker-Davies, R.M.; O'Sullivan, O.; Senaratne, K.P.P.; Baker, P.; Cranley, M.; Dharm-Datta, S.; Ellis, H.; Goodall, D.; Gough, M.; Lewis, S. The Stanford Hall consensus statement for post-COVID-19 rehabilitation. *Br. J. Sports Med.* **2020**, *54*, 949–959. [CrossRef] [PubMed]

18. Capin, J.J.; Jolley, S.E.; Morrow, M.; Connors, M.; Hare, K.; MaWhinney, S.; Nordon-Craft, A.; Rauzi, M.; Flynn, S.; Stevens-Lapsley, J.E.; et al. Safety, feasibility and initial efficacy of an app-facilitated telerehabilitation (AFTER) programme for COVID-19 survivors: A pilot randomised study. *BMJ Open* **2022**, *12*, e061285. [CrossRef] [PubMed]
19. Li, J.; Xia, W.; Zhan, C.; Liu, S.; Yin, Z.; Wang, J.; Chong, Y.; Zheng, C.; Fang, X.; Cheng, W.; et al. A telerehabilitation programme in post-discharge COVID-19 patients (TERECO): A randomised controlled trial. *Thorax* **2022**, *77*, 697–706. [CrossRef]
20. Pehlivan, E.; Palalı, İ.; Atan, S.G.; Turan, D.; Çınarka, H.; Çetinkaya, E. The effectiveness of POST-DISCHARGE telerehabilitation practices in COVID-19 patients: Tele-COVID study-randomized controlled trial. *Ann. Thorac. Med.* **2022**, *17*, 110–117. [CrossRef]
21. Liu, K.; Zhang, W.; Yang, Y.; Zhang, J.; Li, Y.; Chen, Y. Respiratory rehabilitation in elderly patients with COVID-19: A randomized controlled study. *Complement. Ther. Clin. Pract.* **2020**, *39*, 101166. [CrossRef]
22. Al Chikhanie, Y.; Veale, D.; Schoeffler, M.; Pépin, J.L.; Verges, S.; Hérengt, F. Effectiveness of pulmonary rehabilitation in COVID-19 respiratory failure patients post-ICU. *Respir. Physiol. Neurobiol.* **2021**, *287*, 103639. [CrossRef]
23. Büsching, G.; Zhang, Z.; Schmid, J.P.; Sigrist, T.; Khatami, R. Effectiveness of Pulmonary Rehabilitation in Severe and Critically Ill COVID-19 Patients: A Controlled Study. *Int. J. Environ. Res. Public Health* **2021**, *18*, 8956. [CrossRef]
24. Curci, C.; Negrini, F.; Ferrillo, M.; Bergonzi, R.; Bonacci, E.; Camozzi, D.M.; Ceravolo, C.; DEFranceschi, S.; Guarnieri, R.; Moro, P.; et al. Functional outcome after inpatient rehabilitation in postintensive care unit COVID-19 patients: Findings and clinical implications from a real-practice retrospective study. *Eur. J. Phys. Rehabil. Med.* **2021**, *57*, 443–450. [CrossRef]
25. Daynes, E.; Gerlis, C.; Chaplin, E.; Gardiner, N.; Singh, S.J. Early experiences of rehabilitation for individuals post-COVID to improve fatigue, breathlessness exercise capacity and cognition—A cohort study. *Chron. Respir. Dis.* **2021**, *18*, 14799731211015691. [CrossRef]
26. Dun, Y.; Liu, C.; Ripley-Gonzalez, J.W.; Liu, P.; Zhou, N.; Gong, X.; You, B.; Du, Y.; Liu, J.; Li, B.; et al. Six-month outcomes and effect of pulmonary rehabilitation among patients hospitalized with COVID-19: A retrospective cohort study. *Ann. Med.* **2021**, *53*, 2099–2109. [CrossRef]
27. Gloeckl, R.; Leitl, D.; Jarosch, I.; Schneeberger, T.; Nell, C.; Stenzel, N.; Vogelmeier, C.F.; Kenn, K.; Koczulla, A.R. Benefits of pulmonary rehabilitation in COVID-19: A prospective observational cohort study. *ERJ Open Res.* **2021**, *7*, 00108–02021. [CrossRef]
28. Hameed, F.; Palatulan, E.; Jaywant, A.; Said, R.; Lau, C.; Sood, V.; Layton, A.; Gellhorn, A. Outcomes of a COVID-19 recovery program for patients hospitalized with SARS-CoV-2 infection in New York City: A prospective cohort study. *PM R* **2021**, *13*, 609–617. [CrossRef] [PubMed]
29. Hayden, M.C.; Limbach, M.; Schuler, M.; Merkl, S.; Schwarzl, G.; Jakab, K.; Nowak, D.; Schultz, K. Effectiveness of a Three-Week Inpatient Pulmonary Rehabilitation Program for Patients after COVID-19: A Prospective Observational Study. *Int. J. Environ Res. Public Health* **2021**, *18*, 9001. [CrossRef]
30. Hermann, M.; Pekacka-Egli, A.M.; Witassek, F.; Baumgaertner, R.; Schoendorf, S.; Spielmanns, M. Feasibility and Efficacy of Cardiopulmonary Rehabilitation After COVID-19. *Am. J. Phys. Med. Rehabil.* **2020**, *99*, 865–869. [CrossRef] [PubMed]
31. Puchner, B.; Sahanic, S.; Kirchmair, R.; Pizzini, A.; Sonnweber, B.; Wöll, E.; Mühlbacher, A.; Garimorth, K.; Dareb, B.; Ehling, R.; et al. Beneficial effects of multi-disciplinary rehabilitation in postacute COVID-19: An observational cohort study. *Eur. J. Phys. Rehabil. Med.* **2021**, *57*, 189–198. [CrossRef]
32. Spielmanns, M.; Pekacka-Egli, A.M.; Schoendorf, S.; Windisch, W.; Hermann, M. Effects of a Comprehensive Pulmonary Rehabilitation in Severe Post-COVID-19 Patients. *Int. J. Environ. Res. Public Health* **2021**, *18*, 2695. [CrossRef]
33. Zampogna, E.; Paneroni, M.; Belli, S.; Aliani, M.; Gandolfo, A.; Visca, D.; Bellanti, M.T.; Ambrosino, N.; Vitacca, M. Pulmonary Rehabilitation in Patients Recovering from COVID-19. *Respiration* **2021**, *100*, 416–422. [CrossRef] [PubMed]
34. Vitacca, M.; Carone, M.; Clini, E.M.; Paneroni, M.; Lazzeri, M.; Lanza, A.; Privitera, E.; Pasqua, F.; Gigliotti, F.; Castellana, G.; et al. Joint Statement on the Role of Respiratory Rehabilitation in the COVID-19 Crisis: The Italian Position Paper. *Respiration* **2020**, *99*, 493–499. [CrossRef] [PubMed]
35. Vitacca, M.; Lazzeri, M.; Guffanti, E.; Frigerio, P.; D'Abrosca, F.; Gianola, S.; Carone, M.; Paneroni, M.; Ceriana, P.; Pasqua, F.; et al. Italian suggestions for pulmonary rehabilitation in COVID-19 patients recovering from acute respiratory failure: Results of a Delphi process. *Monaldi. Arch. Chest. Dis.* **2020**, *90*, 385–393. [CrossRef]
36. Spruit, M.A.; Holland, A.E.; Singh, S.J.; Tonia, T.; Wilson, K.C.; Troosters, T. COVID-19: Interim Guidance on Rehabilitation in the Hospital and Post-Hospital Phase from a European Respiratory Society and American Thoracic Society-coordinated International Task Force. *Eur. Respir. J.* **2020**, *56*, 2002197. [CrossRef] [PubMed]
37. Alcazar, J.; Losa-Reyna, J.; Rodriguez-Lopez, C.; Navarro-Cruz, R.; Alfaro-Acha, A.; Ara, I.; García-García, F.J.; Alegre, L.M.; Guadalupe-Grau, A. Effects of concurrent exercise training on muscle dysfunction and systemic oxidative stress in older people with COPD. *Scand. J. Med. Sci. Sports* **2019**, *29*, 1591–1603. [CrossRef] [PubMed]
38. Official Recommendations of the American Thoracic Society and European Respiratory Society: Implementation, Use, and Dissemination of Respiratory Rehabilitation. Available online: https://www.ers-education.org/lrMedia/2015/pdf/393777.pdf (accessed on 20 October 2022).

healthcare

MDPI

*Article*

# The Masticatory Structure and Function in Children with Cerebral Palsy—A Pilot Study

**Karolina Szuflak [1,2,*,†], Roksana Malak [3,*,†], Brittany Fechner [3], Dorota Sikorska [3], Włodzimierz Samborski [3], Ewa Mojs [4] and Karolina Gerreth [1]**

1 Department of Risk Group Dentistry Chair of Pediatric Dentistry, Poznan University of Medical Sciences, 60-812 Poznan, Poland
2 Doctoral School, Poznan University of Medical Sciences, 60-812 Poznan, Poland
3 Department and Clinic of Rheumatology, Rehabilitation, and Internal Medicine, Poznan University of Medical Sciences, 61-545 Poznan, Poland
4 Department of Clinical Psychology, Poznan University of Medical Sciences, 60-812 Poznan, Poland
* Correspondence: kszuflak@student.ump.edu.pl (K.S.); rmalak@ump.edu.pl (R.M.)
† These authors contributed equally to this work.

**Abstract:** (1) Background: Muscle tension around the head and neck influences orofacial functions. The data exist concerning head posture during increased salivation; however, little is known about muscle tightness during this process. This study aims to investigate whether or not any muscles are related to problems with eating, such as drooling in individuals with cerebral palsy; (2) Methods: Nineteen patients between the ages of 1 and 14 were examined prior to the physiotherapy intervention. This intervention lasted three months and consisted of: relaxing muscles via the strain-counterstrain technique, functional exercises based on the NeuroDevelopmental Treatment-Bobath method, and functional exercises for eating; (3) Results: the tone of rectus capitis posterior minor muscle on the left side ($p = 0.027$) and temporalis muscle on the right side ($p = 0.048$) before the therapy, and scalene muscle on the right side after the therapy ($p = 0.024$) were correlated with drooling behavior and were considered statistically significant. Gross motor function was not considered statistically significant with the occurrence of drooling behavior ($p \leq 0.05$). Following the therapeutic intervention, the frequency of drooling during feeding decreased from 63.16% to 38.89% of the total sample of examined patients; (4) Conclusions: The tightness of the muscles in the head area can cause drooling during feeding.

**Keywords:** masticatory muscles; strain-counterstrain technique (SCS); NeuroDevelopmental Treatment-Bobath (NDT-Bobath) method; salivation; cerebral palsy (CP)

**Citation:** Szuflak, K.; Malak, R.; Fechner, B.; Sikorska, D.; Samborski, W.; Mojs, E.; Gerreth, K. The Masticatory Structure and Function in Children with Cerebral Palsy—A Pilot Study. *Healthcare* **2023**, *11*, 1029. https://doi.org/10.3390/healthcare11071029

Academic Editor: Abdel-Latif Mohamed

Received: 28 February 2023
Revised: 22 March 2023
Accepted: 29 March 2023
Published: 4 April 2023



## 1. Introduction

Drooling (sialorrhea) is defined as an involuntary flow of saliva from the mouth. After the age of 18 months, it is very often associated with intellectual disability and neuromuscular disorders such as cerebral palsy (CP) [1–5]. Approximately 90% of patients with CP also have some form of oral-motor dysfunction [6], of which 10–58% of these individuals have a problem with drooling [5]. This is due to dysfunctional voluntary oral motor activity, improper swallowing, and oral sphincter deficits. Drooling behavior in patients with CP is rarely caused by hypersalivation [7–9]. Therefore, causes of oral-motor disorders tend to be variable and challenging in therapeutic contexts. Therapists should conduct very complex examinations and interviews with patients. Also, the observation of feeding behavior should be performed. Only then will patients and families have the benefit of therapy to be thankful for. Rehabilitation and feeding therapy is for patients and their families.

Nowadays, the medical field proposes various treatments, such as botulinum toxin injections, surgical procedures, laser photocoagulation, pharmacotherapy, and acupuncture [2,5,10–14]. It is necessary to include safe complementary therapies, which involve interdisciplinary medical teams. Exploration of this subject may open the way for determining additional therapeutic options. Muscle tone is rarely considered a significant factor that may influence the eating behavior of children. Some researchers recognize the auxiliary muscles used during eating, the tension of which may affect the positioning of the head and the process of feeding [15–17]. Nowadays, we still have a shortage of information concerning the tension of muscles around the head or neck and relating to the process of eating and drooling in children.

According to Chávez (2008), Dias (2016) and Gerek (2005), intensified drooling may make it difficult to ingest food [4–6]. The lack of such information and the need for help during the feeding process for individuals may cause moderate to severe secondary malnutrition and limit hydration in patients with CP [18,19]. On the other hand, there are some reports about physiotherapy treatment causing decreased drooling in this group of patients. Kumari (2018) proved, when comparing two groups of participants, that oral motor therapy ($p < 0.0001$) was found to be more effective than oral facial facilitation ($p = 0.0719$) [20]. Moreover, Muammer (2010) investigated a combination of physiotherapeutic interventions, such as electrical stimulation and proprioceptive neuromuscular facilitation (PNF), can be helpful in reducing drooling in children with neurodevelopmental disorders [21]. Moreover, Cocks (2022) concluded that if the orbicularis oris is the primary muscle responsible for closing the lips, expiratory muscle strength training (EMST) could contribute to reducing drooling. Therefore, it was decided to prepare an examination to check the influence of expiratory muscle strength training on drooling for people with Parkinson's disease this showed the significant result that drooling and swallowing improved following training ($p < 0.01$) [22]. Thus, it would be necessary to explore the reason for the occurrence of excessive salivation and drooling in these patients during feeding. This became a research question of whether the muscle tension around the head and neck influences drooling? Therefore, we aimed to study the relationship between excessive drooling during feeding and muscle hypertension and have proposed a complementary treatment for sialorrhea.

## 2. Materials and Methods

We obtained permission from the Bioethics Commission at the Poznan University of Medical Sciences (ref. No. 339/15, dated 9 April 2015). Our study group included children with CP. The type in all subjects' neurological classification of cerebral palsy was quadriplegic. These patients were individuals living in a social welfare home, so their medical records were largely unknown. Even a medical history was also very often unclear. We included only this aspect which was retrospective and capable of examination. The intervention took place in 19 patients (11 males and 8 females; aged 1–14, mean age $\pm$ SD = 6.21 $\pm$ 2.82) during the first examination and before the start of the therapeutic intervention. A total of 18 children were assessed during the second examination following the end of the treatment. One participant was a 14-year-old female who was hospitalized during the second examination, and therefore could not be evaluated. The entire examined group presented the level V in the Gross Motor Function Classification System (GMFCS). GMFCS, as a valid 5- level system and reliable in 85% of cases, serves to classify the severity of motor function in pediatric patients with disability [23]. This means that the patient was not able to exhibit head and trunk control, nor any locomotion activities [8,9,24]. The inclusion criteria were difficulties with sucking, swallowing, and excessive salivation during eating according to the Castillo Morales Questionnaire [3,25]. We only used part of the Castillo Morales Questionnaire as it was not fully translated into the Polish language. Similarly we assessed whether children presented excessive drooling according to The Drooling Quotient Assessment (DQ) of which the reliability is 95% [26]. Patients presented the V level in the Eating and Drinking Ability Classification System (EDACS) which mean that the patient is unable to eat and drink safely—tube feeding may be considered to provide nutrition [27]. We excluded patients with inflammatory processes, tumors, any lethal diseases, and any patients who received any prior interventions to reduce drooling. Please see Table 1 below for additional inclusion and exclusion criteria (Table 1).

**Table 1.** Inclusion and exclusion criteria for participants diagnosed with cerebral palsy.

| Inclusion Criteria | Exclusion Criteria |
|---|---|
| Difficulties with sucking, swallowing, or excessive salivation | No oral motor dysfunctions |
| Children residing in one selected social welfare home in Poznan | Children residing in other social welfare homes than one selected in Poznan |
| Children with CP and severe intellectual disability | Children without CP and severe intellectual disability |
| Written and informed consent from the parent/caregiver for the examination and therapy of the child | No written and informed consent from the parent/caregiver for the examination and therapy of the child |
| Patient's cooperation during examination and therapy | Patient uncooperativeness during exam and therapy |
| Children present at social welfare home on days of examination and therapy | Children absent at social welfare home on days of examination and therapy |
| Group of children with the same regional, demographic, cultural, and ethnic origin | Group of children with other regional, demographic, cultural, or ethnic origin |
| Children with a GMFCS level V | Children with a GMFCS level IV or lower |
| Patients presented the V level in the EDACS | Patients presented the IV level or lower in the EDACS |

We developed the therapeutic intervention based on the strain-counterstrain technique (SCS) and NeuroDevelopmental Treatment-Bobath (NDT-Bobath). SCS is an osteopathic manipulative technique of soft tissues successfully used to relieve musculoskeletal pain and improve dysfunction mobility restrictions [27,28]. NDT-Bobath treatment was developed for treating neurodevelopmental disorders in young and adult people. Since 1940, NDT-Bobath has been based on research about brain functions and neurophysiology [29]. This treatment also included posture and balance training, which aims to improve children to the maximum independence level in each activity daily of living [29].

### 2.1. The Examination

The examination was prepared and carried out by experienced and trained physiotherapists. During the first examination before the therapeutic intervention and also during the second examination after the therapeutic intervention, physiotherapists assessed the muscle tone of each patient's masticatory muscles and auxiliary muscles. The assessor compared muscle tension between the right and left sides of the body by applying a gentle touch when palpating the muscle at a tender point. Each participant was diagnosed using the Gross Motor Function Measure–88 (GMFM-88). This measurement is the gold standard for measuring the quantitative evaluation of motor function in children with cerebral palsy from 5 months to 15 years old. This evaluative tool measures the effectiveness of therapy in improving gross motor function [30–32]. Using the same score of GMFM-88 in a study, we can compare the results of participants from different age groups. This is the reason why we included patients between 1 to 14 years old. At the beginning and end of the study, the examiners also assessed participants with The Drooling Quotient Assessment if drooling appeared and made the feeding of participants difficult.

### 2.2. The Therapeutic Intervention

Subsequently, we performed our therapeutic intervention, which lasted three months. During each day of therapy (two days per week), physiotherapists palpated the muscle tone of the following muscles: masseter, temporalis, sternocleidomastoid, trapezius, scalene, serratus anterior, and rectus capitis posterior minor. For the examination procedure, each patient was placed in a supine position, with the patient's back situated in a comfortable position to ensure the relaxation of the muscles. The therapy involved relaxing muscles responsible for sucking, swallowing, and chewing via the strain-counterstrain (SCS) technique and using the NeuroDevelopmental Treatment-Bobath (NDT-Bobath) method, which supported the proper positioning of the child while feeding the participant and the facilitation of functional sucking and swallowing, and chewing. Then we performed the SCS to relax the tensed muscles. For example, the assessment and therapy of the masseter muscle is carried out with the child's mouth open with a slight translation of the jaw towards the muscle, or the treatment of the sternocleidomastoid muscle takes place with the lateral flexion of the head to one side and rotation to the opposite side. When a physiotherapist selected the most tightened muscle, he put his index finger gently positioned with constant pressure for 90 s based on the SCS [33]. Two of the tensest muscles were relaxed during each treatment. After the SCS was applied, we supported each patient in a proper sitting position and facilitated eating based on the NDT-Bobath. After the period of three months with the therapeutic interventions took place, the second examination assessed the tension of the muscles and gross motor function by GMFM-88 again, and drooling as part of the Drooling Quotient Assessment.

Data were analyzed using STATISTICA 8.1 (StatSoft). To analyze the relationship between muscle tone and the presence of a given function, we used Pearson's chi-squared test. The Mann-Whitney test was used to determine the relationship between the test results according to the GMFM-88 and the occurrence of drooling. Correlation between samples was measured using Spearman's rank correlation coefficient. The results were considered statistically significant at $p \leq 0.05$.

## 3. Results

### *3.1. Muscle Tone and Drooling*

There was a statistically significant correlation between the occurrence of excessive salivation before the therapy and the hypertonicity of the rectus capitis posterior minor muscle on the left side ($p = 0.027$) and temporalis muscle on the right side ($p = 0.048$) (Table 2). We did not observe this correlation until after the therapy. However, the correlation after the therapy between tightness and the occurrence of excessive salivation was considered statistically significant in the scalene muscle on the right side ($p = 0.024$). It is worth noting that about 50% of patients with proper scalene muscle tension did not have drooling. Overall, we observed the tendency of tightness of the scalene muscle and excessive salivation (Table 3). The tension of the remaining muscles was not significantly correlated with drooling.

**Table 2.** The evaluation of dependence between the muscle tension and the occurrence of salivation before therapy (n = 19).

| Muscles | Side | Type of Tension | Lack Salivation | | Excessive Salivation | | *p* |
|---|---|---|---|---|---|---|---|
| | | | n | % | n | % | |
| scalene | left | proper | 3 | 15.79 | 7 | 36.84 | 0.515 |
| | | increased | 4 | 21.05 | 5 | 26.32 | |
| scalene | right | proper | 4 | 21.05 | 6 | 31.58 | 0.764 |
| | | increased | 3 | 15.79 | 6 | 31.58 | |
| rectus capitis posterior minor | left | proper | 1 | 5.26 | 8 | 42.11 | 0.027 * |
| | | increased | 6 | 31.58 | 4 | 21.05 | |

**Table 2.** *Cont.*

| Muscles | Side | Type of Tension | Lack Salivation | | Excessive Salivation | | *p* |
|---|---|---|---|---|---|---|---|
| | | | n | % | n | % | |
| rectus capitis posterior minor | right | proper | 6 | 31.58 | 6 | 31.58 | 0.119 |
| | | increased | 1 | 5.26 | 6 | 31.58 | |
| temporalis | left | proper | 5 | 26.32 | 5 | 26.32 | 0.210 |
| | | increased | 2 | 10.53 | 7 | 36.84 | |
| temporalis | right | proper | 2 | 10.53 | 9 | 47.37 | 0.048 * |
| | | increased | 5 | 26.32 | 3 | 15.79 | |
| masseter | left | proper | 5 | 26.32 | 5 | 26.32 | 0.210 |
| | | increased | 2 | 10.53 | 7 | 36.84 | |
| masseter | right | proper | 3 | 15.79 | 6 | 31.58 | 0.764 |
| | | increased | 4 | 21.05 | 6 | 31.58 | |
| sternocleidomastoid | left | proper | 4 | 21.05 | 6 | 31.58 | 0.764 |
| | | increased | 3 | 15.79 | 6 | 31.58 | |
| sternocleidomastoid | right | proper | 2 | 10.53 | 6 | 31.58 | 0.361 |
| | | increased | 5 | 26.32 | 6 | 31.58 | |
| trapezius | left | proper | 3 | 15.79 | 6 | 31.58 | 0.764 |
| | | increased | 4 | 21.05 | 6 | 31.58 | |
| trapezius | right | proper | 2 | 10.53 | 6 | 31.58 | 0.361 |
| | | increased | 5 | 26.32 | 6 | 31.58 | |
| serratus anterior | left | proper | 6 | 31.58 | 9 | 47.37 | 0.581 |
| | | increased | 1 | 5.26 | 3 | 15.79 | |
| serratus anterior | right | proper | 6 | 31.58 | 8 | 42.11 | 0.361 |
| | | increased | 1 | 5.26 | 4 | 21.05 | |

Pearson's chi-squared test was used; * statistically significant; the *p*-value was significant at $p \leq 0.05$; n—number; %—percentage.

**Table 3.** The evaluation of dependence between the muscle tension and the occurrence of salivation after therapy (n = 18).

| Muscles | Side | Type of Tension | Lack Salivation | | Excessive Salivation | | *p* |
|---|---|---|---|---|---|---|---|
| | | | n | % | n | % | |
| scalene | left | proper | 8 | 44.44 | 4 | 22.22 | 0.494 |
| | | increased | 3 | 16.67 | 3 | 16.67 | |
| scalene | right | proper | 9 | 50.00 | 2 | 11.11 | 0.024 * |
| | | increased | 2 | 11.11 | 5 | 27.78 | |
| rectus capitis posterior minor | left | proper | 5 | 27.78 | 6 | 33.33 | 0.088 |
| | | increased | 6 | 33.33 | 1 | 5.56 | |
| rectus capitis posterior minor | right | proper | 9 | 50.00 | 3 | 16.67 | 0.088 |
| | | increased | 2 | 11.11 | 4 | 22.22 | |
| temporalis | left | proper | 11 | 61.11 | 5 | 27.78 | 0.060 |
| | | increased | 0 | 0 | 2 | 11.11 | |

**Table 3.** *Cont.*

| Muscles | Side | Type of Tension | Lack Salivation | | Excessive Salivation | | $p$ |
|---|---|---|---|---|---|---|---|
| | | | n | % | n | % | |
| temporalis | right | proper | 4 | 22.22 | 4 | 22.22 | 0.387 |
| | | increased | 7 | 38.89 | 3 | 16.67 | |
| masseter | left | proper | 8 | 44.44 | 6 | 33.33 | 0.518 |
| | | increased | 3 | 16.67 | 1 | 5.56 | |
| masseter | right | proper | 7 | 38.89 | 3 | 16.67 | 0.387 |
| | | increased | 4 | 22.22 | 4 | 22.22 | |
| sternocleidomastoid | left | proper | 6 | 33.33 | 3 | 16.67 | 0.629 |
| | | increased | 5 | 27.78 | 4 | 22.22 | |
| sternocleidomastoid | right | proper | 8 | 44.44 | 4 | 22.22 | 0.494 |
| | | increased | 3 | 16.67 | 3 | 16.67 | |
| trapezius | left | proper | 6 | 33.33 | 3 | 16.67 | 0.629 |
| | | increased | 5 | 27.78 | 4 | 22.22 | |
| trapezius | right | proper | 5 | 27.78 | 6 | 33.33 | 0.088 |
| | | increased | 6 | 33.33 | 1 | 5.56 | |
| serratus anterior | left | proper | 8 | 44.44 | 7 | 38.89 | 0.130 |
| | | increased | 3 | 16.67 | 0 | 0 | |
| serratus anterior | right | proper | 9 | 50.00 | 6 | 33.33 | 0.829 |
| | | increased | 2 | 11.11 | 1 | 5.56 | |

Pearson's chi-squared test was used; * statistically significant; the $p$-value was significant at $p \leq 0.05$; n—number; %—percentage.

### 3.2. Motor Function and Drooling

The results from the GMFM-88 were not statistically significantly or correlated with drooling (before therapy $p = 0.375$, after therapy $p = 0.928$). After treatment, the frequency of drooling during feeding decreased from 63.16% to 38.89% of patients (Table 4).

**Table 4.** The comparison of the number of patients presenting salivation before and after therapy.

| | Before Therapy | | After Therapy | |
|---|---|---|---|---|
| | n | % | n | % |
| patients presenting excessive salivation | 12 | 63.16% | 7 | 38.89% |
| total patients | 19 | 100% | 18 | 100% |
| $p$ | 0.375 | | 0.928 | |

The Mann-Whitney test was used; the $p$-value was significant at $p \leq 0.05$; n—number; %—percentage.

## 4. Discussion

We observed tightness in muscles that are related to sialorrhea. Our results show that our suggested therapy treatment positively affected food intake behavior.

We consider the SCS technique to be a useful and quick tool for facilitating muscle relaxation in children. It is painless, and as a result younger patients tended to accept it very well. Furthermore, the shorter time of stimulation ensured that patients are neither so weary nor restricted in their free movement [34]. We can palpate the tensed muscle and, using the SCS, relax it to improve body posture or treat the dysfunction. The NDT-Bobath method is a good choice of treatment since this method seeks to improve gross motor function, especially in children with CP. We also chose this method since it takes into consideration balance and postural control [29]. As previously mentioned, postural control is essential during feeding procedures. According to Acar (2021), the NDT-Bobath method has exercises that may supplement feeding therapy that may improve swallowing and oral motor skills in children with CP [35]. These results should be taken into account when considering how to comprehensively conduct therapeutic interventions with patients who have feeding problems. Our recommended therapy was effective in decreasing drooling. We have shown the following connection between the two therapies: The SCS and NDT-Bobath could be useful in patients with excessive salivation and problems with feeding. Using the above therapies, specialists would ensure their patients' comprehensive treatment.

During our examination we experienced barriers when feeding our patients with CP, which was also experienced daily by their caregivers. An involuntary loss of saliva made feeding non-effective. After the therapeutic intervention and equalization of muscle tone, the drooling decreased from 63.16% to 38.89% of participants, and the comfort and efficiency of feeding significantly increased for our patients. Gerek (2005) conducted a similar study in which 85.7% (n = 7) of patients experienced poor saliva management prior to treatment [6]. The results from this study indicate significant improvements, among others, in saliva control after the NDT-Bobath method was applied. Another examination aimed to determine if Kinesio Taping (KT) and oral-motor training (OMT) influence drooling in children with intellectual disabilities [36]. The therapy was applied for muscles to orbicularis oris, supra-hyoid, and masseter muscles, and the results showed a significant reduction in drooling post-intervention ($p < 0.001$). There was also a Drooling Quotient Assessment (DQ) used to diagnose the drooling as it appears [36]. Similar therapy, based on strengthening the orbicularis oris and expiratory muscle, was conducted in Parkinson's disease patients and, likewise, has a positive effect and reduced drooling [22]. These results also suggest the interdependence of muscle tone and the regulation of saliva, which we also observed.

Several authors suggested that the primary influence on oral function has been the following masticatory muscles: masseter, temporalis, medial pterygoids [37,38]. However, we observed a significant correlation between tightness of the temporalis ($p = 0.048$), rectus capitis posterior minor ($p = 0.027$) and scalene muscles ($p = 0.024$) and excessive salivation. Scalene muscles (lac. musculi scaleni) belong to the flexors group of deep neck muscles. Their tension increases when a person has a forward head posture [39]. In this position, the rectus capitis posterior minor muscles (lac. musculus rectus capitis posterior minor) are in the contraction, so they also have increased tension [17]. We found that a forward head posture may increase the occurrence of excessive drooling. As a result, we positioned each patient using the proper chin-tuck position via the NBT-Bobath method. Thanks to this method, we had a continuation of the previous SCS technique on the scalene muscle [40–42]. Taş (2015) also found a significant difference between head control and drooling and that the intensity of producing salivation was higher in individuals with poorer head control ($p = 0.038$) [18]. Moreover, the authors proved that when drooling severity increased, the BMI index decreased significantly ($p = 0.018$). In addition, the meaning in the group that had better drooling control, the independence of eating ability, was found to be more significant [18]. Studies presented and our examination show the magnitude of drooling therapy for patients with neurodevelopmental disabilities to improve their quality of life and their health level.

According to Chávez (2008), Lobo (2013), and Linden (1998), muscles that are engaged in head positioning may affect ingestion [4,43,44]. Additionally, the positioning of the head may influence masticatory function. Gadotti (2020) also found this when they checked the activity of masticatory muscles—temporalis and masseter—during chewing in the natural head posture and forward head posture through the use of EMG. Examiners observed a trend of tighter masseter and temporalis muscles during chewing in head protraction. They found a significant increase in masseter muscle activity in the forward head posture [45]. Poor head control appears during lower tension in the postural muscles. Contributing factors to drooling include the sitting position, proper positioning of the head, anatomic and dental malformations, tongue activity, decreased oral sensory awareness, the inability to breathe through the nose, as well as the individual's emotional state and ability to concentrate [3,5,7]. This is why during our research all patients were properly positioned from the beginning of the study through the facilitation of the NDT-Bobath method. We placed each patient in a seated position with appropriate head posture which helped in the proper placement of the tongue, head, and neck where the respiratory and digestive tracts begin. In patients who are unable to develop head control, another approach is to develop correct sitting and eating postures by training family or caregivers [18]. Therefore, comprehensive therapy should also focus on balance in the postural muscles, especially in those that contribute to head positioning. Examiners from Marmara University in Turkey, observed this significant finding between trunk muscles and oral motor functions in children with CP [35]. According to our intervention, when feeding a child, the following factors should be taken into consideration: drooling, correct sitting position during feeding, and having proper muscle tone. In addition, Haralur (2014) proves in the examination of fifty participants that incorrect head position will result in misalignment of the jaw or even occlusion disorders. The result was a statistically significant difference ($p < 0.5$) between occlusal contacts in three different head postures [46]. We can conclude that the interdisciplinary medical team should treat subjects who have orofacial dysfunctions.

We were also interested in how each patient's level of GMFCS correlated with drooling. Speyer (2019) concluded in their meta-analysis that a higher GMFCS level was correlated to a higher prevalence of drooling, swallowing, and feeding problems [19]. Conversely, Senner (2004) showed that GMFCS levels were not significantly correlated with the severity of salivation, which also showed in our study [3]. Therefore, we found that a patient's GMFCS level should not necessarily be associated with excessive salivation. Moreover, our findings suggested that drooling in patients with CP is correlated with swallowing difficulties. Senner (2004) also found that drooling behavior is related to swallowing difficulties rather than to an increased production of saliva in patients with CP [3]. In addition, children suffering from dysphagia may be at risk of aspiration-related lung disease, malnutrition, neurodevelopmental deficits, and social problems, including relationships with caregivers [18,19,47]. We can conclude that drooling appears in patients with neurodevelopmental disorders for numerous reasons, so the treatment should incorporate comprehensive and multidisciplinary teams of medical specialists to improve one of the crucial activities of daily living—eating. This pilot study contributed to the importance of many feeding aspects for therapists and also parents or caregivers of children with neurological problems.

Our study has some limitations. The number of study subjects is small because this is a pilot study, and we are going to expand the group in the future. The group of patients could vary in terms of disability. Other neurodevelopmental disorders could be investigated in a future study. However, our study presents only children with a GMFCS level V because excessive salivation generally appears in these subjects [48]. We could use a more measurable tool to diagnose muscle tension. Other procedures, such as an electromyography (EMG), would be difficult for the patients to tolerate since their functional and medical conditions were characterized as severe disabilities [29]. Furthermore, the electrodes would not stay on the skin due to wet issues of excessive salivation. Therefore, the children did not receive an EMG, which would be a more impartial method for measuring muscle tone.

## 5. Conclusions

Therapeutic interventions for eating should take into consideration muscle tension regulation. Excessive drooling may be related to the tension of some muscles in the neck and head. The therapy we proposed could be helpful as a complementary therapy in medicine in patients experiencing excessive salivation.

**Author Contributions:** Conceptualization, R.M., K.S., K.G., W.S., B.F., D.S. and E.M.; methodology, K.S. and R.M.; software D.S.; validation W.S. and K.G.; formal analysis, K.S., R.M., B.F. and D.S.; investigation, K.S. and R.M.; resources, K.S., R.M. and B.F.; data curation, K.S. and D.S.; writing—original draft preparation, K.S., R.M. and B.F.; writing—review and editing, K.S., R.M., B.F., E.M., D.S., W.S. and K.G.; visualization, K.S.; supervision, K.G., W.S. and E.M.; project administration, K.S., R.M., B.F., E.M., D.S., W.S. and K.G.; funding acquisition, K.G., W.S. and E.M. All authors have read and agreed to the published version of the manuscript.

**Funding:** This research received no external funding.

**Institutional Review Board Statement:** The research was carried out with the permission of the Bioethics Committee of the Poznan University of Medical Sciences (permission ref. No. 339/15, dated 9 April 2015).

**Informed Consent Statement:** Informed consent was obtained from all subjects involved in the study. Written informed consent has been obtained from the patient(s) to publish this paper.

**Data Availability Statement:** The data that support the findings of this study are available per request from the corresponding author [K.S. and R.M.]. Some data are not publicly available due to containing information that could compromise the privacy of research participants.

**Acknowledgments:** The authors would like to thank the children who participated in the study and the staff of the social welfare home in Poznan.

**Conflicts of Interest:** The authors declare no conflict of interest.

## References

1. Morris, S.E.; Klein, M.D. *Pre-Feeding Skills: A Comprehensive Resource for Feeding Development*; Communicatio Skill Builders: Tucson, AZ, USA, 1987.
2. Chang, C.J.; Wong, A.M.-K. Intraductal Laser Photocoagulation of the Bilateral Parotid Ducts for Reduction of Drooling in Patients with Cerebral Palsy. *Plast. Reconstr. Surg.* **2001**, *107*, 907–913. [CrossRef] [PubMed]
3. Senner, J.E.; Logemann, J.; Zecker, S.; Gaebler-Spira, D. Drooling, Saliva Production, and Swallowing in Cerebral Palsy. *Dev. Med. Child Neurol.* **2004**, *46*, 801–806. [CrossRef] [PubMed]
4. Chávez, M.C.M.; Grollmus, Z.C.N.; Donat, F.J.S. Clinical Prevalence of Drooling in Infant Cerebral Palsy. *Med. Oral Patol. Oral Cir. Bucal.* **2008**, *13*, 5.
5. Dias, B.L.S.; Fernandes, A.R.; Filho, H.D.S.M. Sialorrhea in Children with Cerebral Palsy. *J. Pediatr.* **2016**, *92*, 549–558. [CrossRef]
6. Gerek, M.; Çiyiltepe, M. Dysphagia Management of Pediatric Patients with Cerebral Palsy. *Br. J. Dev. Disabil.* **2005**, *51*, 57–72. [CrossRef]
7. Sochaniwskyj, A.E.; Koheil, R.M.; Bablich, K.; Milner, M.; Kenny, D.J. Oral Motor Functioning, Frequency of Swallowing and Drooling in Normal Children and in Children with Cerebral Palsy. *Arch. Phys. Med. Rehabil.* **1986**, *67*, 866–874. [PubMed]
8. Erasmus, C.E.; Hulst, K.V.; Rotteveel, L.J.C.; Jongerius, P.H.; Hoogen, F.J.A.V.D.; Roeleveld, N.; Rotteveel, J.J. Drooling in Cerebral Palsy: Hypersalivation or Dysfunctional Oral Motor Control? *Dev. Med. Child Neurol.* **2009**, *51*, 454–459. [CrossRef]
9. Erasmus, C.E.; van Hulst, K.; Rotteveel, J.J.; Willemsen, M.A.A.P.; Jongerius, P.H. Clinical Practice: Swallowing Problems in Cerebral Palsy. *Eur. J. Pediatr.* **2012**, *171*, 409–414. [CrossRef]
10. Lawrence, R.; Bateman, N. Surgical Management of the Drooling Child. *Curr. Otorhinolaryngol. Rep.* **2018**, *6*, 99–106. [CrossRef]
11. Isaacson, J.; Patel, S.; Torres-Yaghi, Y.; Pagán, F. Sialorrhea in Parkinson's Disease. *Toxins* **2020**, *12*, 691. [CrossRef]
12. Serrera-Figallo, M.A.; Ruiz-de-León-Hernández, G.; Torres-Lagares, D.; Castro-Araya, A.; Torres-Ferrerosa, O.; Hernández-Pacheco, E.; Gutierrez-Perez, J.L. Use of Botulinum Toxin in Orofacial Clinical Practice. *Toxins* **2020**, *12*, 112. [CrossRef]
13. Xiong, W.; Cheng, L.; Tang, G.; Hou, X.; Zhu, M.; Lu, L.; Zhong, Z. Acupuncture for drooling in children with cerebral palsy: A protocol for systematic review. *Medicine* **2021**, *100*, e25393. [CrossRef]
14. Bekkers, S.; Leow, T.Y.; Van Hulst, K.; Orriëns, L.B.; Scheffer, A.R.; Van Den Hoogen, F.J. Repeated onabotulinum neurotoxin A injections for drooling in children with neurodisability. *Dev. Med. Child Neurol.* **2021**, *63*, 991–997. [CrossRef]
15. Franklin, D.J.; Smith, R.J.; Catlin, F.I.; Helfrick, J.F.; Foster, J.H. Temporomandibular joint dysfunction in infancy. *Int. J. Pediatr. Otorhinolaryngol.* **1986**, *12*, 99–104. [CrossRef]
16. McPartland, J.M.; Brodeur, R.R.; Hallgren, R.C. Chronic neck pain, standing balance, and suboccipital muscle atrophy—A pilot study. *J. Manip. Physiol. Ther.* **1997**, *20*, 24–29.
17. Sun, M.-Y.; Han, X.; Wang, M.-Y.; Ning, D.-X.; Xu, B.; Xie, L.-Z.; Yu, S.-B.; Sui, H.-J. Relationship between the sectional area of the rectus capitis posterior minor and the to be named ligament from 3D MR imaging. *BMC Musculoskelet. Disord.* **2020**, *21*, 101. [CrossRef]
18. Taş, S.A.; Çankaya, T. An investigation of the relationship of drooling with nutrition and head control in individuals with quadriparetic cerebral palsy. *J. Phys. Ther. Sci.* **2015**, *27*, 3487–3492. [CrossRef]

19. Speyer, R.; Cordier, R.; Kim, J.H.; Cocks, N.; Michou, E.; Wilkes-Gillan, S. Prevalence of drooling, swallowing, and feeding problems in cerebral palsy across the lifespan: A systematic review and meta-analyses. *Dev. Med. Child Neurol.* **2019**, *61*, 1249–1258. [CrossRef] [PubMed]
20. Kumari, P.; Nikkitha, E. To compare the effects of oral facial facilitation and oral motor therapy in decreasing drooling in children with spastic cerebral palsy. *Int. J. Pharm. Biol. Sci.* **2018**, *8*, 397–402.
21. Muammer, R.; Kilic, E.; Hayran, O. The effect of physiotherapy treatment on saliva decrease in children with cerebral palsy. *Indian J. Physiother. Occup. Ther.* **2010**, *4*, 129–131.
22. Cocks, N.; Rafols, J.; Embley, E.; Hill, K. Expiratory Muscle Strength Training for Drooling in Adults with Parkinson's Disease. *Dysphagia* **2022**, *37*, 1525–1531. [CrossRef] [PubMed]
23. Palisano, R.; Rosenbaum, P.; Bartlett, D.; Livingston, M. Gross motor function classification system expanded and revised. In *Canchild Centre for Childhood Disability Research, Mcmaster University*; Institute for Applied Health Sciences McMaster University: Hamilton, ON, Canada, 2007.
24. Einspieler, C.; Bos, A.F.; Krieber-Tomantschger, M.; Alvarado, E.; Barbosa, V.M.; Bertoncelli, N.; Burger, M.; Chorna, O.; Del Secco, S.; DeRegnier, R.-A.; et al. Cerebral Palsy: Early Markers of Clinical Phenotype and Functional Outcome. *J. Clin. Med.* **2019**, *8*, 1616. [CrossRef] [PubMed]
25. Sforza, E.; Onesimo, R.; Leoni, C.; Giorgio, V.; Proli, F.; Notaro, F.; Kuczynska, E.M.; Cerchiari, A.; Selicorni, A.; Rigante, D.; et al. Drooling outcome measures in paediatric disability: A systematic review. *Eur. J. Pediatr.* **2022**, *181*, 2575–2592. [CrossRef]
26. Tschirren, L.; Bauer, S.; Hanser, C.; Marsico, P.; Sellers, D.; van Hedel, H.J.A. The Eating and Drinking Ability Classification System: Concurrent validity and reliability in children with cerebral palsy. *Dev. Med. Child Neurol.* **2018**, *60*, 611–617. [CrossRef] [PubMed]
27. Eileen, D.; Schiowitz, S.; Dowling, D.J. *Counterstrain an, Osteopathic Approach to Diagnosis and Treatment*, 3rd ed.; Lippincott Williams & Wilkins: Philadelphia, PA, USA, 2005; pp. 86–88.
28. Wong, C.K. Strain counterstrain: Current concepts and clinical evidence. *Man. Ther.* **2012**, *17*, 2–8. [CrossRef]
29. Tekin, F.; Kavlak, E.; Cavlak, U.; Altug, F. Effectiveness of Neuro-Developmental Treatment (Bobath Concept) on postural control and balance in Cerebral Palsied children. *J. Back Musculoskelet. Rehabil.* **2018**, *31*, 397–403. [CrossRef]
30. Te Velde, A.; Morgan, C. Gross Motor Function Measure (GMFM-66 & GMFM-88) User's Manual, 3rd Edition, Book Review. *Pediatr. Phys. Ther.* **2022**, *34*, 88–89. [CrossRef]
31. Ko, J.; Kim, M. Reliability and responsiveness of the gross motor function measure-88 in children with cerebral palsy. *Phys. Ther.* **2013**, *93*, 393–400. [CrossRef]
32. van der Heide, J.C.; Hadders-Algra, M. Postural Muscle Dyscoordination in Children With Cerebral Palsy. *Neural Plast.* **2005**, *12*, 197–203. [CrossRef]
33. Meseguer, A.A.; Fernández-de-las-Peñas, C.; Navarro-Poza, J.L.; Rodríguez-Blanco, C.; Gandia, J.J.B. Immediate effects of the strain/counterstrain technique in local pain evoked by tender points in the upper trapezius muscle. *Clin. Chiropr.* **2006**, *3*, 112–118. [CrossRef]
34. Klein, R.; Bareis, A.; Schneider, A.; Linde, K. Strain–counterstrain to treat restrictions of the mobility of the cervical spine in patients with neck pain—A sham-controlled randomized trial. *Complement. Ther. Med.* **2013**, *21*, 1–7. [CrossRef]
35. Acar, G.; Ejraei, N.; Turkdoğan, D.; Enver, N.; Öztürk, G.; Aktaş, G. The Effects of Neurodevelopmental Therapy on Feeding and Swallowing Activities in Children with Cerebral Palsy. *Dysphagia* **2021**, *37*, 800–811. [CrossRef] [PubMed]
36. Mokhlesin, M.; Mirmohammadkhani, M.; Tohidast, S.A. The effect of Kinesio Taping on drooling in children with intellectual disability: A double-blind randomized controlled study. *Int. J. Pediatr. Otorhinolaryngol.* **2022**, *153*, 111017. [CrossRef]
37. Guruprasad, R.; Rishi, S.; Nair, P.P.; Thomas, S. Masseter and medial pterygoid muscle hypertrophy. *BMJ Case Rep.* **2011**, *2011*, bcr0720114557. [CrossRef]
38. Ferreira, M.C.; de Toledo, I.P.; Dutra, K.L.; Stefani, F.M.; Porporatti, A.L.; Flores-Mir, C.; De Luca Canto, G. Association between chewing dysfunctions and temporomandibular disorders: A systematic review. *J. Oral Rehabil.* **2018**, *45*, 819–835. [CrossRef]
39. Kang, J.I.; Jeong, D.K.; Choi, H. The effect of feedback respiratory exercise on muscle activity, craniovertebral angle, and neck disability index of the neck flexors of patients with forward head posture. *J. Phys. Ther. Sci.* **2016**, *28*, 2477–2481. [CrossRef] [PubMed]
40. Hung, D.; Sejdić, E.; Steele, C.M.; Chau, T. Extraction of average neck flexion angle during swallowing in neutral and chin-tuck positions. *Biomed. Eng. Online* **2009**, *8*, 25. [CrossRef]
41. Ayuse, T.; Ayuse, T.; Ishitobi, S.; Kurata, S.; Sakamoto, E.; Okayasu, I.; Oi, K. Effect of reclining and chin-tuck position on the coordination between respiration and swallowing. *J. Oral Rehabil.* **2006**, *33*, 402–408. [CrossRef]
42. Saconato, M.; Chiari, B.M.; Lederman, H.M.; Gonçalves, M.I.R. Effectiveness of Chin-tuck Maneuver to Facilitate Swallowing in Neurologic Dysphagia. *Int. Arch. Otorhinolaryngol.* **2016**, *20*, 13–17. [CrossRef] [PubMed]
43. Lobo, P.P.; Pinto, S.; Rocha, L.; Reimão, S.; de Carvalho, M. Orofacial apraxia in motor neuron disease. *Case Rep. Neurol.* **2013**, *5*, 47–51. [CrossRef]
44. De Laat, A. Scientific Basis of Masticatory Disorders. In *Frontiers of Oral Biology*; Linden, R.W.A., Ed.; KARGER: Basel, Switzerland, 1998; Volume 9, pp. 122–134. [CrossRef]
45. Gadotti, I.; Hicks, K.; Koscs, E.; Lynn, B.; Estrazulas, J.; Civitella, F. Electromyography of the masticatory muscles during chewing in different head and neck postures—A pilot study. *J. Oral Biol. Craniofacial Res.* **2020**, *10*, 23–27. [CrossRef]

46. Haralur, S.; Al-Gadhaan, S.; Al-Qahtani, A.; Mossa, A.; Al-Shehri, W.; Addas, M. Influence of Functional Head Postures on the Dynamic Functional Occlusal Parameters. *Ann. Med. Health Sci. Res.* **2014**, *4*, 562–566. [CrossRef] [PubMed]
47. Lefton-Greif, M.A. Can feeding–swallowing difficulties in children predict language impairments. *Dev. Med. Child Neurol.* **2015**, *57*, 872–879. [CrossRef] [PubMed]
48. İnal, Ö.; Arslan, S.S.; Demïr, N.; Karaduman, A.A. An Investigation of Characteristics Related to Oral Motor and Swallowing Disorders in Children with Cerebral Palsy: A Descriptive Study. *Fiz. Rehabil.* **2021**, *32*, 52–61. [CrossRef]

**Disclaimer/Publisher's Note:** The statements, opinions and data contained in all publications are solely those of the individual author(s) and contributor(s) and not of MDPI and/or the editor(s). MDPI and/or the editor(s) disclaim responsibility for any injury to people or property resulting from any ideas, methods, instructions or products referred to in the content.

healthcare

MDPI

Brief Report

# Ankle Kinematics Characterization in Children with Idiopathic Toe Walking: Does the Foot Model Change the Clinical Evaluation?

**Paolo Brasiliano [1,2], Martina Alvini [2,3], Eugenio Di Stanislao [2,3], Giuseppe Vannozzi [1,2,*], Giuseppe Di Rosa [4] and Valentina Camomilla [1,2]**

[1] Department of Movement, Human and Health Sciences, University of Rome "Foro Italico", Piazza Lauro De Bosis 6, 00135 Rome, Italy; p.brasiliano@studenti.uniroma4.it (P.B.); valentina.camomilla@uniroma4.it (V.C.)
[2] Interuniversity Centre of Bioengineering of the Human Neuromusculoskeletal System, University of Rome "Foro Italico", 00135 Rome, Italy
[3] "ITOP SpA Officine Ortopediche", Via Prenestina Nuova 307/A-Area Industriale, 00036 Palestrina, Italy
[4] Division of Pediatric Neurorehabilitation, "Ospedale Pediatrico Bambino Gesù", 00165 Rome, Italy
* Correspondence: giuseppe.vannozzi@uniroma4.it; Tel.: +39-06-36733522

**Abstract:** Idiopathic toe walking (ITW) is a gait deviation characterized by forefoot contact with the ground, sometimes observed in children, that alters ankle kinematics, possibly leading to health-related issues. When studying foot and ankle gait deviations, the adoption of a single-segment foot model entails a significant simplification of foot and ankle movement, and thus may potentially mask some important foot dynamics. Differences in ankle kinematics between single- (conventional gait model, PiG, or Davis) and multi-segment (Oxford foot model, OFM) foot models were investigated in children with ITW. Fourteen participants were enrolled in the study and underwent instrumented gait analysis. Children were asked to walk barefoot and while wearing a foot orthosis that modified the ankle movement pattern toward a more physiological one without blocking foot intrinsic motion. ITW gait abnormalities, e.g., the absence of heel rocker and the presence of anticipated forefoot rocker, were found/not found according to the foot model. Walking conditions significantly interacted with the foot model effect. Finally, the different characterization of gait abnormalities led to a different classification of ITW, with a possible impact on the clinical evaluation. Due to its closer adhesion to ankle anatomy and to its sensitivity to ITW peculiarities, OFM may be preferable for instrumented gait analysis in this population.

**Keywords:** ITW; multi-segment foot model; pediatric gait; gait analysis; rockers

**Citation:** Brasiliano, P.; Alvini, M.; Di Stanislao, E.; Vannozzi, G.; Di Rosa, G.; Camomilla, V. Ankle Kinematics Characterization in Children with Idiopathic Toe Walking: Does the Foot Model Change the Clinical Evaluation? *Healthcare* **2023**, *11*, 873. https://doi.org/10.3390/healthcare11060873

Academic Editor: José Carmelo Adsuar Sala

Received: 30 December 2022
Revised: 10 March 2023
Accepted: 14 March 2023
Published: 16 March 2023



## 1. Introduction

Toe walking is a gait deviation characterized by forefoot ground contact and by marked ankle plantarflexion over the entire gait cycle. It is a gait pattern that is present in several pathologies, such as autism spectrum disorders, cerebral palsy, muscular dystrophy, and others [1]. At the same time, it is commonly seen temporarily during typical gait development [2]. In some cases, typically developed children who should have developed a physiological heel-to-toe gait may present a toe-walking gait pattern. If a clinical cause cannot be identified, they are diagnosed with idiopathic toe walking (ITW) [1]. Persistent ITW has been hypothesized to lead to limitation in ankle range of motion (ROM) together with issues such as higher risk of falling or psychological discomfort [3–5]. A recent review provided an overview of the available methods used to quantify changes of gait pattern in children with ITW [6]. In 63% of the studies included in the review, parameters obtained through instrumented gait analysis were used as primary outcomes of the investigation. The characterization of the differences compared to normal gait is an essential step to obtain a deep understanding of the pathology; in this context, instrumented gait analysis is mandatory to assess the kinetics and kinematics of the foot and ankle joints. Indeed, the main gait deviations caused by this condition occur at the ankle joint, altering its kinematics [7]. Ankle joint function is usually described in terms of angular excursions and foot rockers: the heel, ankle, and forefoot rocker [8]. Together with the analysis of ankle sagittal moment, the characterization of these rockers has been used to determine the severity of ITW [9]. The severity classification of ITW has been used previously to monitor treatment effects [6]. Moreover, it could be integrated within the clinical evaluation of children with ITW performed by physicians, allowing objective assessment of the status of the condition.

Ankle kinematics is commonly determined using stereophotogrammetry, modeling the foot as one rigid segment (as in the conventional gait models plug-in gait (PiG) [10] and Davis (DAV) [11]). However, in the past years, multi-segment foot models (MSFMs) have been widely used, especially in clinical populations [12]. MSFMs are collectively considered to describe the anatomy of the foot more accurately. When the anatomical description of a body segment changes, the estimation of the adjacent joint kinematics and kinetics changes. In the case of the foot, changing its anatomical description (mono- or -multi-segmented foot) will change the characterization of the ankle and the foot intrinsic joint movement. MSFMs have been found to be effective in distinguishing between normal and pathological feet [12]. Even if the evidence is still preliminary, other uses of the MSFMs have been found in pathological populations: surgery outcome assessment, correlation of foot pathologies with proximal joint movement deviation or other symptoms, association of foot pathologies with patients' reported outcomes, classification of foot types, and MSFM repeatability assessment [12]. Among MSFMs, the Oxford foot model (OFM) has been validated [13] and is commonly used in children [12]. In some cases, MSFMs lead to different characterizations of ankle kinematics at critical points of the gait cycle [14]. Nevertheless, even if the differences in ankle kinematics estimation between mono- and multi-segment foot models have been assessed, their impact on the clinical evaluation of ITW still needs to be verified.

To date, scientific literature has not analyzed the impact of the foot model selection on the resulting ankle kinematics and clinical evaluation in children with ITW. It is noteworthy that in the case of toe walking, the assumption of a rigid and non-deformable foot (i.e., as when using a mono-segment foot model) ascribes the movement of the foot intrinsic joints to the ankle joint, possibly modifying its functional assessment. While MSFMs can more accurately describe the anatomy of the ankle joint and change the estimation of its kinematics, they pose some issues. The motion-capture system resolution must be sufficient to track a high number of adjacent markers, especially when assessing the gait of children with small feet. In addition, the operators must be familiar with the palpation of additional anatomical landmarks compared to the standard mono-segment foot model used in clinical gait analysis. Lastly, the participants may experience the experimental setup as less comfortable (due to a longer preparation time and higher number of markers necessary to record walking trials using MSFM). Given these considerations, before choosing an MSFM over a mono-segment foot model to perform instrumented gait analysis, proof of relevance for a clinical evaluation when using the former over the latter must be obtained.

As a first aim, this study evaluated the effects of using mono- or multi-segment foot models to analyze ankle kinematics in children with ITW. The interest was to verify whether the use of a biomechanical model that better describes the anatomy of the ankle leads to different results in terms of severity classification of ITW as support to the clinical evaluation. To this end, instrumented gait analysis was performed using OFM (version 4 and 5 described in the work by Stebbins and colleagues [13]), PiG, and DAV models on children with ITW walking barefoot. As a second aim, the study verified whether the differences between models are specific to the presence of ITW gait deviations (i.e., verifying whether a model × walking condition interaction exists). For this purpose, children were also asked to walk while wearing a foot orthosis that promoted heel-to-toe gait [15], changing the ITW typical gait pattern towards a more physiological one.

## 2. Materials and Methods

Fourteen children diagnosed with ITW were enrolled in the study (8 females, age = 9 ± 2 years, mass = 37 ± 15 kg, stature = 1.38 ± 0.14 m) following signed consent by their parents. The study received the approval of the local institutional review board (University of Rome "Foro Italico", Rome, Italy, CAR130/2022). Children were diagnosed by a physician of the "Bambino Gesù" hospital in Rome and referred to ITOP "Officine Ortopediche" for screening assessment comprising clinical evaluation with instrumented gait analysis.

During testing sessions, children were asked to walk barefoot (BF) and while wearing a foot orthosis (FO) at their preferred speed along a straight 8 m walkway. A motion-capture system with eight infrared cameras (BTS SMART-DX, Quincy, USA, @250 frame/s) and four floor-embedded force plates (BTS Bioengineering Corp, Quincy, USA, @1000 frame/s) were used to measure gait kinematics and to detect gait events and define gait cycles, respectively. A total of 113 and 115 gait cycles were used for BF and FO conditions, respectively, corresponding to a mean of about 6 complete gait cycles per subject (range 4 to 10). Participants started walking with their preferred leg. A trial was considered valid when a complete foot contact on at least one force platform was obtained. Markers were placed on the child's lower limbs to allow ankle kinematics reconstruction according to the OFM, PiG, and DAV (Figure 1A–D) models, and kinematic data were obtained (Nexus 2.10, Vicon, Oxford, UK). Raw data were filtered using a low-pass fourth-order Butterworth filter (fc = 12 Hz). The orthosis (A.Dyn.O.®, ITOP SpA "Officine Ortopediche", Palestrina (RM), Italy) used is a modular solution that combines a custom-made insole, a carbon fiber flexible plate and a specific orthopedic shoe (Figure 1E). The orthosis is designed to exert a downward force on the hindfoot, with the aim of contrasting the toe-walking pattern without blocking the ankle. More precisely, when the carbon fiber plate is solicited by an external force in the anterior portion (i.e., in the case of a forefoot contact with ground), it stores elastic energy that is successively expressed in the posterior region of the plate. This produces a dorsiflexor moment at the ankle joint, dragging down the hindfoot. The textile design of the shoe used with the orthosis allowed for palpation of all the anatomical landmarks of the models except for the posterior aspect of the calcaneus (CA), which was selected as the posterior edge of the orthosis along the line of the Achilles tendon. In the mono-segment foot models, CA height with respect to the marker placed on the base of the metatarsal head was the only factor influencing sagittal kinematics estimation. The shoe used with the orthosis did not hinder the correct relative positioning of these markers. In the multi-segment foot model, CA was used together with the other markers placed on the calcaneus to determine the sagittal plane of the hindfoot. As far as its position is at the same height of the medial and lateral markers placed on the calcaneus and along the line of the Achilles tendon, it did not affect ankle sagittal kinematics estimation. In addition, the orthosis was firmly fixed to the foot, minimizing its in-shoe movement.

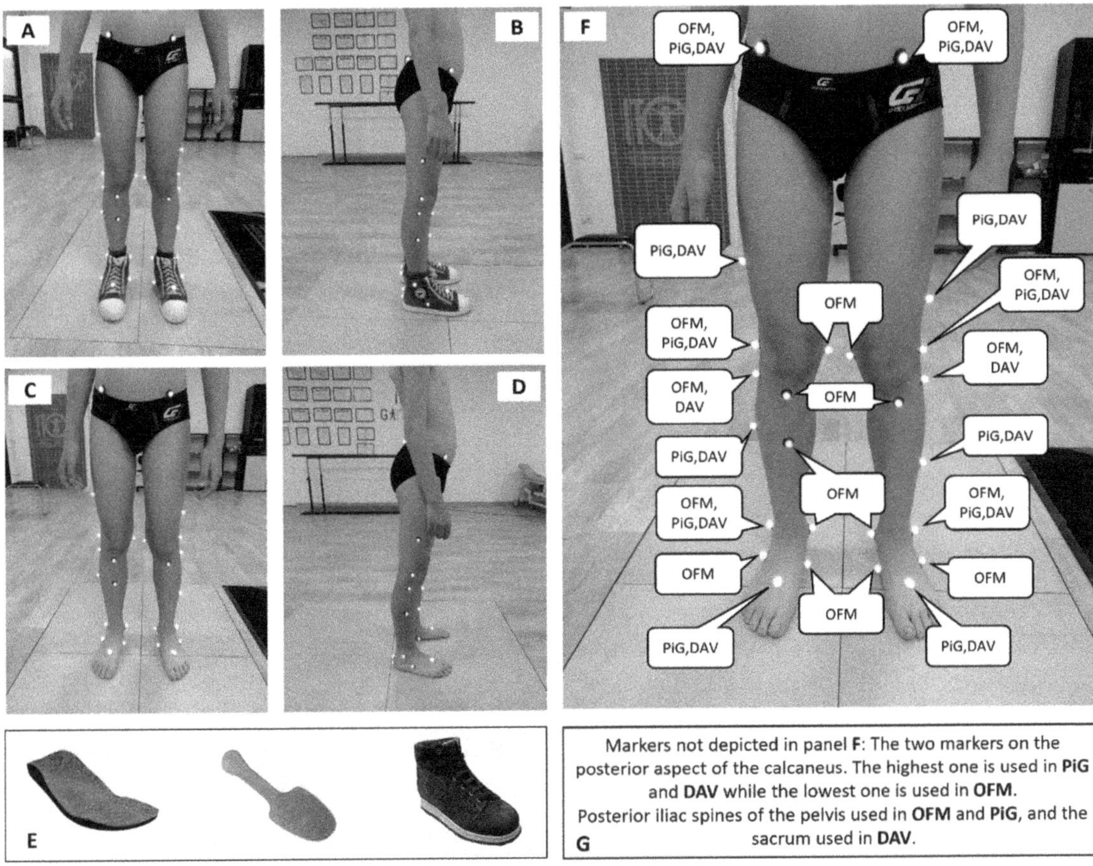


**Figure 1.** Front and lateral view of the used marker set while wearing the foot orthosis (**A** and **B**, respectively) and in barefoot condition (**C** and **D**, respectively). Bottom (**E**): representation of the A. Dyn.O.® orthosis. From left to right: foot orthosis, carbon fiber flexible plate, orthopedic shoe. (**F**) Graphical representation of markers used in the different models, with specification (**G**) for the markers not depicted in panel (**F**). Relevant coordinate systems are described in the Supplementary Materials.

For each subject and each model, a representative gait cycle was selected looking at ankle planta-dorsiflexion angle using the method proposed by Sangeux and colleagues [16]. The method calculates the area between each kinematics trace of a given set of waveforms and a median waveform calculated as the median value of the set at each time instant. Preliminary to the statistical analysis, inter-participant consistency was verified for each model using the linear fit method (LFM) [17]. LFM gives information about the strength of the relationship ($R^2$) between the subjects' kinematic traces. An $R^2$ greater than 0.5 was found for the two conditions, and thus inter-subject consistency was proved. Timing and magnitude of peak plantar and dorsiflexion angles, along with ankle angle at foot contact and plantar-dorsiflexion ROM were measured (Figure 2A) for the subjects' representative gait cycles.

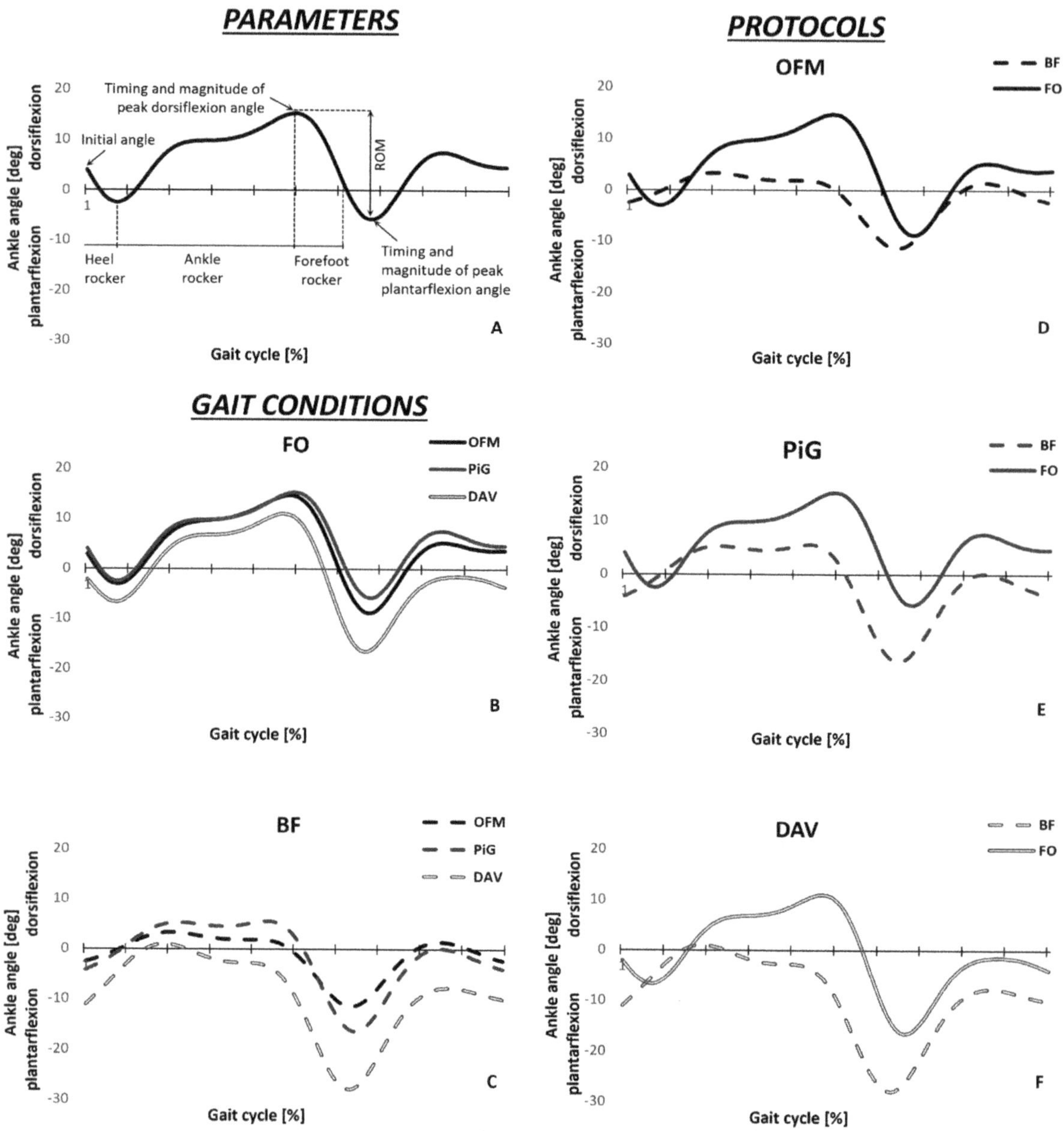


**Figure 2.** (**A**): Graphical representation of calculated parameters on a representative kinematic trace obtained using OFM. In all other panels the mean ankle kinematics of the participants' representative trials estimated using OFM (black), PiG (dark gray), and DAV (dark gray contoured) for FO (solid) and BF (dashed) conditions is represented. In (**B**,**C**), curves from different models are compared for FO (solid) and BF (dashed) conditions, respectively. In (**D**–**F**), curves from different conditions are compared for OFM (black), PiG (dark gray), and DAV models, respectively.

To verify whether the main effects of using mono- or multi-segment foot models existed and whether the differences between models were specific to the presence of ITW gait deviations, i.e., whether interactions between models and walking conditions existed, a 3 × 2 repeated measure ANOVA was performed (SPSS 23.0, Chicago, IL, USA) on the above-mentioned parameters. In case of lack of normality assumption, the non-parametric factorial model was performed using the ARTool R package [18]. Effect size was assessed through η2 values. Significance level was set at 0.05 for all statistical tests, using Bonferroni correction for post-hoc comparisons.

Additionally, for all gait cycles of the BF condition, the presence/absence of a heel rocker and a premature forefoot rocker were investigated as key kinematic features following the most common ITW severity classification [9]. According to this classification, a first rocker is identified with an ankle angle at foot contact higher than −5 deg with a down-going pattern angular excursion within the first 12% of the gait cycle. An early third rocker is defined as the maximal ankle dorsiflexion angle occurring before the 30% of the gait cycle.

## 3. Results

Both the interaction term (upper part) and main effects for models and walking conditions (lower part) are reported in Table 1. The main effects for walking condition and interaction, speculating only on the FO condition, are not commented on, as they do not relate to the aims of this work.

**Table 1.** Summary of statistical results. In the case of model × walking interaction (first part of the table), post-hoc comparisons are detailed for walking condition and model separately. When interaction was not significant (second part of the table), only main effects were reported for walking condition and model separately. RoM: range of motion; FO: foot orthosis condition; BF: barefoot condition; OFM: Oxford foot model; PiG: plug-in gait; DAV: Davis.

| | **Interaction Term (Model × Walking Condition)** | **Interaction Post-Hoc Comparisons for Walking Condition** | **Interaction Post-Hoc Comparisons for Model Type** |
|---|---|---|---|
| Ankle RoM | $F(2,26) = 29.976$ ($p < 0.05$) $\eta 2 = 0.833$ | $OFM_{BF} < OFM_{FO}$ ($p < 0.05$) | $OFM_{FO} < DAV_{FO}$ $PiG_{FO} < DAV_{FO}$ ($p < 0.017$) $OFM_{BF} < DAV_{BF} < PiG_{BF}$ ($p < 0.017$) |
| Time of peak dorsiflexion angle (forefoot rocker) | $F(2,26) = 4.459$ ($p < 0.05$) $\eta 2 = 0.103$ | $OFM_{BF} < OFM_{FO}$ $DAV_{BF} < DAV_{FO}$ ($p < 0.05$) | $PiG_{BF} > DAV_{BF}$ ($p < 0.017$) |
| Ankle peak plantarflexion angle | $F(2,26) = 10.390$, ($p < 0.05$) $\eta 2 = 0.444$ | $PiG_{FO} < PiG_{BF}$ $DAV_{FO} < DAV_{BF}$ ($p < 0.05$) | $DAV_{FO} < PiG_{FO} < OFM_{FO}$ ($p < 0.017$) $DAV_{BF} < OFM_{BF} < PiG_{BF}$ ($p < 0.017$) |
| | **Interaction term (model x walking condition)** | **Main effect forwalking condition** | **Main effect and post hoc for model type** |
| Time of peak plantarflexion angle | $p > 0.05$ | $F(1,13) = 192.012$ ($p < 0.05$) $\eta 2 = 0.811$ BF < FO ($p < 0.05$) | NS |
| Ankle angle at foot contact | $p > 0.05$ | $F(1,13) = 20.265$ ($p < 0.05$) $\eta 2 = 0.609$ BF < FO ($p < 0.05$) | $F(2,26) = 27.980$ ($p < 0.05$) $\eta 2 = 0.683$ DAV < OFM, DAV < PiG ($p < 0.017$) |
| Ankle peak dorsiflexion angle | $p > 0.05$ | $F(1,13) = 99.203$ ($p < 0.05$) $\eta 2 = 0.884$ BF < FO ($p < 0.05$) | $F(2,26) = 7.912$ ($p < 0.05$) $\eta 2 = 0.378$ DAV < PiG ($p < 0.017$) |

Concerning the post-hoc comparisons for the walking conditions, a difference in ankle ROM between FO (25.3 ± 3.6 deg) and BF (16.6 ± 4.8 deg) walking was detected only using OFM (Figure 2D). The timing of the forefoot rocker was found to be significantly different between walking conditions only when using OFM and DAV models (Figure 2D–F). Differences between conditions in peak plantarflexion angle were found using PiG and DAV models (Figure 2E,F).

Concerning the post-hoc pairwise comparisons for the model type in BF condition (Figure 2C), ankle ROM was found to be significantly different across all models, with OFM (16.7 ± 4.8 deg) showing the smallest value, followed by PiG (26.3 ± 6.3 deg) and DAV (31.4 ± 5.1 deg). The timing of the forefoot rocker was found to be different when using PiG (35 ± 14% of gait cycle) compared with the DAV (23 ± 8% of gait cycle), with the former being delayed. Lastly, peak plantarflexion angle was found to be significantly different across all models, with OFM (−12.4 ± 5.2 deg) showing the smallest value, followed by PiG (−17.4 ± 6.4 deg) and DAV (−28.7 ± 6.3 deg).

Concerning the effect of foot models, regardless of the walking condition, DAV model underestimated the ankle angle at foot contact (−7.3 ± 8 deg) compared to OFM (−0.5 ± 7.6 deg) and PiG (1 ± 6.8 deg). It also underestimated the magnitude of peak dorsiflexion angle during the stance phase compared to PiG (6.9 ± 8.2 deg and 12.2 ± 5.6 deg, respectively, Figure 2B,C).

Participants' characterization of heel rocker and premature forefoot rocker are shown in Figure 3A,B. The heel rocker was detected in 35%, 44%, and 26% of all recorded gait cycles using OFM, PiG, and DAV, respectively. A premature forefoot rocker was detected in 61%, 40%, and 79% of all recorded gait cycles, using OFM, PiG, and DAV, respectively.

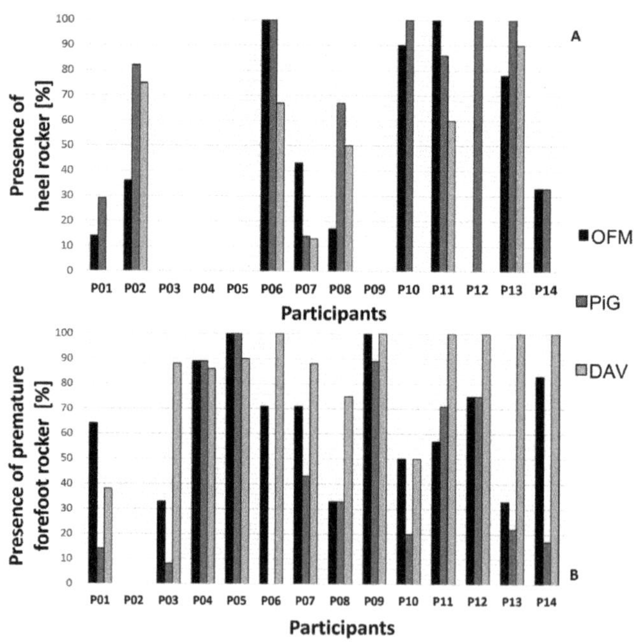


**Figure 3.** Graphical representation of the percentage of the gait cycles in which: (**A**) a heel rocker (up) and (**B**) a premature forefoot rocker (down) were detected using OFM (black boxes), PiG (dark gray boxes), and DAV (light gray boxes) for each participant.

## 4. Discussion

The present work evaluated the role of mono- and multi-segment foot models in describing ankle kinematics as a support to the clinical evaluation and classification of children with ITW walking barefoot and when wearing a foot orthosis.

The characterization of the ITW typical gait deviations changed according to the adopted foot model. As shown by the post-hoc comparisons for the model type, differences in ankle ROM between OFM and PiG were found in BF conditions only, while peak plantarflexion angle difference between OFM and PiG changed its sign in the BF and FO conditions. Moreover, differences in the timing of peak dorsiflexion angle between PiG and DAV were found in BF conditions only. In addition, comparison of walking conditions led to different results according to the model used for ROM, time of peak dorsiflexion, and peak plantarflexion angle. Therefore, the choice of the model changed the characterization of the kinematics parameters used for ITW severity classification (i.e., heel and forefoot rockers, Figure 3A,B).

The significative interaction effects found in this study demonstrate that the choice of biomechanical model is a critical factor when comparing different gait patterns. Indeed, when using a mono-segment foot model to estimate ankle kinematics, the motion of the intrinsic foot joints is ascribed to the ankle joint only. This may be mainly due to the use of a marker on the forefoot to analyze the motion of the hindfoot. Considering that all the models rely on the posterior aspect of the calcaneus to define the primary axis of the foot (or the hindfoot), the differences in the orientation of this axis are related to the second marker used to define it. The OFM uses a virtual marker that belongs to the calcaneus, while PiG and DAV use a marker on the forefoot. This may not largely alter the orientation of the anatomical coordinate system used to define the foot (or the hindfoot), in orthostatic position. Nevertheless, when the foot moves, the axis orientation changes to a greater degree, as it is related to two different bones that are not directly linked one to the other. This causes the ascription of the movement of the foot intrinsic joints to the ankle joint (for a detailed description of the anatomical coordinate systems definition for each model see Supplementary Materials).

Using a less detailed anatomical description of the foot causes alterations in ankle kinematics estimation specific to children with ITW. Figure 2A,B graphically shows how the differences in ankle kinematics estimation may affect the classification of ITW, and potentially the clinical evaluation performed using instrumented gait analysis. Nevertheless, it must be considered that the classification proposed was designed using ankle kinematics and kinetics derived from mono-segment foot model. The inconsistency in the characterization of the heel and forefoot rockers between mono- and multi-segment foot models highlights how a different kinematic estimation may change the clinical evaluation of ITW. Nevertheless, to minimize the differences related to the use of the foot model (rather than to the change in gait pattern), the classification proposed should be used to compare two groups, or the same group in different conditions.

The choice of the biomechanical model may change the clinical evaluation of ITW as well as the assessment of the efficacy of treatments. Indeed, foot models performed differently both when considering barefoot conditions only and when assessing differences between walking conditions (e.g., when assessing the efficacy of treatments).

The results presented must be interpreted in the light of the limitation that only ankle kinematics has been evaluated. Nevertheless, it has been demonstrated that this joint is the one mainly affected by this gait deviation [7]. In addition, only the sagittal component of ankle kinematics was analyzed, since the literature still reports issues about the estimation of the other two ankle kinematics components [19,20]. Moreover, it is the ankle kinematics component that is mainly analyzed in this population. Lastly, even if the use of a foot orthosis tends to restore normal gait patterns in children with ITW, comparison with a group of typically developing children may give additional insights into the effects of the foot model on the clinical evaluation of this population.

To conclude, differences in ankle kinematics estimation between mono- and multi-segment foot models specific to this population have been found. Such discrepancies lead to different classifications of relevant features of this condition, thus changing the clinical evaluation performed using instrumented gait analysis. When feasible, the use of a multi-segment foot model is preferable when analyzing ankle kinematics, due to its more accurate anatomical description of the ankle joint.

**Supplementary Materials:** The following supporting information can be downloaded at: https://www.mdpi.com/article/10.3390/healthcare11060873/s1, File S1: Segments anatomical coordinate systems definition [21,22].

**Author Contributions:** Conceptualization, G.V., E.D.S., G.D.R. and V.C.; formal analysis, P.B.; investigation, G.V., E.D.S., M.A. and V.C.; data curation, P.B.; writing—original draft preparation, P.B., G.V. and V.C.; writing—review and editing, E.D.S. and G.D.R.; visualization, P.B.; supervision, V.C.; project administration, V.C. All authors have read and agreed to the published version of the manuscript.

**Funding:** This research received no external funding.

**Institutional Review Board Statement:** The study was conducted in accordance with the Declaration of Helsinki and approved by the Institutional Review Board of the University of Rome "Foro Italico" (CAR130/2022).

**Informed Consent Statement:** Informed consent was obtained from all subjects involved in the study.

**Data Availability Statement:** The data presented in this study are available on request from the corresponding author. The data are not publicly available due to privacy restrictions.

**Acknowledgments:** The authors wish to thank the following collaborators who were involved in the data collection procedures: Gabriele Denza, Ilaria Pasciuto, Biagio Orefice, Angela Ciaccio, Luigi Catino, and Martina Benedetti.

**Conflicts of Interest:** The authors declare that Giuseppe Di Rosa and Eugenio Di Stanislao are inventors of the foot orthosis and that ITOP SpA Officine Ortopediche is the patent holder. Martina Alvini and Eugenio Di Stanislao are employed in ITOP SpA Officine Ortopediche. All other authors have no conflict of interest associated with this publication.

## References

1. Williams, C.M.; Tinley, P.; Curtin, M.; Wakefield, S.; Nielsen, S. Is Idiopathic Toe Walking Really Idiopathic? The Motor Skills and Sensory Processing Abilities Associated with Idiopathic Toe Walking Gait. *J. Child Neurol.* **2014**, *29*, 71–78. [CrossRef] [PubMed]
2. Sutherland, D. The Development of Mature Gait. *Gait Posture* **1997**, *8*, 163–170. [CrossRef]
3. Sobel, E.; Caselli, M.; Velez, Z. Effect of persistent toe walking on ankle equinus. Analysis of 60 idiopathic toe walkers. *J. Am. Podiatr. Med. Assoc.* **1997**, *87*, 17–22. [CrossRef] [PubMed]
4. Oetgen, M.E.; Peden, S. Idiopathic Toe Walking. *J. Am. Acad. Orthop. Surg.* **2012**, *20*, 292–300. [CrossRef] [PubMed]
5. Caselli, M.A.; Rzonca, E.C.; Lue, B.Y. Habitual toe-walking: Evaluation and approach to treatment. *Clin. Podiatr. Med. Surg.* **1988**, *5*, 547–559. [PubMed]
6. Caserta, A.; Morgan, P.; Williams, C. Identifying methods for quantifying lower limb changes in children with idiopathic toe walking: A systematic review. *Gait Posture* **2019**, *67*, 181–186. [CrossRef] [PubMed]
7. Westberry, D.E.; Davids, J.R.; Davis, R.B.; de Morais Filho, M.C. Idiopathic Toe Walking: A Kinematic and Kinetic Profile. *J. Pediatr. Orthop.* **2008**, *28*, 352–358. [CrossRef] [PubMed]
8. Perry, J. Ankle Foot Complex. In *Gait Analysis: Normal and Pathological Function*; SLACK Incorporated: Thorofare, NJ, USA, 1992; ISBN 978-1-55642-192-1.
9. Alvarez, C.; De Vera, M.; Beauchamp, R.; Ward, V.; Black, A. Classification of idiopathic toe walking based on gait analysis: Development and application of the ITW severity classification. *Gait Posture* **2007**, *26*, 428–435. [CrossRef] [PubMed]
10. Kadaba, M.P.; Ramakrishnan, H.K.; Wootten, M.E. Measurement of lower extremity kinematics during level walking. *J. Orthop. Res.* **1990**, *8*, 383–392. [CrossRef] [PubMed]
11. Davis, R.B.; Õunpuu, S.; Tyburski, D.; Gage, J.R. A gait analysis data collection and reduction technique. *Hum. Mov. Sci.* **1991**, *10*, 575–587. [CrossRef]
12. Leardini, A.; Caravaggi, P.; Theologis, T.; Stebbins, J. Multi-segment foot models and their use in clinical populations. *Gait Posture* **2019**, *69*, 50–59. [CrossRef] [PubMed]

13. Stebbins, J.; Harrington, M.; Thompson, N.; Zavatsky, A.; Theologis, T. Repeatability of a model for measuring multi-segment foot kinematics in children. *Gait Posture* **2006**, *23*, 401–410. [CrossRef] [PubMed]
14. Pothrat, C.; Authier, G.; Viehweger, E.; Berton, E.; Rao, G. One- and multi-segment foot models lead to opposite results on ankle joint kinematics during gait: Implications for clinical assessment. *Clin. Biomech.* **2015**, *30*, 493–499. [CrossRef] [PubMed]
15. Brasiliano, P.; Alvini, M.; Di Stanislao, E.; Vannozzi, G.; Di Rosa, G.; Camomilla, V. Effects of wearing a foot orthosis on ankle function in children with idiopathic toe walking during gait. *Heliyon* **2022**, *8*, e11021. [CrossRef] [PubMed]
16. Sangeux, M.; Polak, J. A simple method to choose the most representative stride and detect outliers. *Gait Posture* **2015**, *41*, 726–730. [CrossRef] [PubMed]
17. Iosa, M.; Cereatti, A.; Merlo, A.; Campanini, I.; Paolucci, S.; Cappozzo, A. Assessment of Waveform Similarity in Clinical Gait Data: The Linear Fit Method. *BioMed Res. Int.* **2014**, *2014*, 214156. [CrossRef] [PubMed]
18. Wobbrock, J.O.; Findlater, L.; Gergle, D.; Higgins, J.J. The Aligned Rank Transform for Nonparametric Factorial Analyses Using Only Anova Procedures. In Proceedings of the SIGCHI Conference on Human Factors in Computing Systems, Vancouver, BC, Canada, 7–12 May 2011; Association for Computing Machinery: New York, NY, USA, 2011; pp. 143–146.
19. Yoo, H.J.; Park, H.S.; Lee, D.-O.; Kim, S.H.; Park, G.Y.; Cho, T.-J.; Lee, D.Y. Comparison of the kinematics, repeatability, and reproducibility of five different multi-segment foot models. *J. Foot Ankle Res.* **2022**, *15*, 1. [CrossRef] [PubMed]
20. Reay, J.; Leboeuf, F.; Hanssen, B.; Chiu, J.; Jones, R. Repeatability of the Oxford Foot Model: Comparison of a team of assessors with different backgrounds and no prior experience of the Oxford Foot Model. *Gait Posture* **2022**, *92*, 191–198. [CrossRef] [PubMed]
21. Vicon. Plug in Gait Reference Guide. 2022. Available online: https://docs.vicon.com/display/Nexus214/PDF+downloads+for+Vicon+Nexus. (accessed on 8 March 2023).
22. Baker, R.; Lebouef, F.; Reay, J.; Sangeux, M. The Conventional Gait Model–Success and Limitations. In *Handbook of Human Motion*; Springer: Cham, Switzerland, 2018.

healthcare

MDPI

Article

# Effectiveness of Vestibular Rehabilitation after Concussion: A Systematic Review of Randomised Controlled Trial

Erasmo Galeno [1,2], Edoardo Pullano [3], Firas Mourad [4,5], Giovanni Galeoto [6] and Francesco Frontani [3,*]

1 Department of Scienze Mediche, Chirurgiche e Neuroscienze, Università degli Studi di Siena, 53100 Siena, Italy
2 Department of Clinical Science and Translation Medicine, University of Rome Tor Vergata, 00133 Rome, Italy
3 Departmental Faculty of Medicine and Surgery, Saint Camillus International University of Rome and Medical Sciences (UniCamillus), 00131 Rome, Italy
4 Department of Physiotherapy, LUNEX International University of Health, Exercise and Sports, 4671 Differdange, Luxembourg
5 Luxembourg Health & Sport Sciences Research Institute A.s.b.l., 50, Avenue du Parc des Sports, 4671 Differdange, Luxembourg
6 Department of Human Neurosciences, Sapienza University of Rome, 00185 Rome, Italy
* Correspondence: francesco.frontani@unicamillus.org

**Abstract:** Introduction: Mild traumatic brain injury (mTBI) affects approximately 740 cases per 100,000 people. Impairments related to mTBI include vertigo, dizziness, balance, gait disorders double or blurry vision, and others. The efficacy on acute or chronic phase and dosage of vestibular rehabilitation (VR) in reducing these symptoms is not clearly stated. To clarify these points, we performed a systematic review of randomised controlled trials (RCTs). Methods: A systematic literature search was performed from 2015 to 2022 on PubMed, CINAHL, Cochrane Trial SPORTDiscus, Web of Science, and PEDRO. Eligibility criteria were RCTs which consider VR, participants with mTBI, and no gender or age restriction. Two blinded reviewers independently selected the study, and a third author was contacted in case of disagreements. Risk of bias was independently screened by two authors and successively checked by the other two authors. Results: Thirty-three full articles were read for potential inclusion and seven records met the inclusion criteria. The authors analysed different outcomes considering DHI, a meta-analysis was carried out, statistical difference was observed ($p < 0.01$), and a mean difference of −6.91 (−9.11, −4.72) in favour of VR was shown. Considering quality of life, the VR group reached a higher score on QOLIBRI. Controversial results were shown about balance and subjective symptoms questionnaire. Differently considering HiMAT, the authors showed a statistically important difference in favour of VR ($p = 0.002$). Conclusion: VR seems useful to reduce symptoms in patients with concussion; however, a huge heterogeneity of the studies and of the outcomes used were found. Therefore, a larger sample is necessary to assess the efficacy of VR.

**Keywords:** vestibular rehabilitation; traumatic brain injury; dizziness rehabilitation; vertigo rehabilitation

**Citation:** Galeno, E.; Pullano, E.; Mourad, F.; Galeoto, G.; Frontani, F. Effectiveness of Vestibular Rehabilitation after Concussion: A Systematic Review of Randomised Controlled Trial. *Healthcare* **2023**, *11*, 90. https://doi.org/10.3390/healthcare11010090

Academic Editor: Mustafa Z. Younis

Received: 16 December 2022
Accepted: 22 December 2022
Published: 28 December 2022



## 1. Introduction

Discussion is ongoing of the proper management of mild traumatic brain injury (mTBI), more commonly termed concussion. There are approximately 740 cases of mTBI per 100,000 people, representing 55.9 million people each year. Sports-related traumatic brain injury (SR-TBI) is a very common occurrence. Each year, there are estimated to be from 1.6 to 3.8 million SR-TBIs, with an incidence that varies among the many types of sports [1]. Given this incidence, a proper dosage and effective conservative treatment seem important. Notably, mTBI is not a pathology that we find only in sports: other causes of mTBI are car accidents and accidental falls. Sensorimotor and vestibular impairments after concussion are well documented. They are classified as either peripheral or central and include vertigo, dizziness, balance and gait disorders, and double or blurry vision, among many others. It has been estimated that 30–65% of patients who have suffered a TBI will suffer vestibular symptoms (dizziness, nausea, vomiting, difficulty in concentrating, etc.). Impairments related to mTBI seem to be positively managed with vestibular rehabilitation (VR) [2,3], which consists in a set of treatments based on exercises which promote adaptation, substitution, habituation, and replacement (Table 1). The objectives of VR concern the improvement of gaze stabilisation, postural stability, symptoms of dizziness, and daily life activities [4]. However, it is necessary to compare this technique with other treatments and no treatment to determine its effectiveness. Murray et al. affirmed that VR's apparent reduction of symptoms in patients after concussion is based on low-quality studies and that randomised controlled trials (RCTs) are lacking [5].

**Table 1.** Brief description of the different vestibular rehabilitation techniques.

| | |
|---|---|
| **Adaptation Exercise** | process where nerve impulses in the brain are able to shift or "adapt" to the incorrect signals from the damaged vestibular system. This gradual shift allows your brain to recalibrate itself. |
| **Substitution** | recovery principle uses other body functions or strategies to replace the missing vestibular function. |
| **Habituation** | process allows you to gradually desensitize yourself to vestibular movement and stimulation if you are repeatedly exposed to it. |
| **Replacement** | different repositioning maneuvers can be performed to help resolve the spinning that occurs due to position changes. |

VR provides treatments oriented to the dysfunctional characteristics of patients (the 'problem-oriented approach') [5]. An in-depth evaluation is followed by the assignment of a personalised exercise programme, based on signs and symptoms related to the dysfunctions of other systems that may be involved as a result of the head trauma [6]. Considering the review of Murray et al. [5], the goal of our study was to analyse the effectiveness of the different techniques of VR, considering only high-quality studies such as RCTs to enable us to determine the effectiveness of VR compared to no treatment or other kinds of treatment. To reach our goal, a systematic literature review was conducted following the Preferred Reporting Items for Systematic Reviews and Meta-Analyses (PRISMA) guidelines [7]. The purpose of this systematic literature review was to analyse the VR dosage considered in the papers and what kind of sensorimotor or vestibular treatment seems most effective. Moreover, we hoped to differentiate the effectiveness of VR on patients with chronic, sub-acute, and acute symptoms. The results are summarised either as a meta-analysis or through a narrative approach.

## 2. Methods

### *2.1. Standards*

The methodology of this review follows the Cochrane Handbook of Systematic Review [8], while the reporting adheres to the updated PRISMA Statement. Search reporting follows the guidelines for PRISMA literature searches reporting (PRISMA-S) [7,9].

The review was a priori registered in the PROSPERO database, registration number CRD42021247187 issued 5 May 2021. The inclusion criteria were that the papers should be full text, in the English language, include an RCT, and consider participants showing vestibular symptoms after concussion.

Eligibility criteria: This study followed the participants, interventions, comparisons, outcomes, and study design (PICOS) framework.

Population: We considered adolescents and adults from 8 to 75 years old suffering vestibular symptoms related to a concussion following a trauma. No gender differences were considered.

Intervention: We considered all types of VR. VR is a specialised form of therapy intended to alleviate the impairments caused by vestibular disorders. Our review included rehabilitation programmes based on VR.

Comparison: The following comparators were eligible: routine care, alternative care, pharmacological care, sham treatment, and wait and see. The most frequent treatments used as comparators were stretching and no intervention.

Outcomes: Outcomes considered were vertigo, dizziness, symptom modification, functional impact of vestibular symptoms, and balance. Outcomes were measured with specific questionnaires or tests related to the impairment or with general questionnaires related to patients' quality of life.

Study design: Only RCTs were included.

### 2.2. Search Strategy and Data Extraction (Information Sources)

The following databases were searched for studies published from 2015 to September 2022: PubMed, CINAHL, Cochrane Trial SPORTDiscus, Web of Science, and PEDRO. The search strategy was carefully designed by including vocabulary terms specific to each database and combined using the Boolean operators AND and OR (Supplementary File S1). The following electronic databases were searched from inception to 1 September 2022: Medline, Web of Science, Cochrane Central Register of Controlled Trials (Cochrane CENTRAL), Cumulative Index to Nursing and Allied Health Literature (CINAHL), SPORTDiscus, and PEDRO. The grey literature was searched by one of the authors (EG). In addition, we screened all the studies included in the review performed by Murray et al. (2016) [5], and we added one paper which matched our inclusion/exclusion criteria.

### 2.3. Study Selection

Titles and abstracts of the studies were screened by two blinded researchers (FF and EP) to identify eligible studies. The screening process was conducted on the rayyan.qcri platform. All the articles were evaluated and selected first by title, then by abstract, and, finally, by full text, according to the inclusion and exclusion criteria described previously. Abstracts deemed to have met the inclusion criteria by at least one reviewer were automatically retrieved as full-text articles. For those studies recommended for exclusion by at least one reviewer, a final decision was made by a third reviewer (EG), and any disagreements were arbitrated and assessed individually. Data extraction tables were created using Microsoft Word, and study design, population characteristics, outcome measures and follow-up intervals, interventions, results, and other relevant data were entered. Data that met the inclusion criteria were extracted by one person (EP) and independently verified by the other authors (FF, EG, FM, and GG). Extracted data were type of study (only RCTs), study characteristics (participants, age, time since concussion, and gender), and intervention (where information was available, prescribed exercise or prescribed VR was extracted). Treatment was described in terms of intensity (frequency, number of sessions, and duration of intervention), outcome measures (vestibular symptoms reported in a specified questionnaire, such as dizziness, gaze stabilisation, vertigo, gait impairments, return to sport (RTS), and quality of life), and results (the results related to the outcome were all reported). The outcomes were defined as short-term (three months), intermediate-term (six months), and long-term (one year). The corresponding author of every selected study was contacted via e-mail twice to check the results of their paper and receive additional information about it.

### 2.4. Statistical Analysis and Narrative Synthesis

A meta-analysis of continuous or dichotomous outcomes was carried out whenever possible. The meta-analysis was performed using Review Manager (version 5.4.1, Cochrane Collaboration, Oxford, England), and the $p$-value was considered statistically significant at $<0.05$.

For outcomes where a meta-analysis was not possible, the result was presented as a narrative synthesis. The narrative approach was proposed considering all the outcomes of interest regarding post-concussion vertigo, dizziness, gaze stabilisation, and RTS reported in the selected papers. We decided to include data from the last follow-up of every paper. Where there were multiple follow-ups, we included data in which results were clearly different from the previous follow-up. We decided to exclude data which were missing, unclear, or unspecified. We included results that were scientifically admissible for every outcome regarding balance, dizziness, gaze stabilisation, quality of life, and RTS.

### 2.5. Risk of Bias

The quality of the included studies was evaluated independently by two reviewers (EP and FF) using the Cochrane Risk of Bias Tool for RCTs. It was successively checked and accepted by the other reviewers (EG and GG).

## 3. Results

The systematic search retrieved 1492 records, with two additional articles retrieved from reference lists and the grey literature. Of these, 175 records were deleted with Endnote, 1126 records were deleted as unsuitable after the title was screened, and 162 were deleted after the abstract was screened. The remaining 31 articles were screened for full text. The study selection process is detailed in the PRISMA flow diagram (Figure 1). Twelve papers were excluded due to their study design, nine were excluded because of the treatment [10–18], and two were excluded because there was no clear distinction between mild, moderate, and severe traumatic brain injury [19,20]. Lastly, it was impossible to retrieve the full text of two papers, which were therefore excluded [21,22]. Six [23–28] records fulfilled the inclusion criteria. In addition, one study was included [29] from a previous review by Murray et al. (2016) [5] (Figure 1) (Table 2).

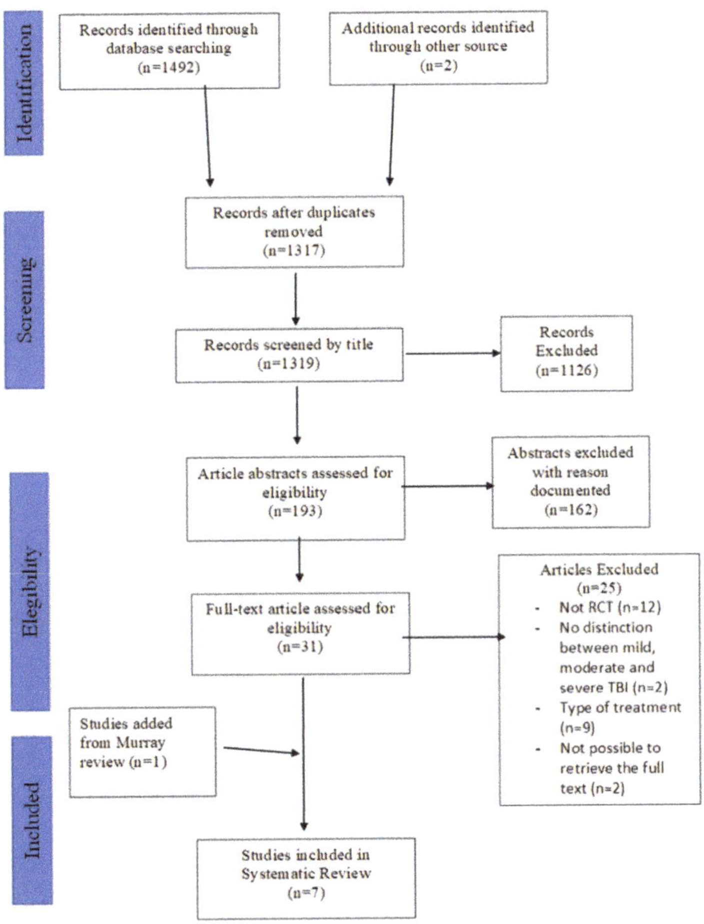


**Figure 1.** PRISMA flow diagram for systematic search. TBI, traumatic brain injury; VRT, vestibular rehabilitation therapy.

**Table 2.** Summary table of main characteristic of the studies.

| Study Author/Year | Type of Study | Sample | Intervention | Outcome Measure | Results |
|---|---|---|---|---|---|
| Soberg H.L. et al. (2021) [26] | Single blind RCT | n = 64 (19 males, 45 females). Mean age was 39.4 (SD 13.0). There was a measure at the baseline (T0) then at the first follow-up (T1) at 2.7 (SD 0.8) months after the baseline. The second follow-up (T2) was 4.4 (SD 1.0) months after the baseline. | Both groups received the TAU Intervention Group: TAU combined with an individualised group-based VR programme, 16 sessions in 8 weeks. VR exercises were tailored and described in another study (27). Control group: only TAU. | QOLIBRI and HRQL were the main outcome measures. RPQ, VSS-SF, and HADS are the secondary outcome measures. | Significant group effect in favour of the intervention group in HRQL on the QOLIBRI. The score at T0 of the QOLIBRI was between 45.4 and 66.7 (SD between 19.2 and 22.7), while at T2, the score was between 55.3 and 66.6 (SD between 20.3 and 24.7). The *p*-value for the QOLIBRI was <0.02. |
| Reneker J.C. et al. (2017) [25] | Double-blind RCT | n = 41. The population included athletes, participating in sports aged 10–23 years with an acute concussion and dizziness diagnosed with PCS. The intervention group (n = 22) with a mean age of 16.5, control group (n = 19) with a mean age of 15.9. The follow-up was made after a 4-week period. | Group 1: The PT designed an individualised and progressive treatment plan. VR included different techniques (including habituation and adaptation), oculomotor control, neuromotor control (including proprioceptive and kinesthetic awareness), and balance exercises were added to each subject's treatment regimen as indicated Generally, each intervention session lasted between 30 and 60 minutes. Group 2: The PT delivered interventions that ranged from sham, sub-therapeutic, and non-progressive therapeutic techniques to minimally progressive therapeutic techniques. | Primary outcomes: symptomatic recovery with PCS and medical clearance for RTP. | The median time for medical release was 10.5 days sooner in the experimental group than in the control group. The median time for PCS recovery was 3.5 days sooner in the experimental group than in the control group. Considering Cox proportional hazards regression for time until medical release for RTP, the experimental group demonstrated a hazard ratio of 2.91 compared to the control group. (95% CI: 1.01, 8.43). |

**Table 2.** *Cont.*

| Study Author/Year | Type of Study | Sample | Intervention | Outcome Measure | Results |
|---|---|---|---|---|---|
| Jafarzadeh, S, et al. (2018) [24] | RCT | n = 20 adult patients (aged 18–60 years). Patients had a mean age of 44.2 (SD 12.6). The follow-up was after 4 weeks of rehabilitation. | Participants were randomly divided into two groups.<br>Control Group: received the usual medical therapy (Betaserc 8 mg pills; at least three pills per day).<br>Intervention Group: received medical therapy and VR after a 4-week period. Different VR techniques were proposed considering the baseline condition of the patients. Different gaze stabilisation and adaptation exercises were used in all patients, although substitution exercises including standing and walking exercise were used only in patients with unsteadiness. More detailed data were summarized in the study. | DHI | Early vestibular rehabilitation programme can decrease vertigo symptoms and increase stability and balance performance. Medical therapy group at week one was 1.8 (SD = 10.9) while at week four was 0.2 (SD = 7.8). The medical therapy and vestibular rehabilitation group at week 1 was −2.0 (SD = 8.7) while at week four was 20.0 (SD = 11.0) with $p = 0.000$. |
| Kleffelgaard I. et al. (2019) [23] | RCT | n = 65 with TBI (45 females and 19 males). Intervention group (n = 32) with a mean age of 37.6 (SD 12.3) and control group (n = 31) with a mean age of 41.2 (SD 13.6). Baseline at 3.5 (mean) months after injury. First follow-up at a mean of 2.7 months. Second follow-up at two months after the end of the intervention. | Control group: (n = 32) did not receive any rehabilitation intervention.<br>Intervention group: (n = 33) received a group-based vestibular rehabilitation. VR exercises were tailored and described in another study (27). The intervention was twice weekly for eight weeks.<br>Both groups received usually multidisciplinary outpatient care. | Primary outcome: DHI<br>Secondary Outcome: HiMAT, VSSV, VSSa, RP3, RPQ13, HADSa, HADSd, and BESS | First follow-up, statistically significant mean differences in favour of the intervention were found in DHI (−8.7 points, 95% CI: −16.6 to −0.9) and HiMAT (3.7 points, 95% CI: 1.4–6.0).<br>The *p*-value was significant for first follow-up: the DHI $p = 0.03$ and the HiMAT $p = 0.002$. No significant difference in other outcomes. |

**Table 2.** *Cont.*

| Study Author/Year | Type of Study | Sample | Intervention | Outcome Measure | Results |
|---|---|---|---|---|---|
| Schneider M.J. et al. (2014) [29] | RCT | Treatment group (n = 15): 11 males, 4 females. Median age: 15 (SD 12–27).<br>Control group (n = 16): 7 males, 9 females. Median age: 15 (SD 13–30). | Both groups performed non-provocative range of motion exercises, stretching, and postural education.<br>Treatment group: in addition, received an individual designed vestibular rehabilitation and cervical spine physiotherapy. VR includes an individualised programme of habituation, gaze stabilisation, adaptation exercises, standing balance exercises, dynamic balance exercises, and canalith repositioning manoeuvres. | (1) Number of days until medical clearance to return to sport.<br>(2) 11-point Numeric Pain Rating Scale score, ABC scale, DHI, SCAT2, DVA, head thrust test, modified motion sensitivity test, FGA, CFE, and JPE. | Return to Sport: OR 10.27, $p < 0.001$ for return to sport in 8 weeks for the intervention group.<br>Intention to treat analysis: OR 3.91 (95% CI 1.34 to 11.34) for the treatment group to be medically cleared to return to sport compared with the control group, ($p = 0.002$). No between-group analyses for secondary outcomes were reported. |
| Kontos A.P. et al. (2021) [27] | RCT | Treatment group (n = 25): 16 females, 9 males. Median age: 15.3 (SD 1.6).<br>Control group (n = 25): 15 females, 10 males. Median age: 15.3 (SD 1.7).<br>The outcomes were recorded at 2 and 4 weeks post-intervention. The participants who were recovered by 2 or 4 weeks stopped the intervention and completed the clinical outcomes. | Both groups performed a behavioural management.<br>Treatment group performed also individual VR and home VR exercises for 30 minutes per day.<br>Control group: performed stretching and physical activity for 30 minutes per day. | VOMS: to assess the VOR, DHI, mBESS, and PCSS | There was a medium treatment effect size for horizontal VOR and VMS (0.09–0.11) and large for vertical VOR (0.16).<br>The subscales of DHI-F demonstrated a medium treatment effect size (0.06–0.1), whereas all other secondary outcomes demonstrated a small treatment effect (0.01–0.06).<br>Significant statistical difference was shown only for horizontal VOR ($p = 0.04$) and vertical VOR ($p = 0.01$). No other significantly differences were shown. |

**Table 2.** *Cont.*

| Study Author/Year | Type of Study | Sample | Intervention | Outcome Measure | Results |
|---|---|---|---|---|---|
| Langevin P. et al. (2022) [28] | RCT | Treatment group: (n = 30): 20 females, 10 males. Mean age: 38.9 (SD 14.56)<br>Control group (n = 30): 21 females, 9 males. Mean age: 39.07 (SD 12.63).<br>The outcomes were recorded at baseline, and after 3, 6, 12, and 26 weeks. | Both groups received education and advice about exercise tolerance and concussion.<br>Control group received 8 sessions in 6 weeks of supervised cardiovascular exercise.<br>Treatment group received the same treatment as control group +1 to 8 sessions of cervicovestibular treatment. The treatment consisted in manual and therapeutic exercises for cervical spine and repositioning manoeuvre, vestibular adaptation, ocular motor exercise, balance, and habituation exercise | PCSS, DHI, NPRS, clearance to return to function, VOMS, and head impulse test (HIT). | No group by time interaction difference was observed for PCSS, DHI, NPRS, and return to function. All the groups demonstrated a statistically significant difference from the baseline. A group by time interaction was observed for horizontal and vertical VOR in favour of the treatment group at 6 weeks ($p < 0.01$). A difference for group interactions was observed for HIT ($p < 0.01$). |

### 3.1. Patient Demographics

All the patients in the included studies experienced vestibular symptoms as the result of a concussion. The concussion occurred within 48 hours to 6 months before the baseline of the studies. A total of 7 RCTs were carried out and included a total of 266 participants (male = 100; female = 146). The gender of 20 participants was not specified [24]. The age of the included participants varied from 9 to 67 years. One study only considered an adolescent population [27], in two studies the sample considered was adolescent or adult [25,29], and the remaining four papers examined an adult population [23,24,26,28].

### 3.2. Types of Interventions

Considering the interventions, we analysed only those studies that considered VR as the main treatment. The comparators for VR were no treatment in three papers [23,26,29], sham or sub-therapeutic treatment in one paper [25], and stretching and physical activity in one study [27]; moreover, one study considered the same educational and physical activity programme for both groups plus VR only in the intervention group [28], and in one paper both groups underwent an identical drug treatment and one experimental group VR was added. [24].

### 3.3. Vestibular Rehabilitation

VR is described as an exercise-based treatment programme designed to promote vestibular adaptation and substitution. The goals of VR are (1) to enhance gaze stabilisation, (2) to enhance postural stability, (3) to improve vertigo, and (4) to improve activities of daily living. VR facilitates vestibular recovery mechanisms: vestibular adaptation, substitution by other eye-movement systems, substitution by vision, somatosensory cues, other postural strategies, and habituation (6).

Seven articles included in this review considered vestibular symptom reduction after a concussion. The protocol was similar in all seven papers, and the authors considered adaptation exercise, substitution exercise, habituation exercise, and balance/gait exercise to treat patients after mTBI. Four of these papers also considered manual techniques applied to the cervical spine [24,26,28,29], but only for patients who complained of cervical pain or range of motion restriction. The other papers considered a group VR with a tailored home-exercise programme. In three different papers [23,27,29], the control group did not receive any treatment. In one paper, both groups received the same medical therapy, but only one was given a VR protocol [24]. In two studies, patients received physical activity treatment [27,28], and in the last one, the control group received sham or sub-therapeutic treatment [25]. Of the studies included in this systematic review, only that by Schneider et al. [29] did not describe the exercise protocol properly. In the other papers, both progression and clinical reasoning for the proposed techniques were clearly stated [24,25,27–29].

### 3.4. Outcomes

We decided to summarise the results in terms of the outcome measures included in the studies. The data extracted were summarised in different sub-groups as follows. In regard to *balance*, the sub-groups are Activities-specific Balance Confidence Scale (ABC-scale), Balance Error Scoring System (BESS), and modified BESS (mBESS). In regard to *dizziness*, they are Dizziness Handicap Inventory (DHI), Motion Sensitivity Quotient, and Vertigo Symptom Scale. *Quality of life* was investigated with QOLIBRI. *Subjective reports of post-concussion* were reported with the Rivermead Post-Concussion Symptom Questionnaire (RPQ), Post-Concussion Scale (PCS), and Post-Concussion Symptom Scale (PCSS). *Gait impairment* was investigated with functional gait assessment (FGA) and the High-level Mobility Assessment Tool for traumatic brain injury (HiMAT). *Gaze stabilisation and vestibular-ocular reflex (VOR)* were investigated with dynamic visual acuity (DVA), the head impulse test (HIT), and the Vestibular/Ocular Motor Screening (VOMS) scale. Other outcome measures were used at the baseline to assess the VOR and other reflexes related to vestibular symptoms, such as the head thrust test, but this measure was not further discussed because it was not analysed as an outcome measure by the authors. The last outcome analysed was *return to sport (RTS)*, defined as medical clearance to return to full sports activity. Heterogeneity of outcome measure and follow-up allowed a meta-analysis only for the DHI score considering short-term outcomes. Adverse responses were not documented.

### 3.5. Risk of Bias

Only one paper showed a high risk of bias [24]. The other papers could be defined as at low risk of bias. All papers except [24] used an adequate sequence generation and allocation procedure, so in six studies there was a low risk of selection bias. Unfortunately, none of the papers showed blinding of personnel or participants, so all papers had a high risk of performance bias. Reporting bias was shown by Schneider et al. and Jafarzadeh et al. [24,29]. No papers except [24] showed attrition bias, and all except [24] gave an adequate overview of withdrawal or drop-outs (Figure 2).

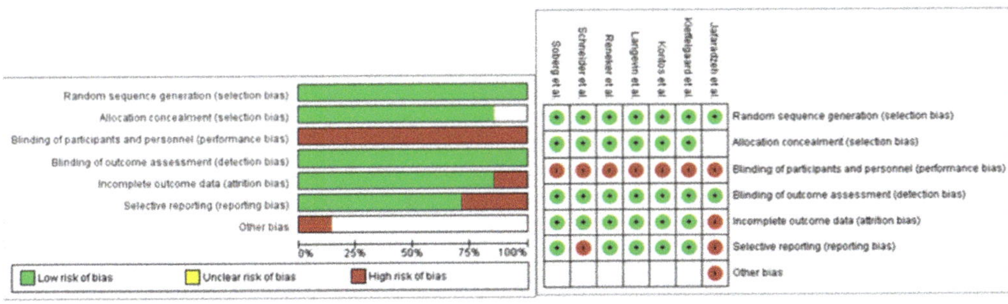


**Figure 2.** Tables representing the risk of bias for the included studies.

### 3.6. *Efficacy of Intervention: Analysis (Synthesis of Results)*

#### 3.6.1. Return to Sport

RTS criteria were analysed in two papers. Schneider et al. [29] found a $p < 0.001$ for medical clearance to RTS in the treatment group within eight weeks of treatment; thus, a ratio of 3.91 times more individuals in the treatment group were medically cleared to RTS than in the control group. Reneker et al. [25] showed a rate of 2.91 in favour of the experimental group in the time-to-medical release RTS, with a median number of days to medical release of 15.5 for the experimental group and 26 for the control group [25,29].

#### 3.6.2. Dizziness

Dizziness was analysed using the DHI scale in five papers [23,24,27–29], the vertigo symptoms scale in one paper [23], and Motion Sensitivity Quotient in one study [29]. A meta-analysis of the DHI scale and data used by Kleffelgaard et al., Jafarzadeh et al., and Kostos et al. was carried out. The data showed a mean difference score of −6.91 (−9.11, −4.72) in favour of the experimental group with a statistically significant difference between groups ($p < 0.001$) (Figure 3). Quantitative analysis of the results reported a statistically significant difference between group mean in DHI at the first follow-up ($p = 0.03$) but no difference at the second follow-up ($p = 0.09$) [23]. The mean difference between groups was −8.7 (−16.6 to −0.9) in favour of the intervention group [23]. Jafarzadeh et al. [24] showed a significant difference in weeks 3 and 4 in favour of the VR group ($p < 0.001$) with a mean change in DHI between the groups of $20 \pm 11$ in the intervention group and $0.2 \pm 7.8$ in the control group at four weeks, during the last follow-up. Schneider et al. [29] reported median DHI changes in the score of −24 in the intervention group and –48 in the control group (just one participant) in those cleared to RTS. Moreover, the authors found a median change of −13 in the intervention group and –21 in the control group in those not cleared to RTS. Kostos et al. [27] reported a small treatment effect for the overall score of the DHI with a mean score of −24.94 (SD 3.72) on the intervention group and a mean score of −17.89 (SD 3.61) on the control group, with no statistically significant difference between groups ($p = 0.18$). Langevin et al. [28] showed no statistical difference between group interaction but only by time interaction for both groups. The DHI score decreased from 45.8 (SD 22.1) in the experimental group and 44.8 (SD 21.87) in the control group to 11.86 (SD 12.16) in the experimental group and 9.63 (SD 9,32) in the control group, respectively. The other dizziness outcome measure employed by Schneider et al. [29] was the modified Motion Sensitivity Quotient. In the treatment group, median changes of −10 and −1.75 were reported in those cleared and not cleared, respectively (to RTS). Conversely, in the control group, median changes of −20 and −7.25 were observed in those cleared and not cleared, respectively (to RTS). Lastly, in regard to dizziness, Kleffelgaard et al. [23] were not able to detect statistically significant changes in the Vertigo Symptom Scale with a mean difference of −2.1 (−4.5 to –0.2) ($p = 0.08$) in the vertigo subscale and 0.4 (−1.4 to −2.1) ($p = 0.69$) in the anxiety subscale.

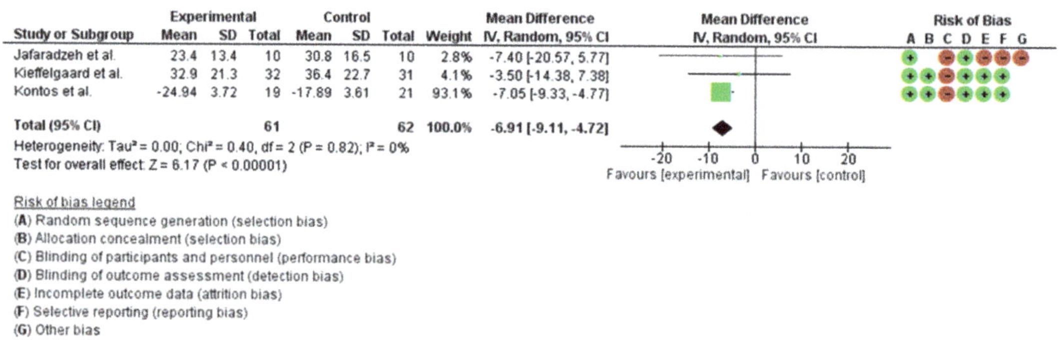


**Figure 3.** Figure representing the results for the meta-analysis for DHI outcome.

### 3.6.3. Subjective Reports of Concussion Symptoms

This outcome measure was reported by PCS, Rivermead Post-Concussion Symptoms Questionnaire, and PCSS. The PCS was used by Reneker et al. [25], who reported that, when accounting for a history of previous concussion, the experimental group recovered at a rate of 1.99 compared to the control group (HR: 1.99; 95% CI: 0.95, 4.15). Kleffelgaard et al. [23] reported no statistically significant difference at either follow-up in the Rivermead Post-Concussion Symptoms Questionnaire. The analysis of the PCSS performed by Kostos et al. [27] showed no statistically significant difference between the group and a small effect in favour of the treatment. PCSS analysis performed by Langevin et al. [28] showed no group by time interaction statistically significant difference between groups for the total score ($p = 0.62$) but a time effect with a significant improvement for both groups. The PCSS score decreased from 62.83 (SD 23.69) in the experimental group and 61.77 (SD 22.59) in the control group to 13.96 (SD 12.63) in the experimental group and 14.67 (SD 16.85) in the control group at 26 weeks post-baseline [28].

### 3.6.4. Balance

Considering balance impairment, the BESS, used by Kleffelgaard et al. [23], showed no statistically significant difference between groups ($p = 0.15$). Considering balance impairment, Schneider et al. [29] reported that 64% of those medically cleared to RTS in the treatment group reached the maximum score of 100/100 on the ABCscale compared with 25% of the control group who were not medically cleared. Considering the mBESS, no difference was found by Kostos et al. [27] with a small effect size in favour of the treatment.

3.6.5. Gait Impairment

Gait impairment and dynamic balance were considered by Schneider et al. and Kleffelgaard et al. [23]. The first author group showed an FGA improvement in the intervention group of 1 in those cleared to RTS and of 3 in those not cleared to RTS. In contrast, in the control group, there was a median FGA change of 3 in those cleared to RTS and of 1 in those not cleared to RTS. Kleffelgaard et al. [23] showed a statistically significant difference at the first follow-up considering the HiMAT with a between group mean difference ($p = 0.002$); no difference was shown at the second follow-up ($p = 0.09$).

3.6.6. Quality of Life

Quality of life was analysed by only one author group, Soberg et al. [26]. Considering the QOLIBRI, the multivariate model showed a mean of 6.5 points higher in the intervention group than in the control group for the change scores on the QOLIBRI.

3.6.7. Gaze Stabilisation

In regard to gaze stabilisation and VOR, Schneider et al. [28] did not perform a specific test between groups of the DVA so the results could not be analysed. The VOMS was analysed by Kostos et al. [27] and showed that a statistically significant difference existed between horizontal VOR ($p = 0.04$) and vertical VOR ($p = 0.01$) but not visual motion sensitivity ($p = 0.07$). However, a medium to large treatment effect was shown in all the reflexes. A statistically significant difference was also shown in the horizontal and vertical VOR by Langevin et al. [28], who showed a group by time interaction difference in favour of the VR group at six weeks only ($p < 0.01$). Moreover, the authors showed a group by time interaction was reported for the HIT ($p < 0.01$) at 12 weeks. For the other reflexes analysed, no differences were reported.

## 4. Discussion

To the best of our knowledge, this is the first systematic review to analyse only RCTs considering VR following concussion. As a starting point, we used the review performed by Murray et al. in 2016 [5]. The use of VR is an emerging topic in rehabilitation. In fact, many existing studies suggest the usefulness of VR in patients with mTBI/concussion who experience persistent vertigo or balance symptoms. The definition of persistent symptoms varies in the literature from seven days to three months. Hence, a huge variety of patients is included in the studies in terms of impairments, and our review reflects this heterogeneity. After TBI, patients are diagnosed within the first few days or even weeks after the traumatic event; however, the optimal time to begin VR following injury remains unclear [5]. Hence, one of the goals of our review was to differentiate between acute, persistent, and chronic cases and to determine potential differences in dosage and treatment over the time which elapses after concussion. Unfortunately, we are not able to clarify this point. In fact, we found that three papers included only acute patients [25,27,29], one paper included a patient with persistent symptoms between 3 and 12 weeks after the concussion [28], and the other three studies did not clearly state the time course from the concussion [23,24,26] and the inclusion on the study, making it difficult to compare the results of these papers considering the differences in time elapsed since concussion.

### *4.1. Acuity and Return to Sport*

The two papers [25,29] which involved acute patients indicate that VR is effective in reducing the time to clearance to RTS. In fact, both papers showed a reduced time to RTS. The paper by Reneker et al. [25] is really interesting: it compares VR to sham and sub-therapeutic treatment, showing that the treatment has an important impact and that there is a significant interaction between treatment and positive history of concussion. The number of sessions was the same in both studies, which considered a maximum of eight treatments, but the frequency was different: one paper considered two treatments per week [25], and the other considered one treatment per week [29]. However, huge differences exist in regard to the RTS definition, so these results should be considered carefully. In the other papers included in this review, the authors did not take proper account of the time elapsed since concussion and the beginning of the treatment, and many different outcomes were used to analyse the effectiveness of VR. Below, we discuss the differences in the analyses of outcome measures.

### 4.2. Dizziness

Considering the DHI, it was possible to perform a meta-analysis of three studies [23,24,27] which showed a significantly statistical difference in favour of the intervention ($p < 0.001$). The mean difference between groups was −6.91 (−9.33, 4.77), and it has recently been suggested that the minimum important difference between groups is 6 [30]. This difference could be considered important not only statistically, but also clinically. In two of the three studies which considered the DHI, the authors found that a statistical difference was present between the intervention and control groups. Unfortunately, the paper by Jafarzadeh et al. [24] had a high risk of bias. Langevin et al.'s [28] analysis did not show any statistical difference between groups for the DHI. In this study [28], the authors considered gradual physical activity for both groups of treatment. Gradual physical activity is considered a fundamental option for the reduction of the symptoms after concussion. So, adding VR to gradual physical activity does not seem to modify significantly the DHI score. In fact, for both groups, a time interaction improvement was demonstrated. Additionally, Schneider and al. [29] showed a difference in the median score of DHI for participants who were cleared to return to sport. Considering the other dizziness outcomes measures used by the authors, it was not possible to collect any differences between groups. So, VR seems effective to reduce symptoms reported on DHI but not so effective when considering Vertigo Symptom Scale.

### 4.3. Subjective Reports of Concussion Symptoms

Four authors analysed different outcome measures on this topic [23,25,27,28]. Reneker et al. [25] showed a favourable VOR in the VR group, taking into account a previous history of concussion. Kleffelgaard et al. [23], Kostos et al. [27], and Langevin et al. [28] did not show any statistically significant differences between groups. Thus, the subjective reports did not seem to follow the improvement shown in dizziness, VOR, and gait impairments but seemed more related to balance, which did not improve significantly in the studies analysed in this paper.

### 4.4. Balance

Kleffelgaard et al. [23] did not find any differences between intervention and the control group considering balance outcomes. Likewise, Kontos et al. [27], who considered the mBESS, did not find any differences between groups. As only two papers considered balance outcomes which could be really important for patients with vestibular symptoms, in the future it could be interesting to focus on this symptom.

### 4.5. Gait Impairments

Schneider et al. and Kleffelgaard et al. [23,29] considered gait impairment as an outcome of VR following a concussion. The authors showed that, in the short term, VR could reduce the gait impairment of patients. The authors considered the same dosage over eight weeks of treatment for each group, but the number of sessions was different: Kleffelgaard et al. [23] considered two treatments per week while Schneider et al. [29] considered one session per week. Schneider et al. [29] also analysed the gaze stabilisation which could affect patients after mTBI, but the results were not properly analysed so it is not possible to describe them.

### 4.6. Quality of Life

Lastly, in patients who were affected by concussion, considering HRQL on the QOLIBRI, a significant effect in favour of the VR was shown with a mean score 6.5 points higher compared to the control group [26].

### 4.7. Gaze Stabilisation and VOR

Three studies considered VOR and gaze stabilisation as outcome measures and showed contradictory results. In fact, Schneider et al. [29] demonstrated no differences in this outcome measure, whereas, in relation to VOR, Kontos et al. [27] and Langevin et al. [28] showed a statistical difference for vertical VOR and horizontal VOR. Hence, these results need further investigation if we are to understand whether VR could be helpful in the short term in reducing VOR reflexes. The HIT analysis performed by Langevin et al. [28] showed a group by time interaction in favour of the VR ($p < 0.01$) at 12 weeks after the baseline.

From current evidence, it therefore appears that VRT is a valid treatment strategy for the management of patients suffering from unilateral vestibular peripheral problems [31]. Considering our results, we could affirm that, in the acute phase, VR seems effective in reducing time to RTS. Moreover, a meta-analysis showed that dizziness seems to be positively influenced by VR in the short term. These results were not confirmed by a qualitative analysis over the long term. Moreover, gait impairment seems to be positively affected by VR in the short term. All these beneficial effects of VR could improve the quality of life of patients, as was shown by Soberg et al. [26], but unfortunately only one paper considers this impairment. However, patients showed no difference in the subjective reports of concussion symptoms, although improvement in quality of life and different outcome measures was shown in almost all the studies included. We consider the prescription and dosage of VR for patients with TBI to be a very important issue, but this was largely addressed in a previous review [5], and we were unable to retrieve any new information on this topic. Clinically, we very often observe a delay in the prescription of VR treatments, and this could pose a problem considering the results of our review. In fact, the effectiveness in the acute phase shown by Reneker et al. [25] and Schneider et al. [29] seems relevant. Considering the papers included in this review proposed a huge range of dosage treatments to patients, we cannot suggest an optimal dosage for administering specific exercises in this category of patients. These factors, together with the disproportionate use of vestibular suppressor medications [32], can certainly affect the prognosis and chronicity of symptoms, as has already been demonstrated in other clinical presentations [33]. Unfortunately, the effectiveness of VR on chronic symptoms is not clear because none of the studies included in the current work only considers patients with chronic symptoms. However, in acute or persistent conditions, VR seems useful in reducing some symptoms related to concussion. Finally, we can affirm that the management of a patient suffering from sensorimotor system disorders after a TBI should include a physiotherapy evaluation. The goal of this assessment is to identify physical, biological, and psychological impairments, as well as functional disabilities, and evaluate, together with the physicians, when to start a rehabilitation programme. Unfortunately, further studies are needed to obtain details concerning the initiation of VR treatment, the dosage, the time course from concussion to the beginning of the treatment, and further RCTs to reinforce the conclusions of our study.

## 5. Limitations

The first limitation was the heterogeneity of the studies, considering the different periods of time which had passed since concussion (the range was 48 hours to 6 months); moreover, due to the different outcomes and follow-up used by the authors, it was not possible to properly compare the efficacy of vestibular treatment. One study did not accurately describe the VR; however, the other studies clearly defined the progression of the exercises prescribed. A larger sample and better codification of the time between concussion and treatment are necessary. The VOR and other vestibular interaction reflexes (OKN, VRS, and others) were not analysed in all the studies, so it could be interesting to add them as outcome measures in future studies.

## 6. Conclusions

VR seems to be a valid approach for the management of patients suffering from dizziness after concussive trauma. VR seems to reduce the time to clearance to RTS in the acute phase and to modify quality of life and gait impairment symptoms in patients who have suffered an mTBI. Moreover, a meta-analysis showed that DHI scores improved significantly in the short term ($p < 0.01$). Considering this relevant outcome, VR could be a valid approach in the short term. We need more studies with higher magnitude and that properly consider the time elapsed since concussion to detect the correct approaches and dosage.

**Supplementary Materials:** The following supporting information can be downloaded at: https://www.mdpi.com/article/10.3390/healthcare11010090/s1, Supplementary File S1.

**Author Contributions:** Conceptualization, E.G., E.P. and F.F.; methodology, F.M., G.G. and F.F.; validation, E.G., G.G. and F.M.; formal analysis, F.F.; investigation, E.P.; data curation, E.P.; writing—original draft preparation, F.F. and E.G.; writing—review and editing, F.F.; visualization, E.P. and G.G.; supervision, E.G., G.G. and F.M. All authors have read and agreed to the published version of the manuscript.

**Funding:** This research received no external funding.

**Institutional Review Board Statement:** Not applicable.

**Informed Consent Statement:** Not applicable.

**Data Availability Statement:** All the data generated or analyzed during this study are included in this published article.

**Conflicts of Interest:** The authors declare no conflict of interest.

## References

1. Mucha, A.; Fedor, S.; DeMarco, D. Vestibular dysfunction and concussion. *Handb. Clin. Neurol.* **2018**, *158*, 135–144. [PubMed]
2. Alsalaheen, B.A.; Mucha, A.; Morris, L.O.; Whitney, S.L.; Furman, J.M.; Camiolo-Reddy, C.E.; Collins, M.W.; Lovell, M.R.; Sparto, P.J. Vestibular rehabilitation for dizziness and balance disorders after concussion. *J. Neurol. Phys. Ther.* **2010**, *34*, 87–93. [CrossRef] [PubMed]
3. Broglio, S.P.; Collins, M.W.; Williams, R.M.; Mucha, A.; Kontos, A.P. Current and emerging rehabilitation for concussion: A review of the evidence. *Clin. Sport. Med.* **2015**, *34*, 213–231. [CrossRef] [PubMed]
4. Han, B.I.; Song, H.S.; Kim, J.S. Vestibular rehabilitation therapy: Review of indications, mechanisms, and key exercises. *J. Clin. Neurol.* **2011**, *7*, 184–196. [CrossRef] [PubMed]
5. Murray, D.A.; Meldrum, D.; Lennon, O. Can vestibular rehabilitation exercises help patients with concussion? A systematic review of efficacy, prescription and progression patterns. *Br. J. Sport. Med.* **2017**, *51*, 442–451. [CrossRef] [PubMed]
6. Herdman, S. *Vestibular Rehabilitation*, 3rd ed.; F.A. Davis Company: Philadelphia, PA, USA, 2007.
7. Page, M.J.; McKenzie, J.E.; Bossuyt, P.M.; Boutron, I.; Hoffmann, T.C.; Mulrow, C.D.; Shamseer, L.; Tetzlaff, J.M.; Akl, E.A.; Brennan, S.E.; et al. The PRISMA 2020 statement: An updated guideline for reporting systematic reviews. *Syst. Rev.* **2021**, *10*, 105906. [CrossRef]
8. Shamseer, L.; Moher, D.; Clarke, M.; Ghersi, D.; Liberati, A.; Petticrew, M.; Shekelle, P.; Stewart, L.A.; PRISMA-P Group. Preferred reporting items for systematic review and meta-analysis protocols (PRISMA-P) 2015: Elaboration and explanation. *Bmj* **2015**, *349*, g7647. [CrossRef]
9. Ardern, C.L.; Büttner, F.; Andrade, R.; Weir, A.; Ashe, M.C.; Holden, S.; Impellizzeri, F.M.; Delahunt, E.; Dijkstra, H.P.; Mathieson, S.; et al. Implementing the 27 PRISMA 2020 Statement items for systematic reviews in the sport and exercise medicine, musculoskeletal rehabilitation and sports science fields: The PERSiST (implementing Prisma in Exercise, Rehabilitation, Sport medicine and SporTs science) guidance. *Br. J. Sport. Med.* **2022**, *56*, 175–195.
10. Varner, C.E.; Thompson, C.; de Wit, K.; Borgundvaag, B.; Houston, R.; McLeod, S. A randomized trial comparing prescribed light exercise to standard management for emergency department patients with acute mild traumatic brain injury. *Acad. Emerg. Med.* **2021**, *28*, 493–501. [CrossRef]
11. Quatman-Yates, C.C.; Hunter-Giordano, A.; Shimamura, K.K.; Landel, R.; Alsalaheen, B.A.; Hanke, T.A.; McCulloch, K.L.; Altman, R.D.; Beattie, P.; Berz, K.E.; et al. Physical therapy evaluation and treatment after concussion/mild traumatic brain injury: Clinical practice guidelines linked to the international classification of functioning, disability and health from the academy of orthopaedic physical therapy, American Academy of sports physical therapy, academy of neurologic physical therapy, and academy of pediatric physical therapy of the American Physical therapy association. *J. Orthop. Sport. Phys. Ther.* **2020**, *50*, CPG1–CPG73.
12. Bailey, C.; Meyer, J.; Briskin, S.; Tangen, C.; Hoffer, S.A.; Dundr, J.; Brennan, B.; Smith, P. Multidisciplinary concussion management: A model for outpatient concussion management in the acute and post-acute settings. *J. Head Trauma Rehabil.* **2019**, *34*, 375–384. [CrossRef] [PubMed]

13. Micay, R.; Richards, D.; Hutchison, M.G. Feasibility of a postacute structured aerobic exercise intervention following sport concussion in symptomatic adolescents: A randomised controlled study. *BMJ Open Sport Exerc. Med.* **2018**, *4*, e000404. [CrossRef] [PubMed]
14. Dobney, D.M.; Grilli, L.; Beaulieu, C.; Straub, M.; Galli, C.; Saklas, M.; Friedman, D.; Dubrovsky, A.S.; Gagnon, I.J. Feasibility of early active rehabilitation for concussion recovery in youth: A randomized trial. *Clin. J. Sport Med.* **2020**, *30*, 519–525. [CrossRef]
15. Kurowski, B.G.; Hugentobler, J.; Quatman-Yates, C.; Taylor, J.; Gubanich, P.J.; Altaye, M.; Wade, S.L. Aerobic exercise for adolescents with prolonged symptoms after mild traumatic brain injury: An exploratory randomized clinical trial. *J. Head Trauma Rehabil.* **2017**, *32*, 79–89. [CrossRef] [PubMed]
16. Chrisman, S.P.D.; Whitlock, K.B.; Mendoza, J.A.; Burton, M.S.; Somers, E.; Hsu, A.; Fay, L.; Palermo, T.M.; Rivara, F. P Pilot randomized controlled trial of an exercise program requiring minimal in-person visits for youth with persistent sport-related concussion. *Front. Neurol.* **2019**, *10*, 623. [CrossRef] [PubMed]
17. Straudi, S.; Severini, G.; Sabbagh Charabati, A.; Pavarelli, C.; Gamberini, G.; Scotti, A.; Basaglia, N. The effects of video game therapy on balance and attention in chronic ambulatory traumatic brain injury: An exploratory study. *BMC Neurol.* **2017**, *17*, 86. [CrossRef] [PubMed]
18. Vegt, C.B.V.; Hill-Pearson, C.A.; Hershaw, J.N.; Loftin, M.C.; Bobula, S.A.; Souvignier, A.R. A comparison of generalized and individualized vestibular rehabilitation therapy in a military TBI sample. *J. Head Trauma Rehabil.* **2022**, *10*, 1097.
19. Tefertiller, C.; Hays, K.; Natale, A.; O'Dell, D.; Ketchum, J.; Sevigny, M.; Eagye, C.; Philippus, A.; Harrison-Felix, C. Results from a randomized controlled trial to address balance deficits after traumatic brain injury. *Arch. Phys. Med. Rehabil.* **2019**, *100*, 1409–1416. [CrossRef]
20. Sisodia, V.; Hamid, J.; Guru, K. Efficacy of vestibular rehabilitation in management of balance deficit in Indian collegiate football players, with sport-related concussion–randomized clinical trial. *Physiotherapy* **2015**, *101*, e1403–e1404. [CrossRef]
21. Hays, K.; O'Dell, D.R.; Cuthbert, J.P.; Tefertiller, C.; Natale, A. Virtual-Reality Based Therapy for Balance Deficits during Traumatic Brain Injury Inpatient Rehabilitation. *Arch. Phys. Med. Rehabil.* **2015**, *96*, e44. [CrossRef]
22. Cuff, S.; Rose, S.; Young, J. Early intervention in pediatric concussion patients with dizziness and balance problems. *Clin. J. Sport Med.* **2014**, *24*, 186–187.
23. Kleffelgaard, I.; Soberg, H.L.; Tamber, A.L.; Bruusgaard, K.A.; Pripp, A.H.; Sandhaug, M.; Langhammer, B. The effects of vestibular rehabilitation on dizziness and balance problems in patients after traumatic brain injury: A randomized controlled trial. *Clin. Rehabil.* **2019**, *33*, 74–84. [CrossRef] [PubMed]
24. Jafarzadeh, S.; Pourbakht, A.; Bahrami, E.; Jalaie, S.; Bayat, A. Effect of early vestibular rehabilitation on vertigo and unsteadiness in patients with acute and sub-acute head trauma. *Iran. J. Otorhinolaryngol.* **2018**, *30*, 85. [PubMed]
25. Reneker, J.C.; Hassen, A.; Phillips, R.S.; Moughiman, M.C.; Donaldson, M.; Moughiman, J. Feasibility of early physical therapy for dizziness after a sports-related concussion: A randomized clinical trial. *Scand. J. Med. Sci. Sports* **2017**, *27*, 2009–2018. [CrossRef] [PubMed]
26. Soberg, H.L.; Andelic, N.; Langhammer, B.; Tamber, A.L.; Bruusgaard, K.A.; Kleffelgaard, I. Effect of vestibular rehabilitation on change in health-related quality of life in patients with dizziness and balance problems after traumatic brain injury: A randomized controlled trial. *J. Rehabil. Med.* **2021**, *53*, 2781. [PubMed]
27. Kontos, A.P.; Eagle, S.R.; Mucha, A.; Kochick, V.; Reichard, J.; Moldolvan, C.; Holland, C.L.; Blaney, N.A.; Collins, M.W. A randomized controlled trial of precision vestibular rehabilitation in adolescents following concussion: Preliminary findings. *J. Pediatr.* **2021**, *239*, 193–199. [CrossRef] [PubMed]
28. Langevin, P.; Frémont, P.; Fait, P.; Dubé, M.O.; Bertrand-Charette, M.; Roy, J.S. Cervicovestibular Rehabilitation in Adults with Mild Traumatic Brain Injury: A Randomized Clinical Trial. *J. Neurotrauma* **2022**, *39*, 487–496. [CrossRef]
29. Schneider, K.J.; Meeuwisse, W.H.; Nettel-Aguirre, A.; Barlow, K.; Boyd, L.; Kang, J.; Emery, C.A. Cervicovestibular rehabilitation in sport-related concussion: A randomised controlled trial. *Br. J. Sport. Med.* **2014**, *48*, 1294–1298. [CrossRef]
30. Friscia, L.A.; Morgan, M.T.; Sparto, P.J.; Furman, J.M.; Whitney, S.L. Responsiveness of self-report measures in individuals with vertigo, dizziness and unsteadiness. *Otol. Neurotol.* **2014**, *35*, 884. [CrossRef]
31. McDonnell, M.N.; Hillier, S.L. Vestibular rehabilitation for unilateral peripheral vestibular dysfunction. *Cochrane Database Syst. Rev.* **2015**, *1*, CD005397. [CrossRef]
32. Langlois, J.A.; Rutland-Brown, W.; Wald, M.M. The epidemiology and impact of traumatic brain injury: A brief overview. *J. Head Trauma Rehabil.* **2006**, *21*, 375–378. [CrossRef] [PubMed]
33. Ponsford, J.; Willmott, C.; Rothwell, A.; Cameron, P.; Kelly, A.-M.; Nelms, R.; Curran, C.; Ng, K. Factors influencing outcome following mild traumatic brain injury in adults. *J. Int. Neuropsychol. Soc.* **2000**, *6*, 568–579. [CrossRef] [PubMed]

healthcare

MDPI

*Article*

# Ataxia Rating Scales: Content Analysis by Linking to the International Classification of Functioning, Disability and Health

**Mohammad Etoom [1,*], Alhadi M. Jahan [2,3], Alia Alghwiri [4], Francesco Lena [5,6] and Nicola Modugno [6]**

1 Physical Therapy Department, Aqaba University of Technology, Aqaba 77110, Jordan
2 School of Rehabilitation Sciences, University of Ottawa, Ottawa, ON K1Y 4W7, Canada
3 Department of Physiotherapy, College of Medical Technology, Misrata 51, Libya
4 Department of Physiotherapy, School of Rehabilitation Sciences, University of Jordan, Amman 11942, Jordan
5 Department of Medicine and Health, University of Molise, 86100 Campobasso, Italy
6 IRCCS INM Neuromed, 86077 Pozzilli, Italy
* Correspondence: metoom@aut.edu.jo

**Abstract:** Ataxia management is mainly based on rehabilitation, symptomatic management, and functional improvement. Therefore, it is important to comprehensively assess ataxic symptoms and their impact on function. Recently, the movement disorders society recommended four generic ataxia rating scales: scale for assessment and rating of ataxia (SARA), international cooperative ataxia rating scales, Friedreich's ataxia rating scale (FARS), and unified multiple system atrophy rating scale (UMSARS). The aim of the study was to analyze and compare the content of the recommended ataxia rating scales by linking them to the international classification of functioning, disability and health (ICF). A total of 125 meaningful concepts from 93 items of the four included scales were linked to 57 different ICF categories. The ICF categories were distributed in body structure ($n$ = 8), body function ($n$ = 26), activity and participation ($n$ = 20), and environmental factors ($n$ = 3) components. UMSARS and FARS were the only ones that have addressed the body structure or environmental factors component. The content analysis of ataxia rating scales would help clinicians and researchers select the most appropriate scale and understand ataxic symptoms and their impact on function. It seems that SARA is the optimal scale for rapid assessment of ataxia or in busy clinical settings. UMSARS or FARS are more appropriate for the investigating the impact of ataxia on overall health, and monitoring ataxia progression and disability.

**Keywords:** patient outcome assessment; ICF linking; content analysis; outcomes measurement; treatment outcome; rehabilitation

**Citation:** Etoom, M.; Jahan, A.M.; Alghwiri, A.; Lena, F.; Modugno, N. Ataxia Rating Scales: Content Analysis by Linking to the International Classification of Functioning, Disability and Health. *Healthcare* **2022**, *10*, 2459. https://doi.org/10.3390/healthcare10122459

Academic Editors: João Paulo Brito and Alessandro Sartorio

Received: 6 September 2022
Accepted: 4 December 2022
Published: 5 December 2022



## 1. Introduction

Ataxia is a group of impairments of the ability to perform coordinated movements due to neurological disorders that can be sporadic or inherited [1]. It has broad and heterogeneous effects on mobility, speech, psychological status, and quality of life [2]. Management of ataxia is mainly based on rehabilitation, symptomatic management, and functional improvement [3]. Therefore, it is important to comprehensively assess ataxic symptoms and their impact on function.

The clinical assessment of ataxia can be performed by a set of ataxia rating scales [4]. Recently, the movement disorders society recommended four generic ataxia rating scales based on using the scales in different ataxic populations and psychometric proprieties [4]. The scales are: scale for assessment and rating of ataxia (SARA) [5], international cooperative ataxia rating scales (ICARS) [6], Friedreich's ataxia rating scale (FARS) [7], and unified multiple system atrophy rating scale (UMSARS) [8]. These ataxia rating scales showed adequate psychometric proprieties represented with feasibility, acceptability, consistency, and reproducibility. Moreover, the scales can be used in different ataxic populations [4].

The recommended ataxia rating scales show similarities and differences in the covered ataxia aspects. For example, the SARA mainly assesses ataxia through motor performance, while ICARS is concerned with assessing of oculomotor disorders. The autonomic functions and bulbar dysfunctions were assessed by UMSARS and FARS, respectively. Accordingly, it is essential to analyze and compare the content of ataxia rating scales. One way to assess and compare the content of rating scales is by linking them to the International Classification of Functioning, disability and health (ICF). The Linking to ICF would provide a structured description and comparison of the content of each ataxia rating scale. Therefore, the aim of this study was to analyze and compare the content of the recommended ataxia rating scales by linking them to the ICF.

## 2. Materials and Methods

### *2.1. Selection of Ataxia Rating Scales*

We have selected four generic ataxia clinical rating scales that were recommended by movement disorders society: SARA, ICARS, FARS, and UMSARS [4].

### *2.2. Description of Ataxia Rating Scales*

(1) SARA has eight items to assess motor performance, speech disturbance, coordination, and limb kinetic functions. The application time is 14.2 ± 7.5 min [5].
(2) ICARS consists of 19 items, divided into posture and gait disturbance, limb kinetic function, speech disorders, and oculomotor disorders. The application time is 21.3 ± 7 min [9].
(3) FARS has 36 items distributed in 4 domains: (I) functional staging of ataxia; (II) activity of daily life; (III) neurological assessment of bulbar, upper and lower limbs, peripheral nerve, and upright stability/gait functions; and (IV) quantitative timed activities—PATA rate, nine-hole pegboard, and timed 25-foot walk test. It needs more than 30 min to be administrated [7].
(4) UMSARS has 30 items comprising four parts, including a historical review of disease-related impairments, motor examination, autonomic examination, and the global disability scale. The application time is 30–45 min [10].

### *2.3. ICF*

The ICF was developed by the world health organization in 2001 to define different aspects of functioning, disability, and health. It aims to provide a common language for disability and health that enables a better understanding of health and health-related states [11].

In the ICF codes, the letters b, s, d, and e, refer to the components of the classification: body structure (s), body function (b), activity and participation (d), or environmental factors (e). The component letter is followed by a numeric code starting with the first level [chapter], second level, third level, and rarely fourth level. The following example illustrated an ICF category in the activity and participation component:

d Activity and participation [component level]
d4 Mobility [first level/ chapter]
d415 Maintaining a body position [second level]
d4154 Maintaining a standing position [third level]

### 2.4. Procedure of ICF Linking

The linking processes were conducted using updated linking guidelines and refinements [12,13] in two phases. All items and their responses in the included scales were surveyed to identify the meaningful concepts for each item independently by the two raters (M.E and A.J) in the first phase. More than one meaningful concept may be acknowledged for an item. A list of meaningful concepts was discussed to be used in the second phases.

In the second phase, each meaningful concept was linked to one or more ICF categories by detecting the most suitable component, first level (chapter), second level, and third level. The ICF categories were independently selected by the two raters. In case of disagreement between raters, a third rater who has an extensive experience in ICF (A.A) [14–16] was referred to resolve the disagreement and provided the rationale for the most appropriate code.

### 2.5. Interrater Rating Agreement

Cohen's kappa statistic was used to evaluate the interrater agreement between the two raters on identification of meaningful concepts, and ICF category linkage process. Cohen's kappa value ranges from 0 to 1, in which 0 indicates no agreement and 1 indicates perfect agreement [17]. Interrater agreement was estimated for meaningful concepts and component level, then first/chapter level, second, and third level category. The analyses were done at a 95% confidence interval.

### 2.6. ICF Linking Indicators

The following ICF linking indicators were calculated to compare scales and their relationship to ICF [18]:

#### 2.6.1. Measure to ICF Linkage

Is the Percentage of Items in a Scale that Can Be Linked to the ICF Category = The Number of Items Linked to At Least 1 ICF Code/Total Number of Items on the Measure × 100%.

#### 2.6.2. Measure of Linking to Unique ICF Codes

Percentage of Items in a Scale that Could Be Linked to Unique and Unrepeated ICF Code = Number of Items that Are Linked to Unique ICF Code/Total Number of Items on the Scale × 100%

## 3. Results

### 3.1. Meaningful Concepts

The most identified meaningful concept was "movement coordination" (20 concepts, 16%), followed by "tremor" and "walking" (8 concepts, 6.4% each).

### 3.2. ICF Linking Results

The meaningful concepts were linked to 57 different ICF categories. Two meaningful concepts were not linked to ICF. They were "stage of disability" from the global disability scale item in UMSARS, and from functional staging of ataxia item in FARS, and they were assigned to "nd-dis".

The 57 different ICF categories were distributed in body structure component ($n$ = 8), body function component ($n$ = 26), activity and participation component ($n$ = 20), and environmental factors component ($n$ = 3). Table 1 summarizes the total number of items, meaningful concepts, ICF components and categories, and ICF indicator results. Table 2 shows the linked ICF categories among the four ataxia rating scales.

**Table 1.** Summary of the frequencies of the meaningful concepts, ICF components and categories, and ICF indicators for the included ataxia rating scale. ICARS, international cooperative ataxia rating scales; FARS, Friedreich's ataxia rating scale; SARA, scale for assessment and rating ataxia; UMSARS, unified multiple system atrophy rating scale.

| Scale | SARA | ICARS | UMSARS | FARS |
|---|---|---|---|---|
| Numbers of items | 8 | 19 | 30 | 36 |
| Number of concepts (Different) | 14 (10) | 26 (15) | 39 (28) | 45 (34) |
| Concept not linked to ICF | 0 | 0 | 1 | 1 |
| Total ICF categories (Unique) | 15 (13) | 33 (16) | 40 (30) | 56 (39) |
| Body structure | 0 | 0 | 1 | 7 |
| Body function | 8 | 21 | 22 | 23 |
| Activity and participation | 7 | 12 | 16 | 22 |
| Environmental factors | 0 | 0 | 2 | 4 |
| | ICF indicators: | | | |
| Measure to ICF linkage | 100% | 100% | 96.7% | 97.2% |
| Measure of linking to unique ICF codes | 6/8 (75%) | 9/19 (47.4%) | 23/30 (76.7%) | 24/36 (66.7%) |

### 3.2.1. Representation of Body Structure

The 8 ICF categories in the body structures component are included in two chapters:
Chapter 3: Structures involved in voice and speech,
Chapter 7: Structures related to movement.

The body structure component was covered only by UMSARS and FARS (Table 2, Figure 1).

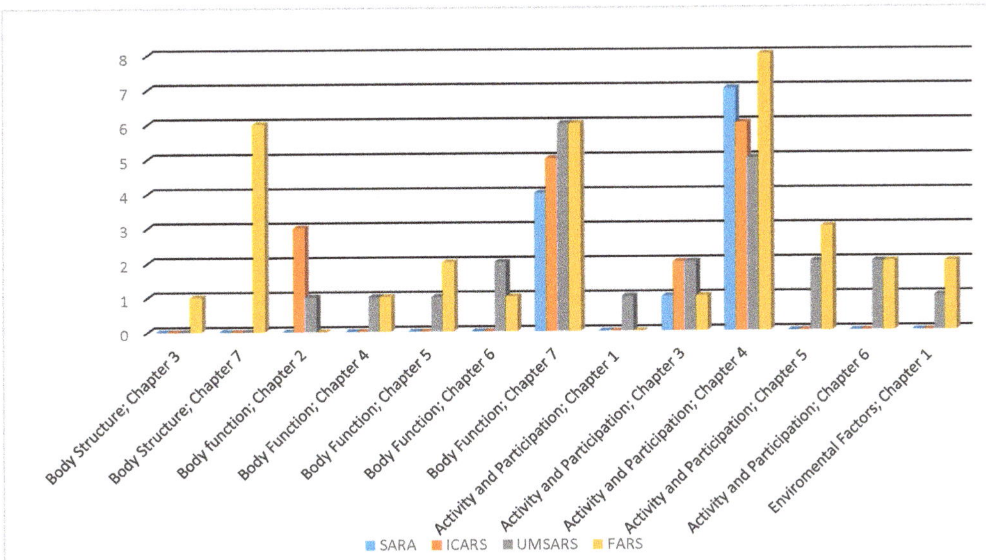


**Figure 1.** Comparison between the linked ICF categories of ataxia rating scales in terms of the covered chapters among ICF components. FARS, Friedreich's ataxia rating scale; SARA scale for assessment and rating ataxia; UMSARS, unified multiple system atrophy rating scale.

#### 3.2.2. Representation of Body Function

The 26 ICF categories in the body function component are included in five chapters:

Chapter 2: Sensory functions and pain,

Chapter 4: Functions of the cardiovascular, hematological, immunological, and respiratory systems,

Chapter 5: Functions of the digestive, metabolic and endocrine systems,

Chapter 6: Genitourinary and reproductive functions,

Chapter 7: Neuromusculoskeletal and movement-related functions.

All the included scales included concepts that are referred to chapter 7. The ICF category "b 7602 coordination of voluntary movements" was linked with all scales. "b 7651 tremor", and "b 770 gait pattern functions" were linked with three out of the four included scales. Chapter 2 was covered by ICARS and UMSARS, while chapters 4, 5, and 6 were covered by UMSARS and FARS (Table 2, Figure 1).

#### 3.2.3. Representation of Activity and Participation

The 20 ICF categories activities and participation are included in five chapters:

Chapter 1: Learning and applying knowledge,

Chapter 3: Communication,

Chapter 4: Mobility,

Chapter 5: Self-care,

Chapter 6: Domestic life.

All the included scales have concepts that referred to chapters 3 and 4. "d 4500 walking short distances" was linked with all scales. "d 4509 walking, unspecified", and "d 465 moving around using equipment" were linked to three out of the four included scales. Chapters 1, 5, and 6 were covered by UMSARS and FARS only (Table 2, Figure 1).

#### 3.2.4. Representation of Environmental Factors

The 3 ICF environmental factors are included in two chapters:

Chapter 1 Products and technology,

Chapter 3 Support and relationships.

The environmental factors component was covered by only UMSARS and FARS (Table 2, Figure 1).

**Table 2.** Frequencies of ICF categories among the four ataxia rating scales. ICARS, international cooperative ataxia rating scales; FARS, Friedreich's ataxia rating scale; SARA scale for assessment and rating ataxia; UMSARS, unified multiple system atrophy rating scale.

| ICF Component | ICF Category | SARA | ICARS | UMSARS | FARS |
|---|---|---|---|---|---|
| Body structure | Chapter 3: Structures involved in voice and speech | | | | |
| | s 3203 Tongue | 0 | 0 | 0 | 1 |
| | Chapter 7: Structures related to movement | | | | |
| | s 7104 Muscles of head and neck region | 0 | 0 | 0 | 1 |
| | s 73002 Muscles of upper arm | 0 | 0 | 0 | 1 |
| | s 73012 Muscles of forearm | 0 | 0 | 0 | 1 |
| | s 73022 Muscles of hand | 0 | 0 | 0 | 1 |
| | s 75002 Muscles of thigh | 0 | 0 | 0 | 1 |
| | s 75012 Muscles of lower leg | 0 | 0 | 0 | 1 |
| | s 760 Structure of trunk | 0 | 0 | 1 | 0 |

**Table 2.** *Cont.*

| ICF Component | ICF Category | SARA | ICARS | UMSARS | FARS |
|---|---|---|---|---|---|
| Body Function | Chapter 2: Sensory functions and pain | | | | |
| | b 2152 Functions of external muscles of the eye | 0 | 3 | 1 | 0 |
| | Chapter 4: Functions of the cardiovascular, hematological, immunological and respiratory systems | | | | |
| | b 4201 Decreased blood pressure | 0 | 0 | 2 | 0 |
| | b 450 Additional respiratory functions | 0 | 0 | 0 | 1 |
| | Chapter 5: Functions of the digestive, metabolic and endocrine systems | | | | |
| | b 51050 Oral swallowing | 0 | 0 | 1 | 1 |
| | b 5253 Faecal continence | 0 | 0 | 0 | 1 |
| | Chapter 6: Genitourinary and reproductive functions | | | | |
| | b 6202 Urinary continence | 0 | 0 | 1 | 1 |
| | b 640 Sexual functions | 0 | 0 | 1 | 0 |
| | Chapter 7: Neuromusculoskeletal and movement-related functions | | | | |
| | b 7152 Stability of joints generalized | 0 | 0 | 1 | 0 |
| | b 7159 Stability of joint functions, unspecified | 0 | 0 | 1 | 1 |
| | b 7300 Power of isolated muscles and muscle groups | 0 | 0 | 0 | 3 |
| | b 7350 Tone of isolated muscles and muscle groups | 0 | 0 | 1 | 0 |
| | b 7500 Stretch motor reflex | 0 | 0 | 0 | 1 |
| | b 755 Involuntary movement reaction functions | 2 | 0 | 0 | 0 |
| | b 7600 Control of simple voluntary movements | 1 | 0 | 4 | 2 |
| | b 7602 Coordination of voluntary movements | 3 | 5 | 0 | 5 |
| | b 7650 Involuntary movement functions | 0 | 1 | 0 | 0 |
| | b 7651 Tremor | 1 | 5 | 2 | 0 |
| | b 770 Gait pattern functions | 0 | 1 | 1 | 1 |
| Activity and participation | Chapter 1: Learning and applying knowledge | | | | |
| | d 170 Writing | 0 | 0 | 1 | 0 |
| | Chapter 3: Communication | | | | |
| | d 330 Speaking | 1 | 1 | 2 | 3 |
| | d 3350 Producing body language | 0 | 0 | 1 | 0 |
| | d 3352 Producing drawings and photographs | 0 | 1 | 0 | 0 |
| | Chapter 4: Mobility | | | | |
| | d 4103 Sitting | 1 | 0 | 1 | 0 |
| | d 4104 Standing | 1 | 1 | 1 | 0 |
| | d 4153 Maintaining a sitting position | 1 | 2 | 0 | 2 |
| | d 4154 Maintaining a standing position | 1 | 1 | 1 | 4 |
| | d 4301 Carrying in the hands | 0 | 0 | 0 | 1 |
| | d 4400 Picking up | 0 | 0 | 0 | 1 |
| | d 4403 Releasing | 0 | 0 | 0 | 1 |
| | d 4500 Walking short distances | 1 | 2 | 2 | 2 |
| | d 4509 Walking, unspecified | 1 | 2 | 0 | 2 |
| | d 465 Moving around using equipment | 1 | 1 | 2 | 1 |
| | Chapter 5: Self-care | | | | |
| | d 510 Washing oneself | 0 | 0 | 1 | 0 |
| | d 5400 Putting on clothes | 0 | 0 | 1 | 1 |
| | d 5402 Putting on footwear | 0 | 0 | 0 | 1 |
| | d 599 Self-care, unspecified | 0 | 0 | 0 | 1 |

**Table 2.** *Cont.*

| ICF Component | ICF Category | SARA | ICARS | UMSARS | FARS |
|---|---|---|---|---|---|
| | | Chapter 6: Domestic life | | | |
| | d 6300 Preparing simple meals | 0 | 0 | 1 | 1 |
| | d 6600 Assisting others with self-care | 0 | 0 | 1 | 1 |
| Environmental Factors | | Chapter 1 Products and technology | | | |
| | e 1151 Assistive products and technology for personal use in daily living | 0 | 0 | 1 | 1 |
| | e 1201 Assistive products and technology for personal indoor and outdoor mobility and transportation | 0 | 0 | 0 | 2 |
| | | Chapter 3 Support and relationships | | | |
| | e 340 Personal care providers and personal assistants | 0 | 0 | 1 | 1 |

### 3.3. Content Comparison

UMSARS and FARS were the only scales that have addressed the body structure or environmental factors component. In the body function component, chapters 4, 5, and 6 were covered by UMSARS and FARS only, as well as chapters 1, 5, and 6 in the activity and participation component. Furthermore, UMSARS and FARS have the highest representation in chapter 7 in the body function component (Figure 1).

The measure of linking to unique ICF codes percentage ranged from 36.8% to 76.6% (Table 1). The ICARS has the lowest measure of linking to unique ICF codes percentage.

### 3.4. Unspecified-ICF Categories

There were three unspecified-ICF categories as follows:

(1) "b 7159 Stability of joint functions, unspecified" that was linked to "Falling" concept in UMSARS and FARS.
(2) "d 4509 Walking, unspecified" that was linked for "changing walking direction" or "tandem walking" concepts in all included scales.
(3) "d 599 Self-care, unspecified" that was linked to "hygiene care" concept in FARS.

### 3.5. Agreement between Authors

Table 3 shows the Kappa agreement at a 95% confidence interval between the two raters. The estimated kappa values for the scales ranged from 0.67 to 0.84 for meaningful concepts identification, and from 0.67 to 1 for ICF categories. The overall Kappa reflects substantial to perfect agreement between raters in the linkage process.

**Table 3.** Kappa agreement (95% confidence interval) at meaningful concepts, and ICF categories for the ataxia rating scales. ICARS, international cooperative ataxia rating scales; FARS, Friedreich's ataxia rating scale; SARA, scale for assessment and rating ataxia; UMSARS, unified multiple system atrophy rating scale.

| Scale | SARA | ICARS | UMSARS | FARS | Overall |
|---|---|---|---|---|---|
| Meaningful concepts | 0.75 (0.486 to 1.000) | 0.668 (0.372 to 0.965) | 0.732 (0.511 to 0.952) | 0.835 (0.655 to 1.000) | 0.762 (0.622 to 0.903) |
| ICF Component | 1 | 0.878 (0.713 to 1) | 0.781 (0.578 to 0.985) | 0.842 (0.669 to 1) | 0.843 (0.749 to 0.937) |
| First/chapter level | 0.732(0.387 to 1) | 0.824 (0.632 to 1) | 0.733 (0.514 to 0.953) | 0.796 (0.605 to 0.988) | 0.747 (0.625 to 0.868) |
| Second Level | 0.714 (0.348 to 1) | 0.721 (0.493 to 0.949) | 0.689 (0.459 to 0.918) | 0.714 (0.499 to 0.929) | 0.705 (0.577 to 0.832) |
| Third Level | 0.717 (0.462 to 0.972) | 0.666 (0.421 to 0.911) | 0.645 (0.405 to 0.885) | 0.675 (0.453 to 0.898) | 0.644 (0.504 to 0.783) |

## 4. Discussion

The current study provides a content analysis and comparison of ataxia rating scales. The selection of recommended ataxia rating scales with sound psychometric proprieties allows for comparison of the content. There is a set of ICF linking studies for vestibular symptoms [16], fatigue [15], fear of falling [19], pain [20], and quality of life outcomes [21]. The majority of studies have linked self-reported questionnaires and included all potential outcomes despite the psychometric evaluations that limit the comparability and choosing of appropriate scales [19]. The current study included performance-based ataxia measures. The included ataxia rating measures show similarities and differences in the covered ataxia aspects as well as the variances in the meaning of the terms and response scale. Therefore, we think that it is important to analyze the content of the included scales. To the best of our knowledge, this is the first study that analyze the content of generic ataxia rating scales. Content analysis by linking to ICF is an important step for content validity. The ICF provides a valuable framework and classification method for coding components of scales by linking them to ICF components and categories [13].

The included ataxia rating scales focus mainly on body function and activity and participation components. Chapter 7: Neuromusculoskeletal and movement-related functions in body function component with "b 755 Involuntary movement reaction functions", "b 7600 Control of simple voluntary movements", "b 7602 Coordination of voluntary movements", "b 7650 Involuntary movement functions", "b 7651 Tremor", and "b 770 Gait pattern functions" categories were the more frequent. In the activity and participation component, Chapter 4 Mobility; "d 4153 Maintaining a sitting position", "d 4154 Maintaining a standing position", "d 4500 Walking short distances", "d 4509 Walking, unspecified", and "d 465 Moving around using equipment" categories were the more frequent. Ataxia is characterized by an inability to perform coordinated movements, and wide range of ataxic involuntary movement, and abnormal gait ataxic patterns [22]. Gait deficits are typically the presenting sign of ataxia [1]. The included scales have a low representation of the body structure and environmental factors component. It is crucial to assess body structure impairments in ataxia such as postural deformities. The involuntary movements and ataxic pattern lead to muscle imbalance and postural deformities and, therefore, falls [23]. The fall rating was assessed only in UMSARS and FARS.

The comparison between outcomes was based on the ICF indicators, and the covered ICF components and categories especially at the first/chapter level. There is a clear superiority of UMSARS and FARS in terms of the covered ICF categories. Moreover, these scales have higher unique meaningful concepts and ICF codes. These scales assess non-ataxia symptoms such as peripheral nervous system, autonomic, and bulbar functions. SARA and ICARS have fewer items and need less time to perform [24]. The redundant items of ICARS did not represent more content diversity, ICARS has repeated concepts and ICF categories more than other scales that reflect in low measure of linking to unique ICF codes, Table 1. Development of a short-form of ICARS based on psychometric evaluations and content would be beneficial. We think that SARA is an optimal scale for rapid assessment of ataxia, or in busy clinical settings. UMSARS, or FARS are more appropriate for assess impact of ataxia on health, functioning, and disability. They are more beneficial for monitoring ataxia progression, the activity of daily life, and independency.

A few limitations of this study should be noted. First, the inclusion of generic ataxia rating scales and exclusion of functional scales, quality of life, and other-related ataxic outcomes was a limitation. The ICF does not fully cover all meaningful concepts. For example, the meaningful concepts "Changing walking direction", "tandem gait", and "falling" were linked to multiple ICF codes to cover the meaningful concept. Furthermore, we noted some complexity in items as the majority of items had more than one meaningful concept. This is because of the wide responses for items. For example, item 1 with its responses in the ICARS have four meaningful concepts. Also, there were undefined ICF categories. The current study linked four ataxia rating scales to ICF. Future studies developing an ICF core set for ataxia are required. An ICF ataxia core set should consider the patient's perspective and different healthcare professionals including neurologists and rehabilitation professionals, such as physiatrists, and physical, occupational, and speech therapists.

## 5. Conclusions

The current study analyzed and compared the content of recommended ataxia rating scales. This would help clinicians and researchers in selecting most appropriate scale and understanding the ataxic symptoms and their impact on function. It seems that SARA is an optimal scale for rapid assessment of ataxia, or in busy clinical settings. UMSARS or FARS are more appropriate for assessing the impact of ataxia on overall health, monitoring ataxia progression, the activity of daily life, and disability.

**Author Contributions:** Conceptualization, F.L. and N.M.; methodology, A.A.; writing—original draft preparation, M.E.; writing—review and editing, A.M.J.; project administration, A.A. All authors have read and agreed to the published version of the manuscript.

**Funding:** This research received no external funding.

**Institutional Review Board Statement:** Not applicable. The study is not involving humans or animals.

**Informed Consent Statement:** Not applicable. The study is not involving humans or animals.

**Data Availability Statement:** The data presented in this study are available on request from the corresponding author.

**Conflicts of Interest:** The authors declare no conflict of interest.

## References

1. Klockgether, T. Sporadic Adult-Onset Ataxia. *Handb. Clin. Neurol.* **2018**, *155*, 217–225. [CrossRef] [PubMed]
2. Xiong, E.; Lynch, A.E.; Corben, L.A.; Delatycki, M.B.; Subramony, S.H.; Bushara, K.; Gomez, C.M.; Hoyle, J.C.; Yoon, G.; Ravina, B.; et al. Health Related Quality of Life in Friedreich Ataxia in a Large Heterogeneous Cohort. *J. Neurol. Sci.* **2020**, *410*, 116642. [CrossRef] [PubMed]
3. Milne, S.C.; Corben, L.A.; Georgiou-Karistianis, N.; Delatycki, M.B.; Yiu, E.M. Rehabilitation for Individuals with Genetic Degenerative Ataxia: A Systematic Review. *Neurorehabil. Neural Repair* **2017**, *31*, 609–622. [CrossRef] [PubMed]
4. Perez-Lloret, S.; van de Warrenburg, B.; Rossi, M.; Rodríguez-Blázquez, C.; Zesiewicz, T.; Saute, J.A.M.; Durr, A.; Nishizawa, M.; Martinez-Martin, P.; Stebbins, G.T.; et al. Assessment of Ataxia Rating Scales and Cerebellar Functional Tests: Critique and Recommendations. *Mov. Disord.* **2021**, *36*, 283–297. [CrossRef] [PubMed]
5. Schmitz-Hübsch, T.; Du Montcel, S.T.; Baliko, L.; Berciano, J.; Boesch, S.; Depondt, C.; Giunti, P.; Globas, C.; Infante, J.; Kang, J.S.; et al. Scale for the Assessment and Rating of Ataxia: Development of a New Clinical Scale. *Neurology* **2006**, *66*, 1717–1720. [CrossRef]
6. Trouillas, P.; Takayanagi, T.; Hallett, M.; Currier, R.D.; Subramony, S.H.; Wessel, K.; Bryer, A.; Diener, H.C.; Massaquoi, S.; Gomez, C.M.; et al. International Cooperative Ataxia Rating Scale for Pharmacological Assessment of the Cerebellar Syndrome. *J. Neurol. Sci.* **1997**, *145*, 205–211. [CrossRef] [PubMed]
7. Subramony, S.H.; May, W.; Lynch, D.; Gomez, C.; Fischbeck, K.; Hallett, M.; Taylor, P.; Wilson, R.; Ashizawa, T. Measuring Friedreich Ataxia: Interrater Reliability of a Neurologic Rating Scale. *Neurology* **2005**, *64*, 1261–1262. [CrossRef]
8. Meissner, W.G.; Fernagut, P.O.; Dehay, B.; Péran, P.; Traon, A.P.-L.; Foubert-Samier, A.; Lopez Cuina, M.; Bezard, E.; Tison, F.; Rascol, O. Multiple System Atrophy: Recent Developments and Future Perspectives. *Mov. Disord.* **2019**, *34*, 1629–1642. [CrossRef]
9. Schmitz-Hübsch, T.; du Montcel, S.T.; Baliko, L.; Boesch, S.; Bonato, S.; Fancellu, R.; Giunti, P.; Globas, C.; Kang, J.S.; Kremer, B.; et al. Reliability and Validity of the International Cooperative Ataxia Rating Scale: A Study in 156 Spinocerebellar Ataxia Patients. *Mov. Disord.* **2006**, *21*, 699–704. [CrossRef]
10. Wenning, G.K.; Tison, F.; Seppi, K.; Sampiao, C.; Diem, A.; Yekhlef, F.; Ghorayeb, I.; Ory, F.; Galitzky, M.; Scaravilli, T.; et al. Development and Validation of the Unified Multiple System Atrophy Rating Scale (UMSARS). *Mov. Disord.* **2004**, *19*, 1391–1402. [CrossRef]
11. Organization World Health. *International Classification of Functioning, Disability and Health*; Organization World Health: Geneva, Switzerland, 2001.
12. Cieza, A.; Geyh, S.; Chatterji, S.; Kostanjsek, N.; Üstün, B.; Stucki, G. ICF Linking Rules: An Update Based on Lessons Learned. *J. Rehabil. Med.* **2005**, *37*, 212–218. [CrossRef] [PubMed]
13. Cieza, A.; Fayed, N.; Bickenbach, J.; Prodinger, B. Refinements of the ICF Linking Rules to Strengthen Their Potential for Establishing Comparability of Health Information. *Disabil. Rehabil.* **2016**, *41*, 574–583. [CrossRef] [PubMed]
14. Whitney, S.L.; Alghadir, A.; Alghwiri, A.; Alshebber, K.M.; Alshehri, M.; Furman, J.M.; Mueller, M.; Grill, E. The Development of the ICF Vestibular Environmental Scale. *J. Vestib. Res.* **2016**, *26*, 297–302. [CrossRef]

15. Alghwiri, A.A.; Almhdawi, K.A.; Marchetti, G. Are Fatigue Scales the Same? A Content Comparison Using the International Classification of Functioning, Disability and Health. *Mult. Scler. Relat. Disord.* **2020**, *46*, 102596. [CrossRef]
16. Alghwiri, A.A.; Marchetti, G.F.; Whitney, S.L. Content Comparison of Self-Report Measures Used in Vestibular Rehabilitation Based on the International Classification of Functioning, Disability and Health. *Phys. Ther.* **2011**, *91*, 346–357. [CrossRef] [PubMed]
17. Gliner, J.A.; Morgan, G.A.; Harmon, R.J. Measurement Reliability. *J. Am. Acad. Child Adolesc. Psychiatry* **2001**, *40*, 486–488. [CrossRef] [PubMed]
18. MacDermid, J.C. ICF Linking and Cognitive Interviewing Are Complementary Methods for Optimizing Content Validity of Outcome Measures: An Integrated Methods Review. *Front. Rehabil. Sci.* **2021**, *2*, 702596. [CrossRef]
19. Bladh, S.; Nilsson, M.H.; Carlsson, G.; Lexell, J. Content Analysis of 4 Fear of Falling Rating Scales by Linking to the International Classification of Functioning, Disability and Health. *PM&R* **2013**, *5*, 573–582. [CrossRef]
20. Tiwari, D.; Clock, C.; Gore, S.; Alsalaheen, B. Content Comparison of Neck Pain Outcome Measures Using the International Classification of Functioning, Disability and Health. *Int. J. Rehabil. Res.* **2022**, *45*, 24–32. [CrossRef]
21. Cieza, A.; Stucki, G. Content Comparison of Health-Related Quality of Life (HRQOL) Instruments Based on the International Classification of Functioning, Disability and Health (ICF). *Qual. Life Res.* **2005**, *14*, 1225–1237. [CrossRef]
22. Pearson, T.S. More than Ataxia: Hyperkinetic Movement Disorders in Childhood Autosomal Recessive Ataxia Syndromes. *Tremor Other Hyperkinetic Mov.* **2016**, *6*, 368. [CrossRef]
23. Moon, Y.; Sung, J.H.; An, R.; Hernandez, M.E.; Sosnoff, J.J. Gait Variability in People with Neurological Disorders: A Systematic Review and Meta-Analysis. *Hum. Mov. Sci.* **2016**, *47*, 197–208. [CrossRef] [PubMed]
24. Saute, J.A.M.; Donis, K.C.; Serrano-Munuera, C.; Genis, D.; Ramirez, L.T.; Mazzetti, P.; Pérez, L.V.; Latorre, P.; Sequeiros, J.; Matilla-Duenas, A.; et al. Ataxia Rating Scales-Psychometric Profiles, Natural History and Their Application in Clinical Trials. *Cerebellum* **2012**, *11*, 488–504. [CrossRef] [PubMed]

healthcare

MDPI

*Article*

# Habilitation of Executive Functions in Pediatric Congenital Heart Disease Patients through LEGO®-Based Therapy: A Quasi-Experimental Study

**Eduardo Espinosa-Garamendi [1,*], Norma Angélica Labra-Ruiz [2], Lizbeth Naranjo [3], Claudia Andrea Chávez-Mejía [4], Erika Valenzuela-Alarcón [5] and Julieta Griselda Mendoza-Torreblanca [2,*]**

1 Unidad de Habilitación Cognitiva, Subdirección Médica, Instituto Nacional de Pediatría, Ciudad de México 04530, Mexico
2 Laboratorio de Neurociencias, Subdirección de Medicina Experimental, Instituto Nacional de Pediatría, Ciudad de México 04530, Mexico
3 Departamento de Matemáticas, Facultad de Ciencias, Universidad Nacional Autónoma de México, Ciudad de México 04510, Mexico
4 Escuela de Psicología, Universidad Panamericana, Ciudad de México 03920, Mexico
5 Fundación Care & Share for Education, Ciudad de México 01050, Mexico
* Correspondence: eduardogaramendi@hotmail.com (E.E.-G.); julietamt14@hotmail.com (J.G.M.-T.); Tel.: +52-55-1084-0900 (ext. 1441) (J.G.M.-T.)

**Citation:** Espinosa-Garamendi, E.; Labra-Ruiz, N.A.; Naranjo, L.; Chávez-Mejía, C.A.; Valenzuela-Alarcón, E.; Mendoza-Torreblanca, J.G. Habilitation of Executive Functions in Pediatric Congenital Heart Disease Patients through LEGO®-Based Therapy: A Quasi-Experimental Study. *Healthcare* **2022**, *10*, 2348. https://doi.org/10.3390/healthcare10122348

Academic Editors: Marco Tramontano and Giovanni Galeoto

Received: 27 October 2022
Accepted: 20 November 2022
Published: 23 November 2022



**Abstract:** Congenital heart disease is defined as an abnormality in the cardiocirculatory structure or function. Various studies have shown that patients with this condition may present cognitive deficits. To compensate for this, several therapeutic strategies have been developed, among them, the LEGO® Education sets, which use the pedagogic enginery to modify cognitive function by didactic material based on mechanics and robotics principles. Accordingly, the goal of this study was to evaluate the effect of cognitive habilitation by using LEGO®-based therapy in pediatric congenital heart disease patients. This was a quasi-experimental study; eligible patients were identified, and their general data were obtained. In the treatment group, an initial evaluation with the neuropsychological BANFE-2 test was applied; then, once a week, the interventions were performed, with a final test at the end of the interventions. In the control group, after the initial evaluation, a second appointment was scheduled for the final evaluation. Our results show that >50% of children presented cognitive impairment; nevertheless, there was an overall improvement in treatment patients, showing a significant increase in BANFE scores in areas related to executive functions. LEGO®-based therapy may be useful to improve cognitive abilities; however, future research should be performed to strengthen the data.

**Keywords:** executive functions; LEGO®-based therapy; congenital heart disease; orbitomedial cortex; RACHS1 scale; cognitive habilitation

## 1. Introduction

Congenital heart disease is defined as an abnormality in the cardiocirculatory structure or in the function that includes the heart and the great vessels; it occurs during embryonic and fetal development and is present at birth, although it is discovered later during the life of the carrier of the malformation [1]. Worldwide, it is considered one of the most frequent congenital anomalies with the highest mortality, since it is estimated that 9 out of 1000 live newborns are affected. Thus, 1.35 million babies are born each year with some type of heart disease, which causes more deaths in the first year of life than any other birth defect [2]. In the United States, it affects 36,000 infants per year [3], and in Mexico, there are between 18,000 and 20,000 new cases per year [4].

Various studies have shown that patients with congenital heart disease may present cognitive deficits [5–7] that are related both to hypoperfusion caused by heart malformation, which causes low oxygenation performance in the frontal and prefrontal cortex [8,9], as well as the factors involved during cardiovascular surgery, one of the main procedures to treat this disease [10].

Cardiovascular surgeries can be stratified through the Risk Adjusted Classification for Congenital Heart Surgery (RACHS-1), which considers the complexity level at the congenital malformation and the surgery risk, among other factors [11]. It has been reported that a higher level on the RACHS-1 scale (from 3 to 6) may result in a higher detriment at a cognitive level in these patients [12,13].

In children with congenital heart disease, the prefrontal region of the brain is affected, which could be related cognitively to executive functions, which are a series of capabilities to control, elaborate goals, planning, do and regulate behavior and cognitive processes effectively [14,15]. By showing affectations in executive functions, such as working memory and the response inhibition process [16], different learning sequences may be altered, including reading-writing functions and mathematical progression. Depending on the stage of life, it could increase the probability of manifesting a higher deterioration in cognitive functions and, consequently, in emotional, behavioral and social functions, limiting his/her quality of life [17].

To compensate for cognitive deficits, therapeutic strategies centered on cognitive habilitation have been developed; their main objective is the growth in cortical plasticity by functional retraining, stimulating the cognitive system to improve or activate this process [18,19]. LEGO® Education are part of these strategies; they use a pedagogic enginery to modify the cognitive function sequence through didactic material based on mechanics and robotics principles [20,21].

Diverse studies have reported an improvement in social and communication skills, specific conduct and family relationships in children and younglings with an autistic spectrum who were treated with LEGO®-based therapy [21,22]. Likewise, children from 4 to 10 years, diagnosed with cerebral paralysis and related motor affections, showed interest in the LEGO® robots, showing changes in their behavior and in their social and language abilities after the therapy [23]. Additionally, Lindsay and Lam (2018) [24] reported that children with different kinds of disabilities showed progress from solitaire plays to parallel and/or cooperative plays as the LEGO® robotic program progressed, helping the children's capacity to interact with their mates and facilitating their social development. However, few studies have reported the use of this tool to improve the cognitive deficit of congenital heart disease patients [25]; thus, the goal of this investigation was to measure the effect of cognitive habilitation by the intervention of assembly and robotic programming with LEGO®-based therapy on the executive functions of pediatric congenital heart disease patients.

## 2. Methodology

Quasi-experimental study in children with a diagnosis of congenital heart disease undergoing heart surgery. The sample selection was at convenience, intentional and with voluntary participation. The protocol was approved by the Research and Ethics Committee of the National Pediatrics Institute (INP; registration number 2020/51).

### *2.1. Participants*

Forty-five patients diagnosed with congenital heart disease who underwent cardiovascular surgery were recruited. Of these 45 patients, 24 remained in the study; 14 were part of the experimental group, and 10 were part of the control group. The children's ages ranged from 6 to 17 years. Children suffering from any relevant psychiatric or psychological disorder were excluded. Patients (or their parents) were free to withdraw from the study at any time.

## 2.2. *Instruments*

### 2.2.1. RACHS-1

The complexity of the surgical intervention was categorized using the RACHS-1 scale. This method allowed the evaluation of the surgical risk depending on the type of heart disease, the type of repair and some other elements that may influence the final result, such as weight, age and associated abnormalities; it is divided into 6 levels or risk categories: level 1 is the least complex, and level 6 is the most [11,26].

### 2.2.2. BANFE-2

To measure executive functions, the Battery of Executive Functions (BANFE-2), in its original version, was applied. This instrument was used for the evaluation of cognitive processes that depend mainly on the orbitomedial cortex, the anterior prefrontal cortex and the dorsolateral cortex. The orbitomedial cortex assesses motor control, inhibitory control and risk selection; the anterior prefrontal cortex is associated with abstract meaning, metamemory and metacognitive control; and the dorsolateral cortex assesses working memory, visuospatial working memory, consecutive and inverse operations, planning, visuospatial planning, cognitive flexibility, productivity of abstract thinking, verbal fluency and sequential planning [27].

### 2.2.3. LEGO® Education Scale

The execution of the intervention was measured with the LEGO® scale, a Likert-type scale, developed by the researchers according to the type of behavioral execution. It was based on executive functions [28] and was classified as follows: 0 = does not execute; 1 = difficult to execute; 2 = executes and 3 = executes with ease. To quantify the validity coefficient of the scale, the Hernández-Nieto (2002) procedure [29] was used, with qualifying scores of 0.80 to 0.90, indicating an acceptable validity and concordance coefficient.

## 2.3. *Process*

Eligible patients were identified and invited to participate. Parents or guardians and patients were provided with information about the study and were asked to sign the informed consent letter. For their registration, the relevant clinical and demographic data were considered, and the complexity of their surgical intervention was classified according to the RACHS-1 scale. Subsequently, a startup session was held to assess and determine the degree of cognitive deficit using the BANFE-2 neuropsychological test (lasting 60 min). In the treatment group, in the second stage, the children were scheduled once a week to carry out between seven and eighteen 60-min interventions (Table 1; Appendix A), assessing their execution using the LEGO® Education scale. At the end of all the interventions, a postintervention evaluation was applied using the BANFE-2 test. In the control group, after the initial evaluation, a second appointment was scheduled for the final evaluation. Assessments and interventions were carried out by neuropsychologists trained in LEGO® Education.

**Table 1.** Intervention of Executive Functions with LEGO®-based therapy (also see Appendix A).

| Session | Target | Activities | Material |
| --- | --- | --- | --- |
| Session 1<br>Free game with programming | Start of initial interaction and get the patient to familiarize with the material and achieve therapeutic interaction | - Colored blocks identification and free assembly.<br>- Assembly and programming of robotics initial assembly.<br>- In case of severe damage start with animal sets assembly.<br>- Simple machine assembly.<br>- Robotics challenge programming: forward and backward sequence at 10 s | - LEGO® DUPLO® bricks<br>- WeDo 2.0 ® Set<br>- LEGO® Simple machines Set<br>- Bingo LEGO® Education Bingo Set |
| Sessions 2 and 3<br>Working and visuospatial memory, inhibitory control | Gradually stimulate the CPDL and COM areas to generate changes in the selective attentional effort reversal process, inhibitory control and short-term memory | - Start with working memory exercise and 2 or 3 pieces blocks assembly.<br>- Stimulate with a visuo-spatial working memory template, blocks of the same color<br>- Spin assembly and challenge settings<br>- Robot assembly and programming with challenge<br>- Simple machine or robotic challenge disassembly and reassembly without support from a template or the therapist | - LEGO® DUPLO® bricks<br>- WeDo 2.0 ® Set<br>- LEGO® Simple machines Set<br>- Assembled blocks template |
| Sessions 4 to 8<br>Working memory, inhibitory control, risk selection and planning | CPA, CPDL and COM areas stimulation to get changes in the effort investment process of the associated functions | - Start with working memory exercise and 3–4 pieces block assembly.<br>- Stimulate with visuo-spatial working memory template, colored blocks.<br>- Sort of color blocks by color and label.<br>- Robot assembly and rogramming with challenge | - LEGO® DUPLO® bricks<br>- WeDo 2.0 ® Set<br>- Assembled blocks template |
| Sessions 9 to 16<br>Follow-up and executive functions integration | Enablement of executive functions and monitoring of their development | - Memory assembly to 6 pieces.<br>- Robot armed and assembly<br>- Math adder for counting and regression<br>- Complex challenge to solve with the robot<br>- Concrete and abstract classification of animals set | - LEGO® DUPLO® bricks<br>- WeDo 2.0 ® Set or SPIKE™ Set<br>- LEGO® Education Animals Set<br>- LEGO® Education More to Math Set |

### 2.4. Intervention Evaluation

The intervention was designed based on the conceptualization and operationalization of neuropsychological variables of the BANFE-2 [27,28], the LEGO®-based therapy [30] and the basic frontal function enablement model [25]. The sessions were carried out individually in the Cognitive Habilitation Unit within the INP facilities. In the 60-min interventions, different functions were worked on in the same session, increasing the complexity of the exercises each week. The children took between seven and eighteen sessions depending on their ability to assemble the more complex robots, i.e., those children who assembled the robots faster took fewer sessions (Table 1; Appendix A).

### 2.5. Statistical Analysis

The scores for patients in the experimental setting were analyzed using the loess smoothing method [31] to estimate the mean of profiles for the scores by RACHS-1. The dependent variables studied were orbitomedial cortex, anterior prefrontal cortex, dorsolateral cortex, and total executive functions. The hypothesis scored with significant differences between the control and treatment groups was examined using analysis of covariance (ANCOVA) [32,33] followed by a Bonferroni test and the Wilcoxon rank sum test [34]. Statistical analysis was performed using R version 3.4.1 and R Studio version 0.99.902 software. We considered a $p$ value $< 0.05$ to be statistically significant.

## 3. Results

### 3.1. Descriptive Analysis of the Population

Table 2 shows a summary of the descriptive characteristics of the study population. In total, we analyzed 24 patients, 10 in the control group (six male and four female) and 14 in the treatment group (eight male and six female). Their average age was 9.5 for the control group (interquartile range, IQR 8.0–12.25) and 8.0 for the treatment group (IQR 6.25–10.0). The stratification with the RACHS-1 scale was as follows: in the control group, five patients were classified as level one; three patients as level two; one patient as level three; and one patient as level four. In the treatment group, one patient was classified as level one; two patients as level two; five patients as level three; and six patients as level four.

**Table 2.** Patient characteristics.

| Characteristic | Category | Control Group | Treatment Group |
|---|---|---|---|
| Sex [1] | Male | 6 (60%) | 8 (57.14%) |
| | Female | 4 (40%) | 6 (42.86%) |
| Age [2] | | 9.5 (8.0–12.25) | 8.0 (6.25–10.0) |
| RACHS-1 [1] | 1 | 5 (50%) | 1 (7.14%) |
| | 2 | 3 (30%) | 2 (14.29%) |
| | 3 | 1 (10%) | 5 (35.71%) |
| | 4 | 1 (10%) | 6 (42.86%) |

[1] Counts and percentages. [2] Median and interquartile range (IQR: 1st quartile–3rd quartile). Treatment = LEGO®-based therapy.

### 3.2. Cognitive Conditions of Pediatric Patients with Congenital Heart Disease

The cognitive condition of pediatric patients with congenital heart disease before and after LEGO®-based therapy is shown in Table 3. The evaluations were focused on the orbitomedial, anterior prefrontal and dorsolateral cortices and on total executive functions. According to the battery of executive functions, the scores increased in nine patients, giving clinical change in diagnoses, whereas in two patients, the score increased, but not the diagnosis. In the orbitomedial cortex, an increase in the score and diagnostic range change were observed in 10 patients, with an increase in the score in one subject, without diagnostic change. In the anterior prefrontal cortex, there was an increased score and diagnostic change in seven participants. Finally, in the dorsolateral cortex, there was an increased score, and the diagnostic range changed in five patients.

**Table 3.** Scores and diagnostics of the neuropsychological executive functions battery in LEGO®-based therapy patients with congenital heart disease.

| | Orbitomedial Cortex | | | | Anterior Prefrontal Cortex | | | | Dorsolateral Cortex | | | | Executive Functions | | | |
|---|---|---|---|---|---|---|---|---|---|---|---|---|---|---|---|---|
| | Pretest | | Posttest | | Pretest | | Posttest | | Pretest | | Posttest | | Pretest | | Posttest | |
| Pat | Score | Diag | Score | Diag | Score | Diag | Score | Diag | Score | Diag | Score | Diag | Score | Diag | Score | Diag |
| 1 | **43** | **SA** | **73** | **MMA** | **85** | **N** | **121** | **HN** | **74** | **MMA** | **98** | **N** | **51** | **SA** | **89** | **N** |
| 2 | **44** | **SA** | **91** | **N** | **70** | **MMA** | **109** | **N** | **108** | **N** | **124** | **HN** | **88** | **N** | **118** | **HN** |
| 3 | **92** | **N** | **136** | **HN** | 117 | HN | 117 | HN | 123 | HN | 119 | HN | 122 | HN | 133 | HN |
| 4 | **44** | **SA** | **86** | **N** | **107** | **N** | **117** | **HN** | 77 | **MMA** | **111** | **N** | **44** | **SA** | **108** | **N** |
| 5 | 100 | N | 99 | N | **48** | **SA** | **83** | **MMA** | 70 | **MMA** | **98** | **N** | **75** | **MMA** | **97** | **N** |
| 6 | 102 | N | 85 | N | 114 | N | 96 | N | 86 | N | 101 | N | 92 | N | 97 | N |
| 7 | **114** | **N** | **136** | **HN** | 117 | HN | 110 | N | 97 | N | 106 | N | **101** | **N** | **133** | **HN** |
| 8 | **125** | **HN** | **136** | **HN** | 117 | HN | 117 | HN | 133 | HN | 134 | HN | **72** | **MMA** | **133** | **HN** |
| 9 | **103** | **N** | **136** | **HN** | **96** | **N** | **117** | **HN** | 108 | N | 89 | N | **44** | **SA** | **133** | **HN** |
| 10 | **44** | **SA** | **136** | **HN** | **107** | **N** | **117** | **HN** | **66** | **SA** | **101** | **N** | **44** | **SA** | **133** | **HN** |

**Table 3.** *Cont.*

| | Orbitomedial Cortex | | | | Anterior Prefrontal Cortex | | | | Dorsolateral Cortex | | | | Executive Functions | | | |
|---|---|---|---|---|---|---|---|---|---|---|---|---|---|---|---|---|
| | Pretest | | Posttest | | Pretest | | Posttest | | Pretest | | Posttest | | Pretest | | Posttest | |
| Pat | Score | Diag | Score | Diag | Score | Diag | Score | Diag | Score | Diag | Score | Diag | Score | Diag | Score | Diag |
| 11 | 92 | N | 103 | N | 117 | HN | 117 | HN | 99 | N | 92 | N | 100 | N | 95 | N |
| 12 | **92** | **N** | **136** | **HN** | **110** | **N** | **117** | **HN** | 116 | HN | 112 | N | **114** | **N** | **127** | **HN** |
| 13 | **44** | **SA** | **115** | **N** | 82 | MMA | 41 | SA | 67 | SA | 45 | SA | 47 | SA | 45 | SA |
| 14 | 43 | SA | 43 | SA | 63 | SA | 56 | SA | 45 | SA | 47 | SA | 45 | SA | 45 | SA |

SA = severe alteration (score of 69 or less); MMA = mild moderate alteration (score from 70 to 84); N = normal (score from 85 to 115); HN = high normal (score of 116 and greater). Pat = Patient; Diag = Diagnostic; ($n$ = 14).

Likewise, the cognitive condition of control pediatric patients with congenital heart disease is shown in Table 4. Notably, in the total executive functions, only one patient changed the diagnostic range, and three patients increased their score very slightly. In the orbitomedial cortex, two patients had slightly increased scores. In the anterior prefrontal cortex, an improvement in diagnosis was observed in five patients, and two children increased their scores. Finally, in the dorsolateral cortex, a change in diagnostic range was observed in one subject, and a very slight score change was observed in five patients.

**Table 4.** Scores and diagnostics of neuropsychological executive functions battery in control patients with congenital heart disease.

| | Orbitomedial Cortex | | | | Anterior Prefrontal Cortex | | | | Dorsolateral Cortex | | | | Executive Functions | | | |
|---|---|---|---|---|---|---|---|---|---|---|---|---|---|---|---|---|
| | Pretest | | Posttest | | Pretest | | Posttest | | Pretest | | Posttest | | Pretest | | Posttest | |
| Pat | Score | Diag | Score | Diag | Score | Diag | Score | Diag | Score | Diag | Score | Diag | Score | Diag | Score | Diag |
| 1 | 43 | SA | 43 | SA | 48 | SA | 41 | SA | 45 | SA | 45 | SA | 45 | SA | 45 | SA |
| 2 | 113 | N | 111 | N | **63** | **SA** | **136** | **HN** | 106 | N | 95 | N | 103 | N | 104 | N |
| 3 | 44 | SA | 44 | SA | 97 | N | 107 | N | 70 | MMA | 81 | MMA | 44 | SA | 44 | SA |
| 4 | 44 | SA | 44 | SA | 97 | N | 97 | N | 51 | SA | 69 | SA | 44 | SA | 44 | SA |
| 5 | 94 | N | 91 | N | **50** | **SA** | **89** | **N** | 86 | N | 111 | N | **81** | **MMA** | **106** | **N** |
| 6 | 124 | HN | 128 | HN | **63** | **SA** | **94** | **N** | 117 | HN | 100 | N | 117 | HN | 105 | N |
| 7 | 113 | N | 110 | N | **74** | **MMA** | **95** | **N** | 130 | HN | 113 | N | 130 | HN | 112 | N |
| 8 | 44 | SA | 44 | SA | **112** | **N** | **122** | **HN** | 75 | MMA | 77 | MMA | 44 | SA | 46 | SA |
| 9 | 114 | N | 103 | N | 103 | N | 103 | N | 79 | MMA | 82 | MMA | 83 | MMA | 84 | MMA |
| 10 | 120 | HN | 136 | HN | 103 | N | 110 | N | **114** | **N** | **127** | **HN** | 116 | HN | 133 | HN |

AS = severe alteration (score of 69 or less); MMA = mild moderate alteration (score from 70 to 84); N = normal (score from 85 to 115); HN = high normal (score of 116 and greater). Pat = Patient; Diag = Diagnostic; ($n$ = 10).

### *3.3. Evaluation of LEGO®-Based Therapy in Pediatric Patients with Congenital Heart Disease*

The children's execution in LEGO®-based therapy was evaluated with the LEGO® scale, also considering their classification on the RACH-1 scale. Figure 1 shows the execution percentages by child. The plot on the top shows the profiles of the execution. Each line represents a patient and is colored by his/her RACHS-1 classification. The plot on the bottom shows the mean of profiles (solid line) computed with the loess smoothing method [31] and their 95% confidence intervals (shaded areas), and the colored line represents the RACHS-1 classification.

In general, the observed scores are higher as sessions progress. The profiles for patients with RACHS-1 in classifications one or two have higher scores than those with classifications three or four. Moreover, in the first sessions (sessions 1 to 5), the scores of the patients show significant differences between patients with RACHS-1 in levels one or two and patients with RACHS-1 in levels three or four, since the 95% confidence intervals for these sessions do not intersect (Figure 1 bottom). However, as the sessions progress, these differences are not so considerable. For sessions 6 to 10, there were no significant differences between patients with RACHS-1 levels one or two and those with RACHS-1 level three, since their 95% confidence intervals intersect; the only significant difference was shown between patients with RACHS-1 levels one or two and those with RACHS-1 level four since their 95% confidence intervals did not overlap (Figure 1 bottom). Finally, from sessions 11 to 14, there were no significant differences between patients according to RACHS-1, although patients with RACHS-1 levels three or four had average scores lower than those with RACHS-1 levels one or two; the advance in LEGO®-based therapy execution seemed closer as sessions progressed (Figure 1 bottom).

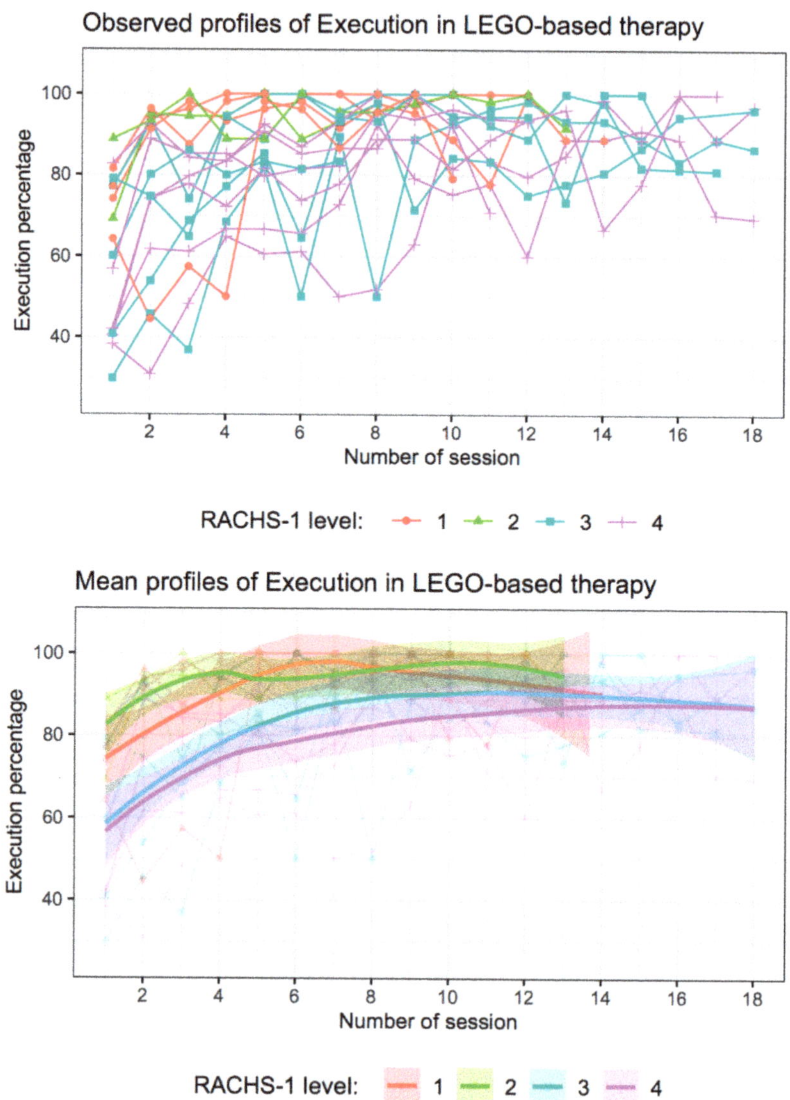


**Figure 1.** Evaluation of execution of pediatric patients with congenital heart disease in LEGO®-based therapy by sessions and RACHS-1 classification. (**Top**): Observed profiles of each patient colored by his/her RACHS-1 level. (**Bottom**): Mean of profiles computed with the loess smoothing method (solid line) and 95% confidence intervals (shaded areas); colored lines represent the RACHS-1 level.

### *3.4. Overall Improvement of Pediatric Patients with Congenital Heart Disease with LEGO®-Based Therapy*

To evaluate the overall improvement of congenital heart disease patients with LEGO®-based therapy, we used 2 × 2 contingency tables constructed with categorized variables from the BANFE-2 pretest and posttest normalized scores of each group. Two categories were established. If the total scores were greater than 84, they were categorized as normal; otherwise, they were categorized as alteration. Figure 2 summarizes the variables related to executive functions of the orbitomedial cortex, anterior prefrontal cortex and dorsolateral cortex and the total executive functions for each group (control or LEGO®-based therapy).

| **OBM** | **Control** | |
|---|---|---|
| | *Posttest* | |
| *Pretest* | Alteration | Normal |
| Alteration | **4** | **0** |
| Normal | 0 | 6 |

| **OBM** | **Treatment** | |
|---|---|---|
| | *Posttest* | |
| *Pretest* | Alteration | Normal |
| Alteration | **2** | **4** |
| Normal | 0 | 8 |

| **APF** | **Control** | |
|---|---|---|
| | *Posttest* | |
| *Pretest* | Alteration | Normal |
| Alteration | **1** | **4** |
| Normal | 0 | 5 |

| **APF** | **Treatment** | |
|---|---|---|
| | *Posttest* | |
| *Pretest* | Alteration | Normal |
| Alteration | **3** | **1** |
| Normal | 0 | 10 |

| **DL** | **Control** | |
|---|---|---|
| | *Posttest* | |
| *Pretest* | Alteration | Normal |
| Alteration | **5** | **0** |
| Normal | 0 | 5 |

| **DL** | **Treatment** | |
|---|---|---|
| | *Posttest* | |
| *Pretest* | Alteration | Normal |
| Alteration | **2** | **4** |
| Normal | 0 | 8 |

| **TEF** | **Control** | |
|---|---|---|
| | *Posttest* | |
| *Pretest* | Alteration | Normal |
| Alteration | **5** | **1** |
| Normal | 0 | 4 |

| **TEF** | **Treatment** | |
|---|---|---|
| | *Posttest* | |
| *Pretest* | Alteration | Normal |
| Alteration | **2** | **6** |
| Normal | 0 | 6 |

OBM = orbitomedial cortex; APF = anterior prefrontal cortex; DL = dorsolateral cortex; TEF = total executive functions. Treatment = LEGO-based therapy group.

**Figure 2.** Overall improvement of congenital heart disease pediatric patients.

It was observed that, in all cases, the patients who had a normal category in the pretest remained in the same category in the posttest. However, in the control group, most of the patients who showed an alteration in the pretest continued with an alteration in the posttest (with the exception of the anterior prefrontal cortex). Furthermore, most patients who received LEGO®-based therapy changed from alteration to normal category (with the exception of the anterior prefrontal cortex); for instance, in the orbitomedial cortex, in the control group, the four subjects categorized as alteration in the pretest continued in alteration in the posttest; however, for the treatment group, two subjects categorized as alteration in the pretest continued in alteration, but four subjects categorized in alteration improved to normal category.

### 3.5. Effect of LEGO®-Based Therapy in Pediatric Patients with Congenital Heart Disease

Figure 3 shows the summary of the BANFE-2 scores for the control and LEGO®-based therapy patients. Plots on the left show the boxplot of the normalized BANFE-2 scores by test and group. Plots on the right show the estimated marginal means of the posttest scores by group, under the mean of the pretest, showing an increase in the LEGO®-based therapy group in all evaluated areas, with the exception of the anterior prefrontal cortex. The significant BANFE-2 scores increased in the treatment group after LEGO®-based therapy in the orbitomedial cortex and in the total executive functions.

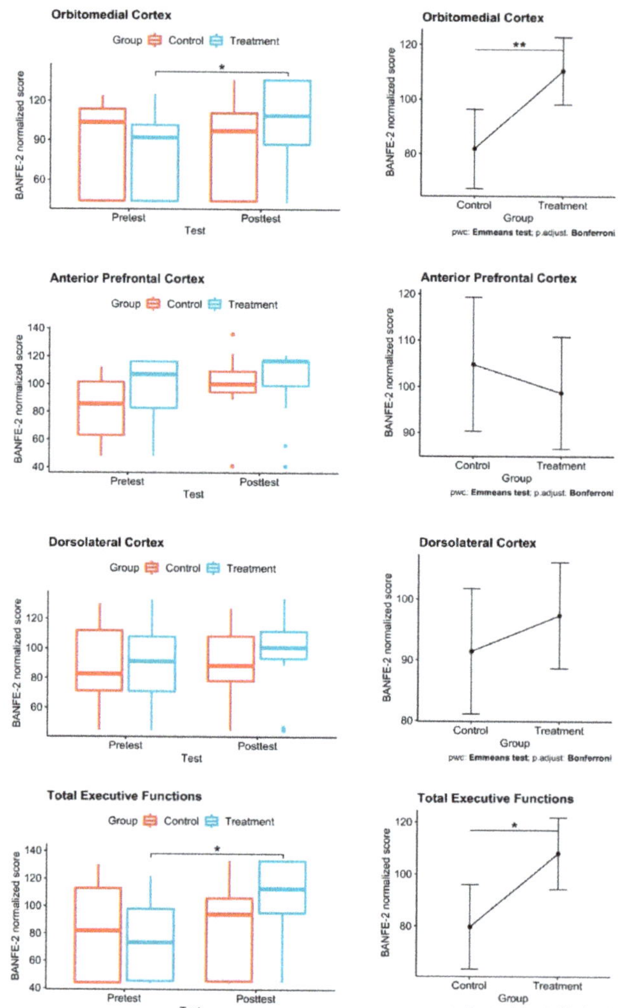


**Figure 3.** Effect of LEGO®-based therapy in pediatric patients with congenital heart disease. **Left**: Box plots depict changes in BANFE-2 scores of congenital heart disease pediatric patients in the control and treatment groups; there was a significant score increase after LEGO®-based therapy in the orbitomedial cortex and in the total executive functions. ANCOVA test; * $p \leq 0.050$, ** $p < 0.01$. **Right**: ANCOVA followed by Bonferroni post hoc test applying multiple testing correction; there is an increase in the adjusted mean score in the LEGO®-based therapy group in all evaluated areas, with the exception of the anterior prefrontal cortex. Control $n = 10$; treatment $n = 14$.

### *3.6. Analysis of Gain Score*

Another procedure to analyze a pretest-posttest design compares the gain scores [32], which evaluates the differences between pretest and posttest for each variable, i.e., gain score = posttest score − pretest score.

Figure 4 shows the boxplots for the gain scores for the evaluated variables by group. For the anterior prefrontal cortex, the boxplots look similar, which means that there is no difference in the gain score between the control and LEGO®-based therapy groups. Something similar happens for the dorsolateral cortex; boxplots do not show differences between the control and treatment groups; however, there is a slight increase (improvement) in the latter.

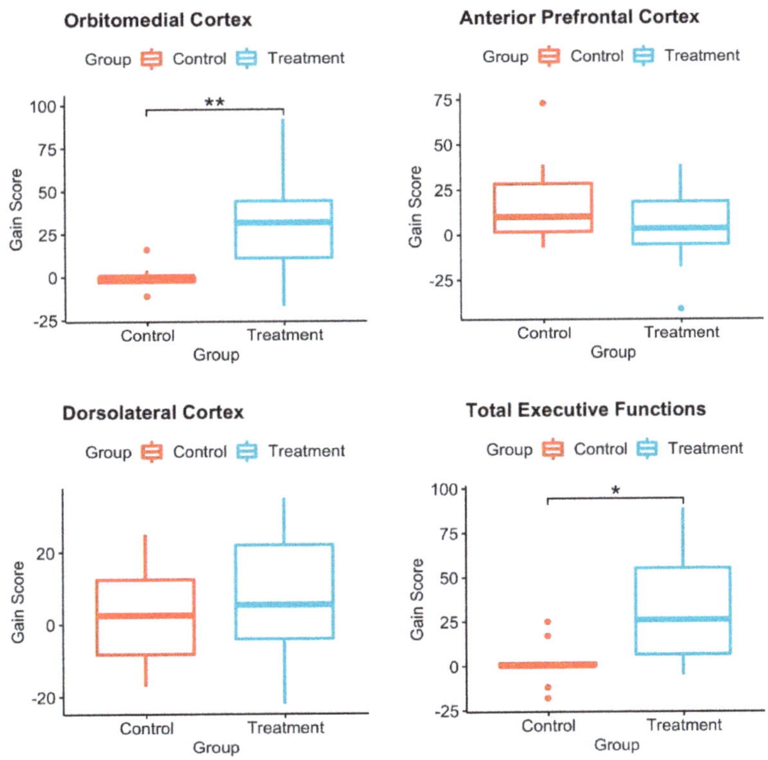


**Figure 4.** Boxplot of the gain scores for the diagnosis variable by group. Box plots depict the differences between pretest and posttest gain scores in the control and LEGO®-based therapy groups. There were significant differences between groups in the orbitomedial cortex and in the total executive functions. Wilcoxon test; * $p \leq 0.01$; ** $p \leq 0.001$. Control $n = 10$; treatment $n = 14$.

Remarkably, for the orbitomedial cortex, the boxplots of the control and LEGO®-based therapy groups were significantly different; for the control, the median was 0, and the first and third quartiles were −3 and 0, but for the treatment, the median was 31.5, and the first and third quartiles were 11 and 44, respectively, which means that for the orbitomedial cortex, children improved their scores on the BANFE-2 neuropsychological test and, therefore, their cognitive abilities. Something similar happens for total executive functions; for control, the median is 0.5, and the first and third quartiles are zero and two, respectively, while for treatment, the median is 26, and the first and third quartiles are 5 and 61, respectively. Then, the boxplot shows a significant difference between control and treatment, with the posttest scores in treatment being higher than those in pretest.

## 4. Discussion

In this research, we evaluated the cognitive deficit presented by patients with congenital heart disease after undergoing cardiovascular surgery and the effect of therapy based on LEGO® Education on frontal executive functions. In the pretest measurement, more than 50% of the participants showed cognitive impairment, either severe or mild to moderate, which corresponds to what is stated in the literature regarding cognitive impairment in patients with congenital heart disease [12,13].

Additionally, we observed that the degree of complexity of the pathology influenced the execution performance of the therapy based on LEGO® Education, since the patients with classification one or two of RACHS-1 obtained higher scores in the execution and required fewer sessions to achieve better performance. In comparison, heart disease patients with RACHS-1 classification three or four had more difficulty in execution and required greater cognitive effort, which involved a greater number of sessions. Thus, the patients most affected by the hypoperfusion sequence and associated surgical factors presented important deficiencies that led to psychological implications [16]. The above could even have repercussions in the academic area due to alterations in learning sequences, which can hinder mathematical and reading-writing skills [35].

Although the affected areas in patients with heart disease occur mainly in the frontal and prefrontal regions, the results showed that it is possible to generate significant changes in the orbitomedial cortex. This indicates that the patients reached a higher level of development than expected for their age in the detection of risk selection, working memory, motor control and inhibitory control [15], implying that basic frontal functions improved from the diagnostic range after the intervention, so it would be expected that this cortex and its functions are working in an optimal process. On the other hand, it was observed that the control group maintained the same diagnosis or increased the coded score slightly, which could mean that the neurons are in their natural maturation process for the age range. Therefore, therapy based on LEGO® Education can favor the group of neurons and processes associated with this cortex to develop more quickly, in accordance with the concepts of concentration, mutual induction and cell irradiation proposed by physiology behavior and the principles of cortical plasticity [36].

Regarding the functions related to the dorsolateral cortex, the scores were not significant, but there was a tendency to have an improvement after the treatment in most of the patients in the therapy based on the LEGO® Education group, unlike the control patients, whose score increased only slightly. This means that the experimental group had a tendency to increase their capacity in working memory, planning, cognitive flexibility, verbal fluency and abstract thought productivity in relation to the control group [15,25]; however, scores could vary due to age ranges and different cardiovascular diagnoses [27,37]. It would be important, in a second approach, to be able to count on a greater number of patients.

Following the development of executive functions, the ranges of improvement in the diagnosis, obtained at the end of the interventions, in the functions related to abstract meaning, monitoring and metacognitive control, which correspond to the anterior prefrontal cortex [15,28], suggest that the patients could maintain proper functioning in the anterior prefrontal cortex and its functions for adolescence and adulthood, which is when the development of this structure culminates.

In relation to other studies, the ascending curve of the execution scale shows that the stimulation of neuronal groups, in this case associated with executive functions with LEGO®-based therapy, promotes their cognitive habilitation process, which coincides with the results of [38,39], which report strategies related to the assembly, programming and elaboration of abstract challenges related to computerized or noncomputerized therapies; however, therapy based on LEGO® Education for executive functions involves multiple cognitive and behavioral processes, as well as computerized and noncomputerized activities, merging these processes in the same intervention [40]. In addition, in previous work, we reported that cognitive intervention, with therapy based on LEGO® Education for executive functions in congenital heart disease patients, had a favorable impact on enabling basic frontal functions, showing changes mainly in working memory and visuospatial and verbal fluency, which are also related to the orbitomedial and dorsolateral cortices [25].

It is worth mentioning that most of the patients started with low execution in the first sessions, and as they progressed, they obtained greater control of the material, with greater motor capacity and in less execution time, thus increasing their scores. Additionally, as the patients progressed through the sessions, they were able to solve more complex programming and robotics problems. In the two cases in which there was no improvement, this could be because the patients finished the program, but sometimes, they missed some interventions, and with this, we observed that they could not maintain working memory or inhibitory control as the patients who were constant in all their sessions. The constancy of work helps the neuronal group associated with executive functions to remain constantly stimulated, achieving greater concentration and irradiation, resulting in a long-term effect.

Additionally, it is important to point out the limitation of this study due to the number of patients. Since this work was carried out shortly before and during the COVID-19 pandemic, many patients who started therapy were unable to continue due to various factors intrinsic to the situation. However, our results showed interesting trends and significant differences that can be corroborated and strengthened in future studies.

Finally, children's parents reported that participants improved their manual motor skills and interaction behaviors, for example, interpersonal relationships. The above could be related to the improvement of skills in the social sphere, as reported in the population with autism and Asperger's [22,41–48]. Therefore, for future studies, it will be important to include socioemotional factors, emotional self-control and motor skill scales in the evaluation.

## 5. Conclusions

Despite the limited number of patients in this study, we observed that cognitive habilitation through LEGO®-based therapy in congenital heart disease patients might generate significant changes in areas related to executive functions, which are impaired due to the disease itself and its treatment. By increasing the functions associated with the frontal and prefrontal cortex at school age, children could improve their cognitive abilities, which may favor learning in academic and functional areas of daily life. In addition, since this was a quasi-experimental study, future research should be done to strengthen and corroborate the data.

**Author Contributions:** Conceptualization, E.E.-G. and E.V.-A.; Data curation, N.A.L.-R. and C.A.C.-M.; Formal analysis, E.E.-G., L.N. and J.G.M.-T.; Funding acquisition, E.V.-A.; Investigation, E.E.-G., N.A.L.-R. and J.G.M.-T.; Supervision, E.E.-G.; Writing—original draft, E.E.-G., L.N., C.A.C.-M. and J.G.M.-T.; Writing—review & editing, E.E.-G. and J.G.M.-T. All authors have read and agreed to the published version of the manuscript.

**Funding:** This research did not receive external funding, but was supported by LEGO® Education with the donation of some game boxes, by the LEGO® Foundation and the EDACOM corporation with the loan of robots and by the Care and Share for Education Foundation with the training of researchers.

**Institutional Review Board Statement:** The study was conducted in accordance with the Declaration of Helsinki and approved by the research and ethics committee of the National Institute of Pediatrics registered under number 2020/051.

**Informed Consent Statement:** Informed consent was obtained from all subjects involved in the study.

**Data Availability Statement:** Not applicable.

**Acknowledgments:** J.G.M.-T. and L.N. are members of the National Research System of Mexico. The authors would like to thank Josué Juvenal Bernal Celis for his help with information gathering and César Temistocles Psihas Mondragón for his valuable translation support. We thank American Journal Experts for the Digital Editing Service.

**Conflicts of Interest:** The authors declare no conflict of interest.

## Appendix A

**Table A1.** Description table of the sets used for the habilitation.

| Set | Description | Picture |
|---|---|---|
| LEGO® DUPLO® bricks | Simple colored blocks for free assembly. |  |
| LEGO® Education Bingo Set | Template based assembly of animals using different shaped blocks. |  |
| LEGO® Simple machines Set | Interpret the 2D building instructions and turn them into a 3D model. Acquire mechanic terms. |  |
| LEGO® Education Animals Set | Different habitat animals and small pieces that can be used to represent their environment. |  |
| LEGO® Education More to Math Set | Mathematical problem solving through simplistic models. |  |
| WeDo 2.0 ® | Multiple types of pieces used to enhance the ability to build and program robots by using one motor. |  |
| Spike Set ® | Multiple types of pieces used to enhance the ability to build and program robots by using two motors |  |

## References


1. Mendieta-Alcántara, G.G.; Santiago-Alcántara, E.; Mendieta-Zerón, H.; Dorantes-Piña, R.; Ortiz de Zárate-Alarcón, G.; Otero-Ojeda, G.A. Incidence of congenital heart disease and factors associated with mortality in children born in two Hospitals in the State of Mexico. *Gac. Med. Mex.* **2013**, *149*, 617–623.
2. Williams, J.L.; Torok, R.D.; D'Ottavio, A.; Spears, T.; Chiswell, K.; Forestieri, N.E.; Sang, C.J.; Paolillo, J.A.; Walsh, M.J.; Hoffman, T.M.; et al. Causes of Death in Infants and Children with Congenital Heart Disease. *Pediatr. Cardiol.* **2021**, *42*, 1308–1315. [CrossRef]
3. Jones, C.E.; Desai, H.; Fogel, J.L.; Negrin, K.A.; Torzone, A.; Willette, S.; Fridgen, J.L.; Doody, L.R.; Morris, K.; Engstler, K.; et al. Disruptions in the Development of Feeding for Infants with Congenital Heart Disease. *Cardiol. Young* **2021**, *31*, 589–596. [CrossRef]
4. Márquez-González, H.; Yáñez-Gutiérrez, L.; Rivera-May, J.L.; López-Gallegos, D.; Almeida-Gutiérrez, E. Demographic analysis of a congenital heart disease clinic of the Mexican Institute of Social Security, with special interest in the adult. *Arch. Cardiol. Mex.* **2018**, *88*, 360–368. [CrossRef] [PubMed]
5. Harvey, K.A.; Kovalesky, A.; Woods, R.K.; Loan, L.A. Experiences of Mothers of Infants with Congenital Heart Disease before, during, and after Complex Cardiac Surgery. *Heart Lung* **2013**, *42*, 399–406. [CrossRef]
6. Day, T.G.; Adwani, S. Congenital Heart Disease in the Teenage Patient. *Paediatr. Child Health* **2015**, *25*, 13–17. [CrossRef]
7. Spillmann, R.; Polentarutti, S.; Ehrler, M.; Kretschmar, O.; Wehrle, F.M.; Latal, B. Congenital Heart Disease in School-Aged Children: Cognition, Education, and Participation in Leisure Activities. *Pediatr. Res.* **2021**. [CrossRef] [PubMed]
8. Sanz, J.H.; Berl, M.M.; Armour, A.C.; Wang, J.; Cheng, Y.I.; Donofrio, M.T. Prevalence and Pattern of Executive Dysfunction in School Age Children with Congenital Heart Disease. *Congenit. Heart Dis.* **2017**, *12*, 202–209. [CrossRef] [PubMed]
9. Sanz, J.H.; Wang, J.; Berl, M.M.; Armour, A.C.; Cheng, Y.I.; Donofrio, M.T. Executive Function and Psychosocial Quality of Life in School Age Children with Congenital Heart Disease. *J. Pediatr.* **2018**, *202*, 63–69. [CrossRef]
10. Bellinger, D.C.; Newburger, J.W. Neuropsychological, Psychosocial, and Quality-of-Life Outcomes in Children and Adolescents with Congenital Heart Disease. *Prog. Pediatr. Cardiol.* **2010**, *29*, 87–92. [CrossRef]
11. Calderón-Colmenero, J.; Marroquín, S.R.; Salazar, J.C. Method for risk adjustment for surgery for congenital heart disease. *Arch. Cardiol. Mex.* **2008**, *78*, 60–67. [PubMed]
12. Schunck, E.D.R.; Schaan, C.W.; Pereira, G.A.; Rosa, N.V.; Normann, T.C.; Ricachinevsky, C.P.; Reppold, C.T.; Ferrari, R.S.; Lukrafka, J.L. Functional Deficit in Children with Congenital Heart Disease Undergoing Surgical Correction after Intensive Care Unit Discharge. *Rev. Bras. Ter. intensiva* **2020**, *32*, 261–267. [CrossRef] [PubMed]
13. Barnés Domínguez, J.A.; Álvarez López, A.; Cabrera Zamora, J.L.; Arpajón Peña, Y. Presencia de Enfermedad Arterial Periférica En Pacientes Con Cardiopatía Isquémica. *Rev. Cuba. Angiol. Cirugía Vasc.* **2020**, *21*, 1–14.
14. Lázaro, J.C.F.; Solís, F.O. Neuropsicología de Lóbulos Frontales, Funciones Ejecutivas y Conducta Humana. *Rev. Neuropsicol. Neuropsiquiatría Y Neurocienc.* **2008**, *8*, 47–58.
15. Lázaro, J.C.F.; Ostrosky-Solís, F. *Desarrollo Neuropsicológico de Lóbulos Frontales y Funciones Ejecutivas*; Editorial El Manual Moderno: Ciudad de México, Mexico, 2012; ISBN 6074482233.
16. Calderon, J.; Bellinger, D.C. Executive Function Deficits in Congenital Heart Disease: Why Is Intervention Important? *Cardiol. Young* **2015**, *25*, 1238–1246. [CrossRef]
17. Hövels-Gürich, H.H.; Konrad, K.; Skorzenski, D.; Minkenberg, R.; Herpertz-Dahlmann, B.; Messmer, B.J.; Seghaye, M.-C. Long-Term Behavior and Quality of Life after Corrective Cardiac Surgery in Infancy for Tetralogy of Fallot or Ventricular Septal Defect. *Pediatr. Cardiol.* **2007**, *28*, 346–354. [CrossRef]
18. Moreno Gea, P.; Blanco Sánchez, C. Hacia Una Teoría Comprensiva de La Rehabilitación de Funciones Cerebrales Como Base de Los Programas de Rehabilitación En Enfermos Con Daño Cerebral. *Rev. Neurol* **2000**, *30*, 779–783. [CrossRef]
19. Ginarte-Arias, Y. Cognitive rehabilitation. Theoretical and methodological aspects. *Rev. Neurol.* **2002**, *35*, 870–876.
20. Sánchez, J. Ingeniería Pedagógica, Nuevo Desafío Para Los Objetos de Aprendizaje. *Cienc. E Ing.* **2011**, *32*, 105–114.
21. Lindsay, S.; Hounsell, K.G.; Cassiani, C. A Scoping Review of the Role of LEGO®-Based therapy for Improving Inclusion and Social Skills among Children and Youth with Autism. *Disabil. Health J.* **2017**, *10*, 173–182. [CrossRef] [PubMed]
22. Hu, X.; Zheng, Q.; Lee, G.T. Using Peer-Mediated LEGO® Play Intervention to Improve Social Interactions for Chinese Children with Autism in an Inclusive Setting. *J. Autism Dev. Disord.* **2018**, *48*, 2444–2457. [CrossRef] [PubMed]
23. Cook, A.M.; Adams, K.; Volden, J.; Harbottle, N.; Harbottle, C. Using LEGO® Robots to Estimate Cognitive Ability in Children Who Have Severe Physical Disabilities. *Disabil. Rehabil. Assist. Technol.* **2011**, *6*, 338–346. [CrossRef] [PubMed]
24. Lindsay, S.; Lam, A. Exploring Types of Play in an Adapted Robotics Program for Children with Disabilities. *Disabil. Rehabil. Assist. Technol.* **2018**, *13*, 263–270. [CrossRef] [PubMed]
25. Garamendi, E.E.; Benítez, L.A.G.; Alarcón, E.V.; Torreblanca, J.G.M. Habilitación de Funciones Frontales Básicas En Cardiópatas Congénitos a Través de LEGO® Education. *Rev. Chil. Neuropsicol.* **2022**, *16*, 11–16.
26. Jenkins, K.J.; Gauvreau, K. Center-Specific Differences in Mortality: Preliminary Analyses Using the Risk Adjustment in Congenital Heart Surgery (RACHS-1) Method. *J. Thorac. Cardiovasc. Surg.* **2002**, *124*, 97–104. [CrossRef]
27. Lázaro, J.; Ostrosky, F.; Lozano, A. Batería Neuropsicológica de Funciones Ejecutivas y Lóbulos Frontales-2. *México Man. Mod.* **2012**, 1–63.

28. Flores, J.C.; Castillo-Preciado, R.E.; Jiménez-Miramonte, N.A. Desarrollo de Funciones Ejecutivas, de La Niñez a La Juventud. *An. Psicol. Psychol.* **2014**, *30*, 463–473. [CrossRef]
29. Hernández-Nieto, R.A. Contributions to Statistical Analysis. *Mérida Univ. Los Andes* **2002**, *119*, 132–134.
30. Barr, A.; Coates, E.; Kingsley, E.; de la Cuesta, G.G.; Biggs, K.; Le Couteur, A.; Wright, B. A Mixed Methods Evaluation of the Acceptability of Therapy Using LEGO® Bricks (LEGO® Based Therapy) in Mainstream Primary and Secondary Education. Autism Res. *Off. J. Int. Soc. Autism Res.* **2022**, *15*, 1237–1248. [CrossRef]
31. Fox, J.; Weisberg, S. Appendix: Nonparametric Regression in R. *SAGE* **2018**.
32. Dimitrov, D.M.; Rumrill, P.D.J. Pretest-Posttest Designs and Measurement of Change. *Work* **2003**, *20*, 159–165. [PubMed]
33. Montgomery, D. *Design and Analysis of Experiments*, 8th ed.; 111 River Street: Toronto, ON, Canada, 2012.
34. Gibbons, J.D.; Chakraborti, S. *Nonparametric Statistical Inference*; CRC Press: Boca Raton, FL, USA, 2014; ISBN 0203911563.
35. Salamanca-Zarzuela, B.; Morales-Luego, F.; Alcalde-Martin, C.; Centeno-Malfaz, F. Psychomotor development in patients with severe congenital heart disease. *Rev. Neurol.* **2018**, *66*, 409–414.
36. Garcés-Vieira, M.V.; Suárez-Escudero, J.C. Neuroplasticidad: Aspectos Bioquímicos y Neurofisiológicos. *Ces Med.* **2014**, *28*, 119–132.
37. Mills, R.; McCusker, C.G.; Tennyson, C.; Hanna, D. Neuropsychological Outcomes in CHD beyond Childhood: A Meta-Analysis. *Cardiol. Young* **2018**, *28*, 421–431. [CrossRef]
38. Takacs, Z.K.; Kassai, R. The Efficacy of Different Interventions to Foster Children's Executive Function Skills: A Series of Meta-Analyses. *Psychol. Bull.* **2019**, *145*, 653–697. [CrossRef] [PubMed]
39. Reyes-Amigo, T.; Bezerra, A.; Gomez-Mazorra, M.; Boppre, G.; Martins, C.; Carrasco-Beltran, H.; Cordero-Roldan, E.; Mota, J. Effects of High-Intensity Interval Training on Executive Functions in Children and Adolescents: A Systematic Review and Meta-Analysis. *Phys. Act. Rev.* **2022**, *10*, 77–87. [CrossRef]
40. Cano de la Cuerda, R.; Collado Vázquez, S. Neurorrehabilitación: Métodos Específicos de Valoración y Tratamiento. Editorial Médica Panamericana: Madrid, Spain, 2012; ISBN 8498354102.
41. Legoff, D.B. Use of LEGO as a Therapeutic Medium for Improving Social Competence. *J. Autism Dev. Disord.* **2004**, *34*, 557–571. [CrossRef]
42. Legoff, D.B.; Sherman, M. Long-Term Outcome of Social Skills Intervention Based on Interactive LEGO® Play. *Autism* **2006**, *10*, 317–329. [CrossRef]
43. Owens, G.; Granader, Y.; Humphrey, A.; Baron-Cohen, S. LEGO® Therapy and the Social Use of Language Programme: An Evaluation of Two Social Skills Interventions for Children with High Functioning Autism and Asperger Syndrome. *J. Autism Dev. Disord.* **2008**, *38*, 1944–1957. [CrossRef]
44. Pang, Y. LEGO® Games Help Young Children with Autism Develop Social Skills. *Int. J. Educ.* **2010**, *2*, E7. [CrossRef]
45. Andras, M. The Value of LEGO® Therapy in Promoting Social Interaction in Primary Aged Children with Autism. *Good Autism Pract.* **2012**, *13*, 17–24.
46. Coxon, S.V. The Malleability of Spatial Ability under Treatment of a FIRST LEGO® League-Based Robotics Simulation. *J. Educ. Gift.* **2012**, *35*, 291–316. [CrossRef]
47. Barakova, E.I.; Bajracharya, P.; Willemsen, M.; Lourens, T.; Huskens, B. Long-term LEGO®-based therapy with Humanoid Robot for Children with ASD. *Expert Syst.* **2015**, *32*, 698–709. [CrossRef]
48. Kolne, K.; Bui, S.; Lindsay, S. Assessing the Environmental Quality of an Adapted, Play-Based LEGO® Robotics Program to Achieve Optimal Outcomes for Children with Disabilities. *Disabil. Rehabil.* **2021**, *43*, 3613–3622. [CrossRef]

*healthcare*

MDPI

*Article*

# Manual Physiotherapy Combined with Pelvic Floor Training in Women Suffering from Stress Urinary Incontinence and Chronic Nonspecific Low Back Pain: A Preliminary Study

Gianluca Giordani [1,†], Sara De Angelis [1,*,†], Annunziata Isabella Parisi [1], Andrea Cosimo D'amico [1], Moira Di Re [1], Chiara Liumbruno [1], Federica Tamburella [1], Danilo Lisi [2], Giovanni Galeoto [3] and Marco Tramontano [1]

1 Santa Lucia Foundation IRCCS, 00174 Rome, Italy
2 UOC Risk Management, Azienda Ospedaliera Rilievo Nazionale Sant'Anna e San Sebastiano, 81100 Caserta, Italy
3 Department of Neurosciences, Sapienza University of Rome, 00100 Rome, Italy
* Correspondence: s.deangelis@hsantalucia.it; Tel.: +39-06-51501420
† These authors contributed equally to this work.

**Abstract:** Stress urinary incontinence (SUI) represents one of the most common subtypes of urinary incontinence (UI) reported by women. Studies have shown an association of SUI with nonspecific low back pain (NSLBP). The primary aim of the present study was to explore the long-term effects of a combined treatment of manual techniques and pelvic floor muscle (PFM) training in women suffering from SUI associated with NSLBP. The secondary aim was to evaluate which manual approach combined with PFM rehabilitation is more effective in improving symptoms related to SUI and in reducing pain perception related to NSLBP. Twenty-six patients suffering from SUI associated with chronic NSLBP were randomly assigned to one of two groups: the postural rehabilitation group (PRg) or the spinal mobilization group (SMg). Both groups performed a manual approach combined with PFM rehabilitation. All patients were evaluated before the treatment (T0), after 10 sessions (T1) and after 30 days from the end of the treatment (T2). The results showed an improvement in both groups in all of the investigated outcomes. Combining manual therapy and PFM training within the same therapy session may be useful for improving both SUI and NSLBP and increasing the quality of life of women suffering from SUI associated with NSLBP.

**Keywords:** stress urinary incontinence; nonspecific low back pain; pelvic floor rehabilitation; physiotherapy; women

**Citation:** Giordani, G.; De Angelis, S.; Parisi, A.I.; D'amico, A.C.; Di Re, M.; Liumbruno, C.; Tamburella, F.; Lisi, D.; Galeoto, G.; Tramontano, M. Manual Physiotherapy Combined with Pelvic Floor Training in Women Suffering from Stress Urinary Incontinence and Chronic Nonspecific Low Back Pain: A Preliminary Study. *Healthcare* **2022**, *10*, 2031. https://doi.org/10.3390/healthcare10102031

Academic Editor: José Carmelo Adsuar Sala

Received: 26 August 2022
Accepted: 11 October 2022
Published: 14 October 2022

**Publisher's Note:** MDPI stays neutral with regard to jurisdictional claims in published maps and institutional affiliations.



## 1. Introduction

Urinary incontinence (UI) is a common health condition in the female population. Although its prevalence increases with age, women of all ages could be affected [1,2].

Stress urinary incontinence (SUI) is defined by the International Continence Society (ICS) as "the complaint of any involuntary loss of urine on effort or physical exertion (e.g., sporting activities) or on sneezing or coughing" [3]. It represents one of the most common subtypes of UI reported by women [2], and it is typically associated with small and momentary leakages that come to an end once the intra-abdominal pressure decreases [4]. Factors such as age, pregnancy, childbirth, and hormone-related conditions have been reported to increase their prevalence [5]. It is related to poor quality of life with negative effects on different dimensions of everyday life including social activities and mental health. Moreover, in addition to having a substantial impact on the health-related quality of life, it is associated with a high level of individual and societal expenditure [6].

Several epidemiological studies have shown an association of SUI with nonspecific low back pain (NSLBP) demonstrating, moreover, that the presence of one condition may predispose the patient to the onset of the other [5,7–12].

Low back pain (LBP) is one of the most common musculoskeletal conditions in industrial countries [5,13]. It has been defined as pain, discomfort, muscle tension, or stiffness localized below the costal margin and above the inferior gluteal folds, with or without leg pain [14–17]. The most common form of LBP is non-NSLBP, a condition characterized by no known pathoanatomical causes [14,18]. Based on the duration of the symptomatology, LBP is defined as acute LBP (ALBP) when the LBP episode persists for fewer than 6 weeks, subacute LBP (SLBP) if the condition persists between 6 and 12 weeks and it is defined as chronic LBP (CLBP) when the symptoms persist for more than 3 months or longer than the expected recovery period [13,17]. Specifically, CLBP represents one of the principal causes of disability worldwide with a high impact on the quality of life [13]. Clinical practice guidelines for treating LBP provide recommendations for physical rehabilitative treatment [13,19]. Different techniques, physical exercises and rehabilitation delivery methods [20–24] have been developed and proved to be efficacious in improving LBP-related disorders, but to date, it has been difficult to affirm the superiority of one approach compared to another [13,19].

Although the mechanism in the development of NSLBP is not fully understood, it could be considered to be associated with changes in the trunk's muscle control, particularly the reduced postural activity of the diaphragm, transversus abdominis and pelvic floor muscles (PFMs), which seem to be related to impairment in the spine's mechanical support, favoring the onset of LBP [25,26]. The crucial role played by PFMs, as an integral part of both trunk and lumbo-pelvic stability as well as in the maintenance of urinary continence, leads PFM dysfunction to be associated both with SUI and NSLBP [5,27]. Thus, PFM rehabilitation may be considered an effective approach in patients with chronic NSLBP and UI [5]. On the other hand, the muscles responsible for spine stability also play an important role in the maintenance of continence [28]. Indeed, manual techniques focused on spinal mobility and postural stability could represent a valid approach both for SUI and NSLBP [29,30]. To the best of our knowledge, there are no studies investigating the short- and long-term effects of different manual technique modalities combined with PFM rehabilitation on NSLBP and UI simultaneously.

In this context, the primary aim of the present study was to explore the long-term effects of a combined treatment of manual techniques and PFM rehabilitation in women suffering from SUI associated with NSLBP. The secondary aim was to evaluate which manual approach combined with PFM rehabilitation is more effective at improving symptoms related to SUI and in reducing pain perception related to NSLBP.

## 2. Materials and Methods

### 2.1. Study Design

This study was a two-arm, single-blind randomized controlled trial (Figure 1).

The Consolidated Standards of Reporting Trials (CONSORT) [31] were followed. This trial was approved by the Local Ethics Committee of Fondazione Santa Lucia (FSL) with protocol number: CE/PROG.593. Participants provided their written informed consent for participation.

A researcher who was not involved in the intervention sessions assessed the patients' eligibility to participate based on the inclusion and exclusion criteria.

### 2.2. Participants

Twenty-six patients (mean age = 54.0 ± 11.2; age range = 31–70) with a diagnosis of SUI associated with chronic NSLBP were recruited and enrolled through the databases of Fondazione Santa Lucia (FSL) based on consecutive sampling at the FSL Institute for Research and Health Care, from September 2020 to July 2021.

The inclusion criteria were women aged 18–75 years with a diagnosis of SUI (medical diagnosis) associated with nonspecific chronic LBP (medical diagnosis). The exclusion criteria were severe pelvic organs prolapse (second stage or higher following the International Continence Society (ICS) classification scheme) [32]; pregnancy; perineal denervation;

inverted perineal command; presence of pelvic pain; fecal incontinence; vaginal infections; associated pathologies involving the central nervous system (CNS); psychotic disorders. All criteria were determined based on medical assessments and diagnoses. All participants did not attend physiotherapy treatment in the 6 months prior to enrollment. Furthermore, the enrolled patients did not take any medicine that could influence the clinical assessments (e.g., NSAIDs) during the period under investigation. The demographic characteristics of the sample are reported in Table 1.

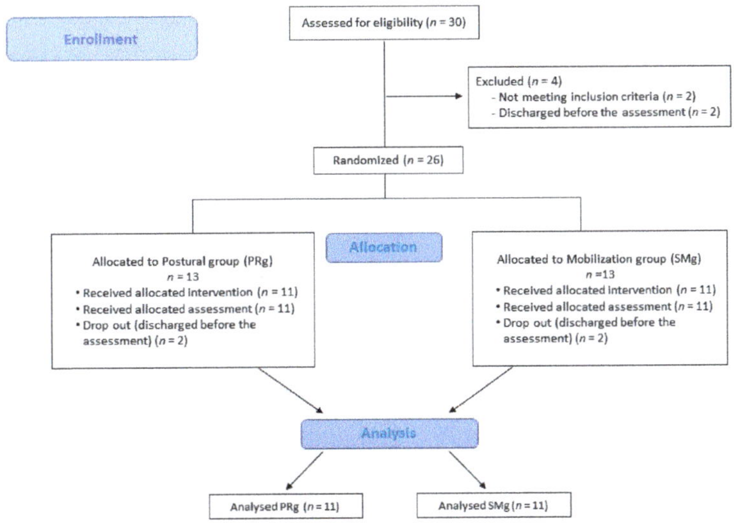


**Figure 1.** Flow diagram of the study design.

**Table 1.** Demographic and clinical characteristics at the baseline of the trial.

| | PRg ($n$ = 11) | SMg ($n$ = 11) | $p$-Value |
|---|---|---|---|
| Age (years) ± SD | 49.6 ± 11.3 | 58.5 ± 9.6 | 0.063 |
| Age (years) | | | |
| 31–40 | 1 | 3 | |
| 41–50 | 0 | 0 | |
| 51–60 | 5 | 5 | |
| 61–70 | 5 | 3 | |
| Time since NSLBP diagnosis (months) ± SD | 1.5 ± 2.3 | 2.0 ± 2.1 | 0.567 |
| Time since SUI symptoms onset (years) ± SD | 4.9 ± 2.9 | 4.4 ± 2.8 | 0.673 |
| ICIQ-SF | 9.6 ± 1.6 | 8.1 ± 3.1 | 0.332 |
| VAS | 4.9 ± 1.6 | 5.7 ± 1.5 | 0.171 |
| Pelvic floor strength | 1.7 ± 0.8 | 2.2 ± 0.8 | 0.332 |

SD = standard deviation. PRg = postural rehabilitation group; SMg = spinal mobilizations group; NSLBP = non-specific low back pain; SUI = stress urinary incontinence; ICIQ-SF = International Consultation on Incontinence Questionnaire-Urinary Short Form, scored from 0 (no leakage of urine and no effect on quality of life) to 21 (greatest severity of symptoms and effect on quality of life) [33]; VAS = visual analogue scale, ranging from 0 (least pain) to 10 (greatest pain) [34]; PFS = pelvic floor strength, graded by the modified Oxford scale which ranges from 0 (no discernible pelvic floor muscle contraction) to 5 (strong pelvic floor muscle contraction) [35]. The $p$-value was significant at $p < 0.05$.

### 2.3. *Interventions*

Two different protocols were designed: one based on the postural rehabilitation associated with perineal exercises (PRg) and the other one based on spinal mobilizations (Table 2) associated with perineal exercises (SMg). For both interventions, each session lasted 60 min. Each 60 min session consisted of 20 min of pelvic floor muscle rehabilitation and 40 min of postural rehabilitation or spinal mobilization, based on the allocation group. Both groups performed 10 sessions of the allocated intervention, organized 2 times a week for 5 weeks. All of the proposed exercises for both groups were carried out by the same experienced physiotherapist.

#### 2.3.1. Postural Rehabilitation

Each session of the experimental approach was composed of 40 min of postural exercise. The postural rehabilitation intervention included specific exercises that promote proper alignment by increasing the efficiency of dynamic movement and limiting muscle imbalance and overcompensation. Participants were asked to maintain two different postures to stretch both the anterior and posterior muscle chains. The first posture (Figure 2a) consisted of lying on the back maintaining the extension of the legs to release the respiratory diaphragm and stretch the anterior muscle chain (i.e., diaphragm, pectoralis minor, scalene, sternocleidomastoid, intercostalis, iliopsoas, muscles of the arms and forearms, and hand flexors). For the second posture (Figure 2b), participants were asked to lie down on their back with their legs flexed to stretch the posterior chain (i.e., upper trapezius, levator scapulae, suboccipital, erector spinae, gluteus maximus, ischiotibial, triceps surae, and foot intrinsic muscles). For each posture, the physical therapist used verbal commands and manual contact to maintain alignment, make the necessary postural corrections to optimize the stretching and to discourage compensatory movements [36,37].

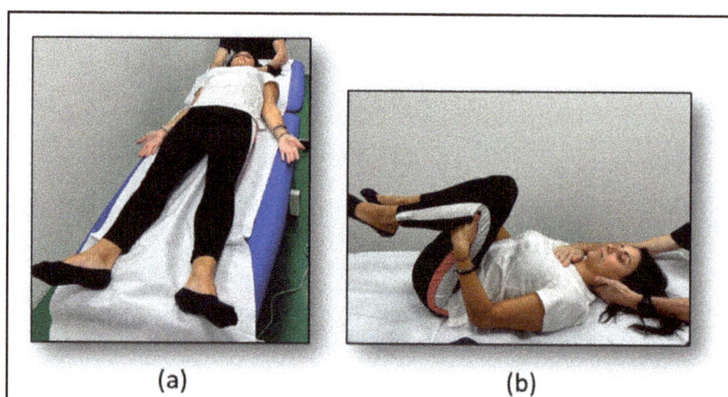


**Figure 2.** Postural rehabilitation intervention exercises. (**a**) Postural rehabilitation first posture; (**b**) Postural rehabilitation second posture.

#### 2.3.2. Spinal Mobilizations

The conventional approach consisted of 40 min of thoracolumbar spine mobilization. Two different mobilizations were carried out. In the first one (Figure 3a), the patient was in a sitting position with both legs out of the bed and mobilization in the anteroposterior direction was provided by the physiotherapist; the second (Figure 3b) consisted of rotational mobilization with the patient in a lateral decubitus position [38].

**Table 2.** Spinal mobilization interventions description.

| Spinal Mobilizations |
|---|
| **Exercise 1** |
| The patient is placed in a sitting position with the legs off of the table. The operator positions himself in front of the patient's knee and grasps him at the level of the dorsal-lumbar spine to be mobilized passing his arms under the patient's armpits. The patient rests the upper limbs on the operator's shoulders so he can relax. The operator mobilizes the tract of the dorsal-lumbar spine of greatest interest by applying a force in the posterior–anterior direction and allowing it to return, following these movements with his own body. (Figure 3a) |
| **Exercise 2** |
| The patient is positioned in the lateral decubitus aligned with the front edge of the table, with the lower limbs flexed and the hand of the decubitus under the head; the limb opposite the decubitus is placed along the patient's side. The operator positions himself in front of the patient, placing the cranial forearm at the level of the ribs and the caudal one at hip level; with his hands he causes the spinous processes of the lumbar vertebrae to be mobilized more. By moving the two forearms away in the direction of the longitudinal axis, the operator mobilizes the affected tract in an inclination opposite to the decubitus. By moving the forearms anteroposteriorly, the operator mobilizes the lumbar area of greatest interest in rotation. (Figure 3b) |

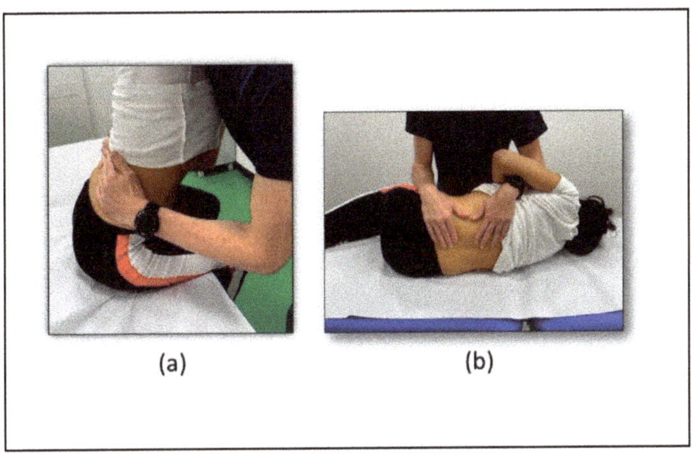


**Figure 3.** Spinal mobilization intervention exercises. (**a**) Spinal mobilization exercise 1; (**b**) Spinal mobilization exercise 2.

#### 2.3.3. Pelvic Floor Muscle Rehabilitation

Perineal exercises were performed in both of the allocated approaches. The protocol consisted of two exercises: 10 min of perineal contraction and relaxation and 10 min of stretch–reflex, for a total of 20 min of perineal exercises. In the first exercise, a slow contraction for 5 s and a slow relaxation for 5 s of the perineal muscles were required. The second exercise required a slow contraction for 5 s, holding of the contraction for 5 s and a slow relaxation for 5 s. For both exercises, the rest time was double the working time, so 20 s for the first exercise and 30 s for the second. All the participants performed the same exercises.

### *2.4. Outcome Measures*

At enrolment, clinical and demographic data were collected. All patients were evaluated before the treatment (T0), after 10 sessions of treatment (T1) and after 30 days from the end of the treatment (T2) in order to evaluate the prolonged effects of the treatment.

The primary outcome measure was the International Consultation on Incontinence Questionnaire-Urinary Short Form (ICIQ-UI SF) [33] to evaluate the severity of urinary loss and the quality of life (QoL). Secondary outcome measures were the pain visual analogue scale (VAS) [34] to assess LBP. Moreover, a digital assessment (bi-digital palpation) of pelvic floor muscle strength (PFS) was performed. PFM strength was graded using the modified Oxford scale, assigning a score from 0–5 [5,35]. All of the assessments were performed by a trained and experienced physiotherapist, different from the one who carried out the rehabilitative interventions.

### 2.5. Sample Size

This sample size complied with the minimum number of participants recommended by a power analysis performed on the preliminary data ($\alpha = 0.05$; $\beta = 0.8$; ES = 0.5) for nonparametric between-group comparisons [39]. This sample size estimation procedure recommends that at least 10 patients be included in each group [40].

### 2.6. Blinding

A researcher not involved in the intervention sessions carried out the randomization. Block randomization was performed with a computer-generated randomization list using a block size. To ensure the concealment of the allocation for the two groups, a computer program that generates random numbers to select random permuted blocks with a block size of eight and an equal allocation ratio was used. The researcher responsible for the randomization process deposited the list in secure web-based storage.

### 2.7. Statistical Analysis

A nonparametric approach was used. The Wilcoxon signed rank test was used for the within-subject comparisons for both groups at times T0vs. 1 and T0vs. T2. The Mann–Whitney U-test was used to compare data between groups at T0, T1 and T2. The IBM SPSS Statistics software (v23, IBM Corp., Armonk, NY, USA) was used.

## 3. Results

Twenty-six patients with a diagnosis of SUI associated with chronic NSLBP met the inclusion criteria and were enrolled in the study. Four of the enrolled subjects left the study before the end for reasons not related to the study. The statistical analysis was performed using the data of twenty-two participants (PRg = 11; SMg = 11) (see Figure 1).

There were no significant differences between groups in demographics and clinical data at the baseline (T0) (Table 1).

The within-subject analysis showed a significant improvement in both groups in all the investigated outcomes (i.e., ICIQ-SF, VAS and PFS). Significant statistical differences ($p < 0.05$) were found both between the baseline and the post-treatment assessment (T1) and between the baseline and the 30 day follow-up (T2). The results of the within-subject analysis are shown in Table 3.

**Table 3.** Within-subject analysis results.

| | PRg | | | | | SMg | | | | |
|---|---|---|---|---|---|---|---|---|---|---|
| | **T0** | **T1** | **T2** | **T0 vs. T1** | **T0 vs. T2** | **T0** | **T1** | **T2** | **T0 vs. T1** | **T0 vs. T2** |
| ICIQ-SF [1] | 9.6 ± 1.6 | 7.1 ± 3.9 | 6.5 ± 4.2 | 0.032 * | 0.026 * | 8.1 ± 3.1 | 6.1 ± 3.9 | 5.4 ± 3.5 | 0.042 * | 0.036 * |
| VAS [1] | 4.9 ± 1.6 | 2.5 ± 1.9 | 2.1 ± 2.3 | 0.005 * | 0.013 * | 5.7 ± 1.5 | 1.3 ± 1.5 | 2.1 ± 2.8 | 0.003 * | 0.006 * |
| PFS[1] | 1.7 ± 0.8 | 3.1 ± 0.9 | 3.4 ± 1.0 | 0.006 * | 0.003 * | 2.2 ± 0.8 | 3.6 ± 1.4 | 3.4 ± 1.4 | 0.011* | 0.041 * |

[1] Mean ± standard deviation of a clinical scale's scores at T0, T1 and T2. PRg = postural rehabilitation group; SMg = spinal mobilization group; ICIQ-SF = International Consultation on Incontinence Questionnaire-Urinary Short Form, scoring from 0 (no leakage of urine and no effect on quality of life) to 21 (greatest severity of symptoms and effect on quality of life) [33]; VAS = visual analogue scale, ranging from 0 (least pain) to 10 (greatest pain) [34]; PFS = pelvic floor strength, graded by the modified Oxford scale which ranges from 0 (no discernible pelvic floor muscles contraction) to 5 (strong pelvic floor muscles contraction) [35]. * Significant at $p < 0.05$.

The between-subject analysis showed no significant difference between the two groups, neither at T1 nor at T2 (Table 4).

**Table 4.** Between-subject analysis results.

| | PRg | | | SMg | | | PRg vs. SMg | |
|---|---|---|---|---|---|---|---|---|
| | T0 | T1 | T2 | T0 | T1 | T2 | Comparison at T1 | Comparison at T2 |
| ICIQ-SF [1] | 9.6 ± 1.6 | 7.1 ± 3.9 | 6.5 ±4.2 | 8.1 ± 3.1 | 6.1 ± 3.9 | 5.4 ± 3.5 | 0.478 | 0.519 |
| VAS [1] | 4.9 ± 1.6 | 2.5 ± 1.9 | 2.1 ± 2.3 | 5.7 ± 1.5 | 1.3 ± 1.5 | 2.1 ± 2.8 | 0.133 | 0.797 |
| PFS [1] | 1.7 ± 0.8 | 3.1 ± 0.9 | 3.4 ±1.0 | 2.2 ± 0.8 | 3.6 ± 1.4 | 3.4 ± 1.4 | 0.270 | 0.949 |

[1] Mean ± standard deviation of a clinical scale's scores at T0, T1 and T2. PRg = postural rehabilitation group; SMg = spinal mobilization group; ICIQ-SF = International Consultation on Incontinence Questionnaire-Urinary Short Form scoring from 0 (no leakage of urine and no effect on quality of life) to 21 (greatest severity of symptoms and effect on quality of life) [33]; VAS = visual analogue scale, ranging from 0 (least pain) to 10 (greatest pain) [34]; PFS = pelvic floor strength, graded by the modified Oxford scale which ranges from 0 (no discernible pelvic floor muscles contraction) to 5 (strong pelvic floor muscles contraction) [35].

## 4. Discussion

The first aim of the present study was to explore the effectiveness of a combined treatment of manual techniques and PFM rehabilitation in women with SUI associated with NSLBP. Specifically, the patient's quality of life and perception of back pain and the strength of the complex of the levator anus musculature (in particular, the pubococcygeus muscle) were assessed. The results show that both of the combined approaches to PFM rehabilitation were useful in improving SUI symptoms. Indeed, 10 sessions, two times a week for 5 weeks, led to an improvement in the quality of life in relation to incontinence and in pain perception in relation to NSLBP. The improvements were clinically significant at the end of the training and also at 1 month after the end of the treatment (i.e., follow-up).

In this study, two manual approaches (manual therapy for NSLBP and PFM rehabilitation for SUI) were combined simultaneously in the same therapeutic session to improve both conditions. Indeed, the muscles responsible for spine stability play an important role not only in trunk and lumbo-pelvic stability but also in the maintenance of continence [28]. Indeed, diaphragm superiorly, PFM inferiorly, transversus abdominis anteriorly, and deep lumbar extensor muscles posteriorly work in synergy in a complex anatomic structure with neurologically directed muscular and fascial components and a specific biomechanical function. For these reasons, the novelty of our preliminary study was to design a global manual approach that is not only focused on PFM rehabilitation but also on the spine. According to other studies, we also found a positive clinical effect in the follow-up, 1 month after the end of the training. Indeed, a previous study [5] reported that PFM rehabilitation alone produces only short-term effects on SUI, and 6–12 weeks of training more than three times a week sessions are recommended for long-term effects.

Furthermore, as previously reported [41], a program that combines pelvic floor muscle exercises with low-load core stability awareness exercises (i.e., abdominal draw-in, heel slide, and heel off exercises) may be helpful in reducing the amount and frequency of UI as well as in improving the QoL for women with LBP who have SUI.

We can hypothesize that a global approach leading to an improvement in the musculoskeletal system and spine stability can produce long-lasting effects on NSLBP and SUI. The secondary aim of this study was to evaluate which manual approach combined with PFM rehabilitation was more effective at improving SUI and reducing pain perception related to NSLBP. Our results showed no clinically significant differences between groups at the end of the training and at follow-up. Although the two proposed manual approaches were different from each other, one was more global and active and one more selective and passive. Reasonably, both treatments play a role in improving trunk muscle stability. Indeed, according to previous studies [26,27], trunk stability has a role in reducing pain and disability in chronic LBP and related symptoms in SUI.

### Limitations

We acknowledge some of the limitations of this study. First, the sample size was relatively small, and this could have affected the statistical analysis. Another important limitation was the use of digital palpation in the PFM strength assessment. Although currently it has been used in clinical practice and no evaluation tool is considered the golden standard [42], many researchers consider digital palpation unreliable, subjective and not sensitive [35]. On the other hand, different studies have shown a correlation between digital palpation and other methods and consider it an objective assessment tool [43]. Thus, because this reproducibility remains questionable, instruments such as biofeedback monitors, manometers, perineometers and dynamometers may be considered for use in future studies as support in the PFM strength assessments.

## 5. Conclusions

In conclusion, combining manual therapy and PFM rehabilitation within the same therapy session may be useful for improving both SUI and NSLBP symptoms and for increasing the quality of life in women suffering from SUI associated with NSLBP.

**Author Contributions:** Conceptualization, S.D.A., M.T., G.G. (Gianluca Giordani); methodology, M.T., S.D.A.; formal analysis, S.D.A.; data curation, A.I.P., A.C.D., M.D.R., C.L.; writing—original draft preparation, S.D.A., F.T.; writing—review and editing, G.G. (Gianluca Giordani), D.L., F.T.; supervision G.G. (Giovanni Galeoto). All authors have read and agreed to the published version of the manuscript.

**Funding:** This research received no external funding.

**Institutional Review Board Statement:** This trial was approved by the local ethics committee of Fondazione Santa Lucia (FSL) Institute for Research and Health Care (Protocol: CE/PROG.593); all participants provided their written informed consent for participation.

**Informed Consent Statement:** Informed consent was obtained from all subjects involved in the study.

**Data Availability Statement:** The datasets used and/or analyzed during the current study are available from the corresponding author upon reasonable request.

**Conflicts of Interest:** The authors declare no conflict of interest.

## References


1. Mostafaei, H.; Sadeghi-Bazargani, H.; Hajebrahimi, S.; Salehi-Pourmehr, H.; Ghojazadeh, M.; Onur, R.; Al Mousa, R.T.; Oelke, M. Prevalence of female urinary incontinence in the developing world: A systematic review and meta-analysis—A Report from the Developing World Committee of the International Continence Society and Iranian Research Center for Evidence Based Medicine. *Neurourol. Urodyn.* **2020**, *39*, 1063–1086. [CrossRef] [PubMed]
2. Reynolds, W.S.; Dmochowski, R.R.; Penson, D.F. Epidemiology of stress urinary incontinence in women. *Curr. Urol. Rep.* **2011**, *12*, 370–376. [CrossRef] [PubMed]
3. Haylen, B.T.; de Ridder, D.; Freeman, R.M.; Swift, S.E.; Berghmans, B.; Lee, J.; Monga, A.; Petri, E.; Rizk, D.E.; Sand, P.K.; et al. An International Urogynecological Association (IUGA)/International Continence Society (ICS) joint report on the terminology for female pelvic floor dysfunction. *Neurourol. Urodyn.* **2010**, *29*, 4–20. [CrossRef] [PubMed]
4. Bardsley, A. An overview of urinary incontinence. *Br. J. Nurs.* **2016**, *25*, S14–S21. [CrossRef] [PubMed]
5. Ghaderi, F.; Mohammadi, K.; Amir Sasan, R.; Niko Kheslat, S.; Oskouei, A.E. Effects of Stabilization Exercises Focusing on Pelvic Floor Muscles on Low Back Pain and Urinary Incontinence in Women. *Urology* **2016**, *93*, 50–54. [CrossRef]
6. Aoki, Y.; Brown, H.W.; Brubaker, L.; Cornu, J.N.; Daly, J.O.; Cartwright, R. Urinary incontinence in women. *Nat. Rev. Dis. Prim.* **2017**, *3*, 17042; Erratum in *Nat. Rev. Dis. Primers* **2017**, *3*, 17097. [CrossRef]
7. Pavón, A.G.; Chao, C.W.; Rodríguez, N.R.; Iglesias, F.J.G. Prevalencia y factores de riesgo de incontinencia urinaria en mujeres que consultan por dolor lumbopélvico: Estudio multicéntrico [Prevalence and risk factors of urinary incontinence in women who visit the doctor with low back pain: Multicentre study]. *Atención Primaria* **2014**, *46*, 100–108. [CrossRef]
8. Welk, B.; Baverstock, R. Is there a link between back pain and urinary symptoms? *Neurourol. Urodyn.* **2020**, *39*, 523–532. [CrossRef]
9. Kaptan, H.; Kulaksızoğlu, H.; Kasımcan, Ö.; Seçkin, B. The Association between Urinary Incontinence and Low Back Pain and Radiculopathy in Women. *Open Access Maced. J. Med. Sci.* **2016**, *4*, 665–669. [CrossRef]
10. Smith, M.D.; Russell, A.; Hodges, P.W. Is there a relationship between parity, pregnancy, back pain and incontinence? *Int. Urogynecol. J. Pelvic Floor Dysfunct.* **2008**, *19*, 205–211. [CrossRef] [PubMed]

11. Eliasson, K.; Elfving, B.; Nordgren, B.; Mattsson, E. Urinary incontinence in women with low back pain. *Man. Ther.* **2008**, *13*, 206–212. [CrossRef] [PubMed]
12. Cassidy, T.; Fortin, A.; Kaczmer, S.; Shumaker, J.T.L.; Szeto, J.; Madill, S.J. Relationship Between Back Pain and Urinary Incontinence in the Canadian Population. *Phys. Ther.* **2017**, *97*, 449–454. [CrossRef] [PubMed]
13. Paolucci, T.; Attanasi, C.; Cecchini, W.; Marazzi, A.; Capobianco, S.V.; Santilli, V. Chronic low back pain and postural rehabilitation exercise: A literature review. *J. Pain Res.* **2018**, *12*, 95–107. [CrossRef] [PubMed]
14. Vrbanić, T.S. Krizobolja—OD definicije do dijagnoze [Low back pain—From definition to diagnosis]. *Reumatizam* **2011**, *58*, 105–107. [PubMed]
15. Firestein, G.; Budd, C.; Gabriel, S.; McInnes, I.; O'Dell, J. *Kelley and Firestein's Textbook of Rheumatology*, 10th ed.; Elsevier: Amsterdam, The Netherlands, 2017; pp. 696–716, ISBN 9780323316965.
16. Koes, B.W.; van Tulder, M.W.; Thomas, S. Diagnosis and treatment of low back pain. *BMJ* **2006**, *332*, 1430–1434. [CrossRef]
17. Burton, A.K.; Balagué, F.; Cardon, G.; Eriksen, H.R.; Henrotin, Y.; Lahad, A.; Leclerc, A.; Müller, G.; van der Beek, A.J. Chapter 2. European guidelines for prevention in low back pain: November 2004. *Eur. Spine J.* **2006**, *15* (Suppl. 2), S136–S168. [CrossRef]
18. Golob, A.L.; Wipf, J.E. Low back pain. *Med. Clin. N. Am.* **2014**, *98*, 405–428. [CrossRef] [PubMed]
19. Oliveira, C.B.; Maher, C.G.; Pinto, R.Z.; Traeger, A.C.; Lin, C.C.; Chenot, J.F.; van Tulder, M.; Koes, B.W. Clinical practice guidelines for the management of non-specific low back pain in primary care: An updated overview. *Eur. Spine J.* **2018**, *27*, 2791–2803. [CrossRef] [PubMed]
20. Lawand, P.; Lombardi, I., Jr.; Jones, A.; Sardim, C.; Ribeiro, L.H.; Natour, J. Effect of a muscle stretching program using the global postural reeducation method for patients with chronic low back pain: A randomized controlled trial. *Jt. Bone Spine* **2015**, *82*, 272–277.
21. Hasanpour-Dehkordi, A.; Dehghani, A.; Solati, K. A Comparison of the Effects of Pilates and McKenzie Training on Pain and General Health in Men with Chronic Low Back Pain: A Randomized Trial. *Indian J. Palliat. Care* **2017**, *23*, 36–40. [CrossRef]
22. Areeudomwong, P.; Wongrat, W.; Neammesri, N.; Thongsakul, T. A randomized controlled trial on the long-term effects of proprioceptive neuromuscular facilitation training, on pain-related outcomes and back muscle activity, in patients with chronic low back pain. *Musculoskelet. Care* **2017**, *15*, 218–229. [CrossRef] [PubMed]
23. Raiszadeh, K.; Tapicer, J.; Taitano, L.; Wu, J.; Shahidi, B. In-Clinic Versus Web-Based Multidisciplinary Exercise-Based Rehabilitation for Treatment of Low Back Pain: Prospective Clinical Trial in an Integrated Practice Unit Model. *J. Med. Internet Res.* **2021**, *23*, e22548. [CrossRef] [PubMed]
24. Castagnoli, C.; Cecchi, F.; Del Canto, A.; Paperini, A.; Boni, R.; Pasquini, G.; Vannetti, F.; Macchi, C. Effects in Short and Long Term of Global Postural Reeducation (GPR) on Chronic Low Back Pain: A Controlled Study with One-Year Follow-Up. *Sci. World J.* **2015**, *2015*, 271436. [CrossRef] [PubMed]
25. Smith, M.D.; Russell, A.; Hodges, P.W. Disorders of breathing and continence have a stronger association with back pain than obesity and physical activity. *Aust. J. Physiother.* **2006**, *52*, 11–16. [CrossRef]
26. Fozzatti, C.; Herrmann, V.; Palma, T.; Riccetto, C.L.; Palma, P.C. Global Postural Re-education: An alternative approach for stress urinary incontinence? *Eur. J. Obstet. Gynecol. Reprod. Biol.* **2010**, *152*, 218–224. [CrossRef]
27. Bi, X.; Zhao, J.; Zhao, L.; Liu, Z.; Zhang, J.; Sun, D.; Song, L.; Xia, Y. Pelvic floor muscle exercise for chronic low back pain. *J. Int. Med. Res.* **2013**, *41*, 146–152. [CrossRef]
28. Quaghebeur, J.; Petros, P.; Wyndaele, J.J.; De Wachter, S. Pelvic-floor function, dysfunction, and treatment. *Eur. J. Obstet. Gynecol. Reprod. Biol.* **2021**, *265*, 143–149. [CrossRef]
29. Grewar, H.; McLean, L. The integrated continence system: A manual therapy approach to the treatment of stress urinary incontinence. *Man. Ther.* **2008**, *13*, 375–386. [CrossRef]
30. Qaseem, A.; Wilt, T.J.; McLean, R.M.; Forciea, M.A. Noninvasive Treatments for Acute, Subacute, and Chronic Low Back Pain: A Clinical Practice Guideline from the American College of Physicians. *Ann. Intern. Med.* **2017**, *166*, 514–530. [CrossRef]
31. Cuschieri, S. The CONSORT statement. *Saudi J. Anaesth.* **2019**, *13* (Suppl. 1), S27–S30. [CrossRef]
32. Madhu, C.; Swift, S.; Moloney-Geany, S.; Drake, M.J. How to use the Pelvic Organ Prolapse Quantification (POP-Q) system? *Neurourol. Urodyn.* **2018**, *37* (Suppl. S6), S39–S43. [CrossRef] [PubMed]
33. Hajebrahimi, S.; Nourizadeh, D.; Hamedani, R.; Pezeshki, M.Z. Validity and reliability of the International Consultation on Incontinence Questionnaire-Urinary Incontinence Short Form and its correlation with urodynamic findings. *Urol. J.* **2012**, *9*, 685–690.
34. Thong, I.S.K.; Jensen, M.P.; Miró, J.; Tan, G. The validity of pain intensity measures: What do the NRS, VAS, VRS, and FPS-R measure? *Scand. J. Pain* **2018**, *18*, 99–107. [CrossRef] [PubMed]
35. Romero-Culleres, G.; Jané-Feixas, C.; Vilaseca-Grané, A.; Arnau, A.; Montesinos, J.; Abenoza-Guardiola, M. Inter-rater reliability of the digital palpation of pelvic floor muscle by the modified Oxford Grading Scale in continent and incontinent women. Fiabilidad inter evaluador de la palpación digital de los músculos del suelo pélvico utilizando la escala modificada de Oxford graduada en mujeres continentes e incontinentes. *Arch. Esp. Urol.* **2019**, *72*, 602–607. [PubMed]
36. Ponzo, V.; Cinnera, A.M.; Mommo, F.; Caltagirone, C.; Koch, G.; Tramontano, M. Osteopathic Manipulative Therapy Potentiates Motor Cortical Plasticity. *J. Osteopath. Med.* **2018**, *118*, 396–402. [CrossRef]
37. Pepe, L.; Milani, R.; Di Trani, M.; Di Folco, G.; Lanna, V.; Solano, L. A more global approach to musculoskeletal pain: Expressive writing as an effective adjunct to physiotherapy. *Psychol. Health Med.* **2014**, *19*, 687–697. [CrossRef]

38. Piermaria, J.; Princi, A.A.; Tramontano, M. *Mobilizzazione, Valutazione e Movimentazione del Paziente—Guida Pratica*; Edi-Ermes: Milan, Italy, 2019.
39. Cohen, J. *Statistical Power Analysis for the Behavioral Sciences*, 2nd ed.; Academic Press: New York, NY, USA, 1977.
40. Mohseni-Bandpei, M.A.; Rahmani, N.; Behtash, H.; Karimloo, M. The effect of pelvic floor muscle exercise on women with chronic non-specific low back pain. *J. Bodyw. Mov. Ther.* **2011**, *15*, 75–81. [CrossRef]
41. Nipa, S.I.; Sriboonreung, T.; Paungmali, A.; Phongnarisorn, C. The Effects of Pelvic Floor Muscle Exercise Combined with Core Stability Exercise on Women with Stress Urinary Incontinence following the Treatment of Nonspecific Chronic Low Back Pain. *Adv. Urol.* **2022**, *2022*, 2051374. [CrossRef]
42. Frota, I.; Rocha, A.; Neto, J.; Vasconcelos, C.; De Magalhaes, T.F.; Karbage, S.; Augusto, K.L.; Nascimento, S.; Haddad, J.M.; Bezerra, L. Pelvic floor muscle function and quality of life in postmenopausal women with and without pelvic floor dysfunction. *Acta Obstet. Gynecol. Scand.* **2018**, *97*, 552–559. [CrossRef]
43. Arab, A.M.; Behbahani, R.B.; Lorestani, L.; Azari, A. Correlation of digital palpation and transabdominal ultrasound for assessment of pelvic floor muscle contraction. *J. Man. Manip. Ther.* **2009**, *17*, e75–e79. [CrossRef]

healthcare

MDPI

Article

# Clinical Items for Geriatric Patients with Post-Stroke at Discharge or Transfer after Rehabilitation Therapy in a Chronic-Phase Hospital: A Retrospective Pilot Study

**Masatoshi Koumo [1], Akio Goda [2,*], Yoshinori Maki [1,3], Kouta Yokoyama [1], Tetsuya Yamamoto [1], Tsumugi Hosokawa [1], Ryota Ishibashi [4], Junichi Katsura [1] and Ken Yanagibashi [1]**

1 Department of Rehabilitation, Hikari Hospital, Otsu 520-0002, Japan
2 Department of Physical Therapy, Faculty of Health Sciences, Kyoto Tachibana University, Kyoto 607-8175, Japan
3 Department of Neurosurgery, Hikone Chuo Hospital, Hikone 522-0054, Japan
4 Department of Neurosurgery, Kitano Hospital, Tazuke Kofukai Medical Research Institute, Osaka 530-0025, Japan
* Correspondence: goda@tachibana-u.ac.jp; Tel.: +81-(0)75-574-4313

**Abstract:** Clinical factors related to destination after rehabilitation therapy for geriatric patients with post-stroke in chronic-phase hospitals have not been elucidated. This study analyzed the clinical characteristics of geriatric patients with post-stroke at discharge/transfer after rehabilitation therapy in a chronic-phase hospital. Fifty-three patients (20 men, 33 women; mean age 81.36 ± 8.14 years) were recruited (the period analyzed: October 2013–March 2020). Clinical data were statistically analyzed among patients discharged to homes or facilities for older adults or transferred to another hospital. In addition, we analyzed the clinical items at discharge and transfer after rehabilitation therapy using a decision tree analysis. Twelve patients were discharged, eighteen were discharged to facilities for older adults, and twenty-three were transferred to another hospital. There were significant differences in the modified Rankin Scale, admission dates, functional independence measure (FIM) score, and Barthel Index score in the three groups ($p < 0.05$). Patients with motor subtotal functional independence scores of ≥14 (chronologically improved ≥5) after rehabilitation therapy for <291 days were more likely to be discharged home. Patients in a chronic-phase hospital who improved within a limited period were discharged to their homes, whereas those who were bedridden tended to be transferred to another hospital.

**Keywords:** chronic-care hospital; destination; functional independence measure; rehabilitation therapy; stroke

**Citation:** Koumo, M.; Goda, A.; Maki, Y.; Yokoyama, K.; Yamamoto, T.; Hosokawa, T.; Ishibashi, R.; Katsura, J.; Yanagibashi, K. Clinical Items for Geriatric Patients with Post-Stroke at Discharge or Transfer after Rehabilitation Therapy in a Chronic-Phase Hospital: A Retrospective Pilot Study. *Healthcare* **2022**, *10*, 1577. https://doi.org/10.3390/healthcare10081577

Academic Editors: Marco Tramontano, Giovanni Galeoto and José Carmelo Adsuar Sala

Received: 11 July 2022
Accepted: 16 August 2022
Published: 19 August 2022



## 1. Introduction

A major concern in Japanese society is the increasing number of older adults requiring care for being bedridden [1]. Stroke is a major cause of a bedridden status for geriatric patients in Japan. In 2017, more than one million Japanese people underwent medical treatment for stroke [1]. Although improved medical treatment for stroke contributed to reducing the mortality related to stroke, it remains the second leading cause of bedridden status among patients and the third leading cause of death in Japan [1]. Therefore, the prevention of a stroke onset and recovery treatment after stroke events, such as rehabilitation therapy, is indispensable in the aging Japanese society. Rehabilitation therapy for post-stroke events is performed in three types of hospitals: acute, recovery, and chronic. Geriatric patients who can be independent or supported in their domestic environment can be discharged home after medical treatment, including rehabilitation therapy during the acute phase of stroke (usually within 2 months after a stroke onset). Meanwhile, patients who cannot be discharged from an acute-phase hospital often require transfer to a recovery or chronic-phase hospital [1].

Previous studies have reported clinical predictors of patients with post-stroke related to destinations (such as home, facilities for older adults, or another hospital) after rehabilitation therapy in acute- and recovery-phase hospitals [2–9]. However, to our knowledge, little is known about the clinical characteristics of geriatric patients with post-stroke at discharge or transfer after rehabilitation therapy in chronic-phase hospitals. Therefore, this study analyzed the clinical characteristics of geriatric patients with post-stroke upon discharge or transfer after rehabilitation therapy in a chronic-phase hospital. We aimed to clarify the clinical characteristics of geriatric patients with post-stroke at the termination of rehabilitation therapy in a chronic-phase hospital.

## 2. Materials and Methods

### *2.1. Study Design*

This retrospective cohort study was approved by the ethics committee of Hikari Hospital (2 April 2021). Informed consent was obtained from all the participants.

We reviewed the medical records of Hikari Hospital between October 2013 and March 2020. The inclusion criteria were as follows: (1) aged 65 years or older, (2) admitted to the chronic-phase ward, (3) discharged by April 2020, (4) diagnosed with a stroke, and (5) receiving rehabilitation intervention. Candidates were excluded if they (1) died during admission or (2) if their clinical data were lacking.

### *2.2. Collection of Clinical Data*

We collected data on the following variables: sex (male/female), age (years), utilization of long-term care insurance (yes/no), the existence of housemates (yes/no), admission dates until discharge (days), initiation time of rehabilitation therapy from stroke onset (days), underlying stroke disease (infarction/intracranial hemorrhage), location of stroke lesion (supratentorial/infratentorial), laterality of stroke lesion (right/left), feeding upon admission (oral/non-oral), period of rehabilitation therapy during admission (days), destination after discharge (home/facilities for the older adults/transfer to another hospital), modified Rankin Scale (mRS) (on admission/at discharge), functional independence measure (FIM) score, Barthel Index (BI) score (at the time of initiating rehabilitation therapy/at discharge), and chronological change in FIM and BI scores.

### *2.3. FIM and BI*

The FIM has two sections: motor subtotal (eating, grooming, bathing, upper body dressing, lower body dressing, toileting, bladder management, bowel management, bed/chair/wheelchair transfer, toilet transfer, tub/shower transfer, locomotion in the form of walking and/or wheelchair use, and stair use) and cognitive subtotal (comprehension, expression, social interaction, problem-solving, and memory) scores. Each item was scored from 1 to 7 according to the patient's activities of daily living (ADLs). The minimum and maximum FIM scores were 18 and 126, respectively.

The BI consists of ten items: feeding, bathing, grooming, dressing, bowel control, bladder control, toilet use, transfer, mobility, and stair use. Each item was evaluated with scores of 0, 5, 10, or 15, according to the patient's ability to perform daily activities. The minimum and maximum BI scores were 0 and 100, respectively.

### *2.4. Statistical Analysis*

The data collected from patients discharged to their homes or to facilities for older adults and those transferred to another hospital were statistically analyzed using Kruskal–Wallis tests (post hoc analysis: Bonferroni correction), one-way analysis of variance (post hoc analysis: Bonferroni correction), and Fisher's exact tests (post hoc analysis: Holm correction). A decision tree analysis was performed using all clinical data items to examine the differences among the clinical items of patients with post-stroke at discharge or transfer. IBM SPSS Statistics for Windows (version 24.0; IBM Corp., Armonk, NY, USA) was used for all statistical analyses. Statistical significance was set at $p < 0.05$.

## 3. Results

This study enrolled 53 patients (male-to-female ratio, 20:33). The mean age ± standard deviation was 81.36 ± 8.14 years. Twelve patients were discharged home, eighteen were discharged to facilities for older adults, and twenty-three were transferred to another hospital. The results of the three-group comparisons are shown in Table 1. The mRS scores upon admission and discharge were significantly higher in the other hospital group than in the other two groups (home and geriatric facilities) ($p < 0.05$). FIM (motor subtotal/cognitive subtotal/total) and BI scores upon admission and discharge were significantly lower in the other hospital group than in the other two groups (home and geriatric facilities) ($p < 0.05$). Chronological changes in the FIM and BI scores were significantly higher in the home group than in the facilities for the older group ($p < 0.05$). For the feeding items, the percentage of non-oral intake was significantly higher in the other hospital group than in the facilities for the geriatric group ($p < 0.05$). The admission dates were significantly longer in the facilities for the geriatric group than in the home group ($p < 0.05$). The transfer FIM score at discharge was significantly higher in the home group than in the other two groups (facilities for the geriatric and other hospitals) ($p < 0.05$).

**Table 1.** Comparison of the fundamental information and measurements among the three groups.

| | Home ($n$ = 12) | Geriatric Facilities ($n$ = 18) | Another Hospital ($n$ = 23) | $p$-Value | Post Hoc Analysis | | |
|---|---|---|---|---|---|---|---|
| | | | | | Home—Geriatric Facilities | Home—Another Hospital | Geriatric Facilities—Another Hospital |
| Age * (years) | 78.8 ± 9.1 | 81.5 ± 8.5 | 82.6 ± 7.4 | 0.419 | 1.000 | 0.5712 | 1.000 |
| Sex † (male/female) | (7/5) | (5/13) | (8/15) | 0.222 | 0.408 | 0.565 | 0.741 |
| Utilization of long-term care insurance † (Yes/No) | (7/4) | (13/4) | (16/5) | 0.703 | 1.000 | 1.000 | 1.000 |
| Housemates † (yes/no) | (10/2) | (10/8) | (18/5) | 0.165 | 0.537 | 1.000 | 0.537 |
| Feeding † (oral/non-oral) | (9/3) | (18/0) | (7/16) | <0.001 | 0.059 | 0.059 | <0.001 |
| Underlying stroke † (infarction/intracranial hemorrhage) | (8/4) | (12/6) | (15/8) | 0.994 | 1.000 | 1.000 | 1.000 |
| Location of stroke lesion † (supratentorial/infratentorial) | (7/4) | (15/3) | (21/2) | 0.136 | 0.6828 | 0.211 | 0.444 |
| Laterality of stroke lesion (right/left) | (3/6) | (9/7) | (8/13) | 0.430 | 0.9927 | 1.000 | 0.9927 |
| Modified Rankin Scale on admission | 4.3 ± 0.5 (4–5) | 4.4 ± 0.5 (4–5) | 4.8 ± 0.4 (4–5) | 0.005 | 1.000 | 0.016 | 0.044 |
| Modified Rankin Scale at discharge | 4.2 ± 0.8 (2–5) | 4.3 ± 0.5 (4–5) | 4.8 ± 0.4 (4–5) | 0.002 | 1.000 | 0.011 | 0.007 |
| Admission dates (days) | 124.9 ± 57.7 (16–207) | 305.1 ± 205.3 (62–906) | 299.3 ± 274.0 (43–1010) | 0.047 | 0.032 | 0.191 | 1.000 |

**Table 1.** *Cont.*

| | Home ($n$ = 12) | Geriatric Facilities ($n$ = 18) | Another Hospital ($n$ = 23) | $p$-Value | Post Hoc Analysis | | |
|---|---|---|---|---|---|---|---|
| | | | | | Home—Geriatric Facilities | Home—Another Hospital | Geriatric Facilities—Another Hospital |
| Initiation timing of rehabilitation therapy from the onset of stroke (days) | 547.2 ± 1109.0 (43–3383) | 86.6 ± 40.5 (35–187) | 122.6 ± 135.9 (34–593) | 0.058 | 0.071 | 0.085 | 0.070 |
| Period of rehabilitation therapy (days) | 119.9 ± 57.1 (13–192) | 298.4 ± 204.8 (56–898) | 273.6 ± 275.6 (29–1004) | 0.079 | 0.102 | 0.166 | 1.000 |
| Motor subtotal FIM score on admission | 31.7 ± 16.0 (13–55) | 24.9 ± 8.5 (17–43) | 16.7 ± 8.1 (13–42) | <0.001 | 1.000 | 0.002 | <0.001 |
| Cognitive subtotal FIM score on admission | 16.0 ± 8.3 (5–30) | 14.4 ± 5.6 (7–26) | 9.6 ± 5.1 (5–26) | 0.007 | 1.000 | 0.014 | 0.046 |
| Total FIM score on admission | 47.7 ± 23.9 (18–85) | 39.3 ± 10.3 (27–59) | 26.3 ± 11.1 (18–58) | <0.001 | 1.000 | 0.007 | 0.002 |
| Motor subtotal FIM score at discharge | 37.8 ± 16.0 (13–87) | 27.7 ± 11.9 (16–53) | 16.5 ± 8.3 (13–42) | <0.001 | 1.000 | 0.004 | <0.001 |
| Cognitive subtotal FIM score at discharge | 17.2 ± 8.8 (5–32) | 15.7 ± 5.5 (7–24) | 9.6 ± 5.3 (5–26) | 0.001 | 1.000 | 0.004 | 0.011 |
| Total FIM score at discharge | 54.9 ± 33.1 (18–119) | 43.4 ± 14.5 (23–77) | 26.0 ± 11.4 (18–58) | <0.001 | 1.000 | 0.004 | <0.001 |
| Chronological change of total FIM score | 8.1 ± 14.7 (−18–44) | 4.1 ± 7.5 (−4–19) | −0.3 ± 2.2 (−7–4) | 0.019 | 0.569 | 0.016 | 0.329 |
| Transfer FIM score on admission (walk/wheelchair/walk and wheelchair) | 1.8 ± 1.5 (1–5) | 1.2 ± 0.7 (1–4) | 1.1 ± 0.4 (1–3) | 0.113 | 0.347 | 0.121 | 1.000 |
| Transfer FIM score at discharge (walk/wheelchair/walk and wheelchair) | 3.3 ± 2.5 (1–6) | 1.2 ± 0.7 (1–4) | 1.1 ± 0.4 (1–3) | <0.001 | <0.001 | <0.001 | 1.000 |
| BI score on admission | 30.8 ± 25.7 (0–85) | 26.1 ± 18.3 (0–55) | 8.5 ± 15.8 (0–55) | 0.002 | 1.000 | 0.008 | 0.001 |
| BI score at discharge | 47.5 ± 36.9 (0–100) | 29.7 ± 20.5 (5–30) | 7.6 ± 16.3 (0–55) | <0.001 | 0.147 | <0.001 | 0.013 |
| Chronological change of BI score | 16.7 ± 16.4 (−5–45) | 3.6 ± 11.7 (−20–25) | −0.9 ± 7.5 (−30–10) | <0.001 | 0.101 | 0.001 | 0.474 |

Mean ± standard deviation (minimum score—maximum score); Home: patients discharged home, Geriatric Facilities: patients discharged to geriatric facilities, Another hospital: patients transferred to another hospital; BI: Barthel index, FIM: functional independence measure Kruskal–Wallis test (post hoc analysis: Bonferroni correction), *: one-way analysis of variance (post hoc analysis: Bonferroni correction), †: Fisher's Exact Test (post hoc analysis: Holm correction).

*Decision Tree Analysis*

A decision tree analysis identified the following discriminators: motor subtotal FIM score at discharge, rehabilitation therapy period, and chronological change in the total

FIM score. The best discriminator was the motor subtotal FIM score (≧14 or <14). Patients with motor subtotal FIM scores of <14 were categorized for transfer to another hospital. In this group, three patients were discharged home, one patient was discharged to a facility for older adults, and eighteen patients were transferred to another hospital. Among the patients with scores $\geq$ 14, the next best discriminator was the rehabilitation therapy period ($\geq$291 days or <291 days). Patients with a motor subtotal FIM score $\geq$ 14 who underwent rehabilitation therapy for at least 291 days were discharged to facilities for older adults. The third-best discriminator was the chronological change in the total FIM score ($\geq$5 or <5). Seven patients with a chronological change in the total FIM score of $\geq$5 were discharged to their homes. The classification accuracy of the decision tree analysis was 79.2% (58.3% for patients discharged to home, 94.4% for those discharged to facilities for older adults, and 78.3% for those transferred to another hospital) (Figure 1).

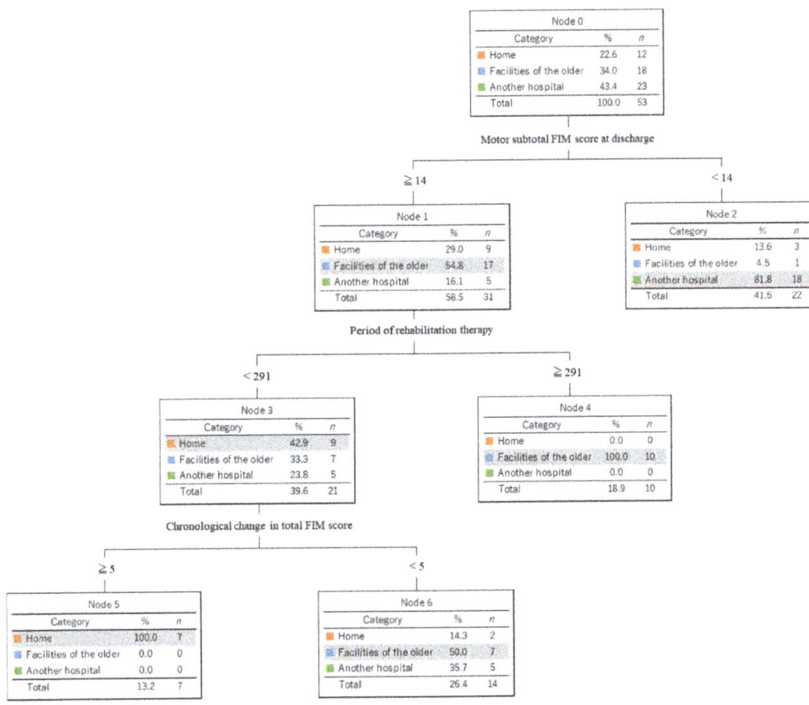


**Figure 1.** Results of decision tree analysis. FIM motor subtotal score, period of rehabilitation therapy, and chronological change of total FIM score were identified as discriminators at discharge or transfer after rehabilitation therapy.

## 4. Discussion

This study analyzed the clinical characteristics of geriatric patients with post-stroke at discharge and transfer after rehabilitation therapy at our chronic-care hospital by comparing three groups of patients: those discharged to their homes, those discharged to facilities for older adults, and those transferred to another hospital. Between the three groups, the ADLs evaluated using the FIM and BI scores, admission dates, and feeding status (oral/non-oral) were significantly different. In addition, the decision tree analysis results showed that patients with subtotal motor FIM scores at discharge $\geq$ 14, period of rehabilitation therapy < 291 days, and chronological change in total FIM score $\geq$ 5 were more likely to be discharged home.

Patients undergoing rehabilitation therapy following stroke events are frequently evaluated using the FIM [2,10–15]. The correlations between the outcome of rehabilitation therapy after stroke events and FIM scores (motor subtotal/cognitive subtotal/total) in acute- and recovery-phase hospitals have been described [4–7,9,16,17]. The BI is also widely used to evaluate patient performance and to predict outcomes related to rehabilitation therapy [8,18,19]. In the present study, the FIM/BI scores at admission and discharge were also significant factors for discharge/transfer after rehabilitation therapy of geriatric post-stroke patients in a chronic-care hospital. Notably, the chronological change in the total FIM score was significant in the decision tree analysis. These results suggest that improvements in physical performance during rehabilitation therapy may result in a discharge home from a chronic-phase hospital. Previous reports identified FIM scores as predictors of discharge destination in geriatric stroke patients [6,20–23]. It has also been reported that improvements in the FIM score during hospitalization can lead to household discharge [24]. The results of the present study were consistent with the reports of these previous studies. Therefore, positive and effective rehabilitation therapy resulting in improved ADLs in geriatric stroke patients is warranted in chronic-care hospitals to increase the likelihood of being discharged home.

The results of the present study identified the period of rehabilitation therapy as the second discriminator of patient destination after rehabilitation therapy. Patients with total FIM scores of $\geq$14 and undergoing rehabilitation therapy for $\geq$291 days were discharged to facilities for older adults. A previous study [25] has also reported that prolonged length of hospital stay is strongly associated with discharge to a geriatric facility for patients with post-stroke sequelae. There are cases in which a discharge home from a chronic-care hospital becomes impossible despite the patient's ability to perform ADLs due to factors such as the caregivers and the home environment. Compared with patients discharged home or transferred to another hospital, patients discharged to facilities for older adults had to wait because of the limited number of rooms at facilities for older adults. Consequently, the patients continued to be admitted and underwent rehabilitation therapy. The discharge of stroke patients to geriatric care facilities is a bottleneck in discharge coordination and is likely to prolong the length of discharge [26]. Therefore, it is useful to pay attention to the prolonged duration of rehabilitation treatment (length of stay) to predict the discharge transition of geriatric stroke patients admitted to chronic-care hospitals.

In this study, a significantly higher percentage of patients transferred to another hospital were parenteral, confirming that feeding status was also important. This may be because the administration of gastrostomy, tubal feeding, and central venous feeding can be complicated for staff working in facilities for older adults [27,28]. Furthermore, the mRS results at admission and discharge showed that patients transferred to another hospital had significantly more severe diseases. Previous studies [29,30] have also reported that the severity of illness, as assessed by the mRS during hospitalization, affects poor discharge outcomes (discharge to another location other than home). Therefore, feeding status and disease severity should be confirmed when predicting where geriatric stroke patients will be discharged from chronic-care hospitals.

*Limitations*

This retrospective study was conducted at a single chronic-care hospital. The number of enrolled patients was limited, possibly because patients in chronic-care hospitals tend to be admitted longer than those in acute or recovery-care hospitals. Future multicenter studies should include a larger number of patients. As multiple rehabilitation therapists evaluated patients' performance, subjective bias could not be completely excluded. In this regard, efforts should be made to minimize bias among evaluators by providing training in evaluation. In addition, this study could not examine the influence of modifiable stroke risk factors, and future studies should collect and analyze a wider range of data. In addition, we did not evaluate the types of hospitals to which the patients were transferred, such as acute-phase or other chronic-phase hospitals. Thus, whether patients were transferred to another hospital because of an improved (or at least stable) status or a sudden aggravated status remains unclear and should be addressed in future studies.

## 5. Conclusions

In this study, patients with post-stroke whose ADLs improved with rehabilitation therapy within a short period were more likely to be discharged to their homes. Meanwhile, a longer period of rehabilitation therapy and low motor subtotal FIM scores were related to discharge to facilities for older adults and transfer to another hospital. Rehabilitation therapy resulting in improved ADLs and early discharge also contributed to a discharge home in the chronic phase after stroke.

**Author Contributions:** Conceptualization, M.K., A.G. and Y.M.; methodology, M.K. and Y.M.; formal analysis, A.G.; investigation, M.K., Y.M., K.Y. (Kouta Yokoyama), T.Y. and T.H.; data curation, M.K., A.G. and Y.M.; writing—original draft preparation, Y.M.; writing—review and editing, M.K. and A.G.; supervision, J.K.; project administration, R.I. and K.Y. (Ken Yanagibashi). All authors have read and agreed to the published version of the manuscript.

**Funding:** This research received no external funding.

**Institutional Review Board Statement:** This study was approved by the ethical committee of the Hikari Hospital (2020-3).

**Informed Consent Statement:** In this study, the data were all anonymized.

**Data Availability Statement:** Not applicable.

**Acknowledgments:** We thank our collaborators at the Hikari Hospital.

**Conflicts of Interest:** The authors declare no conflict of interest.

## References

1. Ministry of Health, Labour and Welfare. Available online: https://www.kaigokensaku.mhlw.go.jp/publish/ (accessed on 9 March 2022).
2. Matsugi, A.; Tani, K.; Tamaru, Y.; Yoshioka, N.; Yamashita, A.; Mori, N.; Oku, K.; Ikeda, M.; Nagano, K. Prediction of advisability of returning home using the home care score. *Rehabil. Res. Pract.* **2015**, *2015*, 501042. [CrossRef] [PubMed]
3. Mirkowski, M.; Pereira, S.; Janzen, S.; Mehta, S.; Meyer, M.; McClure, A.; Speechley, M.; Teasell, R. Caregiver availability for severe stroke results in improved functional ability at discharge from inpatient rehabilitation. *Disabil. Rehabil.* **2018**, *40*, 457–461. [CrossRef] [PubMed]
4. Mees, M.; Klein, J.; Yperzeele, L.; Vanacker, P.; Cras, P. Predicting discharge destination after stroke: A systematic review. *Clin. Neurol. Neurosurg.* **2016**, *142*, 15–21. [CrossRef] [PubMed]
5. Matsugi, A.; Tani, K.; Yoshioka, N.; Yamashita, A.; Mori, N.; Oku, K.; Murakami, Y.; Nomura, S.; Tamaru, Y.; Nagano, K. Prediction of destination at discharge from a comprehensive rehabilitation hospital using the home care score. *J. Phys. Ther. Sci.* **2016**, *28*, 2737–2741. [CrossRef]
6. Koyama, T.; Sako, Y.; Konta, M.; Domen, K. Poststroke discharge destination: Functional independence and sociodemographic factors in urban Japan. *J. Stroke Cerebrovasc. Dis.* **2011**, *20*, 202–207. [CrossRef]
7. Sato, A.; Fujita, T.; Yamamoto, Y. Activities of daily living independence level for home discharge in stroke patients based on number of caregivers: An analysis of the Japan Rehabilitation Database. *Phys. Ther. Res.* **2017**, *20*, 23–27. [CrossRef]
8. Meyer, M.J.; Pereira, S.; McClure, A.; Teasell, R.; Thind, A.; Koval, J.; Richardson, M.; Speechley, M. A systematic review of studies reporting multivariable models to predict functional outcomes after post-stroke inpatient rehabilitation. *Disabil. Rehabil.* **2015**, *37*, 1316–1323. [CrossRef]
9. Sugiura, T.; Sakurai, H.; Sugiura, Y.; Iwata, K.; Kimura, K.; Sakamoto, K.; Matsumoto, T.; Kanada, Y. A study of ADL outcome factors of elderly stroke patients over 85. *Rigakuryoho Kagaku* **2013**, *28*, 623–626. [CrossRef]
10. Heinemann, A.W.; Linacre, J.M.; Wright, B.D.; Hamilton, B.B.; Granger, C. Prediction of rehabilitation outcomes with disability measures. *Arch. Phys. Med. Rehabil.* **1994**, *75*, 133–143. [CrossRef]
11. Inouye, M. Predicting outcomes of patients in Japan after first acute stroke using a simple model. *Am. J. Phys. Med. Rehabil.* **2001**, *80*, 645–649. [CrossRef]
12. Inouye, M.; Kishi, K.; Ikeda, Y.; Takada, M.; Katoh, J.; Iwahashi, M.; Hayakawa, M.; Ishihara, K.; Sawamura, S.; Kazumi, T. Prediction of functional outcome after stroke rehabilitation. *Am. J. Phys. Med. Rehabil.* **2000**, *79*, 513–518. [CrossRef] [PubMed]
13. Koyama, T.; Matsumoto, K.; Okuno, T.; Domen, K. A new method for predicting functional recovery of stroke patients with hemiplegia: Logarithmic modelling. *Clin. Rehabil.* **2005**, *19*, 779–789. [CrossRef] [PubMed]
14. Sonoda, S.; Saitoh, E.; Nagai, S.; Okuyama, Y.; Suzuki, T.; Suzuki, M. Stroke outcome prediction using reciprocal number of initial activities of daily living status. *J. Stroke Cerebrovasc. Dis.* **2005**, *14*, 8–11. [CrossRef] [PubMed]

15. Matsugi, A.; Tani, K.; Mitani, Y.; Oku, K.; Tamaru, Y.; Nagano, K. Revision of the predictive method improves precision in the prediction of stroke outcomes for patients admitted to rehabilitation hospitals. *J. Phys. Ther. Sci.* **2014**, *26*, 1429–1431. [CrossRef] [PubMed]
16. Tanwir, S.; Montgomery, K.; Chari, V.; Nesathurai, S. Stroke rehabilitation: Availability of a family member as caregiver and discharge destination. *Eur. J. Phys. Rehabil. Med.* **2014**, *50*, 355–362. [PubMed]
17. Nguyen, T.A.; Page, A.; Aggarwal, A.; Henke, P. Social determinants of discharge destination for patients after stroke with low admission FIM instrument scores. *Arch. Phys. Med. Rehabil.* **2007**, *88*, 740–744. [CrossRef]
18. Stein, J.; Bettger, J.P.; Sicklick, A.; Hedeman, R.; Magdon-Ismail, Z.; Schwamm, L.H. Use of a standardized assessment to predict rehabilitation care after acute stroke. *Arch. Phys. Med. Rehabil.* **2015**, *96*, 210–217. [CrossRef]
19. van der Zwaluw, C.S.; Valentijn, S.A.; Nieuwenhuis-Mark, R.; Rasquin, S.M.; van Heugten, C.M. Cognitive functioning in the acute phase poststroke: A predictor of discharge destination? *J. Stroke Cerebrovasc. Dis.* **2011**, *20*, 549–555. [CrossRef]
20. Mokler, P.J.; Sandstrom, R.; Griffin, M.; Farris, L.; Jones, C. Predicting discharge destination for patients with severe motor stroke: Important functional tasks. *Neurorehabil. Neural. Repair.* **2000**, *14*, 181–185. [CrossRef]
21. Lutz, B.J. Determinants of discharge destination for stroke patients. *Rehabil. Nurs.* **2004**, *29*, 154–163. [CrossRef]
22. Wilson, D.B.; Houle, D.M.; Keith, R.A. Stroke rehabilitation: A model predicting return home. *West J. Med.* **1991**, *154*, 587–590. [PubMed]
23. Ween, J.E.; Mernoff, S.T.; Alexander, M.P. Recovery rates after stroke and their impact on outcome prediction. *Neurorehabil. Neural Repair* **2000**, *14*, 229–235. [CrossRef] [PubMed]
24. Bottemiller, K.L.; Bieber, P.L.; Basford, J.R.; Harris, M. FIM score, FIM efficiency, and discharge disposition following inpatient stroke rehabilitation. *Rehabil. Nurs.* **2006**, *31*, 22–25. [CrossRef] [PubMed]
25. Clery, A.; Bhalla, A.; Bisquera, A.; Skolarus, L.E.; Marshall, I.; McKevitt, C.; Rudd, A.; Sackley, C.; Martin, F.C.; Manthorpe, J.; et al. Long-term trends in stroke survivors discharged to care homes: The South London Stroke Register. *Stroke* **2020**, *51*, 179–185. [CrossRef]
26. Jones, B.; McClean, S.; Stanford, D. Modelling mortality and discharge of hospitalized stroke patients using a phase-type recovery model. *Health Care Manag. Sci.* **2019**, *22*, 570–588. [CrossRef]
27. Bourdel-Marchasson, I.; Dumas, F.; Pinganaud, G.; Emeriau, J.P.; Decamps, A. Audit of percutaneous endoscopic gastrostomy in long-term enteral feeding in a nursing home. *Int. J. Qual. Health Care* **1997**, *9*, 297–302. [CrossRef]
28. Mitchell, S.L.; Buchanan, J.L.; Littlehale, S.; Hamel, M.B. Tube-feeding versus hand-feeding nursing home residents with advanced dementia: A cost comparison. *J. Am. Med. Dir. Assoc.* **2004**, *5*, S23–S29. [CrossRef]
29. Qureshi, A.I.; Chaudhry, S.A.; Sapkota, B.L.; Rodriguez, G.J.; Suri, M.F. Discharge destination as a surrogate for Modified Rankin Scale defined outcomes at 3- and 12-months poststroke among stroke survivors. *Arch. Phys. Med. Rehabil.* **2012**, *93*, 1408–1413.e1. [CrossRef]
30. Kubo, K.; Kamo, T.; Momosaki, R.; Mitsutomi, K. Development of a Point System to Predict Discharge to Home for Acute Stroke Patients. *PM R* **2021**, *13*, 38–44. [CrossRef]

MDPI AG
Grosspeteranlage 5
4052 Basel
Switzerland
Tel.: +41 61 683 77 34

*Healthcare* Editorial Office
E-mail: healthcare@mdpi.com
www.mdpi.com/journal/healthcare

www.ingramcontent.com/pod-product-compliance
Lightning Source LLC
Chambersburg PA
CBHW061454210926
51850CB00008B/1718
*9783725816309*